# CITY UNDER SIEGE

☆ ☆ ☆

## THE BERLIN BLOCKADE
## AND AIRLIFT, 1948–1949

MICHAEL D. HAYDOCK

BRASSEY'S

*Washington & London*

Copyright © 1999 Brassey's, Inc.

First Brassey's paperback edition 2000

**Library of Congress Cataloging-in-Publication Data**
    City under siege : the Berlin blockade and airlift, 1948–1949 / by Michael D. Haydock.
        p.    cm.
    Includes bibliographical references.
    1. Berlin (Germany)—History—Blockade, 1948–1949. 2. United States—Foreign relations—1045–1953. 3. United States—Foreign relations—Soviet Union. 4. Soviet Union—Foreign relations—United States.  I. Title
        DD881.H34    1999
        943'.1550874—dc21                                      98-10967
                                            943.                CIP
                                            087

ISBN 1-57488-264-3 (alk.paper)

Printed in the United States of America on acid-free paper that meets the American National Standards Institute Z39-48 Standard.

Brassey's
22841 Quicksilver Drive
Dulles, Virginia  20166


10 9 8 7 6 5 4 3 2 1

*To Elizabeth, who made writing
about the past possible, and
to Katherine, who makes writing about
it important*

# CONTENTS

# PREFACE

The Cold War is over. It concluded with the collapse of the Soviet Union in 1991 when decades of totalitarian rule in the name of Marxist class struggle ended there. The Soviet philosophy of government found a place on the ash heap of history that its own ideologues had long maintained was to be the final resting place of the idea of democracy.

Although there are those who argue that it had its beginnings in the Russian Revolution of 1917, the Cold War is generally agreed to have begun at the end of World War II. In a Central Europe just freed from the domination of Nazi Germany, the armies of the victors met. The fact that the Western democracies and the Soviet Union had conflicting visions about the nature of the postwar world began to come into focus. That focus was never entirely sharp. A variety of explanations was offered for Soviet behavior through the nearly half century of cold conflict, and the variation in the proposed response to that behavior was just as wide. It ranged from conciliation to confrontation, and even to serious recommendations for preemptive nuclear first strikes by American forces. And the Cold War did not long remain confined to the dark arena of Central Europe. The Cold War turned hot in the frozen mountains of Korea and in the fetid jungles of Vietnam; it led the world to the brink of nuclear annihilation over the presence of Soviet missiles on an island ninety miles from the United States. It broke out elsewhere in Asia, in Central America, and in the brush and jungles of Africa. There, in the Congo, the echoes of old Cold War struggles and alliances reverberate even as this is being written. It is the same in other places across the face of the globe.

Now that the Soviet protagonist has collapsed, there is a wealth of newly available information on Soviet intentions and motivations during those times. While a full evaluation of that material will require many years, what is perhaps most striking about the revelations that have come since the demise of the Soviet Union and the opening of its long-sealed archives is that there have been so very few revelations. The American and British observers who concluded soon after World War II ended that the Soviet Union had embarked on a path of world conquest have proven to have been remarkably perceptive. The analysis of Soviet behavior presented by George Kennan in 1946 is as penetrating, accurate, and valid today as it was at the time. Its prescription for a measured, firm, pragmatic American response has proven to have been exactly what was required, then and in the long run. Just as Kennan predicted so long ago, it was the Soviet Union, and not democracy, that ultimately collapsed because of internal contradictions and conflicts.

Berlin was one of the first testing points in the Cold War and it remained one for as long as the conflict existed. Nikita Khrushchev once compared the city to a most tender part of human anatomy and said that he had only to squeeze it to make the West scream. But that was not the case. Often squeezed in the course of the Cold War, Berlin always proved to be a nettle that ultimately injured the one doing the squeezing—the Soviet Union.

Like many Americans of my generation, my early life was influenced and shaped by the events of the Cold War and their impact on the world. I can recall even now emerging with a sense of awe and wonder from the dark recesses of a movie theater where John Wayne had just assured the safety of the American West for someone who was wearing a yellow ribbon in her hair. My amazement was not at the Technicolor celluloid exploits of the U.S. Cavalry, but at the real-life exploits of the airmen of the Berlin Airlift that had flashed over the screen in the grainy black and white of the Fox Movietone News before the feature started. Wondering why anyone would attempt to starve a city led me to ask about the Berlin Airlift. The increase in my interest in what was then, and may still be, called "social studies" came as a pleasant and gratifying shock to my teachers. Not very many years later, teachers in the same school would instruct us on the need to crouch quickly under our desks if the schoolroom were suddenly illuminated by a blinding white light. The Soviet Union had developed the atomic bomb, and it seemed that the world would never be the same.

It was the Cold War that gave rise to my own brief and mandatory—for military service was then compulsory—term in the Army and to my continuing membership in the American Legion and VFW. It stimulated my study of history as my primary focus in college and as a continuing passion. As the Cold War ended, I found myself drawn back to its beginnings and the first major test of wills between opposing world views—the dark battleground of Berlin, ruined capital of the Third Reich and bright spark of freedom and democracy in a sea of oppression. Fifty years ago, several courageous and farsighted Western political leaders recognized a danger, accepted its challenge, and refused to let that spark be extinguished. A few thousand soldiers and airmen sustained that spark by the miracle of the airlift. These were defining events in our history. Memories of the costs of appeasement and attempted accommodation with totalitarian aggression were sharper at the time of the blockade of Berlin. A later American president would attempt to rally Cold Warriors with talk of a long, twilight struggle as the conflict dragged on, year after year, without apparent resolution or hope of conclusion. Now that a conclusion has been reached, it can be seen with some clarity that, had the outcome of the first real battle—that of the Berlin Blockade—been different, the course of the war would have been altered. It was my desire to understand and record the events of that momentous time that led to the writing of this book.

My gratitude to Liz and Tom Powell—late of Poughkeepsie, Sylvan Lake, various ports in Florida, and now of Bishopville, South Carolina—is unending. Without their friendship and hospitality, this project could never have been finished.

Many people have helped as I thought about, researched, and wrote this book. The person who gave me the greatest help was my wife, Elizabeth. Without her love, patience, understanding, and encouragement, this project would never have been; without her sharp editorial skills, the product would have been inevitably poorer.

The assistance I received from veterans of the airlift and members of the Berlin Airlift Veterans Association cannot be overestimated. President Ken Herman ensured that I was welcomed at meetings, Secretary Fred Hall made available scarce copies of the association's publication, *Legacy,* and many other members of the association and other veterans shared reminiscences, logs, diaries, photographs, and other materials from half a century ago. Special thanks go to Forrest Ott, Jim O'Gorman, Ken Slaker, Billy Morrisey, Robert Wilcox, Lou Wagner, Fain Pool, Dr. Earl Moore, and "Stu" Studak.

Tim Chopp of the Berlin Airlift Historical Foundation and his wife helped me compile an accurate list of airlift casualties.

A great deal of the research for this book took place in libraries. My thanks go to Alan Aimone of the West Point Special Collections for his courtesy and help, to Professor Susan G. Blandy of Hudson Valley Community College for her guidance through the Internet, and to V. Hugh Morgan of Beavercreek, Ohio, for his assistance in finding suitable photographs of the events and some of the major characters in the drama of the Berlin blockade. The research staff of the library of the State University of New York at Albany was continually helpful, and Edward Voves of the Research Library of the *Philadelphia Inquirer* supplied invaluable material on the life of General Frank Howley that was available nowhere else. Most important of all of the libraries where I worked was the one closest to my home. Gail Sacco and the entire staff of the Voorheesville Library were invariably helpful. It has never ceased to amaze me how they, seemingly by magic but actually by the wonder of interlibrary loans, made the most arcane, esoteric, and obscure research material arrive in a small village in upstate New York.

Professor Michael V. Romanov of the Russian Studies Department of the State University of New York at Albany provided invaluable assistance in attempting to trace the postblockade activities of Soviet principals.

Special thanks go to Peter A. Howley, who shared his memories of boyhood in Berlin as the son of the American commandant, as well as papers and photographs from that time.

At Brassey's, Debra Greinke's appreciation of my objective guided the book to its final form while her knowledge of German saved me from many an embarrassing error that would have detracted from this work. *Danke!*

Finally, to Don McKeon of Brassey's, whose encouragement was inspiring and whose editing was inspired as well as sensitive. The book is far better for the attention he gave it, and I thank him deeply for that.

# PROLOGUE
# BERLIN, 1945

As long as the old trees,
Still bloom on Unter den Linden
Berlin is still Berlin,
And nothing can vanquish us.

These words are the lyrics to the city's unofficial song, written for a musical review around the turn of the century. The linden trees did not bloom in the bitter spring of 1945. They were gone—blasted away by bombs and artillery fire or cut down and burned for firewood—and the city that had been the capital of Nazi Germany lay vanquished.

In the last months of the war, with Soviet armies relentlessly moving into Germany from the east and the armies of the British and Americans, along with the French, swarming across the Rhine, the seizure of Berlin was the one stroke that could end the war in Europe. General Dwight D. Eisenhower, commanding the Allies, had no desire in that final spring of the war to risk the lives of American soldiers to achieve a military objective simply to obtain a political advantage over the West's Soviet ally. In early April Eisenhower wrote to Chief of Staff George C. Marshall, "I regard it as militarily unsound at this stage of the proceedings to make Berlin a major objective, particularly as it is only thirty-five miles from the Russian lines. I am the first to admit that a war is waged in pursuance of political aims, and if the combined chiefs of staff should decide that the Allied effort to take Berlin outweighs purely military considerations in this theater, I would cheerfully readjust my plans and my thinking so as to carry out such an operation."[1]

The combined chiefs of staff made no such decision, and the final assault on Berlin was begun by two Red Army fronts on April 16, 1945. The First Belorussian Front, under the command of Marshal Georgi K. Zhukov, led the attack on the city proper. The First Ukrainian Front, under Marshal Ivan S. Koniev, was assigned to cut off German Army Group Vistula from Berlin and secure the southern flank of the city. By April 21, the leading troops of Zhukov's Third Shock Army, the Second

Guards Tank Army, and the Forty-seventh Army had broken into the outskirts of the city.

In March the Germans had issued a document entitled "Basic Order for the Preparations to Defend the Capital," but it was a paper myth. Its so-called panzer divisions consisted of a dozen or so tanks and armored vehicles, and the only troops available to the city commandant, General Helmuth Weidling, were a few pathetic *Volkssturm* battalions—made up of old men and Hitler Youth teenagers not old enough to have been drafted into the Wehrmacht—some Luftwaffe ground personnel, and the remnants of his own 56th Panzer Corps.

Within the beleaguered city all was chaos. The population of over three million, mostly women, children, old men, and the infirm, huddled most of the time in cellars as bombers devastated the city.

Heavy bombing raids on Berlin had begun just after the Casablanca Conference, at which Winston Churchill and Franklin D. Roosevelt answered the demands of the absent Joseph Stalin for a second front to relieve pressure on the Red Army with a plan for intensified bombing of Germany. Beginning on June 10, 1943, the Royal Air Force conducted night raids over the capital and the U.S. Army Air Force pounded it with heavy bombs during the day. Over three hundred fifty raids were carried out and 75,000 tons of bombs fell on the city before the end of the war. Entire districts of the city were nearly obliterated. In Charlottenburg, near the center of the city, only 604 of the 11,075 residential buildings were left standing. Over one million tons of rubble were left, and a million and a half Berliners were homeless out of a total population of 3.3 million—one million fewer than had lived in Berlin in 1939. While many had fled the city, at least 50,000 were dead in the bombings.

Ruth Andreas-Friedrich and her companion, Leo Borchard, were among the Berliners who did not flee. Ruth, a writer, worked as an editor in the Ullstein publishing house. Leo was a composer and musician who had fallen out of favor with the Nazi regime early. In 1933, the year that Hitler had become chancellor of Germany, Borchard had reminded a newly enrolled Nazi party member in his orchestra that the man had been a socialist until the Führer had come to power. When the orchestra was scheduled to play for Hitler's birthday, the newly minted Nazi denounced Borchard, and the other orchestra members refused to play under his baton. From that time forward, Borchard had not been allowed to appear on stage in Germany. Ruth Andreas-Friedrich and Leo Borchard formed the core of a resistance group known as *Onkel Emil*. When members of the group communicated with each other, it was always in terms of the health of their mythical Uncle Emil. Even in the diaries she kept, Ruth referred to her companions by their code names.[2] While the members of *Onkel Emil* cooperated with other groups, including a small communist one known as

*Gruppe Ernst,* the supposed relatives of Uncle Emil held no particular political beliefs other than anti-Nazism. Like Ruth and Leo, most of the members were professionals. Jo Thaler and Frank Matthis were doctors, and Ruth's nineteen-year-old daughter, Karin, was an entertainer. But their number also included a skilled printer who could forge nearly any document perfectly. His talent was valuable in fostering the main work of the group, sheltering Jews and helping people evade the draft. Military exemption certificates, passes, false identification papers, and ration tickets were part of the man's production during the Hitler years. The fictitious Uncle Emil resided, through the war, in the Steglitz section of Berlin.

On April 20, 1945, Leo and Ruth were returning home along the Bismarckstrasse when they noticed two men in jackboots, storm trooper trousers, and civilian jackets marching in front of them, juggling a long, flat wooden box between them.

"Bazookas," Leo whispered.

Moments later they encountered another pair, similarly attired and burdened, followed by four Hitler Youths wearing broad belts of rifle ammunition over their shoulders.

"Not a very peaceable neighborhood, Steglitz," Ruth commented.[3]

That evening, crouching in a basement only a yard below ground, they endured three bombing attacks. During a break in the bombardment Leo rose.

"I'll see what it looks like outside," he said, and Ruth joined him.

The horizon over the cemetery near their building was the color of blood, tinged by the fires burning in the city. In the east they could hear an unfamiliar rumbling, like nothing they had heard before.

"Artillery!" Leo said. "They're attacking the city."[4]

The approaching Red Army was pouring over 40,000 tons of shells into the city during its final assault, completing the destruction begun by the American and British bombers.

For some of the members of the assaulting army the anticipated entry into Berlin would be a homecoming. One of these was fifty-one-year-old Walter Ulbricht, the son of a tailor from Leipzig. Apprenticed to a cabinetmaker after he had completed his elementary school education, Ulbricht became a member of the Worker's Youth Organization of the Socialist Party. Joining the Spartacus Society of Rosa Luxemburg and Karl Liebknecht in 1919, Ulbricht had helped to found the German Communist Party. He had trained in Moscow during the 1920s and had served as a Communist delegate to the Reichstag from 1928 until Hitler had expelled all Communists from that body after the Reichstag fire in 1933. Ulbricht fled, first to Czechoslovakia, then to the Soviet Union, where he became a member of the National Committee for Free Germany.[5] As the armies of Marshal Zhukov poised to batter their way into the city of Berlin, Walter Ulbricht was with them, wearing the blue-trimmed insignia and blue peaked cap of a colonel in the political corps of the Red Army.

On April 21, 1945, Adolf Hitler directed his final battle, meticulously giving precise instructions for the disposition of largely imaginary forces for a counterattack against the armies facing Berlin and predicting that the Soviets would meet their bloodiest defeat at the gates of the city. His orders called for an "Army Group" under the command of SS *Obergruppenführer* Felix Steiner to smash the spearhead of Marshal Zhukov's drive on the city. The orders were absurd: Steiner was not in communication with the scattered troops he was to command and had no transport available for them, even if he were. The counterattack never materialized.

Early in the morning of April 27, Ruth Andreas-Friedrich was startled by shouts outside the door of her building. When she opened the door she was confronted by seven worn-out soldiers with the runic emblems of the S.S. on their collars. They asked for water.

"We have no water here," she said. "Where's the front?"

"Along the canal," one of the soldiers answered. "They've broken through."

"Well, off with you."

"Where to? We're bottled up. We've lost our squad leader. They'll shoot us if we come without a leader."[6]

At seven o'clock in the morning the battle began to flow around her building. Soviet shells slammed into a nearby water tower, collapsing it in a cloud of dust and smoke. Soldiers, *Volkssturm* civilians, medics, and antiaircraft crews raced past, ducking shell bursts and moving toward the cemetery. At the street corner a man lay on the pavement, arms flung wide in death. Suddenly, silence descended. Ten, then fifteen, then twenty minutes passed, and the street was still deserted. Then the figure of a soldier in an unfamiliar uniform appeared at the corner of the block. He was a Soviet. Within moments he was joined by others, then by several tanks. Andreas-Friedrich, Borchard, and their companions in the house hung a white flag in the front window.

The following day the Soviets were joined by more tanks, and German snipers began harassing them. The apartment building shook and heaved as the Soviet tanks fired. Moments later, rifle butts clattered against the doors. Borchard, who was born in Moscow, answered in Russian, and the occupants were herded before a Soviet colonel whose field headquarters was a nearby cellar.

"You are partisans," the colonel said. "We shall shoot you."

"We're not partisans," Borchard answered.

"Why do you speak Russian?" the colonel asked.

Borchard explained, but the colonel remained suspicious and went on with his questioning. After several minutes, Borchard could stand it no longer.

"For twelve years we have been waiting for you. We've always been on your side."

The colonel was still not convinced.

"You say that you have listened to our radio. Do you know what we do when we announce a victory over you?" he asked.

"You fire a salute."

"Do you know the Russian national anthem?"

"I do."

The men in the command post were staring at Borchard, with faces frozen in iron expressions.

"Sing it to us. If you know it, you should be able to sing it."

As Borchard's voice rose in the dusty air of the command post, Andreas-Friedrich suddenly realized that he was singing for their lives. His voice rang clear in the smoky room.

*"Soyus nerushimyy respublik svobodnych,*
*Splotil na veki velikaya Rusy, . . . "*

The faces of the colonel and his men softened. When Borchard reached the fifth verse, the colonel pushed a half-filled glass of tea across the table to him.

"Drink that, *Tovarich,*" he said, and the men in the room leaped up, slapping Borchard and Andreas-Friedrich on the back, offering them food, laughing, and shaking their hands.[7]

On April 29 Adolf Hitler married his longtime mistress, Eva Braun, in a simple ceremony in the Führerbunker. He then ordered that his favorite Alsatian dog be poisoned. Early the next morning, he shook hands with the remaining staff in the bunker and retired with his new wife to their cramped quarters. At approximately 3:15 in the afternoon, Eva took poison, and, moments later, Hitler placed the barrel of a Walther pistol in his mouth and pulled the trigger. Their bodies were removed from the bunker to the courtyard of the Reich chancellery, where S.S. guards doused them with gasoline and ignited them.

By May 1, 1945, all that was left in the hands of the German army were a few government buildings, a small part of the adjoining Tiergarten, and the area between the Havel River and the zoo. Lieutenant General Hans Krebs, who had served in Moscow as the German military attaché and spoke Russian, was sent to negotiate a truce. At four in the morning, he met with the commander of the 8th Guards Tank Army, General Chuikov, at Schulenburgring near Tempelhof Airport. There he was informed that the Soviets would accept nothing less than unconditional surrender. Krebs noted during the brief talks that it was May 1, a day that both Germany and the Soviet Union shared as a holiday. Chuikov responded coldly that it might be a fine day in Moscow, but that he could not say the same for Berlin. General Kerbs returned to the Führerbunker and, after reporting his failure, committed suicide, in imitation of his fallen leader.

At noon on May 1, two Yakalov Yak-3 fighters of the Red Air Force's 2d Air Army swooped low over the city, skimming along the River Spree at one hundred feet. Turning at the fire-blackened hulk of the cathedral, the fighters bore down on the ruins of the Reichstag. As they passed over the building, two red banners fluttered down from their cockpits. One bore an embroidered greeting to the Red Army troops there. The second bore a single word: VICTORY.[8] Adolf Hitler's body, incompletely incinerated by the makeshift cremation, lay in a shell crater behind the ruins of the chancellery. The capital of the Thousand-Year Reich lay shattered about it.

The following morning, General Weidling crossed the lines separating his troops from the Soviets and surrendered unconditionally.

When the city surrendered, Berlin's water mains were ruptured in 3,000 places, three out of four of its fire stations had been destroyed, and fewer than forty buses and one hundred street cars were functioning. Of the more than 125,000 street lamps that had brightened Berlin's thoroughfares before the war, fewer than 4,000 still stood.

The canals that crisscrossed the city were reeking cesspools into which the effluent of the city's ruptured sewers poured, and the stink of death rose from the cellars of bomb-blasted buildings. Of the 150 bridges that had once linked various parts of the city, 128 had been totally destroyed.

The Soviets had conquered ruins.

# ONE

# THE FACE OF
# DEFEAT

When Lucius DuBignon Clay arrived for his new assignment in the European theater of operations on April 7, 1945, he was wearing the three stars of a lieutenant general. His recent appointment as deputy for military government to Supreme Allied Commander Dwight D. Eisenhower called for that rank. The great-grandnephew of Henry Clay and son of a United States senator, Lucius Clay's fondest memory of his boyhood trips to Washington with his father was of his borrowing privileges at the Library of Congress. He would check out dozens of books at a time. Appointed to the Military Academy at West Point, he had graduated in the class of 1918 but had never held a combat command. He had chosen the field artillery as his branch of service upon graduation, but, along with many other members of the class of 1918, he was arbitrarily assigned to the Corps of Engineers to fill the manpower needs of the Army as it entered World War I. He spent that war supervising training in the United States and reached the rank of captain. The first of the interwar retrenchments by the Army found Clay and his fellow engineers-by-assignment reduced to first lieutenants, a grade in which he remained for eleven years. During that time, he spent four years as an instructor at the Military Academy, did a tour with the 11th Engineers in Panama, and served on detached duty with the U.S. Marines in the Caribbean, earning a letter of commendation from the commandant of the Corps, a singular distinction at a time when medals, decorations, and commendations were rare.[1] He regained the rank of captain only after having been assigned to the headquarters of the Corps of Engineers in Washington in July 1933, where he built a reputation as a brilliant administrator with an extremely retentive mind and the knack for cutting to the core of a problem in a moment.

When the United States entered World War II, Clay repeatedly asked for combat assignments, but his requests were invariably turned down. His reputation as a "get-it-done" engineer kept him in staff assignments: first, as Director of Materiel of the Armed Service Forces under

General Brehon Somervell, and, later, as James Byrne's deputy at the Office of War Mobilization and Reconversion. Byrnes said of Lucius Clay, recommending him to President Roosevelt for the job of deputy for military government, "I found no army officer with as clear an understanding of the point of view of the civilian." [2]

The staff assignments during the war had brought rapid promotion for Clay; he was appointed a temporary brigadier general in March 1942 and given two-star rank nine months later. Now, with the end of the war in Europe in sight, Clay had been chosen to be the American who would administer military government in the United States sector of a conquered Germany.

The decision to divide Germany into separate zones of occupation administered by the victorious powers had developed gradually from seeds planted in mid-December 1941, a time when Allied fortunes were at their lowest ebb. The Japanese had struck at Pearl Harbor only a week before, destroying major elements of the American Pacific Fleet, and Rommel was on the offensive in North Africa. German submarines were hunting unmolested on the seas, exacting a terrible toll on Allied shipping in the North Atlantic and off the American coast.

When British foreign secretary Anthony Eden arrived in Moscow on December 16, 1941, to discuss future Allied cooperation, Hitler's invasion of Russia was only six months old. The German armies had pushed to a point where their advance patrols could see the spires of the Kremlin, where Eden was meeting Generalissimo Joseph Stalin, gleaming in the distance. The panzers of Field Marshal von Kluge's Fourth Army were in the western suburbs of Moscow, and Eden could hear the rumble of artillery fire in the night. [3] Therefore, Eden was surprised when Stalin began their meeting by launching into a long discussion of the Soviet Union's territorial expectations once Germany had been defeated.

The war, the Soviet premier stated, had already cost the USSR untold suffering, and she would have to be compensated. Poland's western border must be fixed at the old Curzon line of 1939, meaning that the Polish territory that the Soviets had occupied under the terms of the Nazi-Soviet Non-aggression Pact, before Hitler turned on his Soviet ally, would return to Soviet control. East Prussia was to be annexed directly and the Baltic states of Latvia, Lithuania, and Estonia and that portion of Finland won in the Russo-Finnish War but now occupied by Germany were all to be returned to Soviet control.

A somewhat shaken Eden reported these proposals to Winston Churchill, who replied, "To approach President Roosevelt with these proposals would be to court a blank refusal, and might cause lasting trouble on both sides." [4] There is no indication that Roosevelt was ever made aware of these early territorial demands of the Soviets. Roosevelt, and most of his advisors, preferred a course of winning the victory first and dealing with postwar settlements later.[5]

By the time of the Casablanca conference between Roosevelt and Churchill, in January 1943, the prospects for the Allies were much better. The Japanese main fleet had been defeated at the critical battle of Midway, and Axis forces had been swept out of North Africa. In the Soviet Union, Field Marshal von Paulis had become entrapped at Stalingrad where, within a month, he would surrender a German army of 200,000 to the Soviets. At Casablanca President Roosevelt announced the Allied demand of "unconditional surrender" by the Axis nations but was otherwise extremely vague as to postwar Allied intentions. It was two months after Casablanca that Roosevelt, in a meeting with Foreign Secretary Eden, first committed the United States to having American troops remain in Germany after the war and to taking part in an occupation.

Presidential advisor Harry Hopkins took notes of a meeting between Eden, Roosevelt, Secretary of State Cordell Hull, and himself, that took place over tea in the President's study. Hopkins recorded in his diary:

> I said I thought that there was no understanding between Great Britain, Russia, and ourselves as to which armies would be where and what sort of administration should be developed. I said that unless we acted promptly and surely I believed one of two things would happen—either Germany would go Communist or an out and out anarchic state would set in.
>
> I said I thought it required some sort of formal agreement and that the State Department should work out a plan with the British and the one agreed upon between us should then be discussed with the Russians.[6]

While Roosevelt agreed with Hopkins's suggestion, the Anglo-American position still had not been agreed upon when the foreign ministers of the three nations met in Moscow seven months later, as a preliminary to the Big Three Conference scheduled to be held in Tehran in November 1943. In Moscow, Secretary of State Hull presented a general document titled "Basic Principles Regarding Germany's Surrender" to Soviet Foreign Minister Vyacheslav I. Molotov. The suggestions contained in the document were extremely general in nature. While it stated that Germany was to be occupied by all three nations, it failed to mention how this was to take place: no zonal boundaries were suggested, and no mention whatsoever was made of the German capital of Berlin. Others had thought the problem through more thoroughly.

In 1943 a British Cabinet committee headed by Deputy Prime Minister Clement Attlee had devised a partition of Germany into three zones of occupation, with the Soviets occupying approximately forty percent of the territory of pre-1937 Germany. The British and Americans were scheduled, under the Attlee proposal, to occupy the western portion of the country, with the British sector in the northwest and the American in the south. The city of Berlin, deep inside the territory proposed to be occupied by the Soviets, was to be jointly occupied as a symbol of Allied unity. The Attlee committee made no mention of access to the city through the territory proposed for Soviet occupation.

Learning of Hull's proposal, Anthony Eden suggested the formation of a European Advisory Commission to consider the problems of the conquered countries in greater detail. Eden proposed that the commission be a negotiating body and the conclusions arrived at be in the form of recommendations to the Big Three. The suggestion of the British foreign minister was eagerly adopted, and the concept of a European Advisory Commission was approved by Roosevelt, Stalin, and Churchill at Tehran.[7] While the Big Three, later joined by General Charles DeGaulle of France, focused on winning the war, the EAC was expected to work on the details of how the occupation of conquered territory would be handled.

President Roosevelt had become aware of the Attlee plan while on board the USS *Iowa,* en route to the Tehran Conference. His immediate reaction was negative, and he marked out his own ideas for zones of occupation on a *National Geographic* map of Europe. The American zone, Roosevelt insisted, should be in the industrial northwest of the country, with the British occupying the south. The Soviet zone, as proposed by Roosevelt, was to be much smaller than proposed in the British draft, and the city of Berlin would lie at the boundary between American and Soviet territory.[8]

President Roosevelt designated John G. Winant, the ambassador to the Court of St. James, to head the American delegation to the European Advisory Council. Winant, a former governor of New Hampshire, had succeeded Joseph P. Kennedy as ambassador to England and was expected to serve on the EAC at the same time that he was fully discharging his duties in England. Winant was assisted by a staff that included George F. Kennan, a career State Department employee.

The Soviet delegate was Fedor Tarasovich, the ambassador to England. Great Britain was represented by Sir William Strang, a permanent undersecretary in the Foreign Office. At the first formal meeting of the commission, held in London on January 14, 1944, Sir William formally introduced the Attlee proposal.[9]

Ambassador Winant had no instructions on the matter of occupation zones in Germany, not having been informed of the president's desires. When the Soviets announced on February 18 that they were prepared to accept the British proposal and spelled out in detail their own plan for a tripartite occupation of Berlin, the ambassador communicated nothing to Washington. He was startled when, three weeks later, he received a plan from Washington that had been devised by a low-level Department of State group known as the Working Security Committee. Set up to gather opinions from the State, Navy, and War departments, as well as the Joint Post War Committee of the Joint Chiefs of Staff, the Civil Affairs Division, and any other interested Washington agency, the WSC had been a wrangling ground for months. The plan forwarded to Winant for presentation to the EAC showed Germany divided into three zones, the boundaries of which radiated out from Berlin at the center. Winant refused even to present it without a supporting memorandum from the Department of State, but his request for such a document went unanswered.[10]

In April, George Kennan was sent to Washington to review the matter with the president. They met on April 3, 1944, and Roosevelt learned for the first time that the Soviets and the British had completely agreed on the original Attlee proposal. He acquiesced on the question of zone boundaries but continued to stress that the United States must occupy the northwestern portion of the country and not the south. The location of Berlin 110 miles inside the Soviet-occupied zone was now fixed. General Clay would have to live with that geographic fact. Discussions of zones of occupation at later meetings of the war leaders—between Roosevelt and Churchill at Quebec and among Stalin, Roosevelt, and Churchill at Yalta—would not even involve Berlin. The question of who would occupy the industrial north of Germany would be resolved in favor of the British, and the inclusion of the French as an occupying power, with their zone carved out of the areas allocated to the British and Americans, would be accomplished. The fact that Berlin would be an enclave under quadripartite administration, deep within the Soviet zone, was never again an object of discussion.

General Clay's job as Eisenhower's deputy for military government was complicated by other policy disagreements at the highest level of the Allied governments as well. When the war in Europe ended, the troops of the victorious British and American armies had penetrated far into the territories that had been designated for Soviet occupation. Both Clay and his superior, Supreme Commander Eisenhower, urged that an orderly withdrawal of troops from these areas and a transfer to Soviet control be undertaken at the earliest possible moment. Both realized that a joint occupation of Germany could not begin until the forces of each of the occupying nations were in their designated zones.

On April 5, 1945, a month before the fighting stopped, Eisenhower requested permission to allow his area commanders to arrange independently for the Soviet entry into the territories captured by American forces that the Soviets were scheduled to occupy. That permission was denied.[11] There was a growing misapprehension and puzzlement about Soviet postwar intentions in the State Department. America's

British allies, historically suspicious about Soviet intentions, were concerned as well.

The British Foreign Office and in particular Prime Minister Winston Churchill were deeply distrustful of the Soviets. They objected to any withdrawal such as Eisenhower proposed and made those objections known to the American government. They believed that the large parts of the Soviet zone now occupied by the Western allies would provide a powerful lever to wring concessions from the Soviets. Even Roosevelt had begun to become mistrustful of the Soviet Union. When he was given a cable critical of Soviet actions from his ambassador in Moscow, W. Averell Harriman, Roosevelt reacted vehemently. He banged his fists on the arms of his wheelchair, proclaiming, "Averell is right. We can't do business with Stalin."[12] His reaction to the specific plan of his British allies to force the Soviets into concessions by refusing to withdraw troops from the Soviet designated zone of Germany is unknown.

On the afternoon of April 12, 1945, while vacationing at the spa at Warm Springs, Georgia, President Roosevelt complained of a terrific headache, then collapsed from a cerebral hemorrhage. He died at 3:45 p.m., and Vice President Harry S Truman succeeded him. Truman was described at the beginning of his career in Washington as "the Senator from Prendergast,"[13] in reference to his connections to the notorious Kansas City political machine, but he had since built a reputation as a diligent, hard-working member of the Senate, particularly for his work in ferreting out waste in war production programs.[14] Speaking to the press the day after Roosevelt died, Truman said, "Boys, if you ever pray, pray for me now. I don't know if you ever had a load of hay fall on you, but when they told me yesterday what had happened, I felt like the moon, the stars, and all the planets had fallen on me."[15]

Harry Truman then went to work gathering in the reins of government. While there were disturbing signs that the Soviet Union was not living up to agreements between the allies, Truman could not see the value of the West reneging on its own commitments, such as the occupation zones of Germany. For the time being, the new president was content to continue the policies of his predecessor.[16]

On May 7, 1945, a formal Instrument of Surrender was signed at General Eisenhower's headquarters at Rheims, and the war in Europe ended. The Soviets insisted that a second surrender ceremony take place in the fallen German capital of Berlin, and it was quickly arranged. At this ceremony, Field Marshal Keitel represented the Germans, and Soviet Marshal Georgi Zhukov and British Air Marshal Tedder signed for the Allies. General Carl Spaatz of the U.S. Army Air Forces and General de Lattre de Tassigny of France were witnesses.[17]

Prime Minister Churchill remained "profoundly concerned"[18] about Soviet ambitions in Europe, stating that "An iron curtain is being drawn down upon their front, and we do not know what is going on behind it."[19] It was his first use of that ringing phrase. Churchill proposed that he and the new American president meet to discuss future relations with the Soviet Union, but Truman flatly refused, arranging instead for a meeting of the Big Three. He firmly informed Churchill that the United States' intention was "to adhere to our interpretation of the Yalta Agreements."[20] His commitment that the United States would withdraw to its designated zone of Germany prior to the Big Three meeting was clear.

☆  ☆  ☆

While politicians and diplomats wrangled over abstract ideas, the people of Berlin were learning the meaning of living in a conquered city. Behind the hardened, frontline veterans of Zhukov's army came hordes of troops intent on exacting retribution from the Germans. Their vengeance took the form of rape and looting on a massive scale.

In a cellar shelter in the Zehlendorf section, the door was beaten in by four Soviet soldiers. Ursula Koster, the mother of six-year-old twins and a seven-month-old boy who were sleeping there with her, was raped by all four after they had looted the shelter. The following morning, as Koster was nursing her baby, two more Soviets appeared, and she was raped again.[21]

Ruth Andreas-Friedrich and a friend, a doctor, from the resistance group *Onkel Emil* ventured forth from their shelter wearing red armbands. They visited a friend, Hannelore Theile, and found her huddled on a couch, crying with her face in her hands.

"One really ought to kill oneself," Theile said.

"Was it really that bad?" Andreas-Friedrich asked.

"Seven. Seven in a row. Like animals."[22]

Another friend, eighteen-year-old Inge Zaun, was raped sixty times.[23]

It was a scene repeated, with minor variations, throughout the city in the spring of 1945, and Berliners would long remember the harsh call of *"Frau kommen,"* a phrase that was often the only German a Soviet soldier knew. It meant, "Woman, come here."

As Ruth and her companion wandered the streets after the encounter, she was shaken, remembering that Goebbels had harangued the German public for years, saying that if the Soviets won the war they would rape and pillage, plunder and murder. She did not want Goebbels to have been right.

"You see," the doctor explained to her, "when we invaded their country, killed their men, carried off their possessions, the *muzhaks* thought: They must be poorer than we are. They must suffer from hunger and need. That they would have understood because it's simple and natural. But it wasn't simple. And it wasn't natural. And when they came to Germany they saw we had houses and even bathtubs and mirrors and fancy furniture. Do you understand now why they got so mad? The plundering and looting, the smashing and pillaging? It's the mirrors that made them mad, the bathtubs and the fancy furniture. One doesn't attack someone if one is so much better off than one's victim."

"But the rapes? You don't rape just because you don't have fancy furniture. And if you do, then certainly not with entire battalions."

"On the contrary," the doctor interrupted, "you do it with entire battalions. That's what it's all about." [24]

The Soviet looting was at first unsystematic and sometimes even comic. Soldiers from Asian republics, unfamiliar with electricity, unscrewed light bulbs from their sockets and carefully packed them in their knapsacks on the theory that they would light when they returned home. Others were seen with dozens of wristwatches on their arms, all pilfered from Germans and set two hours ahead of the time in Berlin, to Moscow time.

Where they did not loot, the Soviet troops frequently destroyed. At the warehouses of the International Red Cross near the suburb of Potsdam, they drunkenly machine-gunned thousands of parcels of drugs and medical supplies. "They came in," recalled a witness, "went into one of the cellars, saw the huge pile of parcels and just tommy-gunned the lot. Liquids of all sorts poured out of the shattered parcels. It was just unbelievable." [25]

At the UFA Film studios, hundreds of drunken soldiers broke into the costume department and emerged festooned in fantastic outfits, firing their guns into the air and dancing in the street. [26]

Even the *Onkel Emil* group was not immune.

Returning home one evening, Leo Borchard and Ruth Andreas-Friedrich encountered open drawers, broken furniture, and chaos. Clothes were scattered throughout their rooms, and phonograph records, broken bottles, and prescription pill containers crunched under their feet as they looked for the source of a terrible stench. Leo Borchard found it in the bathroom.

"Buffaloes must have done this," he said, trying to flush the toilet. There was no water. [27]

Gradually, the Soviet High Command brought their troops under some control. On May 2, 1945, restaurants and cabarets were authorized to reopen as places of entertainment for Soviet troops. The distribution of rations to the civilian population began to be organized, although the ration was a meager 1,248 calories a day for those in the lowest category—the unemployed, the overaged, and those who had somehow incurred the displeasure of the occupiers. Politicians, party officials, and persons performing hard labor were allowed 2,485 calories a day. [28]

Radio Berlin, now under Soviet control, began to broadcast again on May 4, and publication of the *Tägliche Rundschau*, a German language newspaper for the Red Army, began. Soon the *Berliner Zeitung,* controlled by the Soviets, was available for sale in news kiosks.

In each of the twenty boroughs of the city, district mayors were appointed, all sympathetic to the Soviets. The same procedure was followed for the heads of borough departments, and most were elderly and without political experience. Key positions in each of the boroughs, such as that of personnel director, were reserved for members of the Communist Party. The top education posts and leadership of the police always remained in Communist hands.

A sixty-seven-year-old retired municipal architect, Arthur Werner, was appointed lord mayor of Greater Berlin. He had not been a supporter of the Nazis and had been dismissed from his municipal position as an architect when they came to power, but there was nothing else in his background that appeared to qualify him for the post. His appointment came about in a curious fashion.

Werner was pruning fruit trees and shrubs in his garden on May 12, 1945, when a car driven by a Red Army soldier stopped and a German passenger, Karl Marion, got out and approached Werner. Werner, fearing that he was being kidnapped, was hustled into the car and driven to a small house in the eastern suburb of Friedrichsfelde, where he was introduced to a man with a Lenin-like beard, wearing the uniform of the Red Army. The question he posed startled Dr. Werner. "Would you accept the position of Mayor of Berlin?" asked Colonel Walter Ulbricht.

Stunned, desperately tired, and hungry, Werner offered no answer, and Ulbricht invited him to eat and to rest on the sofa. He dozed off and woke up only when several people, led by a heavily bemedaled Soviet general, entered the room. Through an interpreter the general said, "I am General Bersarin, City Commandant of Berlin. Do you wish to be Mayor?" Werner stammered his agreement.[29]

Karl Marion, a dedicated Communist, was appointed Werner's deputy mayor, and six of his thirteen executive department heads were members of the Communist party. The critical post of police president was given to Paul Markgraf, whose experience as a police officer was sparse and many years past. Under the Hitler regime Markgraf had been an army training officer and had risen rapidly once the war broke out. He was a lieutenant colonel and holder of the Knight's Cross of the Iron Cross when his luck as a Nazi ran out. He was among the 200,000 men captured by the Soviets at Stalingrad, and he had almost immediately signed up as a member of the Free Germany Committee. The Soviets flew him back to Berlin soon after the capture of the city.

The tragicomic looting of the first week of the occupation slowed, and systematic stripping and dismantlement of factories for shipment to the Soviet Union as reparations began, even though the Western allies had not yet agreed on the amount and nature of such reparations.

The people of Berlin—hungry, numbed by the defeat of their country, and battered by the cruelty of the initial occupation by the Soviets—hoped for better times. They had not been told that their city was scheduled to be occupied, jointly, by all four of the victors, but they prayed for the arrival of someone other than the Soviets.[30]

## TWO
# "IT'S GOT TO WORK"

A week after the Germans surrendered, General Lucius D. Clay held a news conference in the Hotel Scribe in Paris. His deputy, Major General Frank McSherry, and General Eisenhower's diplomatic advisor, Robert Murphy, were at his side. Clay made it clear to the gathered reporters that the first priority of the occupation would be the dismantling of the Nazi apparatus of government. Long-range plans for Germany and the regeneration of the German people would be considered later.

As his piercing dark eyes swept the crowd during the question-and-answer session after the briefing, Clay was asked of the chances of success in achieving inter-Allied cooperation. His answer was emphatic. Slamming one fist into the palm of his other hand, he said, "It's got to work." He went on:

> If the four of us can't get together now in running Germany, how are we going to get together in an international organization to secure the peace of the world? We are going to have to give and take and do a lot of things which the American public will not believe in, but we cannot go in there with four nations without being prepared to give and take, and if the people at home will recognize that the experiment of four nations means much to the future of the world then we have hope for the future of the job.[1]

It was an expression of pure Rooseveltian idealism.

Leo Borchard, long banned from performing in Germany, announced to his friends over their meager dinner on May 23, 1945, "Tomorrow at ten I have my first rehearsal."[2] The Soviets had moved quickly to reestablish cultural activities in the fallen city, and Borchard had been appointed director of a revived Berlin Philharmonic, with a concert scheduled for May 26 in the hastily repaired Titania Palace.

The concert opened with Mendelssohn's *Midsummer Night's Dream.* It was music that had been forbidden to Germans as "a Jewish

concoction" under the Nazis. As the concert concluded with Tchaikov-
sky's Fourth Symphony, the man seated next to Ruth Andreas-
Friedrich said, in amazement at the survival of beauty among ruins:
"That something like this is still possible."[3]

At home, after the concert, Borchard stood silently on the balcony
and stared up at the stars, completely unable to express his feelings
about it.

☆    ☆    ☆

The Soviets still had not informed the citizens of Berlin that their city
was to be divided into sectors and administered by the military governments of the Soviet Union, Great Britain, France, and the United States.
The negotiations to establish the administration of the city, and of Germany itself, continued to drag.

General Eisenhower made it quite clear to his superiors in Washington that he "could not carry out his mission much longer" in the absence of a four-power agreement and had again suggested that American forces begin their withdrawal from the Soviet designated zones
immediately.[4] The Foreign Office in London suggested instead that the
four commanders-in-chief—Eisenhower, Zhukov, Field Marshal Bernard Law Montgomery for the British, and General Lattre de Tassigny
for France—convene in Berlin to establish the Control Council, then
schedule meetings of that body as they thought necessary. Eisenhower
and Clay were sure that the question of withdrawing troops would be
a major question at the meeting, which was scheduled for June 5. Clay
prepared a cable to Chairman of the Joint Chiefs of Staff George C. Marshall for Eisenhower's signature:

> It is anticipated that one of the questions which will be raised at the
> Berlin meeting, will be the date on which forces will begin their with-
> drawal from the Russian zone. . . . Any cause for delay in the establish-
> ment of the Control Council would be attributable to us and might well
> develop strong public reaction. . . . It is believed desirable that separate
> instructions be given to me as American Commander and to the British
> Commander prior to the Berlin meeting as to how to reply to this question
> if it is raised.[5]

The Joint Chiefs replied, with the approval of President Truman, that
American troops should not be withdrawn from the Soviet zone before
the establishment of the Control Council and the takeover of the western sectors of Berlin. Once established, the Control Council was to deal
with the withdrawal as a matter of military convenience. "Its timing
will be in accordance with U.S. ability to withdraw their forces from
other than their own zone," Marshall cabled in reply, "and British and
Russian ability to take over."[6]

Churchill was not happy with this decision. In a cable to Truman the day before the meeting of the military commanders, he expressed his grave misgivings about "the retreat of the American Army to our line of occupation in the central sector, thus bringing Soviet power into the heart of Western Europe and the descent of an iron curtain between us and everything to the eastward."[7] The phrase "iron curtain" was finding its way into his pronouncements more often.

On June 5, 1945, the commanders of the three Western allied armies flew in separate planes into the bomb-damaged and only partially repaired Luftwaffe fighter airfield at Tempelhof, in the south-central area of Berlin designated for American occupation. Although Montgomery and de Tassigny were actually subordinate to Eisenhower as Supreme Commander at this time, the use of separate aircraft was chosen to emphasize diplomatically that there would soon be independent commands.[8]

Eisenhower was accompanied by General Clay and Ambassador Robert Murphy, and all three delegations were met by General Zhukov's deputy, General Vassily Sokolovsky, and escorted from the airport by Soviet troops to Zhukov's headquarters in the eastern suburb of Karlshorst. As the group moved through the shattered city by car, destruction was all around them and the air reeked of death. The canals were choked with debris and bodies. Under a last-minute order of the Nazis, Berlin's subways had been flooded, and the thousands who had taken refuge there from the bombing and shells had drowned. Their bodies were only now washing out into the canals.

General Clay noted the Berliners they passed en route. They "seemed weak, cowed, and furtive and not yet recovered from the shock of the Battle of Berlin." The city looked to him like a city of the dead.[9]

Clay, like all of the others, was looking forward to the first meeting with General Zhukov, the foremost military leader of the Soviet Union, but he had some misgivings as well. He recalled that the Soviets had insisted on staging a separate surrender ceremony in Berlin, having first refused to take part in the official German surrender at Rheims, and he could not help but wonder what lay ahead.

The meeting was scheduled to begin at noon and shortly before that time General Eisenhower met briefly with Zhukov. In a small ceremony, Eisenhower awarded his Soviet counterpart the grade of Grand Commander of the American Legion of Honor. No reciprocal Soviet award was given.

The appointed hour for the meeting came and passed, and the three Western commanders were kept waiting in their quarters until late in the afternoon. Becoming angry at the delay, Eisenhower and Montgomery sent a joint message to the Soviets demanding that the conference be convened at once or they would leave. The ultimatum produced fast results, and the meeting began soon afterward, only to become mired in Soviet objections to a single phrase in one of the three documents that were to be signed that day. The language was ambiguous but, as the Soviets interpreted it, they would be required to arrest Japanese nationals in their zone of occupation, even though the Soviet Union was not yet formally at war with Japan.

Field Marshal Montgomery recalled later, "I was so fed up with the whole affair that I suggested that the offending word be deleted from the text; this suggestion was at once agreed to by the Russians and everyone else, and to this day I do not know what difference it made."[10]

The first of the three documents to be signed was the "Declaration Regarding the Defeat of Germany," in which the Allied powers specifically stated their assumption of supreme authority in Germany. The second document divided Germany into four zones of occupation and provided for joint occupation of the capital of Berlin. The third set up various organs of administration, providing that supreme authority in Germany would be exercised by the Allied Control Council, made up of the four commanders-in-chief. All decisions of the council were required to be unanimous, and the chairmanship was to rotate on a regular basis.

When, under the glare of arc lamps set up to accommodate newsreel photographers, the formal signing was completed, the leaders adjourned for a private meeting. General Zhukov chaired the meeting, and he opened it by asking if there were any other matters to be discussed.

"The installment of the Control Council in Berlin," Eisenhower replied.

"*Nyet*," Zhukov answered.

He expanded through his interpreter. "Not until your troops are evacuated from the areas in the Soviet Zone they now illegally occupy."

Eisenhower then suggested that both questions be discussed simultaneously.

"*Nyet*," replied Zhukov. "I cannot discuss the first until the second is settled."[11]

It was obvious to all attending that he was acting under orders from his government, and no further discussion took place.

☆ ☆ ☆

Just before the Allied commanders met in Berlin, the Soviets restored electrical power to the borough of Steglitz. Ruth Andreas-Friedrich, Leo Borchard, and the other members of *Onkel Emil* could gather around the radio they had used to listen to broadcasts from London during the Nazi era. For the first time in six years, they didn't feel like criminals for listening.

On the first evening they had power, Borchard spun the dial through the stations. "Beautiful," he said.[12] They stayed up late into the night listening and talking of their hopes that the Western allies would enter their city.

When the texts of the "Declaration of the Allied Powers Regarding the Defeat of Germany" and its accompanying documents were published in the *Tägliche Rundschau,* there were happy faces all over Berlin again, as people began to feel some hope for the future. Berliners had felt lost to the world and had begun to believe that the Soviets would never leave their city. Now a story printed in a Soviet-controlled newspaper told them that the Americans, the British, and the French were coming.

☆　☆　☆

When the news of the Soviet rebuff at the June 7 meeting was relayed to Washington, Harry Truman reacted with characteristic decisiveness. Consulting with Harry Hopkins, who had just returned from a trip that had included Germany, he agreed to a proposal by Hopkins and Eisenhower that withdrawal of American troops from areas of Germany that had been designated as the Soviet zone should begin as soon as possible and that firm arrangements should be made for the simultaneous arrival of Western troops in Berlin. Churchill was informed of this decision and finally gave way.

"Obviously, we are obliged to conform to your decision, and the necessary instructions will be issued," the British prime minister cabled the president. "I sincerely hope," he concluded the cable, "that your action will in the long run make for a lasting peace in Europe."[13]

Churchill's quick and positive response took the Americans by surprise. Surprise became genuine shock when they received Marshal Stalin's reply to a message setting June 21 as the date when American troops would leave the areas that were assigned to the Soviets.

The Soviets were not ready for the Americans to come to Berlin, Stalin cabled. Marshal Zhukov was required to be in Moscow for a victory parade on June 24, and he would not return to Berlin until the end of the month. In addition, "some districts of Berlin have not yet been cleared of mines, nor can such mine-clearing operations be finished until late June." The Soviet premier suggested that July 1 would be a more convenient date.[14]

In Berlin, the systematic looting of industrial plants, under the direction of the Soviet high command, went forward. Entire factories were emptied and their contents loaded onto flatcars for shipment to the Soviet Union. In Tegel, an area being considered for occupation by the French, the buildings of the Borsig company were stripped to the last screwdriver. Over one hundred years old, Borsig AG was known as the hospital of German industry; it repaired the tanks, pumps, steam engines, giant cranes, and other machines used in countless factories. It was essential to the functioning of Berlin's industry, and, except for the shells of its buildings, Borsig AG had ceased to exist.[15]

In any case, there would be little for it to service in the near future. Ninety percent of Berlin's steel industry, 85 percent of the optical and electrical industries, and 75 percent of the printing industry were removed to be sent to the USSR.[16] Berlin's telephone system, which before the war had over 600,000 private phones, was systematically taken apart. When the Americans arrived, only 4,000 telephones were left.[17] Asked about this, one Soviet officer said, "If the Germans wanted telephone service, they should not have started the war."[18]

Even animals were not exempt. Berlin had boasted a dairy herd of 7,000 cattle even at the height of the war. It supplied the milk needs of the city. All the cows were rounded up and driven east by the Soviets.[19]

☆  ☆  ☆

On June 17, 1945, Colonel Frank L. Howley had a very bad day. His military government detachment, A1A1, was attached to the First Airborne Army under Major General Floyd Parks, and the general had ordered Howley to lead a reconnaissance group to Berlin. It was a task that Howley had been looking forward to ever since late autumn of 1944, when his unit was selected to be the military government detachment for Berlin.

Frank Howley had come into military government by a curious path. A graduate of New York University and the Sorbonne in Paris, where he had studied history, Howley had built a career as a successful Philadelphia advertising executive. An avid horseman, he was a reserve cavalry officer, and his unit was activated in 1940, prior to the outbreak of the war.[20] While on maneuvers in Georgia, where he was serving as executive officer of the Third Cavalry Regiment, he discovered that his skill as a motorcyclist was not all that he thought it was. An accident on a dirt road broke his back and pelvis, and, after five months in the hospital, he was given a choice: be discharged as unfit for combat service or transfer to military government. Howley took the transfer.[21]

After training in the United States and England, he was designated commander of a civil affairs detachment and landed at Omaha Beach on D-Day plus 4, with a mixed American-British-French group designated to take over the administration of the city of Cherbourg. Later he headed the civil affairs detachment in Paris and, while on that assignment, was selected for the Berlin assignment.

The unit he commanded was a well-trained, well-educated group of 150 officers and 200 enlisted men. In contrast to a combat unit, the average age of the soldiers in the unit was forty-two—Howley's own age. A former California supreme court justice, Benjamin Scheinman, headed the legal section, and the head of public sanitation and water was John Diggs, a Purdue graduate with twenty-two years of municipal public works experience in Indiana. Most of the officers—engineers, professional policemen, public accountants—were reservists like Howley.[22]

The reconnaissance that Howley undertook on June 17 did not include his entire detachment. Its purposes were to make a brief survey of the sector of Berlin that the Americans expected to occupy, to hire workers to repair buildings for headquarters and barracks, and to make things ready for the main body of troops who were expected to move in within weeks. The group Howley commanded for this assignment was approximately 500 men, who rode in 120 vehicles. Colonel Howley led in a commandeered Horsch staff car, with the Stars and Stripes flapping from a staff on the right fender. At the rear of the column was a company of the Second Armored Division in half-tracks. The group crossed the Elbe River at Dessau on a pontoon bridge that had been built by the American Army engineers. They passed under a tremendous arch that the Soviets had erected later. The arch was decorated with huge portraits of Stalin and Lenin and a banner proclaiming "Welcome to the Fatherland," as if Germany was already a part of the Soviet Union.[23]

Immediately on the other side of the bridge a Soviet woman soldier, snapping red and yellow signal flags, saluted them, and the convoy was joined by a Soviet officer in a battered German staff car who led them down the road to a roadblock. There, the Soviet informed them that they must stop, as they were expected at the local headquarters.

Headquarters was in a rickety, unrepaired German house, where they were greeted by a heavy-set, round-faced Colonel Gorelik. He told them that they could not proceed yet, as there was "a formality." The colonel invited Howley and some of the other American officers to have a drink and ordered German champagne brought in for them. As they drank, a Soviet sergeant came in and, without a word to anyone, went to a piano in the corner of the room and began to bang away at it. After forty-five minutes the Soviet colonel went to the window and asked, "How many vehicles, officers, and men do you have?"

"Roughly 500 officers and men and 120 vehicles," Howley answered.

"The agreement says 37 officers, 50 vehicles, and 175 men," the Soviet responded coldly.

"What agreement?"

"The Berlin Agreement."

Howley had heard of no such agreement. "Perhaps you're confusing some offhand estimate of what we would need with an actual agreement," he ventured.

"There is such an agreement," the Soviet insisted.

"Well, I haven't heard of any agreement," Howley countered, adding that his orders were clear and that hundreds of Americans would be coming in within days.

"Oh. Then I must check headquarters," the Soviet responded, not adding that to do so a car had to be sent to a village twenty miles away where the telephone lines to Berlin ended. Two hours later, the Americans were still waiting.

"Look," Howley said to the colonel, "we have orders to go to Berlin. These orders cover every unit and they don't say, 'If the Russians are willing.' Let's be frank. You're keeping us from going to Berlin and I want to know who is responsible."

The Soviet colonel glared at Howley. "My superior ordered this," he said.

"Then let us speak to your superior."

Within an hour a one-star Soviet general arrived. "The agreement is for 37 officers, 50 vehicles, and 175 men," he said.

Howley asked to see the general's superior, and a very definite and abrupt two-star general arrived. "My orders are that you stay."

Howley demanded to see the two-star general's superior, and the corps commander, a three-star colonel-general with a twitching right eye, arrived at the dilapidated farmhouse. "My colleagues have explained to you that you are to take into Berlin only 37 officers, 50 vehicles, and 175 men. You have more than that. You can do one of two things. You can stay here and conform to the agreement, or you can go back."

Howley replied that, under the circumstances, he would have to await further orders. They came, six hours later, relayed through the Soviets. Howley was to return the excess men and vehicles to his base and proceed to Berlin—with 37 officers, 50 vehicles, and 175 men.[24]

As the reorganized convoy for Berlin left the Soviet field headquarters, Colonel Gorelik emerged and saluted Howley. "I won't count," he said. Howley assured him, "[W]e have exactly 37 officers, 50 vehicles, and 175 men." As the convoy pulled away, led again by the Soviet in the battered German staff car, Colonel Gorelik stood by the side of the road, counting.[25]

The convoy reached the outskirts of Berlin late at night and never entered the city. The Soviet officer in the battered staff car led it to a compound of villas and houses in the suburb of Babelsburg, near Potsdam. The area had been home to many of the members of the German film industry before and during the war, and was being prepared to provide accommodations for the attendees at the Potsdam Conference, which was scheduled to begin on July 17. The compound was guarded by Soviet troops, and Colonel Howley and his men were restricted to the area except for occasional trips to the airport at Tempelhof or journeys back and forth to the American occupied area of Germany. At no time was the complement of men and equipment allowed by the Soviets to exceed the 37 officers, 50 vehicles, and 175 men they insisted were allowed under the nonexistent "Berlin Agreement."[26]

When it had first been determined that the city of Berlin was to be jointly occupied even though it lay deep within the Soviet zone of Germany, no thought had been given to access by the Western allies. That was a detail to be worked out by the commanding officers in the field, but it was a source of major concern to President Truman. Truman wrote later, "It was my own opinion that it would be silly if these arrangements were to lead to an isolated Berlin . . . to which we had no access. I asked Stalin, with Churchill's backing, in my cable of June 14 for free access by air, road, and rail to Berlin . . . as part of the withdrawal of troops previously agreed to by Roosevelt, Churchill, and Stalin."[27]

Stalin made no reference to access in his response, and General Marshall informed Eisenhower of the importance that the president attached to the question of access, instructing that it be settled simultaneously with arrangements for other adjustments. At the same time Marshall requested that the chief of the U.S. Military Mission in Moscow, Major General John R. Deane, check on the matter with the Soviet General Staff.

The question was passed from the Soviet General Staff to the political leaders in the Kremlin and, on June 25, Deputy Foreign Minister Andre Vyshinsky informed U.S. Ambassador Harriman that Marshal Zhukov had been authorized to discuss the matter with General Eisenhower. A meeting in Berlin was suggested for June 29.

General Clay was detailed to attend that meeting as Eisenhower's representative and was given a set of access requirements on June 28. A copy of the requirements was forwarded directly to Marshal Zhukov at his headquarters, so that they could be discussed the following day.[28]

The access that the Western allies sought included the unrestricted right to use two highways between Berlin and the western zones, including the right to repair and construct surfaces and bridges. Also requested were the right to use three rail lines—including the ability to maintain the rights-of-way—and unrestricted air travel, including fighter escorts, to three airfields in Berlin. Finally, Western allied traffic was to be free from border search or control by customs or military authorities.

With General Clay in the American delegation were Major General Floyd Parks, the newly designated commandant of the American sector of Berlin, and Robert Murphy. The British were represented by Lieutenant General Ronald Weeks, deputy to Field Marshal Montgomery. As the French sector of the city had not yet been finalized, no French representative attended.

Zhukov, who outranked all others present, presided and began the meeting by announcing that the first item of business was the withdrawal of American and British troops from the provinces of Thuringia, Saxony, and Saxony-Anhalt. It was quickly determined that the evacuation would begin on July 1. Four days were allowed for completion.[29]

The discussion then turned to access to Berlin, and Zhukov's manner became frosty. He informed Clay and Weeks that the Soviet Union considered access to Berlin a privilege that it was granting the Western allies, not a right to which they were entitled. The demands that had been presented to him on the previous day, Zhukov went on, were excessive.

When Clay pointed out that the requests were not for exclusive use of the roads and rails, Zhukov responded that he had instructions from Moscow on the matter and that the instructions were explicit. The Western allies, he went on, could use one highway, one railroad, and one air corridor. As for airfields, Tempelhof in the American sector and Gatow in the British sector would be available to them.[30]

Clay and Weeks were at a distinct disadvantage. As deputies to Eisenhower and Montgomery, they were not free to break off negotiations and felt obligated to return with some agreement. Further, they were clearly outranked by Zhukov, who was the Soviet Union's greatest military hero. In spite of this, Clay at first declined to accept the Soviet proposal, and he was supported by Weeks. At this point, Zhukov said that the arrangement could be considered to be a temporary one and that it could be brought up later at a meeting of the Allied Control Council. Clay and Weeks accepted this.[31]

General Clay later wrote, "I must admit that we did not fully realize that the requirement of unanimous consent would enable a Soviet veto in the Allied Control Council to block all of our future efforts."[32]

Winston Churchill's nightmare was taking on the form of reality.

# THREE

## INTER-ALLIED "COOPERATION"

Colonel Howley and his military government personnel spent July 1, 1945, on what he described as "the highroad to Bedlam,"[1] traveling to Berlin in a traffic jam of tanks, trucks, and all sorts of other vehicles, while Soviet officers in an assortment of ramshackle vehicles raced up and down the columns, making sure that the Americans were not carrying off any loot from the areas they were leaving.

"The road was paved," Howley recalled, "with Russian drunks"[2] who insisted on sharing toasts of vodka with the Americans. In some cases the reception committees developed such alcoholic stubbornness that the American units had to force their way through them. In one instance an obstreperous Soviet officer tried, without apparent reason, to stop an American column at a bridge, and an American general jumped from his car to dump the Soviet in a ditch so that the Americans could pass.[3]

It began to rain in the afternoon and many of the Americans, dressed in their best Class A uniforms for the occasion, were forced to sleep in the mud. No billets had been prepared for them because the Soviet occupiers of the city had not permitted Howley's detachment to make such preparations. Howley's men had the foresight to come with field equipment—packs and tents—and moved into the Grünewald, a heavily treed park, and set up camp.

The following morning Howley and General Parks called on General Gorbatov, who had recently replaced General Bersarin as Soviet commandant of the city. Bersarin had ridden his motorcycle into the rear of a Soviet truck shortly after he had recruited Doctor Werner as Lord Mayor and had been killed.

Gorbatov, beefy, squat, and red-faced, was a colonel general and a highly decorated combat veteran. He produced a map showing the sectors of the city and asked when the Americans could assume control of theirs. "Right now," Howley answered. General Parks hesitated and, thinking of the upcoming holiday, suggested July 4, adding that a little ceremony would be a nice touch. "Agreed," said the Soviet general.[4]

☆ ☆ ☆

On July 3, Ruth Andreas-Friedrich's doctor friend announced to the members of the *Onkel Emil* cell that he had seen an American near Schlosstrasse. What had been rumored for days was coming to pass. Eagerly, the members of the group pored over a map of Berlin, marking in blue pencil the areas they thought—and hoped—would fall within the American sector. Steglitz was one.[5]

☆ ☆ ☆

Colonel General Gorbatov did not attend the ceremony that the Americans conducted on the Fourth of July outside the former AEG Telefunken factory, now renamed McNair Barracks, even though General Omar Bradley attended and was scheduled to speak. Gorbatov sent his one-star deputy, General Baranov, and General Bradley gave no hint that he was even aware of the snub. In his speech he complimented the Red Army warmly and expressed hope for lasting peace and friendship.

Baranov responded with a speech that credited the Soviets with winning the war single-handedly, breaking the back of the German army at Stalingrad, and capturing Berlin. He thanked the Americans for the equipment they had supplied for this effort.

At the conclusion of the ceremony, the Soviet artillery fired salutes, which the Americans answered, troops of both countries marched past, and flags were exchanged.

Howley returned to his headquarters in the Grünewald, but was summoned almost immediately by General Parks.

"What do you think of that?" Parks asked, handing Howley a message from Marshal Zhukov that read: "In view of the fact that Berlin is to be ruled by an Allied Kommandatura and that Kommandatura is not yet set up, your sector will not be turned over to you until the Kommandatura is set up."

Howley, a man with a low boiling point, was irate. "I think it's a lot of nonsense," he said, noting that it appeared that the Soviets were throwing sand in the allies' eyes again so that they could complete looting the sectors they were scheduled to turn over. "Unless you change your orders," he said to General Parks, "I'll carry them out and occupy our sector according to the agreement." After a moment's thought Parks agreed, adding, "don't get into too much trouble. After all, the occupation is just beginning."[6]

Back at his own headquarters, Howley briefed the men of his military government unit: "We move in at daybreak and set up military government. The Russians don't get up until noon.

"Don't get into a fight, but protect yourselves if you have to. Don't back out and don't make concessions. If the Russians challenge you, tell them you are just obeying orders."[7]

At eleven the next morning, the Soviets awakened to find that a U.S. military government unit had contacted the mayors in each of the six boroughs in the American sector, commandeered their houses for headquarters, hung out American flags, and posted notices announcing the establishment of military government and of courts. The Soviets reacted swiftly, dispatching officers to order the Americans out. After a stiff exchange of salutes, the orders to leave were refused. Faced with a fait accompli, the Soviets yielded.[8]

The American occupation in Berlin had begun, but no one had yet worked out how the occupying armies would cooperate in governing the city itself. On July 10, Generals Clay and Weeks and Marshal Zhukov signed a one page memorandum establishing an allied "Kommandatura" to carry out that function. The word itself was as unique as the organization it represented; it was a coined amalgam of Russian and German.

The building that was selected to house the Kommandatura was at Kaiserwertherstrasse 16, and the chiefs-of-staff of the allied commandants, Colonels Maginnis of the United States, Ryan of Great Britain, and Maslov of the USSR met there on July 16 to allocate space. The allocations were made by drawing lots from Colonel Ryan's service cap. The Americans and Soviets drew office space on the second floor, with a large conference room between them; the British got offices on the ground floor, and space at that level was set aside for the French, who were expected to arrive soon. The basement was set aside as a common mess area.[9]

The men of the 852d Aviation Engineer Battalion under Lt. Colonel Arlon G. Hazen were not particularly happy about their newest assignment. They had been on the continent of Europe since shortly after D-Day, building airfields for the Mustangs and Thunderbolts that swept the Luftwaffe from the skies. At times the bulldozers of the battalion had been rolling onto one end of a former German airfield to begin reconstruction while the enemy was still retreating from the other end. The strip they were assigned to maintain at Asch, Belgium, had come under a heavy strafing attack by the Germans on New Year's Day, 1945, during the Battle of the Bulge. They had just completed construction of a 5,000-foot runway at Fritzlar, Germany, and all of the men thought that it would be their last job. With the end of the war in Europe, they were waiting to be shipped back to the States. On July 1, orders arrived for the 852d to prepare to move to Berlin to reconstruct Tempelhof Airfield.[10]

Tempelhof Airfield is in south-central Berlin, two and one-half miles south of Unter den Linden, in the sector assigned to the American occupation forces. The first military use of the Tempelhof area occurred in the twelfth century, when the militant crusading Order of the Knights of the Temple of Jerusalem founded a monastery there. The borough of Tempelhof still bears on its official seal the black cross on a white field that was the mark of the order.

Aviation came to Tempelhof in 1811, when a merchant named Karl Friedrich Claudius took off from there in a hot air balloon, and the German Army developed an airship unit there during the Franco-Prussian war. At the beginning of 1897, the German military turned over its hangar on the field, which was exactly that—a large grassy plain—to Dr. Woelfert and his German Airship Company for experiments in powered flight in hydrogen-filled dirigibles.

By summer, the doctor was ready for a test flight of his newly perfected Woelfert Airship. Containing 875 cubic yards of hydrogen and powered by an internal combustion engine, the machine carried Woelfert and his mechanic aloft on June 12. The rudder promptly fell off. As the gas in the airship was subject to expansion from the heat of the sun on the envelope, Woelfert had designed the dirigible with a vent to allow any expanding gas to bleed off. Unfortunately, the vent was located less than a meter from the hot engine. The Woelfert airship rose to an altitude of 100 meters—and exploded. The bodies of the doctor and his mechanic landed in a wood lot near the field—Tempelhof's first aviation deaths.[11]

In 1909, Orville Wright demonstrated the wood-and-wire contraption known as the Wright Flyer to the German military at Tempelhof, breaking an altitude record and carrying the first German woman airplane passenger aloft. The plane he flew had been built under license in Berlin, by the German Wright Aircraft Company.[12]

Because of its location in the center of the city, Tempelhof was not used for military purposes during World War I and seemed destined to revert to a grassy open plain under the terms of the Treaty of Versailles, which prohibited both military and civil aviation in Germany. However, the Germans disregarded the terms of the treaty and by 1919 had established a civil air route from Berlin to the new capital at Weimar. In 1923, Doctor Leonard Adler, Berlin's counselor for transportation, convinced the city fathers to convert the disused field into a centralized urban airport with two 10,000-square-foot hangars and an administration building. The airport opened on October 8, 1923, over the protests of the Berliners who lived nearby. They feared that aircraft would crash into their apartment buildings, which ringed the new airport on all sides.[13]

As air travel became an accepted mode of transportation, Tempelhof continued to grow. By the mid 1930s, it was one of the busiest airports in the world—over 1.5 million square meters in size and boasting a hotel, shops, and a rooftop restaurant where diners could watch the planes land and take off. In 1934, the second year of the Nazi regime, Professor Dr. Ernst Sagebiel was commissioned to draw up plans for a new airport, designed to be the center of German aviation. It included the largest building in the world, a sprawling structure in the shape of a C that contained 5,000 offices. Beneath the structure were seven subterranean levels, equipped with manufacturing shops.

Work on that structure, located at the northwest end of the field, began in 1936, and air traffic went on uninterrupted by construction, which stopped with the beginning of the war. The underground shops were used for the production of fighter aircraft, but because of its location, the field was not used for military aviation purposes during the war, except for occasional emergency landings by night fighters. It was not severely damaged by the American and British bombing raids that devastated much of Berlin, as it was not considered a priority target. Curiously, with all of the improvements through the years, Tempelhof Airport had never been equipped with runways—the German civil aviation authorities preferred grass landings—and the bomb damage that did occur to the landing area was easily repaired. The last flight from Tempelhof before the war ended was on April 22, 1945, and the area commander, Lieutenant Colonel Rudolph Bottger, disobeyed his orders to blow up the airport in the face of the advancing Russians and committed suicide.[14]

Shelling by the Soviets caused considerable damage to the buildings of the facility, and looting cleared them of virtually everything that wasn't bolted down—in some cases even machinery that was bolted down disappeared. The Soviets smashed the pumps and piping that kept the underground levels dry, and these soon flooded. Soon after the Soviets took Tempelhof, fires broke out and did considerable damage to most of the buildings.[15]

An advance patrol of the 852d Aviation Engineer Battalion arrived at Tempelhof Airfield by plane on July 4, 1945; by July 11 the entire battalion was on the site, working at repairs to the facility and planning the layout of a new, metal-surfaced runway. It was that job that gave them their biggest problem.[16]

The Army Air Corps design manuals for airfield construction specified that runways be laid out in such a way that approaching aircraft have a glide path with a slope with a ratio of 1 to 40 along which to descend to their landing. That is, the approaching plane should be able to travel forty feet horizontally for each foot of altitude it lost on its approach.

Colonel Hazen's engineers made calculations on every possible runway configuration at Tempelhof and could not achieve that standard. They couldn't even come close. The ring of eight- and nine-story apartment buildings around the field necessitated a far steeper angle of descent at Tempelhof than the manuals allowed. In typical Army fashion, the problem was bumped "upstairs" to a higher headquarters. The answer that came back essentially directed the engineers to do the best they could. Tempelhof was expected to operate as the airfield for the Occupational Headquarters.

The 852d settled on laying out the runway on an east-west axis— the direction of the prevailing wind. The glide angle for the main runway was 1 to 16, less than half that specified in the manual—but the east-west orientation ensured that, most of the time, the pilots landing on the 4,987-foot primary runway would not be troubled by cross winds.[17]

A secondary runway was laid out on the grass, roughly at right angles to the primary, for use in case there were cross winds on the main one. The best glide angle that could be achieved for the secondary was 1 to 10—a quarter of what the manual specified.[18]

The construction of the primary runway also presented a problem to the engineers because of the lack of building material. Berlin is located in the sandy Pomeranian plains, an area singularly devoid of gravel banks or stone quarries, and the procurement of a suitable base for the runway was a problem that the Americans solved by using Berlin's most abundant building material—the rubble of bomb- and shell-blasted buildings. Over 13,000 cubic yards of this rubble provided the runway base and, when covered with a sand and clay mixture, provided an adequate base for the pierced steel plank of the runway surface. The job was finished on August 28. The secondary runway was simply measured and marked out on the grass.[19]

☆   ☆   ☆

The pierced steel planking of the runway was hard on aircraft tires, particularly when planes braked hard, which was necessary given the steep angle and relative high speed of the approach to Tempelhof. The very best approach to the field was from the west but involved careful positioning to avoid the blocks of apartments around the field. The sole open space was over Neukölln's Thomas cemetery, a grim reminder of the inevitable results of an error.

Further complicating the approach was the tall smokestack of a brewery near the edge of the field. The brewery owner held off American efforts to have it demolished by using the same arguments he had been using since Hermann Göring had been minister of aviation—that the brewery made a tremendous economic contribution to the city and that the smokestack was a valuable aesthetic part of the city landscape.[20]

At Gatow, a second airfield available to the Western allies, in the British sector, the approach was clear, but a hazard of another kind existed. Even a minor error in navigation could bring a plane into the neighboring military airfield at Staaken, in the Soviet sector. The main runway at Gatow was also of tire-killing pierced steel plank, laid directly on the sandy soil. Originally a Luftwaffe training field and then, as the war brought the fighting closer to Berlin, a fighter station, the facilities at Gatow were not designed to handle heavy freight. The hardstands, where aircraft could park and off-load cargo, were made of bricks laid in sand and could not hold up under the wear and tear of freight operations. Moreover, Gatow was not served by a rail siding. Freight brought into the field had to be trucked to nearby Lake Havel to be loaded onto barges and shipped through the network of canals that laced through the city.[21]

The 371 square miles of Greater Berlin were divided into the Soviet sector and the area to be occupied by the Western allies by a border that ran roughly northwest to southeast. To the east were the boroughs occupied by the Soviets—Pankow, Prenzlauer Berg, Weissensee, Treptow, and Karlshorst, where they had their headquarters. The line bulged to the west at the inner ring of the city, so that the Brandenburg Gate lay on the border. The American sector, comprising six boroughs including Steglitz as the members of *Onkel Emil* had hoped, was in the southwest, and the British sector in the northwest. In August, a French sector was carved out of the extreme north of the British sector, giving the French the boroughs of Wedding and Reinickendorf.[22]

The central administrative body for the joint allied occupation of Berlin, the Kommandatura, was made up of the four Allied commandants in the city, mirroring on a smaller scale the makeup of the Allied Control Council, which was the supreme authority in Germany. The Soviets had proposed the Kommandatura arrangement and Colonel Howley, at the direction of the American commandant in the city, General Parks, had drawn up a plan for the manner in which he felt it should function. It was based on the supposition that there would be items on which the Allies would not agree and provided, in cases of irreconcilable differences, for each Allied commandant to handle the situation in his own sector in the manner he deemed most appropriate.[23]

On July 7, 1945, General Clay, his deputy General Oliver P. Echols, and the State Department's Robert Murphy flew into Gatow airport to establish headquarters in Berlin and to attend a meeting with the Soviets. The Supreme Commander, General Eisenhower, was on leave in the United States, enjoying two weeks of golf at White Sulphur Springs, West Virginia. Clay met at British headquarters with General

Sir Ronald Weeks and Sir William Strang and discussed Howley's plan for the administration of Berlin. Colonel Howley was called into the meeting of the generals in time to hear it roundly denounced by General Clay.

He had no idea, Clay said, that General Parks was planning to handle the city on a divided basis, and he did not approve of it. Clay insisted that all questions arising in Berlin be settled unanimously by the four Allies.

Howley, a man with a well-earned reputation for outspokenness, took the initiative boldly and injected himself into the conversation. "I know the plan very well," he said, "having worked on it in accordance with general instructions. General Parks has no idea of setting up a little empire in the American sector. After all, we don't know the Communists; we didn't even have diplomatic relations with them until 1932. There are going to be many questions that can't be solved on a unanimous basis. The British, French, and Americans may agree on a million things; there will be many on which the Russians won't agree." [24]

Lucius Clay fixed the brash junior officer in the steely stare that members of his staff knew well, and his voice was cold when he spoke. "You are entirely wrong," he said. "I have just come from Washington, and it is certainly the intention of our government to administer Berlin on a unanimous basis." Clay went on in that vein, and Howley kept his mouth shut, even when he realized that no one had another plan as an alternative to his. [25]

By the time that the preliminary meeting between the British and Americans broke up, they were nearly late for their appointment at Soviet headquarters, and they raced across the city, arriving in Karlshorst a few minutes after they were expected.

Marshal Zhukov, his deputy, Colonel General Vassily Sokolovsky, and a phalanx of experts awaited the Anglo-American party in a large conference room. Marshal Zhukov surprised his guests by assuming a seat at the head of a large conference table almost immediately and saying, "Well, gentlemen, shall we start business?" [26]

The first order of business was the establishment of the Kommandatura, and Zhukov stunned the British and Americans by quickly producing a single-page document outlining the manner in which he proposed it should function. The proposal clearly provided that all decisions of the Kommandatura be unanimous. There was only a brief discussion before Clay turned to General Parks and asked, "Do these translations check out?"

Parks turned to Howley, who had been standing in the background. "Frank, take the interpreters and check this, will you." As Howley was leaving the room, the Soviets noted that he was a full colonel. They sent a one-star general of their own staff to accompany him.

After a brief review Howley returned to the conference room and handed his copy to Clay, who had half-turned to receive it. "Is it okay?" Clay asked.

"Well, as a legal document, it stinks," Howley responded. "But as a rough draft of what you've been talking about, it's all right."

Clay quickly took out his pen and signed across the bottom of the sheet. It was clear that he had no intention of quibbling. American policy was to try to cooperate with the Soviets and to start off on their terms.[27]

"Now, gentlemen, we will discuss the question of the food and coal you will supply for the maintenance of Berlin," Zhukov then said.

Frank Howley later described the atmosphere in the room at that moment as one in which a cold wind had swept in from the steppes. The American and British commanders looked at one another, stunned. It had been anticipated that the food and fuel needs of Berlin would be supplied from the areas in the surrounding Soviet zone from which they had historically come.[28] General Clay recovered first.

"It is not our plan to bring food into Berlin," he said. "For one thing, we don't have food to bring in. Everything Berlin needs should come either from the territory we've just turned over to you, or from the surrounding areas of Brandenburg and northeast Pomerania, where it always has come from."

Zhukov was stern and blunt in his reply: "Let's be realistic, gentlemen. What have you come for, anyway? Let me tell you frankly, we are not going to supply food to Berlin. Our warehouses are almost exhausted. We must have food, and we must have it quickly."[29]

When General Clay noted that there were obvious difficulties with organization and transportation, citing the destruction of many of the bridges over the Elbe, General Sokolovsky said icily, "Why don't you clean up the bridges and use them? That's what we do."[30]

Shortly, it was concluded that the question of supplying food to Berlin would have to be referred to Washington, and Zhukov said, "Well, gentlemen, the meeting is now ended," closing the first working session of what was to be the Allied Control Council.

"Now I would like you to have a tea," the Soviet went on, ushering his guests into an adjoining room where tables were heaped with caviar and other delicacies, along with beer, wine, and vodka. As the American officers were taking their leave, General Clay approached Marshal Zhukov and presented him with a Beretta pistol engraved "From General Clay to General Zhukov." The Soviet glanced at it quickly and then passed it to an aide, who tossed it into a duffel bag.[31]

# FOUR

# SPOILS OF VICTORY AND VICTORY SPOILS

Under the laws of the occupation, the Allies requisitioned what they required for quarters and other uses from the Germans. Houses and apartments were taken with no notice and, if they were occupied, the residents were given only a few hours to leave and were allowed to take only a few personal possessions when they evacuated. No distinction was made between former Nazis and anti-Nazis. In Zehlendorf and Charlottenburg in the British sector, entire blocks were taken over to house troops. The Soviet commandant chose a spacious villa for his own use; curiously, it was located in the sector of the city that was designated for occupation by the Americans, and when they took control, he chose to stay in that location.[1]

The quarters that General Clay selected were at 43 Im Dol in the borough of Dahlem in the American sector. It was a comfortable, ivy-covered house, originally built around the turn of the century in the English country style for a British woman who lived in Berlin. It was unpretentious compared to the mansions requisitioned by the other military governors. Its spacious grounds were surrounded by poplar and beech trees, and the house had a large dining room and two drawing rooms on the main floor for entertaining small groups. Clay decided to live alone, except for his Scottish terrier, George, until his wife could join him from America.[2]

The building had last been occupied by a German businessman who, even though he was not a member of the Nazi party, had many friends who were. The walls were hung with photographs of parties that had been given there, with all of the guests decked out in Nazi regalia. Clay had the photos and the stacks of Nazi literature on the shelves cleared out.[3]

Robert Murphy was assigned a requisitioned house nearby, on Spechstrasse. It had been occupied for two months by a group of Soviet officers who, according to the live-in housekeeper, had consumed the entire 2,000 bottles that had been in the wine cellar and had amused themselves by shooting the place up when they were drunk, paying special attention to the crystal chandeliers. Murphy noted that the walls, ceilings, and family portraits had all been pocked with bullet holes.[4]

The Allied Control Council, at the suggestion of the Soviets, set up its permanent headquarters in the requisitioned Kammergericht court-house at 32 Elszholzstrasse in the American sector. Its 550 rooms had once housed the highest court of Prussia and later the appeals court of Germany. In 1944, one of its courtrooms had been the setting in which the rabid Nazi People's Court Judge Rolan Freisler had berated and be-littled the June 20 plotters against Hitler before condemning them to death by hanging with piano wire. The building had been badly dam-aged in the war—Freisler had been killed in his courtroom by a direct hit from an American bomb not long after the conspiracy trial—and a full battalion of U.S. Army engineers was still at work on repairs when the Allied Control Council met in these quarters for the first time on July 20, 1945.[5]

The Control Council meetings were held in an ornate second floor assembly hall with marble columns and a mahogany parquet floor. The four delegations sat at identical tables arranged in a hollow square around stenographers who recorded the proceedings. The American delegation faced the French, and the British delegation faced the So-viets.

After each meeting the delegates adjourned to a salon adjoining the assembly hall, where white-gloved waiters served a banquet from tables piled high with food. It had become the custom for the presiding country to offer such a feast, and the Soviets soon earned a reputation as the most lavish of hosts, offering beluga caviar, smoked sturgeon, and pink champagne from the Crimea.

Near the circular driveway outside the palace, four sixty-foot flag-poles were arranged in a row, and the place of honor on the far right pole was given to the flag of the country that was presiding at the Con-trol Council that month.

On July 12, Leo Borchard, so recently appointed conductor of the Ber-lin Philharmonic by the Soviets and confirmed by the Americans, re-turned to his companions with shattering news. The Titania Palace, the only concert hall in the American sector and the least damaged one in Berlin, had been requisitioned for use as a clubhouse for American troops. Borchard had no idea what would become of the newly recon-stituted philharmonic now that it did not have a home, but he was determined to do all in his power to make it survive. He began to go around on his bicycle to offices all over the city, seeking support for the orchestra.[6]

☆ ☆ ☆

In the streets of Berlin, Americans met Soviets and Berliners. The first were supposed to be allies; the second, former enemies, and there was a ban on fraternization with Germans. But one place they all came together was in the black market, regulations and bans notwithstanding.

During the war, an informal barter system of goods for services or other goods and a thriving black market had sprung up in Berlin, driven by the scarcity of goods and the vast amounts of paper money available. At the end of the war, the two officially available forms of money were virtually worthless. The German reichsmark had been issued in a paper blizzard during the war; the actual amount of currency in circulation had grown from five billion reichsmarks in 1935 to over seventy billion in 1945.[7] There was very little to buy with all of this paper. Most of the German industrial capacity had been devoted to war production, and that capacity was now shattered by the effects of the war. Germany's capacity to produce goods was only half of what it had been when the war began.

To add to the dilemma, the occupying forces of the victorious Allies issued their own occupation currency. Designed and printed in the United States and England before the invasion, plates to print this currency were given to the Soviets on the express orders of President Roosevelt, over the objections of most people concerned with the project.[8] The occupation marks were designed to be used to pay troops and to make advances to banks and local governments. For purposes of computing pay to the troops, an exchange rate of ten occupation marks to a dollar was established. Each occupation mark was officially worth ten cents.[9]

The Soviet rules for use of occupation marks by Russian troops, many of whom had not been paid in two or three years, were simple and restrictive. Soviet soldiers could not take the occupation marks home with them, and they could not convert them into rubles. The soldiers of the Red Army had a choice—spend the occupation currency in Germany, or see it become valueless.[10]

When the American troops arrived in Berlin, the black market blossomed overnight. The Soviet troops were willing to pay nearly any price for scarce goods—fountain pens, American watches, clothing, cigarettes—and the Americans were willing participants in the trade, as they did not suffer the restrictions on occupation marks that hung over their Soviet allies. American soldiers could convert any number of the nearly worthless occupation marks into American dollars at the official rate of ten to one and send the money home in the form of postal money orders or in remittances through the Army Finance Section.[11] American currency could also be sent from home in letters. A soldier with the gift of a crisp ten-dollar bill from home in his pocket had the choice of converting it to one hundred marks at the official rate of exchange or taking it to the black market, where the same ten-dollar bill would bring one thousand marks, which could be converted back into dollars at the official rate and sent home again in the form of a money order for one hundred dollars—a profit of 900 percent on a simple transaction. It really was not much of a choice.

American operators on the black market had three principal sources of supplies from which they could draw goods. Packages from home, containing watches, soap, cash, and cigarettes, provided goods that could rapidly be turned to a profit in illicit trades. The GI's weekly PX allotment of a carton of cigarettes, ten candy bars, two bars of soap, and other items drew fabulous premiums when traded on the black market. Cigarettes, which quickly became the principal commodity in black-market trading and the unofficial currency and standard of value for all other trading, were the most valuable. A carton of American cigarettes, which a GI could purchase for fifty cents at the PX, was priced at one thousand five hundred marks—one hundred and fifty dollars—on the black market. A GI could sell a carton, take the marks he got for it to a post exchange and buy another carton, and still have the equivalent of one hundred and forty-nine dollars and change left to convert to a postal money order and send home.[12] A single pack of American cigarettes sold for over ten dollars, and even half-smoked butts had a value. Soldiers grew used to gangs of children, and sometime even adults, eyeing them as they smoked, waiting for the opportunity to snatch up the butt after they had thrown it away.[13] The third source of goods for the black market was the U.S. Army itself, in the form of quartermaster warehouses and mess halls, where pilfering and outright theft became a major problem.

Germans were in the black market because they had to be in order to survive. Prices had soared far ahead of wages, and many Germans found that it was impractical to work. A worker with no skills could command, at best, 160 marks a month in wages, and that would purchase no more than eight kilograms of bread. Barter and the black market remained necessities to the Germans as long as their currency was in chaos. Few in the city of Berlin worked longer than they needed to earn enough reichsmarks to match their ration coupons. At the universities, lectures were paid for not by money, but by goods. Three pounds of flour was the going rate per lecture. The noted cabaret comedian, Bruno Fritz, charged eight ounces of bacon and eight of white beans for each performance.

The center of this black-market activity was the Tiergarten, once a well-maintained park but now a parched expanse of sparse grass in front of the burned-out ruins of the Reichstag. When streetcar service was restored, conductors announcing the stop to passengers would as often as not call out, "Black market!" as the tram approached the Tiergarten.[14] From early in the morning until well after dark, the Tiergarten was crowded with people clutching suitcases or pushing carts of all sorts and hawking what they had to sell or barter.

☆　☆　☆

Soviets, Berliners, and Americans met in other places on the streets of Berlin, and their meetings were often less friendly than when they met to haggle at the Tiergarten. Even after the Western allies had taken over their sectors, the Soviets continued to come over from theirs, mostly drunk and in search of loot. During the first week the Americans were in Berlin, several Soviets in a car stopped a young German girl, Gertrude Gretz, who was riding her bicycle through Zehlendorf. She was unfortunately wearing a wristwatch. The Soviets got out of their car and demanded it, hollering "*urhe, urhe,*" the Russian pronunciation of the German word for watch. When Gertrude resisted, one of the Soviets drew his pistol, calmly shot her, and then removed the watch from her wrist. American protests to the Soviets met with denials that Soviet soldiers could have been responsible.[15] During the same week, two hundred Soviet officers and men came into Kreuzberg, in the American sector, and began looting and raping in a large apartment house. Not even a jeepload of American MPs could get them to leave.[16] Not long after that, Captain Charles Leonetti, a former FBI man who was head of public safety in the borough in which the Potsdamer *S-Bahn* station is located, had a shoot-out with five Soviets who were terrifying passengers in the station. He killed two and wounded another.[17] The Soviets protested the incident and the following week complained that a dozen of their men had been shot by American patrols. One was an officer, caught robbing a German home, who pulled a gun on an American MP. The American put eight rounds from his tommy-gun into the Soviet.[18]

The British made it a practice to thoroughly beat any misbehaving Soviets they caught in their sector before dumping them back across the boundary into the Soviet sector. On a soldier-to-soldier basis, the early weeks of the occupation of Berlin were a tense time, and the Americans ordered a further crackdown. All Soviet vehicles seen driving in the American sector after dark were to be stopped by MPs at checkpoints and the occupants questioned about their business.

☆　☆　☆

Things were little better at the level of the Kommandatura. When it first met, on July 11, 1945, the Soviets insisted that the three Western commandants sign a decree that all regulations previously issued by the Soviets would remain in effect unless unanimously revised by the

Kommandatura. With that document, the Western allies accepted the financial, social, and political structures the Soviets had put in place since the end of May. Now they would have to work within them.

At the Allied Control Council, it was no better. It rapidly became apparent that the Soviets and the Western allies had vastly different outlooks on the government and administration of Germany. This is, perhaps, no better illustrated than in the discussions involving Western access to Berlin. The problem was first discussed at the Kommandatura and, when no agreement could be reached there, it was referred to the Allied Control Council.

The Soviets would not budge from Marshal Zhukov's June 29 statement that the allies would be allowed to use only the single road from Helmstedt in the British zone to Berlin as a highway to bring supplies into their garrisons. No other roads through the Soviet zone would be made available.[19]

The Helmstedt-Berlin road was a prewar autobahn that ran in a straight line through wooded hills, then farmlands, into the city of Berlin. There were few settlements, and service facilities on the road were limited. There was a British post forty miles inside the Soviet zone from Helmstedt, and an American one forty miles short of Berlin. People whose vehicles broke down were subject to being picked up by one of the frequent Soviet patrols and being detained for hours for questioning.

The Soviets proved no less intransigent with respect to rail access to Berlin; it was not until the fifth meeting of the Allied Control Council on September 10 that they agreed to allow up to ten trains a day to travel from the British zone into the city, carrying passengers and much of the food and coal needed to kept Berlin fed, heated, and powered. At the meeting of October 3, the number of daily trains allowed was increased to sixteen. Soon after the trains began to roll, the Soviets tried to enter the American trains to check the identity cards and papers of the passengers, but General Clay stopped that practice with a threat to put armed American guards on the trains and a concession that the only Germans who would travel on the trains would be employees of the Western allies and that they would be confined to sealed cars while in transit.

The question of access to Berlin by water, along the network of canals and rivers through which barges carried much of the coal needed by the city's power plants, was never even discussed at the Control Council. As the coal mines were in the Ruhr, under British control, the British arrived at a bilateral written agreement with the Soviets.[20] The agreements on road and rail transportation were never reduced to writing.

The question of access to Berlin by air was not, at first, considered to be important enough to discuss. Pilots of the U.S. Army Air Force and Royal Air Force assigned to fly to Berlin merely took off and flew in and out of the city as they pleased, usually following the route of an autobahn or railroad. There were no navigational aids in the Soviet zone along the route, and there was no unified air traffic control system, and the Soviets soon began to complain of the number of near-misses between their aircraft and those of the Western allies.

The quadripartite Air Directorate of the Allied Control Council drew up a set of recommendations proposing the establishment of three air corridors between Berlin and the West. The northern corridor was in a straight line to Hamburg, and the center corridor pointed to Hannover, both in the British zone. The southern corridor began at the border of the Soviet zone on a line between Berlin and Frankfurt, in the American zone. Each was twenty miles wide and terminated at Berlin in the Berlin air control zone, a circle forty miles in diameter with the headquarters of the Allied Control Council as its center. The movement of all aircraft within the Berlin control zone was to be controlled by the Berlin Air Safety Center, a quadripartite body. These recommendations of the Air Directorate were later approved by the Allied Control Council, without argument, although it took until November 30, 1945.[21]

☆    ☆    ☆

As the summer of 1945 grew hotter in Berlin, some of the occupying forces were making preparations for the arrival of the Big Three—Harry S Truman, Joseph Stalin, and Winston Churchill—for a conference in the suburb of Potsdam, scheduled to begin on July 17. The conference was to settle questions of reparations, war crimes, demilitarization, and others arising out of the defeat of Germany. Most American troops, however, had only one question on their minds: "How many points do you have?"

As early as June 1942, the War Department had begun planning for the eventual demobilization of the United States Army, and by January 6, 1945, the European Theater of Operations had issued "Redeployment Planning Directive Number 1," calling for the reduction of the huge forces on the continent of Europe to an occupation force.[22]

Four classifications of units were set up—those scheduled for occupation duty, those scheduled to be shipped to the Pacific, those slated for a strategic reserve, and those to be demobilized. Immediately after the cessation of hostilities in Europe, individual soldiers were to be issued an adjusted service rating (ASR) card, scored in points based on a number of factors: time in service, time overseas, combat credit based on decorations and battle stars, and parenthood credit.

The point values under the ASR were announced on May 8, 1945, with 85 points being the magic number that spelled discharge.[23] Everyone, including the 19,000 men and women assigned to military government in Germany, began to count their points.

The United States was about to dismantle the largest army it had ever put into the field. The Soviets had no such plans.

☆   ☆   ☆

President Harry S Truman sailed for Europe aboard the cruiser USS *Augusta* on July 7, 1945. He spent the trip across the Atlantic discussing the upcoming conference of the Big Three with his staff. Immediately before he sailed he had met with Secretary of the Treasury Henry Morgenthau, who had been extremely upset not to be included in the delegation. Morgenthau had developed and circulated a plan to strip Germany of her entire industrial capacity and reduce her to an agricultural nation, but Truman did not believe that the plan was workable or in the best interests of Europe. He believed, as did his own close advisors, that a Germany that was economically strong and productive was essential to stability in Europe.

Morgenthau visited the president in the Oval Office on July 5 and said he thought it essential that he be included in the American delegation to Potsdam. If he was not, Morgenthau concluded, he would resign. Truman accepted the resignation on the spot and announced it to the press the next day, appointing Fred M. Vinson, a former seven-term congressman from Kentucky and current head of the Office of War Mobilization and Reconversion, as Morgenthau's replacement.[24]

The *Augusta* docked at Antwerp on July 15, and the presidential party was greeted by a party led by General Eisenhower. The presidential party traveled by car to Brussels where the presidential plane, *The Sacred Cow,* was waiting. From Brussels it flew to Berlin, a three-and-one-half-hour journey during which it was escorted by a squadron of P-47 fighters.

The engineers of the 852d were still reconstructing Tempelhof Airport—on July 15 work on the runway had barely begun[25]—so Truman and his party landed at Gatow, in the British sector. They were greeted by Secretary of War Henry L. Stimson, Ambassador to the Soviet Union W. Averell Harriman, Admiral Ernest King, a host of Soviets, and an honor guard from the 2d Armored Division. The conferees were to be housed in the Berlin suburb of Babelsberg, on Lake Griebnitz, and the ten-mile route from the airport to the three-story villa at 2 Kaiserstrasse assigned to Truman was lined with green-capped Soviet guardsmen standing with fixed bayonets every twenty feet.

The next afternoon the president decided that he wanted to see the fallen capital of the Third Reich, so a motorcade was quickly assembled, and the president, Admiral Leahy, and James Byrnes sped toward the city in a Chrysler convertible. They traveled along the Avis Autobahn and, halfway to Berlin, met the entire 2d Armored Division arrayed along the side of the road awaiting inspection by the president. The line of troops was so long that it took Truman twenty-two minutes to pass in review, riding in the back of an armored half-track.[26]

When the review was over, the party continued into the city, passing miles of desolation populated only by a seemingly endless line of Germans shuffling along beside the highway, dragging or carrying pathetic bundles that were their only apparent worldly possessions. Entering the city, the entire party was struck at once by the pervasive smell of acrid smoldering fires, broken sewers, and corpses unrecovered from the shattered ruins of the buildings.

"I never saw such destruction,"[27] the president wrote in his diary that night—a strong statement from a man who had served in the artillery in France in the First World War and had seen his share. Much the same reaction came from Churchill and his entourage, which toured the city separately on the same day. Stalin made no sightseeing tours in the capital of his former enemy.

By the time the Allied leaders arrived in the Berlin suburb to conduct their negotiations on the fate of Germany, Leo Borchard had negotiated a solution to his small but immediate problem. The occupying Americans had relented, and he could, once again, use the Titania Palace for rehearsals and concerts, although the Americans would continue to use it as a club. They would have to work together.

# FIVE

# MEETING AT POTSDAM

The British prime minister, Winston Churchill, also flew into Gatow Airfield to attend the Potsdam Conference and was accompanied by the opposition leader in Parliament, Clement Attlee. A general election had been scheduled for July 24, 1945, and while Churchill fully expected to emerge victorious, Attlee was included in the British party as a courtesy.[1]

Joseph Stalin, afraid of flying, arrived in Berlin from the east in a eleven-car train. Four of the cars were luxurious coaches that had been removed from a museum where they had been displayed as examples of Czarist excess and reconditioned for the trip.[2]

The conference opened on July 17 in the Cecilienhof palace, the former Berlin summer home of the imperial crown prince and more recently a hospital for war wounded. It was an ivy-covered Neo-Gothic structure of brown stone, and a twenty-four-foot red star of geraniums had been planted by the Soviets near the entrance. At the first session, which began at 5:10 p.m. in the oak-paneled reception hall around a twelve-foot table covered with wine-red cloth, Stalin suggested that Truman chair the meeting, as he was the only head of state present. Churchill agreed.[3]

The agenda for the conference at Potsdam was full, and Truman moved quickly through a list of the items he believed should be discussed. These included establishing a Council of Foreign Ministers to deal with eventual peace treaties with the Axis Powers and the question of how to administer a conquered Germany. The question of reparations hung heavy in the air, and Truman did not waste time in getting to the sorest of subjects—the apparent Soviet failure to adhere to their obligations under the Yalta agreement to establish free, elected governments in the territories they had liberated from the Germans.[4] At the opening session, Churchill demurred on most points, stating that he had not yet had time to study the questions. Stalin voiced objections to many.[5]

On Truman's personal agenda was a proposal he had developed himself—the internationalization of the world's inland waterways, including the Danube and Rhine rivers, the Kiel, Suez, and Panama canals, and the Dardanelles. He saw this move as a way to foster prosperity, and Truman viewed prosperity as a key to peace: "We want a prosperous, self-supporting Europe. A bankrupt Europe is no advantage to any country, or to the peace of the world," he said in introducing his proposal.[6] "The question is not ripe for discussion," Stalin replied, cutting off the discussion on the point.[7]

As the first session neared its end, Churchill suggested that the foreign ministers provide the Big Three with three or four points for discussion each day. That was not what the new president had in mind: "I don't want to discuss," he said. "I want to decide."[8]

☆ ☆ ☆

As the Big Three deliberated in the Cecilienhof, others went about the daily business of surviving in the shattered city of Berlin. Leo Borchard, with use of the Titania Palace restored to the Berlin Philharmonic, began planning a series of concerts.

Colonel Howley's military government team, which he described as "the type needed to revive a city, not by cracking the whip and shouting, but by a few quiet, firm words of expert advice,"[9] made rapid damage assessments and went to work getting essential services up and running again.

As the underground *U-Bahn* was flooded and the surface and overhead *S-Bahn* had been badly damaged by bombs, there was an urgent need for transportation for American troops. It was immediately addressed by requisitioning double-decker buses and painting them olive drab. A shortage of army transportation personnel soon forced William Knowlton, the officer in charge of transportation, to hire Germans as drivers, and they were lured as much by the hot meal that the Americans provided at noon as by the pay that was offered, because Berliners were on a near-starvation diet.[10]

Five ration classes had been established, with the highest allotting 2,500 calories a day to people doing heavy work. The lowest, Class 5, allotted only 1,250 calories a day—300 grams of bread, 7 of fat, and 20 of meat—not really enough for a person to survive.

When Knowlton began to hire German drivers, word got around to former members of the German Third Panzer Division, which had been stationed in Berlin when it surrendered. Knowlton joked later, "If I had gone out in the morning and said, '*Dritte Panzer Division, achtung*,' everybody would have popped to."[11]

The fact that the water system was shattered and that Berlin's sewers were spewing over 200,000 cubic meters of untreated wastes into her network of canals each day, plus the malnutrition of the population, made the threat of epidemic constant and real. At the height of the war, there had been 38,000 hospital beds in the city; now there were only 9,300, and narcotics and anesthetics were in short supply. Howley's team set about creating emergency rooms in temporary quarters and arranging for the release of thirty tons of medical supplies from army stockpiles and the purchase of an additional one hundred tons from civilian sources.[12]

Although there was a policy against refugees entering the city from the east, it was impossible to enforce, and many of the displaced persons were infested with lice. Delousing stations were set up, and each of the newcomers was sprayed with DDT.

Colonel Howley, well aware that some 30,000 infants were among the German civilians for whom he was responsible, worked out a deal with the Soviet authorities. They would supply fresh milk from the dairy herds they had confiscated and driven out of Berlin in exchange for flour, which the United States was beginning to bring into its sector.[13]

Among the first flour that arrived in the city was a shipment from the Abilene Flour Mills of Kansas. Each sack bore a legend stenciled on by the midwestern grain mill workers: "We come not as liberators, but as conquerors."[14]

This was not a sentiment that was shared by the president from Missouri. Truman offered the Potsdam Conference a broad plan for restarting the German economic machine. It called for treating the conquered country as an economic whole and ignoring the occupation zone boundaries in the trade of goods. The Soviets, in possession of great assets in the coal mines of Silesia and the vast farmlands of the northeast, rejected the proposal out of hand.[15]

Discussions on the question of reparations made no better progress. At Yalta, Stalin had advanced the figure of ten billion dollars as what he expected from Germany as reparations. At Potsdam, he stated early in the conference that ten billion was his starting point in discussions of reparations.[16]

On the question of the territories in the east—Bulgaria, Romania, and Poland—that had been "liberated" by the Red Army, Stalin and Churchill clashed bitterly. Churchill complained that, in Bucharest, the British mission was penned up as if an iron fence had descended around them.[17]

"All fairy tales," said the Soviet dictator.[18]

At the close of that particular session, President Truman rose and walked around the table to Stalin, accompanied by Chester Bohlen, his interpreter. Truman had learned by cable of the successful test of the atomic bomb at Alamogordo, New Mexico, and he casually mentioned to Stalin that the United States "had a new weapon of unusual destructive force."[19] As Truman recalled in his memoirs, "The Russian Premier showed no special interest," but said that he hoped that "we would make good use of it against the Japanese."[20] Stalin was in fact well aware of American progress toward perfecting the atomic bomb, through the efforts of the Soviet spies who were working within the Manhattan Project. Marshal Zhukov, who was present at a meeting between Stalin and Foreign Minister Molotov later that evening, recalled Molotov's reaction when he was told by Stalin of Truman's disclosure: "We'll have to talk it over with Kurchatov [the Soviet atomic bomb project chief] and get him to speed things up," the foreign minister said.[21]

The Potsdam Conference recessed on July 25, 1945, when Churchill returned to England to await the outcome of the election he expected to win in a landslide. The results were a disaster for Churchill's Conservative party. With Churchill's government defeated, the war leader left office, and Clement Attlee returned to Potsdam to head the British delegation as the new prime minister–designate. He brought with him Ernest Bevin, whom he proposed to name secretary of state for foreign affairs. Bevin was a complete contrast to the cosmopolitan and urbane Anthony Eden, the man whom he replaced. The son of a farm laborer and the village midwife of Winsford, in Somerset, Bevin had left school at the age of eleven, never to return. Hired out as a farm laborer himself, he had worked afterward as a dishwasher, streetcar conductor, and truck driver and had become active in the largest of Britain's trade unions, the Transport and General Worker's Union, in 1905. By 1937, he had been elected general secretary of the Trades Union Congress and in 1940 had accepted the post of minister of labor and national service in the war cabinet that Winston Churchill had formed. In that position he had been the principal architect of Britain's "total mobilization" plan.[22] Very obese, suffering from a severe cardiac condition, and speaking in a loud voice in an accent that betrayed his working class origins, Bevin did not immediately impress the American delegation; Truman noted that Bevin appeared "to be a tough person to deal with."[23]

☆　☆　☆

Ruth Andreas-Friedrich and Leo Borchard learned of Churchill's defeat while Andreas-Friedrich was on the balcony of their shattered apartment, trying to cook a meager dinner over a small fire. She called the election results an "outrageous ingratitude." "It's not ingratitude," he rejoined. "It only proves how objectively the English deal with politics. For war, Churchill had been their best man. For peace, particularly if it is to be an allied peace, Churchill as a Conservative might not do so well. Attlee is a Laborite. Between Social Democrats and Communists there shouldn't be insurmountable differences."[24]

☆ ☆ ☆

Attlee and Bevin played no significant role in the final discussions at Potsdam; members of Truman's staff began to refer to the plenary sessions as meetings of the "Big Two," and even Sir Alexander Cadogan, the British permanent undersecretary for foreign affairs, snidely called them meetings of the "Big Two and a Half."[25]

As the conference wound down, it was clear that it would accomplish little of what President Truman had hoped. The question of peace treaties was left to a newly formed Council of Foreign Ministers and the matter of free elections in Poland and the other "liberated" territories was papered over with language that seemed to require them but could not be enforced.

It was determined that each of the individual Allied military commanders would administer his own zone of Germany independently but would cooperate through the Allied Control Council on matters affecting the country as a whole. It was a compromise doomed from its inception.

Reparations were to be taken by each country from the zone it occupied, with the proviso that the Western allies would give over to the Soviets 15 percent of the industrial capacity of their zones in exchange for various raw materials, and an additional 10 percent with no reciprocal payments.[26]

On the day before the conference ended, President Truman made one last effort to have his waterways proposal considered, requesting only that it at least be mentioned in the final communiqué of the conference.

"Marshal Stalin," the President said. "I have accepted a number of compromises during this conference to conform to your views and I make a personal request now that you yield on this point."

"*Nyet,*" the Soviet leader exploded, even before Truman had finished speaking. "No, I say No," he repeated, speaking English for the only time in the seventeen days during which the Big Three met.[27]

Truman turned red and muttered to Secretary of State Byrnes and the rest of the American delegation, "I cannot understand that man."[28] In fact, Harry S Truman was beginning to develop a very keen understanding of the nature of his erstwhile ally, Joseph Stalin, and of the Soviet Union. In his diary that night he noted that Stalin's regime was "police government pure and simple. A few top hands just take clubs, guns and concentration camps and rule the people on the lower levels."[29]

The Soviet Union had, through the long course of World War II, concentrated its efforts in Europe. In the east, it maintained neutrality with

Germany's Axis ally, Japan. At Yalta, Stalin had agreed to enter the war against Japan, and the Western allies were gratified by this. But Truman, as he left Potsdam, had reached a conclusion. Given his recent experience, he was determined that the Soviets would have no part in the control of Japan after the war. "Our experience with them in Germany and in Bulgaria, Rumania, Hungary, and Poland was such that I decided to take no chances in a joint setup with the Russians." Truman had concluded, "The Russians were planning world conquest."[30]

☆   ☆   ☆

The newspapers in Berlin published the final communiqué of the Potsdam conferees under banner headlines, and Ruth Andreas-Friedrich imagined that she was seeing a dove of peace as she read the news.

"Don't see it too soon," one of her companions warned, ticking off on his fingers the problems with the agreement: "For the satisfaction of Russian reparations claims, dismantling of industrial plants in the Russian zone. . . . Reparation claims of the Western Allies covered by assets and resources in the Western-occupied zones. . . . What do you think? Which resources are the Germans to fall back on, under this program, in order to, as it is stated in the resolutions, maintain their existence without outside help?"[31]

Andreas-Friedrich's concern with Potsdam was overshadowed by more immediate things. Borchard's concerts at the Titania Palace and at the Popular Opera became more and more popular, with a varied audience of American troops, British troops, and German civilians from all sectors of Berlin. In the green room after the concerts, musicians and officers of the occupying powers mixed and discussed Tchaikovsky, Strauss, and Beethoven, and Leo Borchard and Ruth Andreas-Friedrich were often invited to dine with Americans and with British officers, in spite of the ban on fraternization. Borchard, after all, was licensed by the authorities to perform in concert and was a proven anti-Nazi.

On August 24, 1945, the staff car of an English colonel wisked Andreas-Friedrich and Borchard to a villa in Grünewald after one of the philharmonic performances. They dined on sandwiches of real meat, sat in comfort, and drank whiskey while talking of Bach and Germany with their English host. The evening passed quickly, and curfew was approaching before they were even aware of it. They became alarmed at the thought of violating an occupation law.

"I'll take you home," the colonel said, calling for his staff car.

On Kaiserplatz, at a railroad overpass, they approached a group of soldiers waving flashlights, and the colonel sped past, still discussing music with Borchard. They were talking about the *Third Brandenburg Concerto.*

"Next time I'll bring you Bach's . . . ," Borchard was saying as a sound like pebbles hitting the car startled Andreas-Friedrich. The car skidded to a halt fifteen yards from the overpass, and Andreas-Friedrich leaped from the back seat, pulled open the front door on the passenger's side, and saw that her lover, Leo Borchard, had just been shot in the head.[32]

The men waving flashlights at the overpass were American military police manning a checkpoint, with orders to stop any car passing their position after eleven o'clock at night and to fire at any car that failed to halt. The evening before there had been a shoot-out between Soviet and American troops, and the American MPs' nerves were on edge in the tense atmosphere between the Allies. Leo Borchard, an ardent anti-Nazi who had survived twelve years in the capital of the Third Reich he detested, died accidentally at the hands of Germany's liberators.

The Philharmonic Orchestra performed a program at the Popular Opera on the night of August 25. Arranged and rehearsed by Borchard, the orchestra was under the baton of a Romanian, Sergiu Celibidache. The program included works by Tchaikovsky and Richard Strauss, and the central piece was to have been Beethoven's *First Symphony*. The new conductor substituted Chopin's "Funeral March" for the Beethoven piece and Ruth Andreas-Friedrich sat through the concert, wondering why she could not cry.[33]

# SIX

# THE BEAR SHOWS ITS CLAWS

On September 6, 1945, only twenty-eight days after returning from Potsdam, Secretary of State James F. Byrnes sailed for Europe again, this time aboard the *Queen Elizabeth*. The ship was newly released from her wartime duties as a troopship and repainted from the dull gray of the Royal Navy to the red-funneled, black-and-white colors of the Cunard line. Byrnes's destination was London and the first meeting of the Council of Foreign Ministers, which had been established at Potsdam.[1]

A conservative Democrat from South Carolina, "Jimmy" Byrnes, not Harry Truman, had nearly succeeded Franklin Roosevelt in the White House. As Roosevelt's director of war mobilization, he was the odds-on favorite to be selected to replace Henry Wallace as Roosevelt's running mate in the 1944 election. He had even asked his old friend from their Senate days, Harry Truman, to make the speech placing his name in nomination at the convention in Chicago. During four days of back-room maneuvering at the convention, Truman had stood by his commitment to back his old friend Jimmy; it took a telephone call from the president to make him accept the vice-presidential nomination.[2] Byrnes had been with Roosevelt at Yalta, but, tired and bitter over having been deprived of the vice-presidential nomination, he resigned as director of war mobilization and returned to his private law practice in Spartanburg. A week later, on the funeral train bearing Roosevelt's body to Hyde Park, New York, President Harry Truman asked Byrnes to serve as secretary of state.[3]

The London meeting included the foreign ministers of the five permanent members of the United Nations—the United States, Great Britain, France, the Soviet Union, and China—and its first order of business was drafting peace treaties with the former Axis powers. It was expected that the treaty with Italy, which had deserted its Axis partners and become a cobelligerent with the Allies, would be considered first and that treaties with Bulgaria, Hungary, Romania, Austria, and Germany would be discussed later.

No expert in foreign affairs, Byrnes did have the advantages of an agile mind, legal training and courtroom experience, good debating skills, and a politician's tactical sense and keenness. He viewed the process of negotiating peace treaties as more or less like maneuvering a bit of New Deal legislation through Congress—wheeling and dealing to pick up votes in favor of what he was proposing. Nothing went as Byrnes expected.

The chairmanship of the conference rotated among the foreign ministers, and Soviet foreign minister V. I. Molotov opened the meeting by launching a series of procedural wrangles, jockeying for concessions from the Western powers to exaggerated Soviet demands. Before the peace treaty with Italy could be discussed, Molotov insisted, it must be agreed to divide up the Italian navy, hand the city of Trieste over to the Yugoslavs, make the former Italian colony of Tripolitania in North Africa a Soviet trusteeship, and agree on Italian reparations to the USSR.[4] With respect to the Axis allies Romania, Bulgaria, and Hungary, the price demanded was Western acceptance of the puppet regimes put in place by the conquering Soviets. He would not consider talk of a treaty with Germany until treaties with all of the other belligerents had been concluded.[5]

These positions of the Soviets were not ones that Britain and the United States could support or agree to. Ernest Bevin of Great Britain was particularly upset by the Soviet proposal for a trusteeship over Tripolitania and later demands for a base on Turkish soil near the Dardanelles.

The conference went on for over two fruitless weeks until Molotov surprised everyone by abruptly demanding that France and China be excluded from any further discussions because no representative of either government had been present at the Potsdam Conference.[6] This was a direct insult to General Charles DeGaulle, who had secured a much publicized Treaty of Friendship with Stalin during a personal trip to Moscow in 1944, and Georges Bidault, the French foreign minister, was furious. The only thing that prevented him from walking out was his knowledge that such an act would give the Soviets precisely what they were looking for.

Molotov's next sudden and unexpected demand was that the United States agree to the establishment of a second Allied Control Council to govern Japan. Byrnes, ever a clever parliamentary tactician, if not an accomplished diplomat, arranged for the next chairman in rotation, Dr. Wang Shih-chieh of China, to adjourn the next session without setting a date for the next meeting. The maneuver took Molotov completely by surprise, and the first, albeit abortive, conference of the Council of

Foreign Ministers ended with nothing resolved.[7] Policymakers in Washington, some of whom had long harbored suspicions about Soviet aims, saw the Soviet actions as confirmations of their fears and began to worry even more about Soviet postwar intentions.

☆ ☆ ☆

In Germany, General Clay was trying to bring order to a world where the American army was in the throes of the chaos of victory and the Germans he was expected to govern were suffering the chaos of defeat.

There is a military maxim taught at staff schools that a poor plan well executed is more likely to succeed than a good plan that is carried out poorly. In Germany at the end of the war, there were a number of plans for the government and administration of the country. Some were good, some poor, and most in conflict. Their existence and proliferation led to the development of a condition described by an informal military epithet: SNAFU—situation normal; all f---ed up. It was to the United States Army that the resolution of the problems fell.

Traditionally, the U.S. Army has not been organized, trained, or geared for the job of civilian administration. Its prior major experience in the field—Reconstruction in the south after the Civil War—was ultimately not a success, and it had had little time to hone military government skills in its short occupation of Germany after World War I. Military units from the level of battalion upward long functioned with four staff positions under the commander. These were G-1 (administration), G-2 (intelligence), G-3 (operations), and G-4 (supply). When victory over the Axis Powers could be foreseen and the prospect of having to govern occupied territories loomed, a fifth staff function was added to the traditional four. This was G-5—military government. It grew at a phenomenal rate and attracted a wide variety of personnel. Combat officers who had been injured or wounded and could not return to their previous units found slots in G-5, even though they might completely lack the background for it. Academics, lawyers, and civilian specialists of all types, mostly directly commissioned and lacking in all but rudimentary military training, also entered G-5. But military government was often considered an orphan stepchild of the army, and combat commanders whose troops had conquered an area of Germany were reluctant to see their conquest pass into the hands of people they usually regarded only as civilians in uniform.[8]

Soon after his arrival in Europe, General Clay had convinced General Eisenhower that if the United States was to carry out a successful occupation, military government had to be removed from the General Staff and placed in a completely separate structure, reporting directly to the commanding general in Europe. Clay argued that Eisenhower should have two coequal deputies, one for military matters and one for military government. While Eisenhower approved the plan, many un-

der him did not accept its wisdom and continued to resist its implementation. These included, not surprisingly, General Walter Bedell
Smith, Eisenhower's deputy for military affairs. Smith insisted that
Clay report to Eisenhower through him as chief-of-staff, but Clay successfully resisted.[9]

The initial arrangement was less than ideal as combat commands
retained their G-5 functions, which were parallel to those of Clay's military government, and there were no clear lines of communication between the two. With some maneuvering by Clay, Major General Clarence L. Adcock was appointed G-5 on Eisenhower's staff and, as Clay's
lifelong friend and Military Academy classmate, Adcock kept Clay
fully informed of the combat command's G-5 activities, even though
Adcock reported to Smith. "General Smith was too damned intelligent
not to know what was going on," Clay wrote later, "and it was not what
he wanted." Smith did not, however, want a showdown on the issue,
according to Clay.[10] By September 1945, Clay and Adcock had agreed
to merge their staffs, and from that time forward, Adcock was effectively Clay's deputy.[11]

That arrangement was helpful but did nothing to alter the fact that
military government was an organization parallel to the rest of the
army in Germany. The military governor commanded no combat
troops—those fell under the theater commander—and did not staff the
garrisons. Military government troops, mostly officers, were expected
to work with indigenous personnel—the Germans themselves—to reestablish essential services and to govern the conquered territory. General Eisenhower, commander of the newly designated United States
Forces European Theater (USFET), left the administration of military
government to Clay. Eisenhower's successor, General Joseph McNar-
ney, continued that policy, devoting his attention to the dwindling
number of combat troops in his command and allowing Clay a relatively free hand.[12]

The policy Clay had to administer was spelled out in instructions
issued by the Joint Chiefs of Staff in a document known as JCS 1067. It
began, "Germany will not be occupied for the purpose of liberation but
as a defeated enemy nation," and pointed out that "it should be brought
home to the Germans that Germany's ruthless warfare and the fanatical
Nazi resistance have destroyed the German economy and made chaos
and suffering inevitable and that the Germans cannot escape responsibility for what they have brought on themselves."[13]

The principal objective of JCS 1067 was to ensure that Germany
would never again become a threat to the peace of the world. It specified that this would be accomplished by the elimination of Nazism and
militarism, the apprehension and trial of war criminals, industrial demilitarization, continuing control over Germany's industry, and preparation for the eventual reconstruction of German political life on a

democratic basis. A paragraph specifically required that the army perform these tasks while remaining aloof from any entanglements with the Germans themselves. It was known as "nonfraternization," and it took a while for the high command to realize that it was totally inconsistent with the other requirements of JCS 1067. It is impossible to live in and administer a country if you can have no contact with the natives.

The individual soldiers recognized the inconsistency instantly and on an elemental level, as they were in daily contact with Germans. Some of the contacts were in the black market; more were of the "boy-meets-girl" variety. When the army command decreed that enlisted men would be fined sixty-five dollars for talking to Germans, GIs quickly came to refer to such conversations as "asking the sixty-five-dollar question."[14]

In the face of reality, the rules against fraternization began to bend. As early as June 8, 1945, General Eisenhower announced that the ban was obviously not intended to apply to "very small children."[15] In Berlin, one of the first things that the Americans did after this pronouncement was to organize a sports program for German youth under sixteen years of age and begin to teach them the quintessential American sport of baseball. The first German teams—the Tigers, the Bears, and Mickey *Mäuse* (mice),—were organized on August 14, and within weeks there were over five thousand children involved. On September 10 the Soviet representative at the Kommandatura, Colonel Dalada, lodged a protest that the American baseball program could be regarded as quasi-military training, which violated the regulations regarding the Germans. Colonel Howley politely but firmly rejected the Soviet assertion.[16]

Soon after the decision on children, the ban on fraternization was further eroded when it was announced that the fact that a soldier had contracted a venereal disease could not be used as proof that he had been fraternizing. By July 14, 1945, the high command allowed army personnel to "engage in conversation with Germans on the street in public places" and allowed "normal contacts" on August 6. While there were few other issues on which Berlin's quadripartite governing body could agree, the Allied Control Council announced the end to nonfraternization as an official policy on October 1, 1945.[17] The ban on fraternization was the first of the directives in JCS 1067 to be modified in light of actual circumstances in Germany.

By the time the decision on fraternization was made, Robert J. Lauenstein was working as an interpreter at the Department of Justice mission in Berlin. He had a very good reason to be working there. He was in love.

Lauenstein had fought his way across Europe as a Technician Fourth Class with the 208th Combat Engineers, and the unit ended the war near Dessau. On July 8, 1945, he and his buddies had decided that getting a keg of beer would be a good way to spend the afternoon, and Lauenstein was picked by lot to run the errand. It was then that he met Anna Maria Christina Heinke, a twenty-two-year-old ballet dancer from Dessau. Her father had died in the Nazi camp at Arnstat, and Anna Maria had spent the war working in the Junkers aircraft factory near her home, having been drafted for the job as punishment for her father's anti-Nazi statements. In spite of the ban on fraternization, Robert and Anna Maria talked and over a period of weeks fell in love. When it came time for Lauenstein to be released from service, he took his discharge in Germany and found the Justice Department job in Berlin to be near Anna Maria. With the announcement of the end of the ban on fraternization, Anna Maria Heinke and Robert Lauenstein made an announcement of their own. They became engaged.[18]

☆  ☆  ☆

In Berlin, some were less interested in the blossoming of love than in the flowering of politics after the long winter of repression under the Nazis.

Frank Matthis, one of the original members of *Onkel Emil,* came home on October 16 with a armful of newspapers.

"Now we've got them," he said, throwing the papers on the table.

"Whom?" Ruth Andreas-Friedrich asked.

"The parties. The political mouthpiece of popular will, if you prefer it more poetical," Frank replied, reeling off the names of the newspapers and the political parties they represented.

"Strange," said Andreas-Friedrich's daughter, Karin. "They all call themselves 'Party of Germany' and three out of four call themselves 'Democratic.' Since the end of the war, to us Germany consists only of Berlin and democracy only of orders issued in agreement—or rather in disagreement—by the occupying powers. Why all this pomp?"

"Because this 'pomp' expresses our willingness to assume political responsibility," Frank explained. "Because freedom begins by assuming responsibility."

"But they don't allow us to assume any responsibility," Heinke answered.

Frowning, Frank responded, "But that doesn't relieve you of the duty to care about the future," adding that he had joined the Social Democrats.

"But why the Social Democrats?" the others asked.

"What other choice is there? I am too much of a scientist to join the Christian Democrats. I'm not Soviet enough for the Communists of today. Mass misery requires social solutions. Social democratic ones."[19]

The wartime alliance of the Big Three—the United States, Great Britain, and the USSR—was a fragile thing even when the partners were faced with a vicious German enemy. With their major adversary defeated, the grand alliance began to unravel under the tensions and strains of securing peace, and that unraveling was first revealed at the deliberations of the Allied Control Council. During the war the Soviets had often made blunt statements of their aim to destroy Germany and its war potential, but the Western allies were encouraged to believe that these aims would be sought in the context of the alliance. With the Soviets occupying a large portion of Germany, reality set in.

Overrun by Soviet troops, the German province of East Prussia was given over to Polish administration, and the government of Poland established by the Soviets did not include representatives from the group of Polish exiles who had fought the war from London. The western border of the reconstituted Poland was established by the Soviets at the line of the Oder and Neisse Rivers and, while this had been discussed at Yalta in February 1945, it had by no means been agreed to. During the Potsdam conference, the Western allies protested this unilateral Soviet action to no avail. Their protests were met with stoic refusal by Stalin even to discuss the matter. The question of the Polish borders was left to be resolved by the foreign ministers at a general peace conference, but sure signs of discord and distrust between the allies had begun to appear.

The Soviet policy of dismantling or stripping German industrial installations and shipping them east before the Allies had agreed on a formula for reparations was another grave cause for concern by the West. While apparent agreement on the subject of reparations was reached by the conferees at Potsdam—that each occupying power would satisfy its reparations requirements primarily from its own zone, provided that enough resources were left to allow the Germans to exist without outside assistance—it was a formula to which the Soviets assented only after they were promised that the Western allies would dismantle and send them 25 percent of the industrial plants in the Western zones of occupation. There was growing evidence that the Soviets were exacting reparations in their zone in violation of the Potsdam agreements, leaving Germany little or nothing on which to build a peaceful, healthy economy.

The disagreements on reparations were a manifestation of the basic difference in approach of the Soviets and the Western allies to the problem of ensuring that Germany would never again threaten the peace of Europe. The Soviet view was that it would be best to bleed Germany white, thereby making sure that it would never again have the strength to become a threat. The Americans, in spite of the apparent harshness of JCS 1067, recalled the chaotic economic conditions that had allowed Hitler's rise to power in the 1930s and believed that the key to future European peace lay in a prosperous and democratic Germany. The British generally shared that view, stressing the reintegration of Germany into a world of civilized nations. The *London Times* even editorialized that "the critical and inescapable fact is that an industrially productive Germany is essential to the material prosperity of most of Europe. If Germany is to be converted into a primitive and third-rate industrial nation, it is the population of Europe who will foot the bill."[20]

The harsh view of the Soviets was understandable, if unwelcome by America and Great Britain. The incessant Soviet demands for reparations and their desire to reduce Germany to a pauper state were rooted in the devastating losses that the Soviet Union had sustained during the war. No other European country had suffered so much at the hands of the Germans. Over 20 million Soviet citizens died in the conflict, and economic damage was widespread. In 1939, 17.5 million horses served as draft animals on Soviet farms. By the end of the war, over seven million had been lost. The number of cattle had dropped from 63 million to 47 million, and two-thirds of the pigs in the country were dead. The output of oil in the Baku region, the scene of bitter fighting, was off by 50 percent, and huge hydroelectric projects in the Donets Basin and on the Don River—projects that had cost millions and had been the pride of Soviet Five-Year Plans in the 1930s—had been intentionally destroyed in 1941 to deprive the advancing Germans of their output. The death in battle of so many young men had lowered the potential industrial work force from 30.4 million in 1940 to around 27 million by the end of the war.[21]

The Soviets found support for their position from the French, who were very much "junior partners" to the Big Three but were included in the occupation of Germany through agreements reached at Yalta. France had known three German invasions in seventy years. In the Franco-Prussian War of 1870, France had tasted defeat quickly, and her provinces of Alsace and Lorraine had been annexed to the German Empire. Most of the blood shed in the Great War of 1914–18 had fallen on French soil, and the youth of the nation had been squandered in the mud of a trench system that stretched from the English Channel to the Swiss border. In 1940, Hitler's panzers had swept through the French army, forcing a humiliating peace that had left the country truncated and writhing under the Nazi boot for over four years. France, now led by General Charles DeGaulle, had one overriding aim—to see that a rearmed and militant Germany would never again pose a threat to France. The manner in which this could be accomplished, the French maintained, was to excise the industrial heart of the Teutonic nation and graft it onto France. The Ruhr, with its rich veins of coal and industrial might, should be annexed by France, just as the Poles had been allowed to annex lands in the east.

While the Soviets would not go so far as to endorse the idea of incorporation of the Ruhr into France, they knew that they had a willing partner on the Allied Control Council in obstructing any move toward a German industrial revival, and preventing that revival was an important step in the accomplishment of a long-range Soviet goal.

Stalin had said at a June 4, 1945, meeting of a group of German veterans of the Comintern that he expected that there would be "two Germanys" for a time. Then, provided that American troops withdrew from Europe, British influence in the West could be undermined so that, in the end, there would be a united, "friendly" Germany, leaning toward the USSR.[22]

That aim would color what happened in Germany, and Berlin, for years to come.

## SEVEN

# "I'M TIRED OF BABYING THE SOVIETS"

On August 25, 1945, the nightmare day following Leo Borchard's death, Ruth Andreas-Friedrich desperately tried to arrange a proper funeral, with the aid of their friend the English colonel. In her daze of disbelief and dispair, it suddenly occurred to her that she must tell Borchard's childhood friend, Makar Ivanov, of the tragedy. Borchard had known Ivanov as a child in Moscow. Now Ivanov was an interpreter for the Soviet forces in the city and lived on Friedrichstrasse. The English colonel drove Andreas-Friedrich there.

Ivanov's building was guarded by a Soviet sentry, deeply suspicious of visitors arriving in the car of an English colonel, but the sentry agreed to summon Ivanov, who was shocked at the news of Borchard's death. He quickly arranged to take a leave from work, but as Andreas-Friedrich, the colonel, and Ivanov prepared to drive away, a Soviet officer ran up to the car, pulled open the door, and shouted something at Ivanov.[1]

Arrangements for a funeral in Berlin in 1945 were complicated. Andreas-Friedrich attempted to obtain a coffin and was told that American soldiers were buried in tarpaulins and the authorities could see no reason for treating a German any better.[2] Not until August 29 could she complete all of the arrangements and lay the body of Leo Borchard to rest. On the Monday following the funeral, Makar Ivanov decided to ask for a few more days of leave from his job with the Soviets. He went to his office that morning, assuring Ruth Andreas-Friedrich that he would return by early afternoon. She never saw him again.[3]

She heard nothing of Ivanov for nearly a month. Then, on September 23, an anonymous messenger said to her, "Help him, for Christ's sake. They are breaking their clubs over him. They say he's a spy." A week later she gave the messenger a bottle of brandy and two hundred cigarettes to use as bribes to get information. He brought news to

Andreas-Friedrich that Makar Ivanov was to be put on trial for espionage on behalf of England.[4]

☆  ☆  ☆

At the Allied Kommandatura in Berlin, the Western allies and the Soviets wrangled over running the city. One of the universities in Berlin is in the square known as Bebelplatz, on Unter den Linden in the Soviet zone of the city. It is the site where Nazi propaganda minister Josef Goebbels presided over the public burning of over 200,000 books on May 10, 1933. An equestrian statue of Frederick the Great stares out over Bebelplatz from one side of the square. Diagonally across the street from the Great Elector are the statues of the scholars Wilhelm and Alexander von Humboldt. Wilhelm Humboldt was instrumental in founding the university on Bebelplatz in 1810.

When the Soviet authorities reopened the university, they erected a less permanent monument: a banner declaring, "At this University Studied the Founder of Scientific Communism, Karl Marx."[5] The Western allies repeatedly requested that the university be brought under quadripartite control, and the Soviets repeatedly rejected the requests. A group of Berlin academics led by Professor Eduard Sprangler even petitioned the Western allies to force the Soviets to agree to four-power control, but the petition was rejected. With so many other sources of friction between the Western allies and the Soviets, there was no desire to add another.

The operation of Radio Berlin was another source of conflict at the Kommandatura. When the Western allies arrived in the city, the Soviets already had the powerful transmitter back in operation. The Americans, British, and French all thought that the radio station would be operated jointly. The Soviets flatly refused to consider the idea, even though the transmitter and studios were located on Masurenallee in the British sector and the antenna was in Tegel in the French sector. The Soviets offered their Western allies one hour of air-time each day, and the offer was grudgingly accepted, under protest.[6]

Returning German soldiers and civilian refugees from the eastern territories now occupied by the Soviets were an ongoing problem for the military government in Berlin. The soldiers, wearing their only clothes—their now-forbidden Wehrmacht and Luftwaffe uniforms—crowded the streets. With winter approaching, the Soviets showed no sympathy when it was pointed out to them that the uniforms were the only clothing that the veterans had. "No clothes?" a Soviet delegate commented. "Well, let them wear underclothes."[7]

The civilian refugees included large numbers of Polish Jews; by late 1945 over five thousand had entered the city and were concentrated in the Soviet sector. As such migration was forbidden, they were there illegally and were not entitled to either ration cards or shelter, and the question of how to treat them came up at the Kommandatura but defied resolution. On December 22, 1945, the American commandant, General Parks, ordered that the preparation of a new camp begin, just in case they were sent to the American sector.[8]

Incidents involving armed Soviet soldiers entering the Western sectors to loot and rape continued to be reported, and each time they were brought up at the Kommandatura, they were met with Soviet denials. The four powers wrangled over the issuance of postage stamps in the city,[9] over efforts to bring the black market under control,[10] over such arcane details as whether Germans should be allowed to have tattoos removed,[11] and over the important issue of food. The Americans concluded that the lowest category of rations, 1,248 calories per day, was below subsistence level. They proposed to raise it.

In arguing the proposal before the Kommandatura, Colonel Frank Howley, the deputy commandant, used a common American metaphor. "You can't kick a lady when she's down," he said.

"Why, my dear Colonel Howley," replied Colonel Dalada, the Soviet deputy, "that is the best time to kick them."

"You mean food is political?" Howley asked, unbelievingly.

The Soviet was smiling when he responded, "Of course."[12]

The workings of the Allied Kommandatura in Berlin mirrored in microcosm those of the Allied Control Council where Clay, as deputy military governor, took part as the main United States representative. In Berlin, the American commandant of the city was in charge of both the garrison and the military government, but the commandants changed frequently, and Howley, deputy commandant and commander of the military government detachment, was the usual American representative at the Kommandatura. It was a position that gave him a unique perspective and led him to an early conclusion that the Soviets had little interest in interallied cooperation.

In one early discussion, Howley and his Soviet counterpart, General Kotikov, were trying to reach agreement on a mundane issue—the color of automobile license tags. Kotikov launched into a long-winded discussion of Marxist philosophy and the world class struggle.

"Look," Howley said. "Let's get down to business. You and I won't live to see the end of the class struggle, but we can settle this automobile tag business today."

Kotikov grinned back at him and replied, "Maybe you won't live to see the end of the class struggle, but I will."[13]

Howley had come to Berlin feeling that the Germans were the enemy. Now, while still unwilling to embrace the Germans as allies, he concluded that the real enemies were the Soviets.[14] General Clay was also beginning to view the Soviets in a less favorable light than before but was still determined to try to make four-power cooperation in Germany work.

On October 3, 1945, Ruth Andreas-Friedrich went to the head of a Russian agency to inquire about Makar Ivanov and was received by the major in charge. She believed that she could explain why Ivanov sought leave from his job with the Soviet authorities to drive off in the car of an English colonel.

"Makar Ivanov," she began. "It must be a misunderstanding. A series of mistakes." She identified the agency for which Ivanov worked and its location.

"Which agency?" the Russian major inquired. He said that he knew of no such agency at that location, smiling at Andreas-Friedrich with eyes that betrayed nothing.

At that moment, she knew that nothing on earth could save Borchard's friend.[15]

☆  ☆  ☆

As secretary of state, Jimmy Byrnes was kept fully informed of the activities of the Allied Control Council by his old friend, General Clay, with whom he had worked in the Office of War Mobilization. Byrnes was not happy with the stalemate with the Soviets that was developing in Germany and believed that it could be best resolved in the context of a peace treaty with the Germans.

Byrnes had developed a reputation in the Department of State and in the administration as being full of surprises. In late November 1945 he pulled a big one. Without consulting with the president, Assistant Secretary Dean Acheson, or any other members of the State Department staff, he proposed to Soviet foreign minister Molotov that the Big Three ministers meet in Moscow in December. The invitation excluded the French, tacitly conceding to the Soviets part of what they had sought in the London meeting of September.[16]

Ernest Bevin learned of the proposal only through his Moscow ambassador, Sir Archibald Clark-Kerr, and was furious. Bevin objected to the very thought of such a meeting. Hardened by his years of trade union negotiations, Bevin believed that the best tactic was to sit tight and wait until the Soviets came around. He knew, however, that if he refused to attend the meeting, it would be perceived as British foot-dragging in seeking a peaceful world. He reluctantly went to Moscow, convinced that it was a mistake and deeply angry with Secretary Byrnes for having dragged him into the situation.[17]

George Kennan, second man on the American embassy staff in Moscow, described Bevin's attitude at the conference: "Bevin look highly disgusted with the whole procedure. It was easy to see by his face that he found himself in a position he did not like and was well aware that nothing good could come out of the meeting."[18] On the other hand, Molotov "sat leaning forward over the table, a Russian cigarette dangling from his mouth, his eyes flashing with satisfaction and confidence. He had the look of a passionate poker player who knows that he has a royal flush and is about to call the last of his opponents."[19]

By the time the conference concluded on December 27, Byrnes had accomplished little. The Soviets promised some minor cosmetic changes in their Bulgarian and Romanian puppet regimes in return for Western recognition, but no progress was made on either Germany or another point that was important to the Americans: the withdrawal of Soviet troops from northern Iran, an area they had occupied during the war. During the protracted negotiations, Byrnes even agreed to set up an Allied Control Council to consult with General MacArthur in Japan, although MacArthur's firmness and imperious approach to the occupation there would ensure that American administration of that fallen enemy would not be subject to Soviet manipulations.[20] Even that concession did not move the Soviets.

In return for his meager accomplishments, Byrnes found that the Moscow meeting he had forced on the British had done much harm. Charles DeGaulle, never trustful of his allies, was thoroughly alienated by the exclusion of France and more determined than ever to take an independent course. The British were thoroughly disgusted over the whole affair, particularly as it had accomplished nothing meaningful. Most important, by failing to keep President Truman informed of what he was doing, Jimmy Byrnes had lost the confidence of his commander in chief. As he left the meeting in Moscow, Byrnes cabled Charlie Ross, the White House press secretary, to set up a radio address in which he proposed to inform the nation of what had been accomplished. The president was in the room when Charlie Ross took the call.

"Who's on the phone?" he asked.

"Byrnes," Ross said, and the president instructed his press secretary how to respond to the secretary of state.

"The President asks me to tell you," Ross relayed, "that you had better come down here posthaste and make your report to the President before you do anything else."[21]

The meeting took place on the presidential yacht *Williamsburg,* and it was not cordial. Harry S Truman was not a man who enjoyed being kept in the dark by his subordinates. Byrnes left a collection of documents with the president, and after he had read them, Truman called Byrnes to the White House on January 5 for a second meeting, during which Truman read his secretary of state a letter he had composed in longhand. The letter castigated Byrnes for not having kept him informed and expressed Truman's growing discontent with Soviet actions: "There is no justification for [the Russian program in Iran]. It is a parallel to the Russian program in Latvia, Estonia and Lithuania. It is also in line with the high-handed and arbitrary manner in which Russia acted in Poland."[22]

The president went on to state his sense of Soviet intentions: "There isn't a doubt in my mind that Russia intends an invasion of Turkey and the seizure of the Black Sea Straits to the Mediterranean. Unless Russia is faced with an iron fist and strong language another war is in the making. . . . I'm tired of babying the Soviets."[23]

Jimmy Byrnes's days as secretary of state were numbered, although it was not a change that the president was prepared to make immediately. He assured Byrnes that he could stay on in the post through the negotiation of peace treaties with the minor Axis powers, but Harry Truman already knew exactly who he wanted to appoint in Byrnes's place when the time was ripe.

That man was General of the Army George Catlett Marshall.[24] As chief of staff, Marshall had been the primary architect of the American military effort that had won the war. Now that the president's focus was beginning to turn from the Rooseveltian concept of peace through mutual understanding to the problem of dealing with a Soviet threat to international security, Truman wanted the State Department's diplomatic efforts directed by General Marshall.

As winter settled firmly over Berlin just before Christmas, a rumor swept the city. The inflated, nearly worthless reichsmark was to be further devalued on January 1. The advice that Berliners offered each other was varied and contradictory. Some tried to use up their reichsmarks, paying off debts or buying resalable goods, and some paid their rent in advance.[25]

The Berliners' quandary was unsolvable. Ruth Andreas-Friedrich noted, "Between ruins, hunger and the black market, slowly the respect for money and the value of money have been equally devalued."[26]

The new year came, and the rumors of devaluation proved false. Measures to deal with the condition of the German economy had reached a stalemate at the Allied Control Council and had become inextricably intertwined with the negotiations for a peace treaty. Ruth had other things to occupy her as Berliners settled in to endure the first winter after the defeat of Germany. Having followed her friend Frank into the ranks of the Social Democratic party, she became involved in the campaign to prevent its merger with the Communists.

## EIGHT

# A LONG TELEGRAM

Otto Grotewohl, the leader of the Social Democratic Party (*Sozial-demokratische Partei*, SDP) in Germany, did not initially favor any move that would unite his party with the Communists, although there were vocal members of both parties who did, and such a merger was Communist party policy. In a speech in September 1945, Grotewohl said that the necessary preconditions for such a merger were not present.[1]

However, the Soviet military administration and the German Communists had determined that such a merger was in their best interests and began to pressure the SDP to unite with the communist KPD (Kommunistische Partei Deutschland). Marshal Zhukov personally intervened to have Grotewohl's son, Hans Günter, released from a British POW camp, and Grotewohl was plied in other ways by the Soviets.[2] On February 11, 1946, he forced through a vote at a meeting of the Central Committee of the SDP calling for a merger of the two parties into a new Socialist Unity Party, the *Sozialistische Einheitspartei,* or SED. The move was denounced by Kurt Schumacher, the one-armed veteran of ten years in a Nazi concentration camp who was now the leader of the SDP in the Western zones. Schumacher remembered that before Hitler rose to power in 1933, the KPD had acted as an agent of the Soviet Comintern and had regarded the Social Democrats, and not the Nazis, as its true enemies in Germany. The same Walter Ulbricht who was now calling for unity had often cooperated with the Nazis in their attempts to bring down the Weimar Republic, which the SDP had vainly supported.[3] The planned merger also provoked an immediate and violent reaction among SDP members in Berlin, with many opposing the idea. An SDP party conference on the proposal was called by the Berlin members for March 1. The Western allies, America included, remained aloof from the debate, considering it to be an internal German matter and one of the preliminary steps toward their eventual democratization, as spelled out in the Potsdam Accords.[4]

In the meantime, the Americans in Berlin were celebrating. On February 27, 1946, the American Office of Military Government hosted a reception and lavish buffet for news correspondents to celebrate what the office considered to be "the successful completion of the first phase of our Berlin mission."[5] A press release prepared for the occasion summed up what OMG considered to be its major accomplishments:

> When Allied Military Government went into effect on 12 July 1945 Berliners had almost exhausted their food supplies. Three million people, a population almost half as large as the entire population of Bavaria, was [sic] packed into a city which had received frightful destruction.
>
> Dysentery was killing 65 out of every 100 babies born in the city. Typhoid and diphtheria were making huge inroads due to the weakened condition of the population. Sewers dumped directly into the city's waterways. There was no drinking of water without boiling—and no fuel to boil it.[6]

The list went on to cite the lack of postal service, public transportation, trade and commerce, and electricity, before turning to the reason for the celebration:

> Out of innumerable Kommandatura conferences the shape of things to come became apparent.
>
> Now the waterways are free of pollution. Water is sufficiently chlorinated to guard the health of the population. More than 5,000,000 kilowatt hours of electricity are available daily. A police force of 14,000 is gaining in skill and proficiency. The entire population has been inoculated against typhoid. Almost three and a quarter million persons are being fed by a system which works with efficiency. Monthly gas production has been upped 75 percent to 17,091,000 cubic meters. More than 800 streetcars are in operation and one and a quarter million riders use them daily. Nazis have been cleaned out of positions of importance and some 1,200 dyed-in-the-wool Nazis are now working on debris clearance.
>
> Above and beyond the technical accomplishments of Military Government in Berlin is the phenomenon of a city successfully run by four nations. Here is a record of successful international adjustments and sympathetic understanding.[7]

The press release did not note that the "innumerable" meetings were more often marked by disagreement than by accord, nor did it note the growing and bitter debate at the Kommandatura about a new constitution for the city and the establishment of a new, elected civil government. The existing government consisted entirely of officials who had been appointed by the Soviets in the immediate wake of their seizure of the city, and the Americans had already dismissed the district leader in Steglitz for being a Soviet lackey and giving the Americans "considerable chin music," in Colonel Howley's colorful phrase.[8] The British and French had also had occasion to dismiss Soviet appointees in their sectors, and the Western allies were in agreement on the need for free elections in the city.[9]

The glowing press release did not mention the problem of the Polish Jewish refugees that had so plagued the deliberations of the Kommandatura in the previous month. The British made it clear in the discussions that they would not accept the displaced persons in their sector; their resources were strained providing food and shelter for the existing population as it was. On January 5, 1946, the Soviets indicated that they had a solution to the problem. They proposed to relocate the refugees forcibly to a detention camp at an undisclosed location in the Soviet east; by January 8, over two thousand Jews had been seized by the Soviets and removed from the city. The terrified remainder fled from the Soviet sector into the American, most of them finding shelter in an abandoned and dilapidated pavilion on a lake called the Wannsee, where they huddled, unfed and poorly clothed, in the cold and snow.

On January 10, General Clay settled the matter without further reference to the Kommandatura or the Control Council. He issued an order that every refugee in the American sector would be cared for by American authorities. With the continuing reduction in American military forces in Germany, former camps and installations were becoming vacant, and the Polish Jews were moved into a facility from which the 3d Battalion, 309th Infantry, had recently departed.[10]

☆ ☆ ☆

In Moscow in February 1946, George Kennan was suffering from a variety of physical ailments—a cold, sinus problems, a fever, and trouble with his teeth—and was on sulfa medications when the telegram reached his sickbed informing him that the Treasury Department was bewildered by Soviet unwillingness to adhere to the rules of the World Bank and International Monetary Fund.[11] The Department of the Treasury was not alone in Washington in its concern and agitation about the Soviets. Most people at high levels in the American government had noted the February 9, 1946, speech by Premier Stalin announcing the first postwar Five-Year Plan. The Soviet leader declared, in classic Leninist terms, that the real causes of World War II had been the demands and contradictions of the capitalist-imperialist monopoly and that those same forces were still at work outside the Soviet Union. Stalin proclaimed that the Soviet Union must be able to guard against all eventualities and that an absolute priority would therefore be given to rearmament. Consumer goods, Stalin directed, would wait. The speech heralded the end to any pretense of continued cooperation with the West.[12]

For the eighteen months he had been with the Moscow embassy, Kennan had "done little else but pluck at people's sleeves, trying to make them understand the phenomenon . . . which our government and people had to learn to understand if they were to have any chance of coping successfully with the problems of the postwar world."[13] Now, someone had asked the right questions, and Kennan was determined to take the opportunity to give them an answer.

Dictating to Dorothy Hessman, his secretary, Kennan composed an eight-thousand-word reply and divided it into five separate telegrams, so that it would not appear outrageously long. The sections dealt with the basic features of the Soviet postwar outlook, the background of that outlook, the relation of the outlook to official Soviet policy, the projection of Soviet attitudes with respect to front organizations, and the implications of all of this for American policy.

"Soviet leaders," Kennan wrote, "are driven by necessities of their own past and present positions to put forth a dogma which pictures the outside world as evil, hostile and menacing, but as bearing within itself germs of creeping disease and destined to be wracked with growing internal convulsions until it is given a final coup de grace by the rising power of socialism."[14] Kennan advised the State Department to look for the Soviet Union to give priority to increasing the strength and prestige of the Soviet state, to advance Soviet territorial gains where possible, to participate in such organizations as the United Nations only with a view toward pursuing Soviet aims, and to work toward the weakening of the power and influence of the West. "In general," he advised, "all Soviet efforts . . . will be negative and destructive in character, designed to tear down sources of strength beyond Soviet control."[15] This, Kennan felt, was in keeping with a basic Soviet instinct that there can be no compromise with a rival power and that constructive work can start only when Communist power is dominant. The prescription he proposed to counter the Soviet Union was essentially a complete reversal of the foreign policy of the Roosevelt years, when compromise, understanding, and cooperation were sought. It was a call to waken to a new danger.

Kennan's "long telegram" arrived at the State Department on February 22 and was read by the former United States ambassador to the Soviet Union, W. Averell Harriman, who was in Washington to confer with department officials prior to taking up his new post as ambassador in London. Harriman rarely bothered to praise the work of his subordinates, but after reading Kennan's dispatch, Harriman sent him a congratulatory wire and passed a copy of the text on to Secretary of the Navy James Forrestal. To the navy secretary, it was something that he had long been seeking—a clear and convincing explanation of heretofore bewildering Soviet policy and behavior. Forrestal immediately distributed copies of Kennan's analysis to the Joint Chiefs of Staff and other senior military officials.[16] The "long telegram" began to spread through the upper echelons of American government. In Berlin, a demonstration of just the type of Soviet behavior Kennan warned about was beginning to take shape.

☆ ☆ ☆

Ruth Andreas-Friedrich was one of the 1,500 representatives packing the hall at the SDP party conference at the Admiralpalast at nine o'clock on the first of March. When Otto Grotewohl announced that the executive committee had endorsed the unification of the worker's parties in the Soviet zone, the representatives began to jeer.

"You didn't ask us," the hall erupted. "Lackey! Go back to Karlshorst, Otto."

As Grotewohl attempted to explain his position, he was drowned out by rising voices.

"We don't want a forced unification. We won't let ourselves be raped."

As Grotewohl stumbled on, the voices in the hall rose angrily. Finally they demanded a strike vote. It passed overwhelmingly. There would be a vote of the entire party in Berlin on the merger—if the vote was approved by the Kommandatura. "For the first time in thirteen years we've defended our freedom," Ruth heard one worker say as the meeting broke up.[17]

Neither the Communists nor the promerger Social Democrats felt that they could come out against a referendum on the question, so their efforts turned to persuasion and coercion of the potential voters. The *Tägliche Rundschau,* the Soviet-backed newspaper, editorialized against "opponents of unity,"[18] and the city was flooded with propaganda material from promerger forces. The city council of Soviet appointees threatened all opponents of the merger with the loss of their jobs, and the district party leaders in Tempelhof and Kreuzberg were dismissed from their posts for opposing the merger. The antimerger forces could, at first, find no medium to voice their concerns and position. The official party newspaper, naturally, supported the line of the leadership. Pleas for help from the Western allies fell on apparently deaf ears. "This is a domestic German matter," American and British friends of the dissidents said evasively.[19]

Communist party members began to spread rumors that the Western allies were preparing to leave Berlin and that the party merger would be forced when they left, with dire consequences for anyone who had resisted it. The Communist-controlled police arrested several antimerger activists, and they disappeared. At the same time, the Soviets temporarily suspended the dismantlement of factories in their sector and allowed the families of German prisoners of war to send them mail, to give the impression that their rule was softening.[20]

In spite of the official hands-off attitude, many junior American and British officers offered encouragement to the antimerger forces, meeting with them in cold, badly lit, damaged buildings, because regulations prohibited such meetings in official quarters.[21] Ultimately, when the Soviet and German Communist coercion became too blatant to be ignored, the United States–licensed newspaper *Tagesspiegel* began to present the position of the opposition in its columns, and the British sanctioned the establishment of an independent Social Democratic newspaper, *Der Sozialdemokrat,* then furnished several tons of newsprint to allow it to publish. In answer to the intimidation tactics of the Communist strong-arm squads in the British sector, eleven of the agitators were arrested. Outright coercion eased after the arrests.[22]

A week before the referendum, General Clay announced at a press conference that the unification of the KPD and SDP into the new SED would be recognized by the American occupying forces only if it was agreed to by the party membership as a whole in the upcoming vote.[23]

The polls opened throughout the city early on March 31, but those in the Soviet sector closed within half an hour, with the Soviets citing unspecified failures to comply with "regulations" as the reason.[24] Social Democrats trudged from the eastern sector into the western ones to cast their ballots, and by the time the polls closed, over 24,000 out of a total party enrollment of 36,000 had voted. Over 19,000 said "No" to the merger.[25] It was a resounding defeat for the Soviets in their maneuver to absorb and silence opposition in Berlin. Colonel Howley concluded that it was "a healthy sign that a group of individuals, who disagreed with their leadership, should insist on expressing themselves against those leaders and what they considered a wrong policy, doing so in an open and democratic process."[26]

☆   ☆   ☆

On the same day that the vote was taken, mail service from Berlin to foreign countries was restored. This allowed an obscure professor of communal science at the University of Politics in Ankara, Turkey, to begin to watch the developments in the German capital through letters from his friends. He had the keen personal interest of a former Berliner, and he longed to be back in Germany.

Born in North Schleswig in 1899, son of a Prussian sea captain, Ernst Reuter had taken an active interest in politics from an early age. His articles in a Social Democrat newspaper criticizing the kaiser's foreign policy had led to his conscription and assignment to the Eastern front early in World War I, a conflict that claimed the lives of three of his brothers.

Wounded in September 1916, he became a convert to Communism while recovering in Russian hospitals and served as the chairman of a committee of German Communist prisoners of war. By the time he was nineteen, Reuter had met Lenin and Trotsky and was serving as commissar of the large German colony that lived near the Volga. His immediate boss in that position was Joseph Stalin, then serving as Bolshevik minister of nationalities.

The Communists marked Reuter for great things, and he returned to Germany at the end of the war under the alias Ernst Friesland. Joining the radical Communist *Spartakusbund,* he edited its newspaper, was chosen to be the secretary of the German Communist party in Berlin, and was named leader of the Berlin KPD in 1921. Later that year, when the party split over the formation of a "popular front" to withstand the possibility of the revolutionary putsch, Reuter became a vigorous opponent of the rigid discipline of the Communist Third International directed from Moscow. He quit the Communist party, being succeeded as secretary general by Wilheim Pieck, the man who now headed the KPD in Germany, and joined the ranks of the Social Democrats. Reuter edited the Social Democrats' newspaper, *Vorwärts* (Forward), and became chief of the transportation and utilities branch of the government of Berlin. Elected to the Reichstag in 1930, Reuter was chosen mayor of the city of Magdeburg the next year but found himself confined to the Lichtenburg concentration camp as soon as Hitler came to power in 1933. He was released, then rearrested and sent back to the camp, and gained his freedom again in 1935, only after the London City Council and several other organizations intervened with the Nazis on his behalf. Knowing that his future in a Germany ruled by Adolf Hitler was dubious, he accepted an offer from the government of Turkey to work in the economics and transportation ministry and had supplemented that work with a university post since 1938.[27]

In the Soviet zone that surrounded Berlin, the SDP disappeared immediately after the executive committees of both parties ratified the merger; the SED was promptly recognized as the only socialist party. The SDP was simply prohibited by the occupying Soviets from carrying out any activities. Within the city of Berlin, things were not so simple, as the new SED and the reorganized SDP both applied to the Kommandatura for official recognition as legal political parties. When the Soviet commandant moved that the SED application be granted and that of the SDP be tabled, he was sharply informed by General Phillipe Lançon, the French representative, that the SED was nothing more than the old Communist party with a new name, not a substitute for the SDP. The matter was referred to the Allied Control Council and ultimately back to the Kommandatura, where what appeared to be a compromise was reached. Both of the parties were to be recognized.[28]

It was a compromise that was in reality a Soviet defeat, because it shattered Soviet plans for eliminating Social Democratic opposition.

With the SDP members who had been in favor of the merger now absorbed into the SED, the reorganized SDP was more militantly anti-Soviet than ever.

On March 28, the Kommandatura had issued an order that the municipal authorities draw up a new city constitution. Fresh from their party election victory, the SDP leaders began to plan eagerly for the general elections that would follow.

NINE

# THE IRON CURTAIN

"Early elections," General Clay had written Colonel Howley, "are an American creed," and Howley emphasized that fact when he brought up the question of a new city constitution at the Kommandatura early in March 1946. He then suggested that the best way to prepare for the elections was to set a target date, adding that the Soviets approved of specific timing, as indicated by their use of five-year plans.[1] The Allied commanders referred the question to the Kommandatura committee on local government, and it did not come up again until April.

When it did, the Soviet commandant, General Kotikov, tried to avoid any possible suggestion of a specific date, stating that Berlin was in the heart of Prussia, where, he said, the most rabid elements of fascism and militarism survived. He went on to specify that the candidates all be "workmen"—shorthand for members of the Communist party. "I don't want to see repeated in Berlin the experience of other parts of Europe," Kotikov stated during one discussion, indicating to Howley that he had in mind recent elections in Hungary, where the non-Communist Smallholders Party had gained a majority, and in Romania, where the Communist candidates had not fared well.[2] The matter of elections in Berlin, like so many others, was referred to the Allied Control Council in a report that indicated that the three Western military governors favored early elections and the Russian disagreed. Surprisingly, Marshal Sokolovsky overruled his deputy in Berlin, and the Allied Control Council directed that the elections be held after the current city leaders had submitted a draft constitution.[3]

The Americans had good cause to be dissatisfied with the regime that had been installed by the Soviets while they were the sole occupiers of the city. In those departments where Communists did not serve as the heads, there were Communist deputies, and the deputies did what the Soviets directed them to do regardless of what the Kommandatura or their nominal department heads had ordered. In one instance an American liaison officer witnessed the deputy mayor, Karl Marion, throw a stack of papers dealing with city finances on the desk of *Ober-bürgermeister* (Lord Mayor) Werner's desk, saying, "I want these signed!" The old architect protested mildly: "But I haven't read them yet. You cannot expect me to sign them without reading them. That would be irregular." Marion shouted, "Sign!" The old man did.[4]

The Berlin police were another problem, being under the command of Paul Markgraf, who considered that he took his orders from the Soviet commandant, not the Kommandatura. Markgraf's police were often implicated in political strong-arm tactics and even in kidnappings of individuals who disappeared into the Soviet zone without a trace.

The draft constitution that was finally submitted to the Kommandatura called for the citywide elections of 130 members of a municipal assembly. Members would hold office for two years, and the assembly was charged with the election of a *Magistrat,* the administrative governing body, and the selection of the *Oberbürgermeister* and three deputies to head the *Magistrat.*

☆   ☆   ☆

While the representatives of the four Allies were struggling to set up a municipal government in Berlin, the future of Germany itself was a concern at higher levels. By early 1946 it had become apparent to the Western allies, and to the United States and Britain in particular, that the occupation of Germany was costing them enormous amounts of money. Assistant Secretary of the Treasury Hilldring estimated that the out-of-pocket expenses of the occupation to the United States were two hundred million dollars per year,[5] and it would later be estimated that the United States and Britain were spending a total of seven hundred million dollars per year to provide food for the western portion of the country.[6]

The occupation was costing so much because Germany was failing to prosper, for two basic reasons. First, the four zones of the country were not operating as an economic whole, in spite of the declarations at Potsdam. That meant that a strong economy could not develop. The Soviets and the French were blocking any efforts at the Allied Control Council toward the economic unity of Germany. Second, the rapidly spiraling inflation of the nearly worthless reichsmark prevented any restoration of Germany's capital assets.

The lack of economic integration of the zones was most acute with respect to the British and the American zones. The British zone contained the vast majority of German heavy industry—its coal mines and steel mills—and the American zone contained most of the more sophisticated manufacturing industries that were the natural users of the heavy products of the British zone. The two zones were economically complementary, and the lack of coordination held back development in both, so conditions in both were deteriorating rather than improving. Former president Herbert Hoover undertook a survey of the American and British zones on behalf of President Truman during the summer of 1946 and reported, "The housing situation in the two zones is the worst that modern civilization has ever seen. . . . Over half of the 6,595,000 children and adolescents . . . are in deplorable condition. . . . The increasing death toll among the aged is appalling."[7]

If the situation in Germany was grim, it was little less so in victorious England. During the war, food rations had varied—a few ounces of fresh meat, four to eight ounces of bacon, one to eight ounces of cheese each week. Milk, eggs, and oranges were distributed as available, which they rarely were, and each person was entitled to one tin containing four pints of dried milk every eight weeks. Dried eggs had become a staple food in wartime Britain. In February 1946 they disappeared from the shops as the Labor government attempted to negotiate a loan from the United States to replace the lend-lease arrangements of the war. Next, the cumulative dislocation of war and war debts, droughts, and bad harvests across the globe caused a worldwide wheat shortage. In Great Britain, bread and potatoes were rationed—something that had not occurred even in the darkest days of the war.[8]

When war had come in 1939, Great Britain had plentiful dollar and gold reserves, and her international debts amounted to £469 million. When the war ended, her reserves were depleted, and the nation was £3.5 billion in debt. The British government was desperate to stop the economic hemorrhage that its zone of Germany had become and was growing increasingly concerned about Soviet designs on postwar Germany and the world. The clearest expression of those concerns would be voiced not by the Labor government but by the leader of His Majesty's loyal opposition, Winston Churchill.

☆  ☆  ☆

Major General Harry Hawkins Vaughan was a proud alumnus of Westminister College, a small liberal arts school in Fulton, Missouri. He owed his military rank less to martial prowess than to the fact that he was an old friend of fellow Missourian Harry S Truman. He was happy to talk to the president when Frank "Bullet" McClure, head of Westminister College, asked for his help in lining up a speaker for a March commencement ceremony. The speaker Vaughan helped to obtain was Winston Churchill, who was introduced by Truman.

The president and the former prime minister arrived in Fulton together on the presidential train. Just before the speech there was a crisis. Fulton was a dry town, and Churchill, one of the greatest orators in the history of the English language, was long accustomed to taking a drink to moisten his throat just before speaking. Harry Vaughan was dispatched by the president to find a pint of whiskey. The eminent Englishman later said, "I didn't know if I was in Fulton, Missouri, or

Fulton, Sahara."[9] With his parched throat eased, Churchill delivered what he characterized as "the most important speech of my career."[10]

"The United States stands at this time at the pinnacle of world power. It is a solemn moment for American Democracy," he began, going on to talk in general terms of the need for an overall concept to clarify strategic thinking. He dwelt heavily on the special relationship between Great Britain and the United States.

Late in his oration, he turned to the "shadow that has fallen upon the scene so recently lighted by allied victory," saying that nobody knew, or could know, the limits of Soviet expansiveness. "From Stettin in the Baltic to Trieste in the Adriatic, an iron curtain has descended across the Continent. Behind that line lie all the capitals of the ancient states of Central and Eastern Europe. Warsaw, Berlin, Prague, Budapest, Belgrade, Vienna, Bucharest and Sofia," Churchill rumbled. "I do not believe that Soviet Russia desires war. What they desire is the fruits of war and the infinite expansion of their power and doctrines.

"The last time I saw it all coming," he said near the end of the speech, referring to his speeches in Parliament on the rise of Hitler, "no one paid attention. . . . If all British moral and material forces and convictions are joined with your own in fraternal association, the highroads of the future will be clear, not only for us but for all, not only for our time but for a century to come."[11]

The speech was not a critical or political success. When he arrived at Columbia University in New York City later on his American trip, he was met with picketers carrying signs decrying him as a warmonger. Newspapers across the United States editorialized against what they viewed as "entangling alliances" such as the one between Britain and the United States suggested by Churchill in Fulton.[12]

Three months after the leader of the opposition spoke in Missouri, British foreign minister Ernest Bevin was in the lounge at the Luxembourg Palace in Paris, with his large laborer's hand wrapped around a glass of scotch and water. There was a brief break in the proceedings of the Council of Foreign Ministers, which was meeting in Paris as a prelude to the peace conference that would make final decisions on treaties with Italy, Bulgaria, Romania, Hungary, and Finland. The problems with a treaty with Germany remained unresolved.

"A drink is good anytime," Bevin ruminated, "but it's better when you need it."

When a fellow drinker asked him how it was going, Bevin responded, "I don't know. I just sit back and listen. I know that if I fall back on the wisdom of the U.S. I will be all right. Jim [Byrnes] will have a formula."[13]

On July 11, Secretary of State Byrnes announced a plan that he hoped would break the deadlock on the German treaty and the stagnation of the German economy. The United States, he said, was ready to merge its zone of Germany with any or all of the other three zones as a means of furthering economic recovery, so that Germany could meet its reparations obligations and again become self-sufficient. The next day, Ernest Bevin stated that the British would accept Byrnes's offer. Instructions were sent to the military commanders of the occupation to work out the details of the merger.

☆   ☆   ☆

"The sausage is at stake" is a phrase in the colorful slang of Berlin that means "this is it; this is the big one." Berliners were saying "*Es geht um die Wurst*" about the elections in the fall of 1946.

The SED was intent on winning the whole sausage and campaigned vigorously. The party distributed free coal briquettes, each stamped with the party logo, to Berliners facing the coming winter. Schoolchildren received notebooks inscribed, "Instead of using this paper for a campaign pamphlet, the Socialist Unity Party of Germany gives you, dear Berlin child, this notebook."[14] SED posters covered walls, kiosks, and telephone poles, and squads of toughs roamed the streets, haranguing and intimidating voters.

The Soviets threw their full weight behind the SED campaign. Early on, they suddenly announced that all fresh fruit and vegetables collected in the Soviet zone outside Berlin would be distributed exclusively in the Soviet sector of the city. It was planned that the leaders of the SED would then approach the Soviets with a request that they bring in fruit and vegetables for all four sectors, in view of the failure of the Western allies to feed their sectors. The Soviets would grant the request, making it known that they had done so in deference to the wishes of the SED, the party of the people, for the good of the city of Berlin. It was a bald attempt to show that life was better there than in the rest of the city.

Colonel Howley learned of the plan and protested at the Kommandatura as soon as the initial order was issued. He made certain that the German press gave heavy coverage to the plot. "Instead of being a hero for all the work I've done to bring vegetables into the Russian sector," Kotikov screeched at Howley during a meeting, "you have made me look like a villain for keeping them out of the other sectors." Howley reminded him that any action regarding food was reserved for the Kommandatura. Then he played his trump. "Would you object to my bringing in fresh oranges, lemons, and grapefruit from California for the American sector only? Of course you would." Kotikov had to admit that America could flood Europe with food and that no food at all could be brought in from the Soviet Union because of the shortages there. In Moscow, the official rations were the same as they were for the citizens of Berlin. The equitable sharing of fresh produce from the Soviet zone among the four sectors of the city was restored.[15]

Ruth Andreas-Friedrich confided to her diary the fears, frustrations, and despair of a Berliner living in a city surrounded by the forces of an increasingly hostile enemy:

> Who are we to stand up against the pressure of a world power? [The Eastern zone] encloses Berlin on all sides. Only a narrow corridor, a single-track railway line, connects it with the West. Our vegetables, our fruit, our potatoes—nearly all our food is obtained from the neighboring provinces. In a twinkling the occupying power there could sever our life-line. All they need to do is prevent a few trains from passing through. . . . If necessary, will the Western Allies supply three million Berliners with potatoes? With fruit, vegetables, coal and electricity? Or will they tell us that this problem, too, is a "German domestic matter?" "Help us!" We keep repeating the refrain.[16]

There was little obvious help from the Americans early in the campaign. Frank Howley was absent from the Kommandatura meeting on the day that a formal complaint filed by the SDP, with encouragement from American and British political officers, was presented. The complaint detailed tactics that the SDP said Soviet authorities were using to block their campaign. For example, the Soviets demanded that the text of all speeches be submitted to them, in Russian as well as German, before they were delivered. Halls that were selected for meetings suddenly became unavailable at the last moment, and meetings were canceled with no notice. Local committees were banned, complained the SDP. The Soviets objected to the complaint, and in Howley's absence, the Kommandatura rejected the SDP plea. It came as a hard blow to the party, which was trying to rebuild after the divisive merger vote of the spring.[17]

Meanwhile, the Soviet military administration distributed 30 million cigarettes to Berliners and issued a bottle of schnapps to each man and a half bottle to each woman in the city. Sixty thousand pairs of leather shoes were issued to schoolchildren, and ration-free clothes appeared in shops. Radio Berlin stayed on the air late into the night, broadcasting a seemingly endless list of names of German prisoners who had been released from captivity in the Soviet Union; the columns of the *Tägliche Rundschau* were filled with the names in the next morning's edition.[18] Electric power, supplied from the Soviet sector, faded out for several hours each day in the Western sectors, with the explanation at the Kommandatura that there were "technical difficulties," or with no explanation at all.[19] The implications were clear: if the city didn't vote for the SED, the Soviets would find means to retaliate.

The Berliners likened the campaign waged by the SED to the 1932 campaign by the Nazis, with the same stage management and flamboyant appeal to mass emotion, but the new party received at least one dose of its own vituperative medicine when anonymous pamphlets appeared all over the city, bearing a message of macabre humor. "Were you raped by a Russian?" the pamphlets asked. "If so, vote for the SED."[20]

The Americans, already disturbed by the Soviet restrictions on broadcast time allowed on Radio Berlin, had developed an alternative known as the *Drahtfunk.* It was a broadcasting process that transmitted a signal over telephone lines, from which it could be picked up by ordinary radio sets. It was far less than satisfactory, because reception was horrible. In the first few weeks that the *Drahtfunk* was in operation, it received only eight letters—all complaints. One irate woman was so upset by the bad reception that she said she allowed her husband to listen to the programming only when she was out of the house on errands.

During the summer, the Soviet authorities used the facilities of Radio Berlin to foster the election efforts of the Communist candidates. Continuing arguments at the Kommandatura failed to convince the Soviets to expand the air time allotted to the West. On September 5, theAmericans opened a regular broadcast station, Radio in the American Sector, which was soon known to everyone as RIAS. RIAS immediately began coverage of the upcoming elections, although it carefully avoided making what could be construed as attacks on any of America's fellow Allies in the city. That would have been a violation of the rules of the occupation; neither Germans nor fellow victors could voice such criticism.[21] But it was a policy that was wearing thin for Colonel Howley.

In early October 1946, Howley and the heads of six of his sections hosted a luncheon for Joseph B. Phillips, the foreign editor of *Newsweek* magazine, who was visiting Berlin. Howley and his aides painted the same bright picture of improving municipal services that the OMGUS February press release had. However, Phillips got the distinct impression that the American officers were involved in a running fight with their Soviet counterparts and that in every important field, from commerce to freedom of information to education, these disagreements were holding up progress in the city.

"Get this right," Howley said to Phillips near the end of the luncheon. "What we've been telling you doesn't come from any prejudice against the Russians. We came here with a job to do—to get this city operating. . . . On the level of our jobs it wasn't any concern of ours whether the Germans wanted to be Communists or Hottentots or what have you. We just wanted to get the job done. But we've found that our program for getting the job done runs into obstacles at every turn and the obstacles always come from the Russians."[22] Phillips's report to his readers conveyed the growing tension in the gray city.

☆  ☆  ☆

The Americans finally began to pump supplies into the city to try to counter the influence of the massive Soviet effort. A million boxes of matches were distributed by the Americans, along with 155,000 pairs of shoes and 16,000 bicycle tires. It had long been a sore point with Berliners that the American soldier, with his seemingly endless supply of cigarettes and more than ample PX rations, was a symbol of plenty in a sea of want. Many had watched in despair as scores of German laborers poured tons of precious building materials into an American dining facility named Truman Hall, not far from the Oscar Helene Heim Children's Hospital, which was still without a roof over a year after the Americans had entered the city. Along with the matches and bicycle tires, the Americans now supplied the city with 5,000 tons of building steel, 1,900 tons of cement, and 1,200 square meters of window glass.[23]

The people of Berlin have a reputation for progressive, liberal political thought and independence; as the most industrialized city in Germany, thousands of workers had flocked there during the Industrial Revolution, and those workers consistently voted for socialist parties. During the time of Bismarck and the kaiser, Berlin was noted for its leftist leanings, and in the years of the Weimar Republic, Berliners consistently supported parties of the left, in opposition to the rising tide of Nazism. They never gave Hitler's party a majority while there were elections in Germany.[24] Even during the war, they continued to greet one another with the traditional "*Guten Morgen,*" rather than the mandatory "*Heil Hitler.*"[25] That kind of independence showed again in the first free municipal election in the city in fourteen years.

On October 21, 1946, 92 percent of the eligible voters in the city of Berlin cast their ballots. It was an overwhelming defeat for the Communist SED. The Social Democrats polled 48.7 percent, the Christian Democrats 22.2 percent, and the Liberal Democrats 9.3 percent. The Social Unity Party (SED) drew only 19.2 percent citywide and only 21 percent in its Soviet sector stronghold. It was a showing that did not equal even that of the Communists in the last pre-Hitler elections.

☆ ☆ ☆

Max Rokhlin was a German Communist who had been involved in assisting the Soviets in reconstructing the German chemical industry in Berlin. On the evening of October 21, the day after the defeat of the SED at the polls, he received a call to report to the headquarters of the NKVD—the Soviet secret police. When he arrived, he was greeted by Colonel General Ivan Serov and shown a list of Germans he was expected to contact immediately, to inform them that they were expected to leave for the Soviet Union at once to continue their work there.

"Why, Comrade Colonel General, must they go?" asked Rokhlin and a colleague who had also been summoned.

"Beria's orders," was the flat reply, curtly citing the dreaded name of the head of the Soviet secret police.

Rokhlin and his colleague requested a moment to go outside and discuss the order, and when they returned to Serov's office, they asked the general to call the Soviet chemical industry minister, Mikhail Pervukhin, because they were certain that he would think that the deportations were a bad idea.

Serov reached Pervukhin by telephone and said, "Your men don't agree with Beria's orders," and then handed the receiver to Rokhlin.

"What's wrong with you; follow orders!" the minister said with finality.[26]

Rokhlin did, convincing many of his fellow chemical workers to pack and leave for the Soviet Union without protest.

At 3:30 on the morning of October 22, the Hirschgarten area of the Soviet sector was cordoned off by Soviet troops. Earlier that summer, at the height of the election campaign, technicians at the Oberspreewerk—a factory specializing in high-frequency radio equipment and radar—had been invited to move into very good housing in the area at very low cost and were given extra rations and bonuses. Now, two hundred of the Oberspreewerk specialists and their families were dragged from their beds and loaded into trucks and then hustled off to trains that carried them east before the sun rose. They were not the only ones: skilled workers from the GEMA, EFEM, AEG-Kabelwerk, and Askania factories were rousted out and shipped away as well. In most cases, the workers were allowed to take their families with them, but the Soviets were not particular about which women went with which men. In some cases they seized workers' maids or sisters, thinking they were wives, and deported them as well.[27] When some of the workers protested, Soviet officers said, "All Berliners are fascists, otherwise they would have voted differently."[28]

The deportation operation had apparently been planned by the Soviets for a long time, and it was not confined to Berlin. Many of the deported workers had been required, months earlier, to sign contracts obliging them to migrate to the Soviet Union to work, and similar contracts were ready for the immediate signatures of the deportees who had not entered into such previous agreements. Deportations also took place in Bitterfeld, Halle, and Dessau. In all, some ninety-two trains carrying thousands of scientists, technicians, and other skilled workers rolled east into the USSR that night.[29]

To the people of Berlin and to the Western allies, it appeared to be a clear-cut case of retribution for the resounding defeat of the SED at the polls. And now the Soviets began a propaganda campaign against the West alleging an attempt to restore a militaristic Germany by the planned merger of the British and American zones.

## TEN

# COPS AND SPOOKS

General Lucius Clay strode into the meeting of the coordinating committee of the Allied Control Council "loaded for bear," of the Soviet variety. Angry at the mass deportations of workers following the Berlin elections, the Western allies had filed stiff protests, and the American general was ready to follow up on them. He began with an extract from the charter of the International Military Tribunal, then in the process of trying Nazi war criminals, citing Article 6-B, "War Crimes." "Such violations," he read, "shall include, but not be limited to, murder, ill-treatment or deportation to slave labor. . . ." Following that, he quoted a statement by General Roman Rudenko, the chief Soviet prosecutor at Nuremberg, describing wartime deportations as "the most heinous crime committed by the Nazis." He concluded by saying that the Anglo-American position was that the Soviets had signed this charter and should now live up to their word.

The Soviet representative responded angrily that the Soviet Union had done nothing wrong and read vehemently from Allied Control Council Proclamation Number Two, which the Soviets had drafted and the Allies had signed in the afterglow of the Potsdam conference:

German authorities will carry out . . . such measures of restitution, reinstatement, restoration, reparation, reconstruction, relief, and rehabilitation as the Allied representatives may prescribe. For these purposes the German authorities shall . . . carry out such repair, building and construction work whether in Germany or elsewhere, and will provide transport, plant, equipment, and materials of all kinds, labor, personnel, and specialist and other services, for use in Germany or elsewhere, as the Allied representatives may direct.

The Soviet representative waited patiently as the Western military governors called for their own copies of Proclamation Number Two to verify the text. He had quoted correctly. The document bore the signatures of Eisenhower, Montgomery, Zhukov, and Koenig. The Western protest was dropped.[1] The Soviets, relying on the early agreements on administration of the city of Berlin and of Germany as a whole, had stymied the West again.

However, the elections of 1946 showed that political interest in the city of Berlin was not just a matter for a few thousand party leaders and members. Of the 2.3 million Berliners who were entitled to vote, over 92 percent actually cast ballots. Many had done so to express their fear and dislike of the Soviets.

Smarting from the rebuke they had received at the polls, the Soviets turned their efforts to attempting to maintain the leading position in Berlin's political life that they had seized when they captured the city. They tried to limit the authority of the new city government, basing their position on the provisional constitution, which provided that the appointment and discharge of "leading persons in city government" could take place only with the approval of the Kommandatura. The Soviets maintained that this included the mayor and councilmen, while the Western allies held that the language applied only to persons holding appointed positions. When the new city assembly chose a *Magistrat*—the executive body consisting of a mayor and department heads chosen from among the assembly members—the Soviets refused to seat the new officers and would not accept the resignations of the old ones. The Kommandatura wrangled over the makeup of the *Magistrat* for six weeks before it reached a compromise. The new officials were allowed to take office only after the Western allies had agreed to the Soviet exclusion of three of the proposed members, including Professor Ernst Reuter, who had recently returned to the city from Turkey.

The new government was a coalition of the four political parties in the city, with the Social Democrat Otto Ostrowski as lord mayor. Members of the three democratic parties held fourteen of the seventeen top positions, but three went to members of the SED. The head of the police, Paul Markgraf, retained his post and continued to maintain his earlier position that he was not subject to any orders issued by the new city government. The police, Markgraf said, came directly under the Kommandatura, and he would report only to that body.

An effective police force was vital to the city because Berlin was a dangerous place. Criminal gangs roamed the streets preying on the weak and poor, and violence by black market operators was common. In 1946, over 177,000 crimes were reported to the police citywide. Forty-six thousand of these took place in the American sector.[2] The civilian police force of the city was ill-equipped to deal with the crime problem and was, in many cases, a part of the problem.

When the Soviets captured the city, they recruited the police department and rebuilt it from practically nothing. They placed hard-core Communists in most of the critical positions, as well as in the rank and file. However, the force, no matter how politically tainted, lacked nearly everything necessary to control ordinary criminal activity. Its personnel were largely untrained for police work, and they had no uniforms, weapons, communications, records, or other equipment. Many of the former police stations were in ruins from the Allied bombing raids and Soviet artillery attacks during the war.

The police force, expected to number 11,000 men, had a turnover rate that saw it lose and replace 10,000 of its personnel by the end of 1946. A quarter of these left because they found better jobs, and another quarter were discharged either because of crimes they committed while policemen or on the basis of past criminal records. The other 5,000 were forced out because it was learned that they had been Nazis.[3] It was during the initial period of rebuilding the force that the basic conflict among the Allies about the nature of the police emerged. It came down to a question of whether Berlin was to become a police state.

The Western allies, and the American military government in particular, were committed to the establishment of a police force that was both effective and democratic, with the primary purposes of maintaining public order and apprehending criminals. Since the days of Prussia and the German emperor, the police of Berlin had been centralized and had served as a political tool of the rulers, as much concerned with furthering the policies of the government and suppressing individuals suspected of subversion as with enforcing civil laws and keeping the peace—the role the Americans envisioned for the new force. During the Nazi era, the police force had been completely subjected to party control, and the American military government wished to prevent any possibility of this happening in the future. The British, with a long tradition of severely limited police powers at home, shared the American view. The Soviets did not. Their view of the role of the police in society was closely akin to that of the defeated Nazis. Ideology aside, there was little to differentiate the outlook or methods of the Gestapo from those of the Soviet NKVD.

Berlin police headquarters was located in the Soviet sector, under the Nazi-turned-Communist police president Paul Markgraf, who exercised tight and biased control as the head of the force. An early assistant, Social Democrat Karl Heinrich, was summoned to his chief's office one day and was arrested there by Soviet security agents. Heinrich disappeared, and inquiries to the Soviets by the Western allies concerning his whereabouts went unanswered, as did most of their other questions on police activities.[4]

Will Tremper was an ambitious and articulate seventeen-year-old who managed to find himself a job as the police reporter for *Der Tagesspiegel,* the German-language newspaper that was licensed to operate in the American sector. Tremper tried to get an interview with police president Markgraf but was constantly refused. Then Tremper uncovered the police president's Nazi career, including that fact that he was a holder of the Knight's Cross of the Iron Cross, and the story ran under bold headlines in his paper. After it was published, an interview was granted, and Tremper went to police headquarters in the Soviet sector to get Markgraf's reaction to the revelations. But the police president didn't show up for the interview; the Soviet military police commander and two of his men arrived instead, and Tremper was arrested.

Tremper's editor at *Der Tagesspiegel* contacted Colonel Howley's headquarters and told the press officer there what had happened. Later that afternoon, on Howley's orders, two officials of the SED in Schöneberg, in the American sector, be taken into custody by American military police. At ten o'clock in the evening, the Soviet and American military police met in the middle of the Potsdamer Platz, where Tremper was exchanged for the two SED men.[5]

The Heinrich disappearance and the Tremper affair were not isolated incidents. From the very beginning of the occupation, people in Berlin had disappeared mysteriously, most never to be heard from again. Sometimes they were snatched from the streets by men who drove up in cars, leaped out, forced them into the back seat, and then drove off. Sometimes there was a knock on the door in the night, and an individual would be spirited away. Often, one of the party knocking on the door would be a uniformed German policeman from the Soviet sector.

It occurred that way in what Colonel Howley dubbed "The Case of the Four Missing Judges," an event that brought into sharp focus the Soviet efforts to bring even the lowest level of the judiciary in the city under their control.

The four judges were members of the *Amtsgericht,* the municipal court of the city. In each case there was a knock on the door in the dead of night, and a German policeman and a civilian asked the judge to accompany them to police headquarters. None of the four was ever seen again. The head of the courts complained to the Kommandatura that he was having difficulty getting judges to serve because of this type of terror. When the Kommandatura took up the matter, the British reported that several judges had sought protection from them, and one told of being threatened by the Soviet secret police unless he showed favoritism toward the local Communists. That judge chose instead to flee to the British sector.

Faced with Soviet denials that such things could happen, nothing could be achieved at the Kommandatura, and an investigation could only conclude that the judges had been arrested illegally by "persons unknown."[6] Kidnappings of this sort remained a constant danger in Berlin, with journalists and others who were outspoken against the Communists as primary targets.

The American military police and intelligence staff knew many of the Soviet secret police operatives by sight and would frequently pick them up for questioning when they were in the American sector, knowing that their real purpose was to participate in yet another kidnapping. This sort of preventive detention was a policy formulated by Colonel Howley to show the Soviets that they could not rule the city by police terror. The policy was tacitly approved by Major General Frank Keating, the current commandant in the city, who had taken over from General Parker in May 1946. Keating shared Howley's dark thoughts about their Soviet "allies." There was even an official name for such detainees, complying with the official dictates of maintaining the fiction of smooth inter-Allied cooperation. The Soviet agents were referred to as "unidentified persons who speak fluent Russian."[7] Keating knew some of the Soviet operatives so well on sight that he had given them nicknames, calling one "Pinkerton" and another "Dick Tracy."[8] The policy of detaining undercover Soviet police had repercussions, however, as not even Americans remained safe from kidnapping or long detention by the Soviets, as hostages for their operatives.

In mid 1946, army warrant officer Samuel L. Henderson and his wife, Helen, who had recently arrived from the United States, wanted a dog as a pet. They innocently went to a shop just inside the Soviet sector and disappeared. Three days later, army officers Harold Corbin and George Wyatt, on a train trip to Oranienburg in the Soviet zone north of Berlin, disappeared as well.

Informed of the disappearances, General Keating contacted Soviet commandant Kotikov, demanding the release of the Americans. First Kotikov denied that the Hendersons were being held; then he suggested that they might be located if two Soviet operatives that the Americans were holding were released at the same time. Keating, knowing that the two Soviets had recently been picked up, was able to deny officially that he was holding them, because they had been apprehended by military police who were not under his direct command. Thereupon, General Kotikov called in Soviet agent number 791, an individual Keating recognized and had nicknamed "The Angel" because of his uncanny resemblance to an American wrestler of that name.

"The Angel" insisted that the two Soviets and an additional eighteen falsely accused Soviet citizens were being held in a prison located at Tempelhof Airport. The central communications center for the American sector police and a lock-up were located at Tempelhof. But Keating knew that the two Soviets were not there, so he responded, "OK Comrade Alex, let's go to Tempelhof and have a look-see." When a ninety-minute tour of the facility with the two Soviets produced no evidence of illegally detained Soviet citizens, Kotikov informed his American opposite number that the Hendersons would be released in a few days, provided that the detained Soviets were also released.

On July 15, over two weeks after they had innocently set off in search of a pet dog, the Hendersons were released. The same day, the Americans released two Soviet officers wearing civilian clothes, along with their German chauffeur.[9] Captain Harold Corbin and Lieutenant George Wyatt were held for an additional twelve days, questioned constantly, and poorly fed. When the details of their captivity were made public, the Soviets promptly charged that their two officers, released in exchange for the Hendersons, had been "treated like criminals while under American custody." The Americans replied that the Soviets had been forcing German employees of the U.S. Army to turn classified documents over to them.[10] This was a bureaucratic way of saying that the men were spies, without uttering that word about an ally.

The cloak-and-dagger intrigue in the city reached a point where even Hollywood recognized its dramatic possibilities and produced a pot-boiler entitled "Night People," set in Berlin and focusing on the kidnappings. Gregory Peck played the lead, a character based on Captain Richard Lake of the American military government, the public safety officer who served as liaison with the 759th Military Police Battalion in the city.[11]

No one seemed exempt from the terror of Markgraf's police. In March 1946, the city was shocked when eight young students from Humboldt University disappeared for Soviet questioning. That shock was compounded when Heinz Kionka, Markgraf's assistant and the vice president of police, also vanished without a trace.[12]

After Kionka's disappearance came a tug-of-war over the appointment of a new vice president of police, with the Soviets backing Hans Seidel, who had already begun to show his colors as a Communist hatchet man. The Western allies favored the appointment of Dr. Johannes Stumm, who had been a police officer during the days of the Weimar Republic and was highly respected by the citizens of Berlin.

The Soviets demanded a four-power investigation of Doctor Stumm's alleged collaboration with the Nazis, and the United States brought a series of charges against Seidel. When the parallel investigations were complete, Stumm had been exonerated. The Soviets had agreed to a face-saving agreement that Seidel would be discharged and never again employed in any capacity by the police, though the discharge would not otherwise be a blot on his record. Even after Doctor Stumm was cleared, the Soviets would not agree to his appointment to the post of vice president, although they did agree to pay him the salary and allowed him to perform the duties of the job.[13]

Because of Markgraf, the Western allied commandants had little control over the German police in their own sectors, so they proposed at the Kommandatura that the entire police force be reorganized. The initial proposal met with a Soviet veto and was passed on to the Allied Control Council, where a compromise was reached on October 4, 1946.

Markgraf remained in overall charge of the police, but an assistant police president was appointed in each of the Western sectors, with those
officials reporting directly to the individual sector commandants, as
well as to police headquarters.[14]

☆   ☆   ☆

The people of Berlin faced the second winter of Allied occupation in a
city with rampant crime, a divided police force, and a new and untried
city government that was preoccupied with the mundane but vital task
of ensuring that they would survive the worst winter in a generation.
The winter had begun early, with arctic winds sweeping blizzards in
from the north. The canals of the city froze, stalling vital coal shipments to industries and power plants, and the temperature dropped to
−30°C. for weeks on end. With the supply of coal limited, over 1,000
factories and businesses closed completely, and 150,000 workers were
idled. Over 700,000 Berliners got through the winter only by relying on
welfare relief, and the *Magistrat* was forced to open public "warming
shelters" for citizens without sufficient heat at home.

Even the rigors of the bitter winter could not crush the spirit of some
Berliners. By December 21, electrical power to Ruth Andreas-
Friedrich's apartment had already been cut off, and the superintendent
had just announced that the pipes had burst in seven places. Andreas-
Friedrich was resigned to another winter of the degrading task of wrap-
ping body wastes up in small paper packages and disposing of them
discretely in the ruins of the city.

As they were breakfasting that frigid morning on a thin slice of bread
and lukewarm ersatz coffee, her friend Frank asked, "Would you like a
Christmas tree?"

"Very much, except there aren't any, unless you're registered as having many children or as a victim of Fascism."

"Or if you have a saw," Frank responded.[15]

That afternoon, Andreas-Friedrich and Frank found a tree in the Soviet sector, just below the Tetlow Lock. Boarding a subway station at
the Dreilinden Station, they entered the compartment reserved for passengers with oversized luggage. It was crowded with people, most of
whom were sheepishly holding illegally cut fir trees.

On Christmas Eve, with members of the *Onkel Emil* group gathered
around the tree, Andreas-Friedrich heard the story of one of the refugee
trains from Poland from Jo Thaler, who was now working in the hospital where the refugees were treated. Fifty-three persons on the train had
frozen to death. One hundred eighty-two were badly frostbitten, and
twenty-five had required amputations.[16]

During the long and dreadful winter of 1946–47, the hospitals of
Berlin treated 40,000 cases of hypothermia, and 1,100 people froze to

death in the streets or in the ruins of the buildings of the once-proud capital.[17] A new graffito appeared in chalk on the ruins of the Reichstag: "Blessed are the dead, for their hands do not freeze."[18] In their sufferings in the cold, the people of Germany were again at one with Europe.

## ELEVEN
# THE DEAD OF WINTER

The winter of 1946–47 locked not only Germany but all of war-ravaged Europe in the grasp of ice, snow, and subzero temperatures the like of which the continent had rarely seen before. In Britain, the weather was so savage that it nearly brought the country to its knees. In December, England's largest auto plant closed due to a lack of power. By February, the government ordered a three-week shutdown of virtually all industrial plants, throwing 2.3 million people temporarily out of work and imposing the severe strain of increased welfare payments on the exchequer. The Thames had frozen all the way from Windsor Castle to the sea, cutting off shipping into London, and coal barges could not move fuel to power stations by way of the canal system. Electricity to households was cut to three hours every morning and three in the afternoon. The frigid winter was a body blow to the reeling British economy, and in the cabinet debate raged as to where Britain could cut her draining overseas commitments. In the early months of 1947 it seemed that the sun never set on Great Britain's responsibilities and expenses.

The Labor government was committed, as a matter of party doctrine, to a withdrawal from imperial responsibilities, and for nearly two years Foreign Minister Bevin had been fighting in the cabinet against cuts in military spending that would force a drastic reduction in British commitments overseas. The prime minister had always taken his side in the past. However, Britain was now nearly bankrupt. Her exchequer had been drained by the cumulative effects of two world wars and the Great Depression, and the pound sterling retained its value only through massive infusions of American and Canadian dollars. Now, without even the electric power to run her factories, Great Britain was no longer a nation that could sustain its previous projection of military power throughout the world. Prime Minister Clement Attlee abandoned his support of Bevin and focused his attention on ending British commitments in India, Palestine, and Greece—the country where

Britain had served in the role of protector since the war of independence in 1820.

Greece was among the most devastated nations on the continent at the end of World War II. Assaulted first by the Italians and then by the Germans, the country had endured a brutal four-year occupation during which the invaders relentlessly pursued and punished the Greek guerrillas, both Communist and Royalist, who took up arms against them. The nation's industries were destroyed, its farms lacked seeds and tools, and the interim government had to resort to printing inflationary amounts of paper money just to keep the country afloat. The royal government of King George II, regarded by many Greeks as corrupt and oppressive, had spent the war in exile, supported by the British. Elections in the spring of 1946 put a Royalist prime minister, Constantine Tsaldaris, in power, and following a referendum in September, the king and his royal entourage had returned. That had caused simmering discontent to erupt into a full-scale civil war, with Communist insurgents concentrating their grip in the north, on the borders with the adjacent Communist states of Bulgaria, Yugoslavia, and Albania. At the end of 1946, Great Britain had 40,000 troops stationed in Greece and was providing massive financial and military aid to the government. While the commitment of troops had been somewhat reduced by early 1947, support of the Greek government remained a severe drain on the British economy. Prime Minister Attlee was determined that it end, along with other responsibilities England had long shouldered.

On February 14, 1947, Ernest Bevin was forced to announce to the House of Commons that, after forty years of rule in Palestine, Great Britain would surrender its mandate there and refer the matter of partition of that territory to the United Nations. Less than two weeks later, Prime Minister Attlee announced that, come what may, British rule in India would end in June 1948. The following day, Lord Inverchapel, the British ambassador in Washington, delivered a stunning note to Acting Secretary of State Dean Acheson. The Labor government of Britain, it stated, found it necessary to end its financial support of Greece and would begin to withdraw its troops there by April 1. Even with Secretary of State George Marshall out of town attending the bicentennial celebration of Princeton University, the reaction in Washington was fast and furious. The departments of State and Defense, along with the Joint Chiefs of Staff, drew up recommendations for American action in time for them to be presented to Marshall when he returned to Washington on Monday morning, February 24, 1947. By Monday evening, basic policy recommendations for emergency aid to Greece and Turkey had been prepared. They were submitted to the president on the following day.

Harry S Truman knew that American action was urgently required to prevent a possible communist takeover in Greece in the wake of the

British departure, because the leaders in the Kremlin were casting about for a solid position in the Mediterranean. If their demand for a mandate over the former Italian colony of Tripolitania in Libya had not been enough to convince the president of this, there was the recent Soviet action toward Turkey as further proof.

Turkey had remained neutral until very late in the war, enjoying a brisk trade with the Germans as well as the Allies, which Stalin regarded as a hostile act. When Turkey finally declared war on the all-but-defeated Axis powers in February 1945, it proposed a treaty of alliance with the Soviets. However, the USSR insisted that any such pact be preceded by the Turks returning the provinces of Kars and Ardahan to the Soviet Union and agreeing both to major modifications to the Montreux Convention regulating navigation into the Black Sea by way of the Dardanelles and to the stationing of Soviet troops on those straits. The Soviets made similar demands at the Potsdam Conference, and variants of these proposals had surfaced ever since, including one that would give control of the straits to the powers with coasts on the Black Sea—Turkey, the Soviet Union, and two Soviet puppet states, Bulgaria and Romania.

That proposal, and the increasingly strident calls for its adoption in the Soviet press, thoroughly alarmed the State Department. After consulting with Secretary of the Navy James Forrestal and the Joint Chiefs, Acting Secretary of State Dean Acheson had presented the draft of a sternly worded note of protest to the Soviets to President Truman for his approval. Expecting to have to convince Truman of the import of the matter, Acheson had prepared for the meeting carefully, having papers for a full background briefing on hand. He didn't even get to finish reading the text of the note. "I don't need to hear any more," the president said partway through the presentation. "We're going to send it."[1]

While he realized that urgent action about Greece was necessary, President Truman also knew what a difficult task bringing about that action would be. In the elections of November 1946, the Republicans had gained 56 seats in the House and 13 in the Senate, giving them control of both houses of the Congress for the first time since the 1920s. A Congress whose members had campaigned for tax cuts and reduced expenditures was not likely to be in the mood for international adventure. It would be the president's task to change that mood.

On Thursday, February 27, the president met with the Republican leaders of Congress in the White House, where they were briefed by Secretary of State George Marshall and Assistant Secretary Dean Acheson, who painted the situation in terms of an approaching apocalypse. The assistant secretary said that the world had not been so polarized since the days of Rome and Carthage and that the choice that existed was between democracy and individual liberty on the one hand and dictatorship and absolute conformity on the other. Acheson predicted that, if Greece fell, Iran, Asia Minor, and Egypt would be next, followed by France and Italy. He warned that two-thirds of the world would soon be Communist.

After Acheson's plea, most of the members of Congress who were present expressed willingness to support the president, but House Speaker Joseph Martin was opposed.[2] Referring to Acheson's summary, the influential head of the Senate Foreign Relations Committee, Arthur H. Vandenberg, said: "Mr. President, if you will say that to the Congress and the country, I will support you and I believe most of its members will do the same."[3]

Loy Henderson, another State Department participant in the meeting, remembered Vandenberg's comment as being far more blunt and trenchant. "Mr. President," Henderson recalled the Senator saying, "the only way you are going to get this is to make a speech and scare the hell out of the country."[4]

It would not be an easy sell for the president. Only a week after Vandenberg's assurance, Congress slashed $4.5 billion dollars from Truman's budget for the coming year, and Truman's ideas on aid to Greece got a cool reception from a larger meeting of members of Congress at the White House on March 10.[5] Truman was determined to go ahead anyway, convinced that the fate of democracy might be decided in Greece. He instructed Acheson to prepare a draft of a speech to Congress. George Kennan, now in Washington, criticized Acheson's draft as being too strong, while Clark Clifford, a White House aide, thought it too weak. Truman had his own ideas on the speech, carefully editing the drafts in pencil. He wanted no hedging. He believed that the speech had to be clear and free of hesitation or double-talk. Truman intended it to be America's answer to the surge of expansion of Communist tyranny.[6]

While the State Department, White House assistants, and the president were laboring over the speech, Secretary of State George Marshall was in Moscow, meeting with his counterparts from the Soviet Union, Great Britain, and France. The primary purpose of the conference was a discussion of the fate of Germany, and there was little agreement between the Anglo-American representatives and the Soviet foreign minister.

While both sides agreed that they favored a united Germany under one government, they could not agree on the nature of the German government or even on how it was to be brought into being. Marshall proposed that any provisional regime be a weak confederation of the existing state and provincial governments, with carefully limited powers.

Foreign Minister Bevin followed Marshall's lead in this, as both the Americans and the British believed that such an arrangement would forestall the possibility of a repetition of Hitler's rise to power.

The Soviets objected nearly to the point of frenzy, denouncing the plan as a plot by capitalists and an ultraconservative Roman Catholic Church to protect Nazis and reactionaries and to consolidate their power. Molotov proposed instead a strong central government built on the basis of "democratic" elections, which the Western leaders recognized as being those in which only parties that had been approved by the Communists could take part. The discussions on the future shape of German government were futile.

The talks on reparations made no more progress than those on the form of government. Molotov continued to assert that the Soviet Union had been promised ten billion dollars in reparations at Yalta. Both Marshall and Bevin continued, correctly, to deny that there had been any such commitment. When the Soviet foreign minister demanded that outstanding reparation payments be made to the USSR from the current production in the Western zones of Germany, both Marshall and Bevin flatly refused, for two reasons. First, such payments were uncalled for under any previous agreement. Second, in spite of their resolve not to finance Germany from their own treasuries, both Britain and the United States were in fact doing so, in order to prevent disease, unrest, and starvation.

The economic merger of the British and American zones, first proposed by former secretary Byrnes and agreed to by the two governments in December, was too recently instituted to have had its desired effect, and it was not running as smoothly as hoped. Furthermore, the ravages of the harsh winter that was just ending had proven a further financial drain on the occupying powers.

Molotov sometimes ignored these assertions and, at other times during the conference, maintained that the Western allies would not have to support the Germans if they properly organized their zones. At one point, he even accused the Western nations of wanting to preserve Germany's industrial base for the benefit of their own banking interests and to use that power to endanger Communist states to the east of Germany. Marshall had a concise answer to the Soviet demands. "The United States is opposed to policies which will continue Germany as a congested slum or an economic poorhouse in the center of Europe."[7]

The Moscow conference of the foreign ministers was in hopeless deadlock, wrangling day after day over the same issues and arriving at no agreements, when President Harry S Truman appeared before a joint session of the Congress in Washington on March 12 to address the problems of Greece and Turkey. It was an electrifying speech, enunciating what came to be known as the Truman Doctrine:

At the present moment in history, nearly every nation must choose between alternative ways of life. The choice is too often not a free one. One
way is based on the will of the majority. The second is based on the will
of a minority forcibly imposed on the majority. It relies on terror and
oppression, a controlled press and radio, fixed elections and the suppression of personal freedom.

I believe that it must be the policy of the United States to support free
peoples who are resisting attempted subjugation by armed minorities or
by outside pressures.

I believe that we must assist free peoples to work out their destinies
in their own way. . . .

Should we fail to aid Greece and Turkey in this fateful hour, the effect
will be far-reaching to the West as well as to the East. We must take immediate and resolute action.

If we falter in our leadership, we may endanger the peace of the
world—and we shall surely endanger the welfare of our own nation.

Great responsibilities have been placed upon us by the swift movement of events.

I am confident that the Congress will face those responsibilities
squarely.[8]

The specific action that the president called for in this case was the
allocation of $400 million in aid to Greece and Turkey for a period to
end on June 30, 1948. When Truman concluded his speech, the heavily
Republican Congress rose to its feet to give the Democratic president a
standing ovation. It was not, however, a unanimous endorsement of the
policy that the president had announced. It was, as Acheson observed,
a tribute to a brave man who had brought the problem before them in
plain and simple terms.[9]

Many editorial writers in the United States, whether they favored
the president's position or not, viewed Truman's speech as casting
down a gauntlet before the Soviets. It was truly that. At the conference
in Moscow, however, the gauntlet wasn't picked up by the Soviet nego-
tiators. *Isvestia* and *Pravda,* the official Soviet Communist newspapers,
railed against the president's speech, but the Soviet delegation never
mentioned it during the formal sessions or in informal conversations.
It was not mentioned by Stalin either, during the one meeting Secretary
Marshall had with the Soviet dictator. On April 14, hoping to get the
stalled negotiations moving, Marshall revived a proposal Secretary
Byrnes had made a year earlier—a twenty-five-year treaty to keep Germany disarmed—but Molotov dismissed the proposal out of hand. The
following evening Marshall met with Stalin, beginning the discussion
with remembrances of their wartime meetings and an expression of
regret at the apparent cooling in relations between their two countries.
Then he told Stalin he had concluded that the Soviet Union was not
interested in the disarmament treaty and he would so report to the

president. Continuing, but not mentioning Truman's speech, Marshall firmly stated it was the intention of the United States to give all the assistance it could to nations threatened with economic chaos.[10]

Stalin listened while doodling wolves' heads with a red pencil on the pad before him.[11] When he spoke, it was to discount the failure of the conference. "These are only the first skirmishes and brushes of reconnaissance forces on this question," he said.[12]

☆  ☆  ☆

In Berlin, the skirmishes and brushes about the nature of the future government of the city were being played out on a more immediate and personal scale, and they revealed, in microcosm, the Soviet idea of "democratic" government.

The new lord mayor, Otto Ostrowski, attempted to steer a middle course between the East and the West in municipal affairs, so that the major effort of rebuilding the shattered city could be carried out and the terrors of the bitter winter could be confronted. He found his hands were tied by the preexisting, Soviet-created governmental structure, where the large majority of jobs were held by Communists. "What I would really like," he remarked wistfully to Colonel Howley one day, "is a Kommandatura clarification of the term 'leading city official.' Here I am, elected Lord Mayor of Berlin, and when I enter the City Hall in the Russian sector, even the charwomen don't answer when I say 'good morning.' "[13]

Ostrowski was warned by the Soviet command in the city that he must not oppose the Communists in his government and was summoned to the Soviet headquarters two or three times a week, alternately plied with liquor and good fellowship and threatened with exposure of details of his private life. Ostrowski had divorced his Jewish wife during the war, and although the Western allies had investigated this event and determined that it was a personal decision, not a pro-Nazi one, the Soviets warned him that they would depict him as a Hitlerite. A weak man, Ostrowski capitulated to the threats, agreeing in writing and without the approval of the Social Democratic Party to cooperate fully with the SED. When news of the agreement became public, Ostrowski was denounced by the leadership of the SDP as a renegade and a traitor, while the Communist SED leaders made long speeches on the floor of the city assembly defending him. His written agreement with the SED was brought to a vote in the assembly on April 11, where it was repudiated by a vote of eighty to twenty.

Colonel Howley called in the lord mayor and the leading members of the SDP to hear their views firsthand. Ostrowski defended his action on the grounds of expediency, and the other leaders heatedly maintained that close cooperation with the Communists could lead only to being swallowed up by them. The recent attempt of the SED to absorb the Social Democrats, successful in the Soviet zone but thwarted in Berlin, was fresh in everyone's mind.

Howley, in keeping with official policy, informed the SDP leaders that the election of a lord mayor was a purely German affair and that the American military government had no intention of either defending the incumbent or supporting any other candidate. Facing impeachment by the SDP, Ostrowski resigned—or tried to. The Soviets wouldn't allow it.

When Ostrowski's resignation letter, along with a letter from the assembly announcing it, arrived at the Kommandatura, General Kotikov requested time to study the matter. His request took the form of a four-hour harangue that consisted mostly of a denunciation of the SDP. The next day, the Soviet-licensed newspapers in the city repeated most of the general's tirade and accused Colonel Howley and the other Western powers of meddling in Berlin politics and instigating the lord mayor's resignation. It was a new instance of the Soviets openly attacking the other occupying powers, and Howley finally hit back openly. Calling in the press, Howley repeated what he had told the SDP—that the election of a lord mayor was a German affair. Then he added caustically that there would be considerably less trouble in Berlin if another power did less mixing in politics.[14]

The Soviets continued to stall on the question, putting forward a proposal that they would accept the resignation only in return for the right to approve Ostrowski's successor in advance. The Western representatives on the Kommandatura realized that this would amount to a Soviet veto, so they refused to accept the proposal. Ultimately, the question was forwarded to the Allied Control Council.

At that level, General Clay was still holding out hope that quadripartite government could work. He agreed to the Soviet condition that Ostrowski's successor be approved in advance, noting for the record that it applied in this case only and did not represent a precedent for future actions.

The decision caused an intense reaction in the press of both the East and the West. Predictably, the Soviets praised it. The Western press denounced it as having sold democracy short. It also came as a hard and discouraging blow to Colonel Howley, who had maintained consistently on the basis of his experience in Berlin that the Soviets would try to control the city's elected government by means of the veto.[15] He was soon to be proven right.

☆  ☆  ☆

Secretary of State George C. Marshall left the meeting of foreign ministers in Moscow in a dark and frustrated mood. While no one from the

State Department had expected that the conference would arrive at the final terms for a German peace treaty, they had all hoped for some progress. There had been absolutely none.

Charles Bohlen, who had acted as Marshall's translator and advisor at the conference, recorded the secretary's reaction to the lack of results of the meeting:

> [Marshall] came to the conclusion that Stalin, looking over Europe, saw the best way to advance Soviet interests was to let matters drift. Economic conditions were bad. Europe was recovering slowly from the war. Little had been done to rebuild damaged highways, railroads, and canals. Business alliances severed by years of hostilities were still shattered. Unemployment was widespread. Millions of people were on short rations. There was a danger of epidemics. This was the kind of crisis that Communism thrived on.[16]

On the plane returning from Moscow to Washington, Marshall talked constantly of the importance of finding some initiative to prevent the complete breakdown of Europe. Marshall activated a State Department Policy Planning Staff to develop such an initiative. George F. Kennan, then on detached duty from the State Department as head of the National War College, was recalled and placed in charge. On April 30, Kennan and Marshall met in the secretary's office, where Marshall expressed his desire to develop a sound program for European recovery. At the close of the conference Kennan asked if there were any special instructions.

"Avoid trivia," Marshall replied.[17]

# TWELVE
## AVOIDING TRIVIA

Raised in Milwaukee and a graduate of St. John's Military Academy there, George Kennan had become fascinated with Russia after a boyhood visit with his distant relative and namesake, George Kennan, an explorer, journalist, and lecturer. His famous relative's book exposing the cruelties of the Czarist Siberian prison camps had caused him to be declared persona non grata in Russia. The younger Kennan attended Princeton, where he was a shy and undistinguished student who participated in few campus activities. "I may not have been the most undistinguished student Princeton ever had," he said later, "but I was most certainly the least memorable."[1]

After college, Kennan joined the Foreign Service, held posts in both Germany and Russia, and mastered the languages of both countries. He was a career diplomat of twenty-one years and had spent most of World War II in the embassy in Moscow, growing more and more disturbed at what he felt was a naive American policy toward the Soviets.

To Kennan, being in the Foreign Service meant making a thorough study of the country to which he was assigned—not merely its current politics, but its history, music, language, customs, and mores—and understanding the inner nature of the place. He had little patience with an American policy toward the Soviets that he saw as marked by "wishful thinking." He took a pragmatic and realistic view of the aims of the USSR.

To Kennan, the American people did not even remotely understand a Soviet Union that, he believed, held a "neurotic view" of the world where they would engage "in patient but deadly struggle for the total destruction of any rival power, never in compacts or compromises with it."[2] Kennan contended that it was useless to try to establish a normal, diplomatic, give-and-take relationship with the Soviets. Such a strategy simply wouldn't work.

A singularly bleak and disillusioning view, Kennan's analysis found little welcome in Washington during the war and in the immediate postwar period. Only later, with the Soviets acting out the forbidding role that Kennan had assigned them, was his analysis given credit and accepted as correct. The "long telegram" he had dispatched in February 1946 had circulated widely in official Washington, and many people were impressed with Kennan's lucid analysis of Soviet behavior. He was summoned home from Moscow and assigned to lecture at the National War College. It was from that assignment that Secretary Marshall called him to head the study by the Policy Planning Staff. The secretary made it clear that he wanted the report in ten days to two weeks.[3]

The group was given a large meeting room adjacent to the secretary of state's office. It contained only a large conference table, chairs, and floor-to-ceiling bookcases. There were no telephones to interrupt the quiet deliberations of the group, and an atmosphere of reasoned and deliberate academic study marked the meetings in spite of the deadline they were working under.

The planners drew on a number of previous analytical studies and the judgment of many experts. Within the framework of George Kennan's analysis of the Soviets, the Policy Planning Staff determined that there were only three courses open to the United States: fight the Soviet Union, with the intention of destroying it; permit Communism to expand indefinitely; or adjust American policy to halt Soviet gains. Rejecting the first as impractical, given the military strength of the Soviet Union, and the second as an unacceptable policy goal for the United States, they fixed on the third avenue as the correct one. Then they addressed the means to achieve that goal.

The problem was not, the planners concluded, a purely military one. A bellicose approach would only strengthen Communist arguments that capitalism was eager to deprive "the masses" of justified social advances. Sensing that the disturbances in the world came from basic economic maladjustments and "a profound exhaustion of spiritual vigor,"[4] Kennan's group concluded that the only sensible approach was to attempt to foster healthy societies, primarily through a program of economic aid.

On May 23, the Policy Planning Staff submitted its report to Secretary Marshall. It was simple, clean-cut, and brilliant. It proposed an offer of massive American economic aid to all of Europe, with no ideological overtones, as a positive effort to restore the economy. According to the report, two details of any such plan were indispensable. The Europeans themselves must take the initiative in working out the details, and the program that they developed must be one that would do the whole job so that it would be the last such program that the United States would be called upon to underwrite in the foreseeable future.[5]

It was fortunate that the policy planners concluded that the response to Soviet aggressiveness was not expected to be a military one, for within a year after the German surrender, the American army that had swept through Europe from the beaches of Normandy had melted away and been replaced by the skeletal army of occupation. The conquering army had consisted of sixty-one divisions, each of which numbered over 10,000 men. Forty-two of the divisions were infantry, fifteen were armored, and four were airborne.[6] The demobilization of those forces after the war has been characterized as "an organized rout,"[7] and by the end of 1945 there were three armored and seven infantry divisions left on the continent.[8] Those units were in such a sorry state that Eisenhower's chief of staff, General W. Bedell Smith, conceded in a report that "the forces in this theater are unable to perform any serious offensive operations. The capacity to carry on limited defensive operations is slightly better."[9] The major function of the United States Army in Europe was not, however, armed conflict, as there did not appear to be an enemy in sight. The purpose of the army was the occupation of a conquered land, and it turned to a concept it had once employed in the Philippines to carry out that task. It created a constabulary.

Recognizing that the primary purpose of an occupying army is the maintenance of law and order, the War Department addressed that need by forming the United States Constabulary, a crack outfit of 30,000, and continued to allow its combat units in Europe to wither. For example, by November 1946, the Army's policy of personnel rotation without replacement had so depleted the ranks of the 78th Infantry Division in Berlin that the unit was reorganized and reduced in size to a battalion—the 3d of the 16th Infantry Regiment—with an authorized complement of 860 soldiers. That battalion was made a part of the small Berlin Military Post of under 3,000.

The newly formed United States Constabulary was commanded by gravelly-voiced, profane, and bombastic Major General Ernest M. Harmon. Harmon was a perfect choice for the command.

A cavalry veteran who had seen action with one of the few armored units the United States had fielded in World War I, Harmon later developed a reputation for taking lagging divisions and whipping them into a high state of effectiveness in short order. Given command of a slack 2d Armored Division, one of his first acts was to bellow a string of contemptuous profanities and scrawl "How long has this shit been going on?" at the bottom of a recommendation for a decoration for a division staff officer.[10] The revitalized 2d Armored Division he commanded during the Battle of the Bulge won what many considered the greatest American tank victory of the war.

When Harmon took command of the forming constabulary on January 20, 1946, he began a whirlwind inspection tour of its installations. At one, accompanied by the colonel in charge of the detachment, he stopped in front of a soldier in baggy pants in the formation.

"Sleep in them, soldier?" Harmon barked.

"No, sir," the soldier answered.

"Transfer him by tonight, Colonel."

Moving on, Harmon asked another man, "How much do you like it here?"

"Not much, sir."

"This one too, Colonel."[11]

By weeding out troops, Harmon was ensuring that the constabulary would consist of men who looked like, acted like, and were happy to be soldiers. He also insisted that their uniform be distinctive and took a strong hand in its design. Scrapping the waist-length "Eisenhower" jacket that other soldiers wore, he put his troops back into the long-skirted, brass-buttoned blouse of the prewar army and prescribed the visored service cap for off-duty wear. On duty, the constabulary wore a fiber helmet liner, buffed and polished to a high sheen, encircled by triple stripes of yellow-blue-yellow, and bearing the distinctive patch of the constabulary—a blue *C* on a yellow circle, bisected by a red flash of lightning. Detractors said that the uniform made the troopers look like "highly polished potato bugs,"[12] and the constabulary was universally referred to by other occupation troops as "the Circle C cowboys" because of their distinctive patch.[13] But the tiny constabulary represented the best that there was of the army in Europe.

While a major organizational problem had been corrected on March 15, 1947, with the appointment of Lucius Clay as commander of U.S. Forces in Europe as well as military governor, thereby consolidating the commands, the units other than the constabulary were disasters. Being a member of an occupying army was "a demoralizing experience for most soldiers," according to an army psychologist touring Europe to check on morale. "The work habit has deteriorated and it has developed a hard, pragmatic, and cynical moral attitude in the average soldier."[14]

Within a year of war's end, American soldiers in Europe were contracting venereal diseases at the rate of 246 cases per 1,000 men per month, and the rate jumped to 306 per 1,000 by autumn of 1946—nearly one soldier in three. In one extraordinary unit of 1,000 men, more than 1,200 cases were reported in one month, indicating that some soldiers were hardly cured of one infection before contracting another.[15] American troops in Europe were also getting themselves killed in motor vehicle accidents at a rate twelve times that in the United States.[16]

Assaults on women by American soldiers were so frequent that American women attached to the occupation took to wearing armbands to identify themselves as Americans to prevent being harassed. The soldiers' practice of "fanny-slapping"—leaning out of moving jeeps to swipe at the bottoms of fräuleins they passed—became so prevalent that the commanding general had to issue a sternly worded general order to curtail it.[17]

Accounts of rape, assault, murder, drug dealing, and black-market activities screamed from the headlines of *Stars and Stripes* and the European edition of the *Herald-Tribune.* The army sent General J. Lawton Collins to Germany on a public relations mission. He frankly admitted to reporters during a press conference in Berlin that his task was to attempt to persuade them to devote their attention to "the real picture in Germany instead of merely the superficial picture of the pregnant fräuleins, venereal disease, and scandal."[18] Unfortunately for the success of General Collins's mission, one of the largest scandals involving looting by Americans broke while he was in the middle of his tour. A Women's Army Corps captain, Kathleen Durant Nash, and her husband, Colonel J. W. Durant, were accused of stealing jewels worth three million dollars from a requisitioned castle under control of the WAC.[19]

The air forces, still a part of the army but lobbying for establishment as an independent service, were in no better shape. By mid 1946, air power in Europe had been reduced to one tactical reconnaissance wing, one bomber group, two squadrons of night fighters, and six groups of fighters.[20] One of those fighter groups was the 66th, stationed at the air base at Fritzlar that the 852d Aviation Engineering Battalion had thought would be their last construction assignment in Europe. Now, the neighbors of the base were startled and annoyed by the thirty to forty explosions that rocked the area each day. While the pilots of the 66th flew routine patrols and training missions, demolition experts on another section of the field were cramming up to ten pounds of high explosives into shiny airplanes that had been stripped of engines and instruments and blowing them up. When officials finally explained to the curious what was happening, they said that the planes were obsolete or obsolescent and that it was cheaper to destroy them than to crate them up and ship them back to the States or to guard them when they were not being used.[21]

The United States Army Air Forces had mustered over 64,000 aircraft at the end of the war. By mid 1947, with the fight for its establishment as an independent arm of service won, the combat fleet of the new United States Air Force consisted of a mere 1,500 planes. Its plan called for seventy air groups, which would vary in size depending on the function of the unit. Fifty were proposed to be combat groups and the rest transport, weather, mapping, or reconnaissance units, but budget cuts forced reduction of the planned number of groups to fifty-five. None of these was up to full strength, and most were classified as having "low combat efficiency."[22] They were the equivalent of thirty wartime groups.

The picture with respect to Air Force personnel was nearly as bleak. Out of a projected total of 401,000 members, the new service had only 380,000 in uniform. Of a planned 48,000 reserve pilots, only 22,500 had been trained. Continuing "economies" led to the closing of nearly half of the training centers that were to have produced the pilots.[23]

☆   ☆   ☆

Late on the morning of June 5, 1947, Harvard Yard, the large open area of the campus between Harvard University's Widener Library and the Memorial Chapel, was crowded with 7,000 people for the school's 286th commencement. The procession that entered was led by the marshal of the university and the sheriff of Middlesex County, Massachusetts, who carried a ceremonial sword. They were followed by Harvard president James B. Conant, Provost Paul H. Buck, and the members of the Governing Board, all resplendent in academic gowns whose colors and cut denoted their academic rank and distinctions.

The deans of the various colleges of Harvard followed. Then the prospective recipients of honorary degrees entered the Yard in solemn dignity. They included General of the Army Omar Bradley, the poet T. S. Eliot, Senator James J. Wadsworth of New York, father of the atomic bomb J. Robert Oppenheimer, Georgia newspaper publisher Hodding Carter, Jr., and Secretary of State George C. Marshall. When the procession ended, the sheriff of Middlesex County called for order by rapping his sword on the stage three times. The ceremony began. After traditional speeches in Latin by members of the graduating class, President Conant awarded the honorary degrees, conferring the degree of Doctor of Law on Secretary Marshall.

Later, while the graduates and their families enjoyed a box lunch on the lawn, Marshall joined the other honorees and special guests at the Fogg Museum for the university's traditional luncheon. Marshall's speech to the group outlined the problems of economic chaos that Europe was facing and announced the need for Western assistance to resolve it on a cooperative basis. Any such program, he stated, "should be a joint one, agreed to by a number of if not all European nations." What would come to be known as the Marshall Plan had been born.[24]

European reaction to the Marshall speech was almost immediate. On June 7, the British government announced that it warmly welcomed the proposal and urgently wished to follow up on it. Britain stated that it was willing to take the lead in calling for a conference of countries interested in participating.[25] The French ambassador, Henri Bonnet, called at the State Department a week after the speech to state his nation's interest. He made the suggestion that the countries of Europe outline their basic resources and their needs, stressing those that Europe could not meet itself.[26] Polish ambassador Josef Winiewicz emphasized that he had no official instructions when he called on the State Department for information but indicated that there was great public interest in Poland about the remarks of Secretary Marshall. He said that the only thing he had seen about the Soviet attitude was an article he had read that did not exclude Soviet participation or indicate opposition. He must not have seen the article in *Pravda, Ukraine* on June 11, 1947, in which the writer attacked the Truman Doctrine as being "spread in bloodstains on the slopes of the Thessalian Mountains where Greek Government troops, equipped by British and Americans, obliterate from the face of the earth insurgent villages" and denounced Secretary Marshall's speech as "evidence of even wider plans of American reaction, of a new stage in Washington's campaign against forces of world democracy and progress."[27]

A meeting of the foreign ministers of Britain, France, and the Soviet Union began in Paris on June 26. One of the items on the agenda was the invitation to twenty-two European nations to attend a July conference to discuss Secretary Marshall's offer. Foreign Minister Vyacheslav Molotov immediately made the attitude of the Soviets quite clear. On arriving, virtually the first thing Molotov did was to ask the two other foreign ministers what they had been doing behind his back. Then he proposed that the three ministers ask the United States how much money would be available for European recovery and if it was likely that Congress would approve it. Next he argued that the European countries should not be required to list their resources but merely set forth a list of their needs. By July 2, Molotov was publicly declaring that the smaller nations of Europe were facing "Big Power" domination and interference with their national sovereignty.

Finally, the Soviet delegation broke off all negotiations and ordered that all Eastern European countries refuse to participate. The government of Czechoslovakia had already accepted an invitation to attend the planned conference, but members of the Czech government, including the Communist prime minister Klement Gottwald and the anti-Communist Social Democrat foreign minister Jan Masaryk, were summoned to a meeting in Moscow. After an audience with Stalin, Czechoslovakia withdrew from participation.[28] The French, the British, and the others were determined to go ahead, even with the realization that this meant the division of Europe into two opposing blocs.

The implications of this determination for Berlin were grave. As Germany would be represented at the July conference by the three Western military governors, it was clear that Marshall Plan aid would split the country in two, and the "Iron Curtain" that Churchill had spoken about in his speech in Fulton, Missouri, would descend across the country dividing it at the Elbe River. Berlin would become an island of Western influence deep in hostile territory.

The people of Berlin were well aware of these implications. In her journal for Tuesday, July 8, 1947, Ruth Andreas-Friedrich noted, "Every day new facts make it clear just how inexorably the countries east and west of the Elbe are evolving in different directions."[29] The next day she noted that England and France had not lost hope and had sent invitations to twenty-two nations to discuss the Marshall Plan. Two days later, hearing of the Czech withdrawal and the refusal of Yugoslavia, Romania, Poland, Bulgaria, and Albania to participate, she wrote, "Sooner than we anticipated, the fronts on either side of the 'curtain' have been consolidated. Eastern bloc against Western bloc. Satellite states of the Soviet Union against satellite states of U.S. capital. One thing is sure: The dividing line runs through the middle of Germany."[30]

☆ ☆ ☆

The newly created United States Air Force was busy in the summer of 1947, attempting to develop and maintain its efficiency within the limits of its constrained budget. It was also designing its own sky-blue uniform and inventing its own special holiday. August 1, the anniversary of the founding of the old Army Air Forces, was designated as Air Force Day, and the fledgling service put on a spectacular show of military might. Massed flights of more than one hundred B-29s took place over Chicago, Milwaukee, Detroit, and other cities. In New York, one hundred forty airplanes put on an aerial show, and seven B-29s made a speed run from Tokyo to Washington with only one stop en route.

There was a downside to the day as well. In order to have enough aviation gasoline to perform the holiday aerial showmanship, all routine training flights for the month preceding Air Force Day had been canceled.[31]

# THIRTEEN

# FROM RIFT TO RUPTURE

Professor Ernst Reuter had risen rapidly in city politics since his return to Berlin from his Turkish exile in the late fall of 1946: he was now the city councilman in charge of transportation. The SDP now put his name forward as a possible candidate for lord mayor to succeed the disgraced Ostrowski. Immediately, a campaign of vilification began against him, orchestrated by the Soviets. Posters appeared in the streets asking, "Do you want a Turk for mayor?" The Soviet liaison officer at the *Magistrat* told the Liberal Democratic Party (LDP) members that Reuter was noted for his anti-Soviet attitude and that they could not vote for him without thereby showing anti-Soviet tendencies.[1] The CDU (Christian Democratic Union) members of the assembly were also warned.

Berlin's democratic political leaders were not, however, willing to be intimidated. On June 24, 1947, the city assembly chose Reuter as the new lord mayor. Reuter garnered 82 percent of the votes, even in the face of the knowledge that the Soviets were opposed to him and that the assembly had no assurances that the Western allies would back them. The Soviets, as expected, vetoed the nomination at the Kommandatura, and the matter was referred to the Allied Control Council, where the veto was upheld.

The Control Council decision was another grave disappointment to Deputy Commandant Howley, and he began to think seriously about leaving the military and returning to Philadelphia, "to learn more about democracy at its historic source."[2] He was not only weary but also well aware that his chances of any further promotion in the army were slim. The official line was that a reserve colonel could hardly expect to be made a brigadier general when there were so many regular officers waiting for their first star—a line of reasoning that had been firmly outlined to Howley by his superiors.[3]

Disappointed in the failure of the West to back its choice for lord mayor, the *Magistrat* remained defiant nonetheless. It now refused to name anyone to the post, appointing instead Social Democrat deputy lord mayor Louise Schroeder to act as lord mayor. The appointment was at first accepted by all of the occupying powers, and Frau Schroeder began to sign official documents as "Acting Lord Mayor."

Louise Schroeder was a tiny, gray-haired woman of nearly sixty, who had been one of the first women ever elected to the Reichstag and who had spent most of the war in a concentration camp. Beneath her benign facade, there was a will of iron, and she stoutly carried out the program of the majority SDP, impervious to threats from the Soviet authorities. Finding that this diminutive woman was totally resistant to their intimidation, the Soviets withdrew their original recognition of her right to act as head of the Berlin government, now insisting that she was only a deputy mayor and making the process of communication between the Allied powers and the city government hopelessly complicated. Western messages to the lord mayor's office in city hall, located in the Soviet sector, were returned to the sender with the notation that no such individual existed.

This absurd situation led Colonel Howley to tell General Kotikov sharply, at a Kommandatura meeting, "If you want to abandon Military Government, it's okay with me, but if you want the Kommandatura to issue any orders at all to the City Government, you better find some way of doing it." Ultimately, the Soviets agreed that communications to the chief city administrator could be addressed "*Magistrat*" and that they would ultimately be delivered.[4]

In the meantime, Ernst Reuter continued to serve as the city's head of transportation and had cards printed that identified him as "Elected Lord Mayor, but forbidden to serve."

☆　☆　☆

Colonel Frank Howley was completely fed up by autumn. He had had his third stormy argument with the military governor, General Clay, in late September and could see no future in remaining in Germany or in the military. He knew that his chances for promotion were nonexistent, and he was completely convinced that his personal perception of the Soviets and their aims was in total disagreement with the government's official position.

Howley had disagreed with Clay before. One clash had occurred in September, when Howley had ordered a group of Communists thrown in jail overnight for having called a mass meeting in the American sector without seeking the approval of the military government. The Soviets had protested at the Allied Control Council, and Clay had promised to investigate the incident. When, during their meeting, Clay accused Howley of running a Gestapo city, the colonel angrily retorted that he wasn't doing anything of the kind and stormed out of the general's office. When he returned to his own office and his temper had cooled,

Howley sent a report to Clay confirming exactly what he had told the general at the meeting—that there was a standing order that political gatherings such as the one he had directed be broken up required prior approval by military government and that permission had not been sought in this case. He was summoned back to the general's office after the report arrived and was sternly invited to go home if he couldn't follow General Clay's orders. Clay had ended the stormy session on a kinder note, however. "I want you to know, Frank, that I wouldn't call you up here if I didn't think the world of you," he said.[5]

Now, just two weeks later, Howley had been called on the carpet before Clay again. This time the conflict was over a staff study that Howley had ordered drawn up, dealing with the steps he thought were necessary to curb Communism in Berlin. The first paragraph of the study pointed out what Frank Howley had come firmly to believe in his two years of dealing with the Soviets in Berlin—that they were neither friends nor allies. It further noted that the Communist party was by no means a democratic one. At the end of the meeting Frank Howley submitted his resignation from active duty. He was going home to Philadelphia.[6]

☆ ☆ ☆

By early autumn of 1947, the bright hope that had been kindled by Secretary Marshall's Harvard speech was still glowing, but less brightly than before. It would take time for a full-scale European recovery plan to be shepherded through Congress, and the need for relief was immediate. American corn and Canadian wheat crops were far below expectations, driving up the prices of food worldwide, and there was a danger that the European countries would exhaust their dollar reserves and slide into anarchy before a comprehensive plan could be passed. In Germany, coal production in the Ruhr, the vital key to German economic prosperity, lagged badly as the miners protested the rations of 1,550 calories a day they were allocated. American analysts seriously feared that the democratic governments of France, Italy, and Greece might founder and that the Communists in those countries might seize power in the wake of an economic collapse. Sent to Europe on a fact-finding mission in late summer, George Kennan reported when he returned that the economic situation in Britain was "deteriorating with terrifying rapidity" and that it was "tragic to a point that challenges description."[7]

☆ ☆ ☆

The Communist parties of the suffering continent had no interest in improving conditions. For a week beginning on September 21, representatives from Poland, Yugoslavia, Hungary, Romania, Bulgaria, Czechoslovakia, France, and Italy, called together by the Soviet Union, met in the province of Lower Silesia, which had been stripped away from Germany and given to Poland at the end of the war. The site was the Szklarska Poreba Palace, one of Hermann Göring's former hunting lodges.[8]

Soviet Politburo member Andrei Zhdanov, the head of the Soviet delegation, opened the meeting by charging that the imperialist camp led by the Americans wished to dominate the world, by war if necessary. He called on his fellow delegates to do their utmost to block this effort by preventing the recovery of the economies in their countries under capitalism. When the conference ended, its final manifesto condemned the Truman-Marshall plan as "the European sub-section of the general plan for the policy of global expansion pursued by the United States in all parts of the world."[9]

Soviet denunciations of the policies of the United States and its allies continued. On November 21, 1947, four days before the Big Four foreign ministers were scheduled to meet again in London, Marshal Sokolovsky monopolized the meeting of the Allied Control Council in Berlin with a harangue that lasted for hours and sounded like a drill sergeant dressing down a group of sloppy recruits on a parade ground.

The West, Sokolovsky declared, was allowing the Germans to rebuild an army and had allowed former German military bases to remain in the country. The Western powers were allowing major Germans weapons factories to exist, so that the British and American zones of the country could be converted into a military base. Sokolovsky charged that the Americans and British were taking "invisible reparations" by paying artificially low prices for the goods that they exported from Germany, while depriving the Soviets of reparations to which they were entitled. Ignoring conditions in the Soviet zone, Sokolovsky accused the Western powers of violating the Potsdam accords that stipulated that all democratic parties should be licensed to operate by banning the Socialist Unity Party from operation. Then he turned to economics, condemning the U.S.-British bizone and their recent agreement to foster more efficient operation of the coal mines in the Ruhr and in heavy industries. He insisted that these bilateral agreements were reached "behind the back of the Control Council."

Turning to the Marshall Plan, he said that it aimed at a "subjugating of the economy of the American, British, and French occupation zones in Germany to American and British monopolies and at converting those regions of Germany, and primarily the Ruhr, into a war industry base of Anglo-American imperialism in Europe." The purpose of all of this, Marshal Sokolovsky concluded, was to achieve a means to bring pressure on European states that refused to be enslaved by the Americans and the British.[10]

At the foreign ministers' conference, Molotov repeated much of what the Soviet representative in Germany had said to his counterparts, adding some vituperation of his own. The rift among the Allies over the future of Germany had become a rupture.[11]

Among the press corps in Berlin were Marguerite Higgins and Jim O'Donnell. In the rough and tumble world of journalism, Higgins and O'Donnell were friendly competitors. Higgins worked for a daily newspaper, the *New York Herald-Tribune,* archrival of the *New York Times.* O'Donnell, Berlin bureau chief for *Newsweek,* had *Time* magazine as his main competition, and he would often give Higgins leads on stories with the understanding that she wouldn't file them until they could appear simultaneously in *Newsweek* and the *Tribune.* The arrangement worked very well until Cardinal von Preysing, a Roman Catholic cleric and former member of the German resistance, made up his mind to speak out against the Communists as he had against the Nazis. He gave an advance copy of his sermon text to Jim O'Donnell who, on this occasion, decided to hold it back from Higgins until the last minute. O'Donnell filed his story on Saturday for his magazine's coming Wednesday deadline but Higgins, dining with O'Donnell and his wife that evening, came across a copy of the sermon. Saying that she would be back later, Higgins excused herself from the dinner party between courses and rushed off to file her own account of the cardinal's text. The story, under her byline, would hit the streets of New York in the *Herald-Tribune* in the Sunday edition, nearly a week before O'Donnell's *Newsweek* piece appeared.

Learning from a maid that Higgins had seen the copy of the cardinal's speech and suspecting why she had left in such a rush, O'Donnell waited for her to return. When Higgins reappeared at the dinner party, O'Donnell told her that he thought he had a great story lined up to share with her, but that it had fizzled out. A cardinal had been planning to speak out against the Communists, but the cleric had backed out at the last minute.

Higgins went dead white and excused herself a second time, dashing off to try to kill the story she had just filed. When she left, O'Donnell called Drew Middleton of the *New York Times* bureau in Berlin and gave him the story. Higgins succeeded in having her story pulled, but the presses in New York were already rolling with the first edition, so it was a difficult and expensive process for her bosses. When they saw virtually the same story appear under Middleton's byline in the *Times* that day, Higgins received a harsh cable from the home office. "What's going on there?" it asked. "Are you drinking?" Marguerite Higgins nearly lost her job over the episode.[12]

At the time, General Clay was in Washington testifying before an unsympathetic Senate Foreign Relations Committee, pleading that food shipments to Germany be increased before starvation reached the proportions that it had taken on in the Nazi concentration camps. The committee was plainly against "feeding Germans," a sign of growing domestic disillusionment with American involvement in Europe. Clay returned to his hotel that evening feeling sick that he hadn't convinced the committee and that thousands of innocent people would die as a result.

Even as Clay was pleading, Marguerite Higgins was playing another dirty trick on Jim O'Donnell. Touring the Ruhr area together, they had accompanied Mayor Carl Arnold of Düsseldorf to a hospital where 220 people had died of starvation in the past two days.

"Don't pull a Cardinal von Preysing on me," O'Donnell said to Higgins. "You can have the story, but we'll both file on Wednesday." Higgins agreed but, when she was several hours late for dinner, O'Donnell knew that she had broken her promise.

"What have you done?" he asked her.

"I couldn't live with my conscience if I'd sat on that story. Can you imagine how many people might die between now and Wednesday?"[13]

The following day, in Washington, General Clay returned to the committee hearing and sensed immediately from the faces of the members that something had changed. Glancing down at the table, he saw a copy of the *Herald-Tribune* with Marguerite Higgins's starvation story on page one.

"Somehow it brought the disaster into focus for them in a way that I could not," he told Jim O'Donnell many years later. "The food was sent. Who knows how many lives were saved?"[14]

☆ ☆ ☆

With the increased stridence of Communist denunciations of the West, the tide in Congress began to swing. Before the end of the year, not only had the package of aid to Greece and Turkey under the Truman Doctrine been approved, but $522 million in temporary aid to Italy, France, and Austria had been voted for as well.[15]

The president and his advisors knew that they still faced a hard fight in Congress before they could hope to win approval of the European Recovery Act, as the Marshall Plan was formally known. Asked if he objected to the plan being named for Marshall rather than him, Truman publicly stated that the credit should justly go to the man who had conceived it. Privately, to his political friends, he confided, "Can you imagine its chances of passage in an election year in a Republican Congress if it is named for Truman and not Marshall?"[16] Liberal Democrats and followers of Henry Wallace were denouncing it as the "Martial Plan" and saying that it was merely an anti-Soviet ploy that would breed war. Conservative Republican senators, led by Robert Taft, grumbled that it was a global New Dealism that threatened to bankrupt the

United States. Its most fervent champion was Senator Arthur Vandenburg, the Republican chairman of the Foreign Relations Committee.

George Kennan, as darkly pessimistic in his view of the Soviets as
Colonel Frank Howley, looked beyond the immediate problem of passage of the program and predicted that there would be a strong and
violent reaction from the Soviet Union when it appeared that the Marshall Plan would be set up and put into operation. He announced to
his colleagues that he expected that the reaction would come in
Czechoslovakia.[17]

Following the failure of the London conference, Clay moved quickly to
bolster German morale and productivity. Claiming that conditions
were worse than at any time since Germany's surrender, Clay and the
British military governor, General Brian Robertson, revised the makeup
of the bizonal economic commission, formed an economic high court,
and established a central bizonal bank. Clay also began to push vigorously for currency reform, knowing that the nearly valueless German
mark was a major part of the problem the country was facing. Without
a reliable, stable currency in which people could place their trust, no
long-range economic progress was possible. A country in which half of
the business transactions took place on the black market was fiscally
hopeless. Clay knew that the "cigarette economy" must end soon.

General Clay also had an urgent personnel matter to attend to. Colonel Frank L. Howley's bags were packed, his relief from active duty had
been approved, and orders for his transportation back to the States had
been cut. He and his family looked forward to spending Thanksgiving
at home in Philadelphia, where he would be free from his duties as
director of the Berlin office of military government and deputy commandant of the city. When he left, only General Clay would remain of
the top level officials who had entered Berlin after its fall two and one-
half years before. Howley had served as deputy under six different
commandants and had seen most of the members of his handpicked
military government detachment depart for home before him. Of the
one hundred fifty officers and civilian experts in the original group,
only eight remained. None of the highly trained enlisted personnel
were left. Howley was looking forward to the prospect of civilian life,
free from the strain of daily conflict with the Soviets and frequent disagreements with his own commanders.

Two days before Howley was scheduled to leave, General Clay again
summoned him to his office. The general broke the ice by asking him
a routine question about one of the members of the military government team, but he didn't even seem to listen to the answer he
was given. Then, as Howley stood up to leave, Clay suddenly asked a

question Colonel Howley was completely unprepared for: "Frank, how would you like to come back on active duty as commandant?"[18]

Howley's orders for his return to the United States were changed from ones calling for a permanent relocation to a new set granting him a three-week leave. On December 1, 1947, Howley officially became the American commandant at the Allied Kommandatura in Berlin.[19]

He had barely settled into the routine of his new position when George Kennan's prediction came true.

FOURTEEN

# "THE CONTROL COUNCIL NO LONGER EXISTS"

As 1948 began, General Lucius Clay's mind was not fixed on dire predictions; dire reality was more than enough to preoccupy him. In the Ruhr, the food shortage had reached such proportions that rations had been cut from the "guaranteed" level of 1,550 calories per day, a little over one-third of the average American diet, to 1,000 calories. Workers in the major cities had walked out in 24-hour protest strikes, and both American and German officials feared there would be food riots. General Clay urgently requested the appropriation of $700 million for food imports from America. The request was for more than the combined American and British appropriations for 1947 and would come entirely from American sources, as the Americans had assumed the entire responsibility for supplying Germany under the revised bizonal plan.[1] In exchange, the United States was given charge of direction of policy. Clay argued that an increase in rations was absolutely necessary before production in Germany could be increased.

The general also recognized that the increased imports were not the real solution to the problem. At least 10 percent of the imports each month failed to reach the rationed consumer. That food, and at least 40 percent of German domestic agricultural production, was being siphoned off into the black market. The American military government estimated that 731,000 head of cattle, 4,255,000 pigs, and 1,333,000 sheep had vanished into that illegal sector of the economy.[2] Overall, 50 to 60 percent of the production in the Western sectors of Germany was traded illicitly, and the people of the country were still reluctant to work merely to earn more of the worthless reichsmarks that were in circulation. Nothing could be bought with them. The people devoted their time and energy instead to acquiring, stealing, or hoarding anything of real value, in order to trade on the black market. It was a seemingly endless cycle, and General Clay knew that the only thing that would break it was reform of the German currency.

He had known this as early as 1946 and had suggested currency reform at the Allied Control Council in January 1947, but the idea had been unacceptable to the Soviets unless they were given plates for the new currency, so that they could print it at will. Remembering the experience of the occupation marks and knowing that the Soviets were still printing them at their plant in Leipzig without informing their allies of the amounts produced, the West refused to consider this and went ahead with plans for its own new marks. Working with the German economic council, which had been set up as a part of the bizonal administration, new currency was printed in the United States beginning in October 1947. It was shipped in great secrecy to Germany, where it was to be stored in bank vaults until a decision was reached on when to introduce it. Clay knew that such a decision had to come soon and that the decision needed to be made in spite of the Soviet attitude, which was growing harsher every day.

To add to their disagreement on German currency reform and their general disparagement and discouragement of the Marshall Plan, the Soviets now began a formal attack on the Anglo-American bizone. At the January 20, 1948, meeting of the Allied Control Council, Marshal Sokolovsky announced firmly that his government regarded the arrangement as constituting the establishment of a separatist German government and was therefore a gross violation of previous inter-Allied agreements. At the next two meetings of the council, the currency reform question dominated the agenda, with Clay operating under an instruction from Washington that the American policy objective was to reach quadripartite agreement, provided it could be obtained promptly. Events elsewhere in Europe were beginning to overshadow momentarily the problems in Germany, however. George Kennan's dire prediction was coming true.

When 1948 began, the people of the Western zones of Germany, and of Berlin in particular, were looking with horror and apprehension at what was happening in the countries to the east. Where the Soviets were the occupiers after the war, old regimes had been swept away. Where coalitions of Communists and more democratic parties had been formed, most had by now been supplanted by one-party rule. The peasant party leader Stanislaw Mikolajczyk of Poland had been driven into exile, as had Ferenc Nagy of Hungary, even though his Smallholders Party had won an absolute majority in elections in 1945. The democrat Nikola Petkov had been hanged in Bulgaria, and Iuliu Maniu of Romania was in a Communist prison. In the republic of Czechoslovakia, the moderate peasant and middle-class parties were struggling to survive a rising Communist tide.[3]

A small country, Czechoslovakia had been founded in the wake of the First World War through the efforts of the patriot Thomas Masaryk, only to become the first of Hitler's European victims. The country was dismembered under the Munich Pact, with the Sudetenland ceded to Germany. Later, what remained was fully incorporated into the Third Reich as the Protectorate of Bohemia and Moravia. President Eduard Beneš and Jan Masaryk, the cosmopolitan son of the founder, were ejected from the rump of the nation by the Nazis in 1938 and conducted a government-in-exile in London throughout the war, with the younger Masaryk serving as spokesman for the government. When the Czech capital of Prague was captured by Soviet troops near the end of the war, Beneš and Masaryk returned to their country and attempted to build a multiparty, democratic state as a model for both the East and the West. A democratic constitution was adopted; the president of the republic was a democrat, while the prime minister was a Communist, and several parties held seats in the cabinet. However, the government was an uneasy coalition, and the fact that democracy in Czechoslovakia was a fiction had been demonstrated when Stalin ordered it not to participate in the Marshall Plan; Klement Gottwald, the Communist prime minister, immediately agreed.

Gottwald, born in a small village in Moravia in 1896, had run away from an apprenticeship to a cabinetmaker and had become a Communist and devoted admirer of Stalin early in his political career. In 1929, when the first Communists entered the Czech parliament and had been asked about their program, Gottwald had looked directly at President Beneš and said, "My answer is simple. We are here to break your necks and I promise you most solemnly we will do it."[4]

Gottwald sat out World War II as Stalin's guest in Moscow and returned to Prague with the Red Army in 1945, becoming the leader of the party. It soon became apparent that he was ready to dispense with even the pretense of democracy in Czechoslovakia. Elections were due to be held in May 1948, but the Soviets were determined that they would not proceed. The experience of democratic elections elsewhere, and especially in Germany, had not been to the Communists' benefit. The vice foreign minister of the Soviet Union, Valerin A. Zorin, was dispatched to Prague early in February to "consult" with Czech Communist leaders during a crisis that had been precipitated when the Communist minister of the interior, Vaclav Nosek, removed eight non-Communist police officials in the capital and replaced them with members of his own party.

At a meeting of the Czech cabinet on February 13, several Social Democratic members complained about the packing of the police force with Communists and demanded that Prime Minister Gottwald order the fired officials reinstated. When Gottwald had still not acted by

February 20, the ministers resigned en masse in the belief that their resignations would force the appointment of a new government. They were fatally wrong.

Gottwald announced that he had uncovered a plot against the state and invoked emergency powers. Communist-led police looked on with apathy as party mobs sacked the headquarters of the Social Democrats. President Beneš, old and suffering from prostate problems that were inoperable due to his diabetes, refused to call out the army to suppress the riots for fear of inciting a civil war. He did, however, manage to block a new slate of cabinet officers that Gottwald had presented to him in the wake of the riots, by simply refusing to accept the resignations of the old cabinet. Then, threatened by the Communists with a general strike, the president accepted the list, and his country slipped under totalitarian rule for the second time. With the exception of Jan Masaryk, the cabinet was composed entirely of members of the Communist party.

The aged president left the capital immediately for his summer home at Sezimova Usti while the new government announced that his close friend, former minister of justice Dr. Prokop Drtina, was hospitalized with serious injuries after having attempted suicide by jumping out a window.[5]

Jan Masaryk let it be known publicly that he intended to stay on in the cabinet as a voice of moderation, but he privately arranged for his American mistress, author and journalist Marcia Davenport, to leave for London, telling her that he expected to follow shortly. The couple arranged to meet at Claridge's Hotel in about ten days.[6]

The events in Czechoslovakia stunned the world with their rapidity and brutality and they occurred while the Congress of the United States was engaged in a lengthy debate on the military budget for the country. The armed forces remained depleted; the United States Army, made up of over 8 million soldiers during the war, now mustered only 1.6 million, and the high command had made it known to Congress that, in the event of a conflict, it would be impossible for more than a division of troops to be committed without a partial mobilization. The newly established command known as United States Air Forces in Europe (USAFE) was so weak that its commander, General Curtis LeMay, feared that it "would be stupid to get mixed up in anything bigger than a cat-fight at a pet show."[7] His eleven operational combat groups, totaling 275 aircraft, faced over 4,000 Soviet planes.

Until the Czech coup, there had not seemed to be any great urgency in a buildup of military strength, and ever since the end of the war, State Department and even military personnel had discounted the possibility of war with the Soviet Union occurring in the immediate future. General Clay, at least, was having second thoughts, and he was growing uneasy from his vantage point in Berlin. In a dispatch to the U.S. Army director of intelligence on March 5, 1948, he wrote:

> For many months, based on logical analysis, I have felt and held that war was unlikely for at least ten years. Within the last few weeks, I have felt a subtle change in the Soviet attitude which I cannot define but which now gives me the feeling that it may come with dramatic suddenness. I cannot support this change in my own thinking with any data or outward evidence in relationships other than to describe it as a feeling of new tenseness in every Soviet individual with which we have official relations. I am unable to submit any official report in the absence of supporting data but my feeling is real.[8]

By now, the government of France, reacting to Soviet foreign minister Molotov's behavior at the meeting of the Council of Foreign Ministers the previous November and impelled by economic considerations, had agreed to the merger of the French zone of Germany with those of the Americans and British. This opened the way to the establishment of a West German state, with the right to participation in the Marshall Plan. Representatives of the United States, Great Britain, and France, joined by delegates from Holland, Belgium, and Luxembourg as interested parties, convened again in London even as the government of Czechoslovakia was falling. Their initial communiqué, issued on March 8, stated:

> The continuous failure of the Council of Foreign Ministers to reach quadripartite agreement has created a situation in Germany which, if permitted to continue, would have increasingly unfortunate consequences for Western Europe. It was therefore necessary that urgent political and economic problems arising out of this situation in Germany should be solved.[9]

The communiqué went on to state that, while Four Power agreement was in no way precluded, "delay in reaching these objectives can no longer be accepted."[10] It was clear that, no matter what the Soviet objections, the West was prepared to proceed on its own course in establishing a stable and economically viable West German state.

The March 7 birthday of Thomas Masaryk had been a holiday in Czechoslovakia ever since the death of the old patriot who won freedom for his country after World War I. A ceremony was held at his grave at Lany, forty miles south of Prague, on March 7, 1948, and Communist politicians made speeches at his grave most of the day. When they left, one figure remained. It was his son, Jan, the foreign minister. His head was bowed and he was weeping.

When Jan Mazaryk finally left the graveside, it was not to return to Prague. He drove instead to Sezimov Usti and spent the next two days with the president, who had not left his country home since agreeing to the Communist cabinet the preceding month. On March 9, Masaryk drove back to the capital and his third floor apartment in the Czerin Palace, where the Czech foreign ministry is located.[11]

At 6:45 a.m. on March 10, 1948, the body of Jan Masaryk was discovered in the snowy courtyard, three stories below the narrow window of his bathroom. Masaryk was in pajamas, and the bathroom window above the crumpled body was open. The Czech government announced that Jan Masaryk had committed suicide.[12] The jittery world had again been stunned.

In the same week as the coup in Czechoslovakia, Stalin sent a personal letter to Juho Paasikivi, the president of Finland, asking him to come to Moscow to discuss a "pact of friendship." Nearly eighty and ill, Paasikivi agreed to a treaty of friendship with Finland's Soviet neighbors, making the Soviet Union Finland's major trading partner and giving the Soviets the right to establish naval bases on Finnish territory on the strategic Baltic sea lanes.

On March 11, 1948, the Norwegian foreign minister, Halvard Lange, disclosed to the British and American ambassadors in Oslo that he had received information from three reliable sources that Norway was the next country that could expect to receive demands from the Soviet Union. He suspected, Lange told the ambassadors, that the Soviets would seek base rights in the Finnmark region of Norway, which they had liberated and occupied all the way up to the North Cape during the latter stages of the war. He also confided to the ambassadors that the Norwegian cabinet had agreed to refuse any demands that the Soviets might make.[13]

☆   ☆   ☆

March 18 was planned as a holiday in Berlin, celebrating the centenary anniversary of the Revolution of 1848 and the victory of the liberal movement in Germany. The four major political parties in the city had planned a joint rally to mark the event. Then the SED announced that it was convening a meeting of the People's Congress for that day. Facing the prospect of being absorbed in a Communist demonstration, the democratic parties chose to hold their own rally. The site they selected was the plaza in front of the ruins of the Reichstag, as if to remind Berliners that they had seen Hitler's totalitarian regime wipe out their liberties only a few years earlier.

Although it was a cold and rainy day, over sixty thousand Berliners gathered to listen to and cheer the speakers. Franz Neumann, leader of the SDP, spoke of there being concentration camps in the East and of the resemblance of the People's Congress to the "action committee" that had so recently snuffed out democratic expression in Czechoslovakia. Jacob Kaiser, a trade unionist whom the Soviets had removed from his post with the CDU in the East, warned against a totalitarian triumph in Germany, and Karl Hurbert Schwennicke, leader of the Liberal Democrats, averred that freedom-loving people could not compromise with Communism, because "the gallows" follows such compromise, as it had in Prague.

Ernst Reuter, unacknowledged mayor of the city, was the closing speaker. Noting the war of nerves going on in the city, he reminded his audience that Berliners had always been known for the strength of their nerves. Recognizing that Prague had fallen in a Communist coup and that Finland was being threatened, Reuter drew sustained applause when he said, "But if one should ask us who will be next, we can answer firmly and confidently: it will never be Berlin." When the applause died down, he concluded, "And if the world knows this, then we will not be abandoned by the world."[14]

☆　☆　☆

General Clay's royal-blue Cadillac Fleetwood swept into the courtyard of the headquarters of the Allied Control Council at 32 Elszholzstrasse at 2:15 on the afternoon of March 20, 1948. He was accompanied by Robert Murphy, Major General Robert Hays, and his chief of staff, Brigadier General Charles Gailey. The silver Rolls Royce belonging to British general Brian Robertson had already arrived, and the blood-red banner with the golden hammer and sickle flapped from the rightmost flagstaff of the four in the front of the building, indicating that Soviet military governor Sokolovsky was the chairman for this, the eighty-second meeting of the Control Council. In the two rooms adjoining the meeting chamber, a buffet of hors d'oeuvres, caviar, champagne, and vodka was laid out for the delegates to consume at the end of the session. Soviet hospitality after the meetings was lavish as always.[15]

Clay and his group were already at their seats under the fresco depicting Justice surrounded by cherubs that graced the ceiling of the conference room, as were the French team of General Pierre Koenig and Robertson's British delegation, when the Soviets came in. Usually punctual, Marshal Sokolovsky and his five aides were four minutes late.

Sokolovsky, his dress tunic dazzling with its forty decorations, lit one of the long black Russian cigarettes he chain-smoked and called the meeting to order. Immediately, he demanded the others consider a resolution attacking Western policy in Germany.

Koenig protested at once that any such resolution was out of order. His government in Paris was debating that issue, and any consideration of it at the level of the Allied Control Council was highly improper. Clay and Robertson were quick to agree with their French colleague. "This only proves once more that the United States, British, and

French representatives here no longer consider the Control Council as quadripartite authority in Germany," Sokolovsky countered. "They regard it as a suitable screen behind which to hide unilateral actions in the Western zones—actions directed against the peace-loving people of Germany."

Marshal Sokolovsky had just accused the Western commanders of perfidy.

"I wish to protest," General Robertson said, "against the strong language the chairman has used in describing the attitude of his colleagues," adding that he thought it best if all members refrained from using the Control Council as a vehicle for propaganda.

"I will not even attempt to reply to these charges," Clay said. "A mere casual examination of the record will show when, where, and by whom the Control Council's efforts to govern Germany have been blocked."

Sokolovsky abruptly withdrew the item from consideration and immediately launched into another attack, demanding that the other delegates report on any directives they had received at the February meeting in London.

Clay, Robertson, and Koenig in turn protested that any such directives were confidential and the marshal was out of order in making the request.

"I insist," the Soviet lashed back, "on the members informing the Control Council what took place in London. What proposals were made? What decisions have been taken on the matters under consideration?"

The Western military governors gave no answer. Sokolovsky snatched up a prepared statement from the table in front of him.[16]

"I am compelled to make the following statement," he said, and began to read from the typewritten document. "The Control Council no longer exists as an organ of government," was a line that appeared early, but the Soviet marshal continued so rapidly that even the skilled interpreters could not follow him.

General Robertson tried to interrupt, but the Soviet ignored him. When Sokolovsky finished reading, he and the rest of the Soviet delegation shoved back their chairs and rose, sweeping their papers up from their table.

"I see no sense in continuing today's meeting and declare it adjourned," Sokolovsky stated, and led the Soviet delegation from the room.[17] No date had been set for the next meeting. With everything to the east clamped firmly behind the Iron Curtain that Winston Churchill had spoken of in Fulton, Missouri, the Four Power mechanism for the administration of Germany had just been shattered by the Soviets.

Word of the Soviet walkout spread rapidly, with many learning of it from their primary news source, the 4:00 p.m. broadcast of RIAS—Radio in the American Sector. It sent a shudder through the city.

# FIFTEEN

# TIGHTENING THE NOOSE

With the breakup of the Allied Control Council, Frank Howley put the staff of the Office of Military Government Berlin into overdrive. By March 25, 1948, they had come up with a basic assumption plan that the colonel dubbed "Operation Counterpunch," providing for the buildup of food and coal stocks in the Western sectors and for emergency restrictions on power should the Soviets cut the supply that flowed from their sector. The main power plant in the American sector, ruined by Allied bombing raids in the war, still had not been repaired.

Meeting with his fellow commandants, Howley laid out the elements for them carefully. General Jean Ganeval, the French commandant, said, "I can't believe that the Russians would do such a cruel thing."

British commander Edwin Herbert was pessimistic. "They won't do it," he said, "and even if they do, we never could hold out." Herbert predicted that a Soviet blockade of food and supplies would drive the West from the city by the first of October.[1]

☆ ☆ ☆

On the evening of March 30, Lieutenant General Mikhail L. Dratvin, the deputy Soviet military governor, sent a set of identical memoranda to the American, British, and French members of the Control Council. Beginning at midnight the following day, the notes stated, all military transport along the single rail line from Helmstedt to Berlin and on the single highway corridor linking the city with the West would be subject to inspection by Soviet guards. All travelers, including Allied military personnel, would have to show individual identification papers; Soviet troops would inspect the contents of all freight trains.

General Clay reacted quickly, protesting the Soviet order and cabling Chief of Staff Omar Bradley in Washington on the morning of March 31, "Am instructing train commandants to resist by force any Soviet entry into military trains if necessary."[2] By nine o'clock that evening, he was still in telecommunication with the American capital and was unhappy with the final answer he received. The trains should proceed, he was told, but he could not increase the number of guards on them, nor could the guards fire unless the Soviets opened fire first.

By the time he got that answer, the Frankfurt-am-Main to Berlin Express was already rolling through the night toward the Soviet checkpoint at Marienborn. It got there at 2:00 a.m. and was greeted by armed Soviet guards. The train commander, a colonel, refused to allow them aboard to inspect the papers of the 300 soldiers who were passengers, and the train was shunted to a siding by the Soviets. By 9:00 a.m. it had been joined on sidings by two more American trains and the westbound French and British ones. The train commanders urgently communicated with their headquarters in Berlin by telephone, while one train, after stopping briefly and being boarded by Soviet soldiers, passed out of the station and on to the West. It was commanded by a youthful second lieutenant, John H. Asbury.

The sets of orders Asbury had been given were contradictory. The first directed him to get the train through from Berlin to Bremerhaven; the second told him to ensure that no Soviets boarded the train. At the Marienborn checkpoint, the Soviet lieutenant in charge gave Asbury a hard choice: allow Soviet soldiers to board and inspect papers or have the train sit in the station, forbidden to go forward or to return to Berlin. After a few moments of discussion, Asbury allowed two Soviet officers on board, where they performed a cursory check of identification papers. The train was then allowed to proceed.

The other trains stood on their sidings until 8:20 p.m. Then they proceeded—back in the direction from which they had come. When the Berlin-to-Bremerhaven train under John Asbury reached its destination, the young lieutenant was informed that he was to be court-martialed immediately.[3]

General Clay had decided that if he could not force the trains through the illegal Soviet controls, he would stop using them altogether. The 61st Troop Carrier Group, equipped with C-47s, the military transport version of the venerable Douglas DC-3, was stationed at Rhein-Main air base in Frankfurt. Clay ordered the group to begin immediately flying in supplies for the American garrison in Berlin. Before the first supply-laden C-47s took off with their three-ton cargoes, the fliers of Major Albert Schneider's 53d Squadron undertook a special mission. The 53d's C-47s flew empty from their base to Berlin, where they circled the city. Then they returned to Rhein-Main. Their mission was to test Soviet reaction. Most of the flight was at 5,000 feet over the Soviet zone, where they would have been easy targets for antiaircraft fire or Soviet fighters, should the Soviet Union have chosen to try to block their flight. The men of the 53d took to calling themselves "Clay's Pigeons."[4]

The Soviets began to make aggressive and unprovoked gestures within the city as well. On April 1, 1948, a squad of Soviet soldiers moved over one hundred yards into the British sector to set up a roadblock near Gatow airport. The British commandant responded by confronting them on three sides with armored cars and 400 infantrymen, leaving them only one avenue of retreat—back to their own sector. They took it.[5]

On Friday, April 2, the Soviets posted armed guards in the building in the American sector that housed the central railway administration. As the main headquarters for railroad operations in the Soviet zone of Germany, they had been using the building since the beginning of the occupation, even though it was located in the American sector of the city. The armed guards were something new, and Frank Howley was not about to accept armed Soviet troops in his sector. Thirty MPs surrounded the site on Howley's orders, informing the Soviets inside that they could leave if they wished, but no more armed soldiers could enter. Before long, three truckloads of heavily armed Soviet infantry arrived on the scene. The commandant telephoned Clay, who was attending a reunion party of West Point graduates stationed in Berlin when he took the call.

"Double the guard," Clay ordered. When the American reinforcements arrived, the additional Soviets departed, leaving one general and eight soldiers stranded in the building. On Sunday, they came out, exchanged polite salutes with the American MPs, and departed.[6]

By the time they did, General Clay had called the Soviets' bluff again. He ordered a military freight train bound for Berlin not to stop for inspection at the checkpoint. When the Soviets allowed the train to proceed unmolested, Clay resumed rail shipments of supplies to the city. In the three days that the trains had not run, the twenty-five operational C-47s of the 61st Troop Carrier Group had flown 125 tons of supplies into the city. It was more than enough to sustain the American garrison. A similar airlift, quickly mounted by the RAF and dubbed "Operation Knicker," sustained the British garrison during this brief period.

The Soviets maintained their right to inspect the papers of Allied soldiers in transit between Berlin and the West, however, so Clay continued to move his personnel by air, as did the British. Tensions mounted further on April 7. A regularly scheduled Vickers Viking of British European Airways, carrying ten passengers and crew, was on its approach to Gatow airport when it was buzzed by a Yak-3 from a nearby Soviet fighter field. After the initial pass, the Yak turned to make another and collided head-on with the civilian plane. The Soviet pilot and all aboard the airliner were killed.

An immediate protest was filed. Both British general Brian Robertson and Clay ordered that future flights to and from Berlin be accompanied by fighter escorts.[7] Marshal Sokolovsky was at first apologetic about the incident. Within days, however, he was blaming the crash on the British.[8]

In the charged atmosphere of the moment, Second Lieutenant Asbury couldn't know what to expect of his court-martial. He could be dishonorably discharged and even sent to a federal prison if he were found guilty of disobeying orders. However, on April 12, the board found that his orders had been contradictory and mutually exclusive, as Asbury's defense counsel maintained. He was acquitted.[9]

☆ ☆ ☆

At the Kommandatura the Soviets continued to be obstructive. Police president Paul Markgraf was called before the Public Safety Committee because of the alleged criminal record of Assistant Chief Schubert, whose post was in the Soviet sector. Markgraf constantly evaded the questions that the British representative, Colonel James Stewart, put to him.

To add to the problem, Colonel Kotishev, the Soviet representative on the committee, kept interrupting Stewart's questions. Finally, Kotishev stood up and loudly proclaimed, "This is not a committee meeting, but a police investigation." Then he stormed from the room, followed by his aides.[10]

The May 13 meeting of the Kommandatura dispelled any hope that the recent exchange of notes between the Western allies and the Soviets on Soviet moves in Germany would improve matters in the body responsible for the administration of the city. Of the three items on the agenda, one was dropped for lack of agreement, one was uselessly referred to the moribund Allied Control Council, and a third was debated for several hours with no results. The only thing the four commandants agreed to was the date for the next meeting.[11]

Abductions in the city continued as well, as the Soviets increased their harassment of Allied personnel. On the last weekend in April, three American sergeants visiting the Soviet War Memorial in the British sector were taken into custody by the Soviet guards and forcibly removed to the Soviet sector. There they were held for sixty hours under conditions that one American official described as ones "in which a pig might feel comfortable."[12]

On June 2, five soldiers with submachine guns, commanded by a Soviet captain, arrested the deputy chief of the civil administration section of AMG while he was shopping for a camera in the Soviet sector. Harry L. Franklin was held by the Soviets for sixteen hours. When he was released, he said, "I feel that my detention, after my identity was clearly established, is an outrage and was probably intended as such."[13]

The Communists also began a campaign calling for a nationwide plebiscite on German unity in reaction to the Western plans to merge their zones and allow the new state that was created to participate in the Marshall Plan. Members of the SED began circulating petitions calling for a vote on national unity. Germans and the Western allies both feared that the petition campaign would "give the communists the opportunity to go door-to-door, gathering the names and addresses of those who are for or against communism"[14] and that the lists might be later used for Communist blackmail. Their fears were not eased when Communist district leader Arthur Lehmann told a mass rally, "Perhaps the time will come when the card you receive for signing must be shown in order to prove that you really stand on the side of the people."[15]

The petition drive was therefore banned in the Anglo-American bizone and in the American sector of Berlin. OMGUS Berlin announced that Germans in the American sector would be protected against molestation and intimidation and added for good measure that anyone entering their sector to distribute the SED petitions would be arrested.

At the same time, rumors were spread through the city that the Western allies planned to leave in the near future. The citizens knew that if the Americans, British, and French left, anyone who had cooperated with them would face reprisals. Soviet automobiles carrying high-ranking officers cruised frequently through the Western sectors, giving the impression that they were picking out new billets to be requisitioned when the Western allies departed.[16]

The attempts of the Soviets to dominate political activity in the city extended even to the university, where students attempted to maintain an atmosphere of freedom of thought. The student body had founded an independent monthly magazine, *Colloquium,* which was often openly critical of the Soviets and their educational and political authorities. Otto Stoltz, Otto Hess, and Joachim Schwarz were the three editors and, in April 1948, they published an attack on Soviet repression of student unrest in Leipzig. The ministry of education, acting without precedent, ordered the expulsion of the three students and sparked a revolt in the process.

On April 23, over two thousand students from Berlin's university flocked to a meeting in the Hotel Esplanade, just inside the British zone, to applaud calls for the *Magistrat* to take over the university and for the establishment of a new university in the West. The RIAS relayed the speeches throughout the city.

By May 10, the *Magistrat* had taken up the cause and called on the Soviets to place the university under municipal control. The inevitable answer was negative, and the *Magistrat* gave what support it could to the foundation of a new university, even though there were no funds and it was doubtful that such an institution would be sanctioned by the Kommandatura, where the Soviets enjoyed the veto.

The students were undeterred. In early June they called a meeting of anyone interested in the project. They acquired a small vacant house in Dahlem, and with a table, a scattering of chairs, and a single telephone, they set about trying to build a new university, dedicated to "the pursuit of truth for truth's sake."[17] Within days they had hundreds of prospective students, and a faculty was beginning to take shape as professors and instructors from the Soviet zone moved to the West and teachers who were working overseas committed themselves to return to Berlin.

Through the spring and early summer of 1948, the Soviets gradually increased their pressure on the city. On April 20, they announced a new set of restrictions on barge traffic into Berlin, and they tightened requirements on travel by Germans. On June 11, all rail traffic into the city was again blocked for a day. When it resumed, the Soviets announced that the bridge over the Elbe River, on the single highway into the city from the West, was in need of urgent repairs. Traffic was diverted over back roads to a ferry that could carry only two vehicles per trip.

Through all of the harassment, General Clay kept working on his plans for currency reform. The details were arranged; in the three Western zones, but not Berlin, the old reichsmark would be replaced by a new "deutsche mark" at a drastic ratio of one new mark for ten of the old. There was hope that the spiraling inflation and black market economy that had been stymieing German recovery would end. The British and French had agreed to announce the deutsche mark on Friday, June 18, after the banks had closed. The military governor was counting on Frank Howley to brief the Kommandatura at a special meeting that the currency reform would not immediately affect the city.[18] The special meeting had not yet been scheduled. Although rumors of the coming currency reform buzzed through the city and the country, the June 18 announcement date was still a closely guarded secret, and Clay did not want to give the Soviets a great deal of advance warning.

☆  ☆  ☆

The agenda of the June 16 regular meeting of the Kommandatura was heavy with mundane items: an item about personnel at Spandau Prison, where the major Nazi war criminals were confined following their convictions at Nuremberg; a question on the reorganization of the courts; a problem dealing with the recognition of nonpolitical organizations; and a dozen others.

Colonel Howley was in his seat at ten o'clock in the morning and was surprised to see that Colonel Alexei Yelizarov, the deputy Soviet military commandant, was sitting in for General Kotikov. At Yelizarov's side was Maximov, the Soviet political advisor. Yelizarov explained to the French general Jean Ganeval, who was chairing the meeting, that the commandant was indisposed.

The meeting dragged on through the day until, at 7:00 pm, a Soviet commissar whom Howley didn't recognize entered the room and engaged in a whispered conversation with Yelizarov. The newcomer was wearing an embroidered Ukrainian shirt under his commissar's tunic, which Howley thought added an exotic touch to the proceedings. After a moment, Yelizarov asked for a recess. He, Maximov, and the oddly garbed stranger left the room. Howley and the others climbed the stairs to a third-floor dining room where sandwiches and coffee were always kept ready during the meetings. Looking down from the window, Howley caught a glimpse of Yelizarov, smoking a long black Russian cigarette, escorting his visitor to a large Horsch staff car. Howley sensed that something big was in the wind and feared that the Soviets had somehow learned the details of the Western currency reform plans.

When the meeting resumed, Yelizarov launched into a blistering attack on the Western powers' approach to trade unions. Debate on the subject went on until 10:00 pm, when the item was dropped from the agenda for lack of agreement. Three-quarters of an hour later, Howley proposed that the meeting adjourn at 11:00 p.m., as it had been in progress for nearly thirteen hours. The Soviet refused, demanding a full-scale discussion of General Kotikov's "Fourteen Points for the Amelioration of Worker's Conditions in Berlin," a subject that had been fruitlessly debated for the last eight months. Many of the fourteen points could be resolved only by the Control Council, which was the final arbiter of all labor questions, and that fact was pointed out to the Soviet delegation. It made no difference. The Soviets were adamant, so the debate began.

At 11:15 p.m. Colonel Howley had sat through enough. Rising, he cut through Colonel Yelizarov's angry recitation and addressed the chairman: "Half an hour ago I suggested that we end our meeting. I'm tired. I am going home and I am going to bed. With your permission, General, I will leave my Deputy, Colonel Babcock, to represent me."[19] It was a common custom for deputies to represent their superiors at meetings of the Kommandatura, just as Kotikov was represented by his at this meeting. General Ganeval nodded his assent.

As soon as Howley left the room, Yelizarov slammed his papers to the table and shouted, "It is impossible to continue this meeting after an action which I can only claim as a hooligan action on the part of Colonel Howley. I consider we should finish."

"I will close the meeting if so requested," General Ganeval responded.

"If Colonel Howley will not apologize, I will remain here no longer," Yelizarov yelled, scooping up his scattered papers and heading for the door.

"It is the Russians who are acting improperly," the chairman called after him. "We haven't set a date for the next meeting."

Amid the general hubbub it was difficult to make out the Soviet's response. Some thought he said, *"Nyet."* [20] Others thought they also heard "There will be no more meetings as far as I am concerned." [21]

Four Power control in Berlin had just ended.

☆   ☆   ☆

Frank Howley made it a point to stop at the U.S. Press Club in Zehlendorf after every meeting of the Kommandatura. He felt that the reporters deserved a briefing on what was happening, and there was the added inducement that the Press Club made a good martini. Arriving at midnight, Howley found only Marguerite Higgins of the *Herald-Tribune,* John Thompson of *Newsweek,* and a handful of others in the main room. Everyone else had gone for the night, thinking it was too late for any story to break. Howley barely had time to order his drink when he was called away to the telephone.

Colonel Babcock was on the other end of the line, excitedly telling him about the chaotic breakup of the meeting. Howley returned to the main room to give the few late-drinking reporters a scoop they had not expected.

Conceding that this seemed to be the end of the Kommandatura, Howley concluded, "if any joker thinks the Americans, British, and French are going to be dealt out of Berlin he has another guess coming." [22]

When he had finished the briefing, Howley returned to the lobby of the Press Club and called Lucius Clay. The general was irate and ordered Howley to report to him at his quarters at 43 Im Dol immediately, in spite of the lateness of the hour.

Howley found General Clay angrier than he had seen him in the three years they had worked together. He dispensed with their customary greetings when Howley entered.

"You have done a terrible thing," was the first thing Clay said.

Howley stood rigidly at attention and did not respond.

"And the worst of it is, you're not even sorry about it."

Howley shot back, "You're damned right I'm not."

Clay dismissed the American commandant coldly, requiring that he return at 8:00 the next morning. [23]

# SIXTEEN
# THE COLOR OF MONEY

At eight the next morning, Frank Howley sat in front of General Clay, being reminded by the military governor that he had been counting on Howley to review the currency reform plan with the Kommandatura and that the Soviets would now probably refuse to attend. The commandant was instructed to withdraw his remarks made to reporters the previous evening indicating that the Soviet action meant the end of the Kommandatura.[1] Howley tried to explain that all the Soviet walkout meant was that the Kommandatura now had the same status as the Allied Control Council—no one would know if it existed or not, and the Soviets would say it existed when that suited their purposes and that it didn't when that suited them. Howley had, in fact, expected the breakup of the Kommandatura for some time. Speaking anonymously to a reporter for *Stars and Stripes,* the commandant had predicted it late in May. He cited the fact that the Soviets were boycotting the vital public safety committee because of the ongoing dispute about the police chief, and he noted that they were now refusing to schedule meetings more than one session in advance. "I think he [the Soviet commandant] does run meeting to meeting," Howley had told the reporter. "My guess is Kotikov doesn't know when he'll receive orders to get out."[2] Colonel Howley had been right, and now he was on the carpet before the military governor again.

Howley explained, in defense of his actions, that he had taken all he could stand from the Soviets. General Clay was pacing the floor in front of him.

"Your job is to sit there and take it."

Howley's temper boiled over again and, expecting to be fired on the spot for insubordination, he shot back angrily at his commanding officer, "I thought my job was to keep them from stealing the city of Berlin."

Clay did not respond as Howley expected he would. After a moment of silence the military governor looked at his subordinate and said softly, "All right, Frank, I guess you've had your quota of conferences for one day. Go home and get some rest."[3]

There was little rest, however, for members of OMGUS Berlin at the beginning of June 1948. All were busy ensuring that the stockpiles of supplies in the city were building up. Already the warehouses of Berlin held seventeen days' supply of bread grains and flour, thirty-two days' worth of cereal, twenty-five of meat and fish, and forty-two of potatoes.[4] Medical supplies adequate for the needs of the city for six months had been laid up, thanks to the efforts of Dr. Eugene Schwartz, chief medical officer in the American sector. In January, Schwartz had heard of a drunken boast made by a Soviet general at a christening party for his newborn daughter. Referring to the Americans, the general had said, "If those swine aren't out of Berlin by June, we'll close every access there is."[5] Dr. Schwartz had taken the report seriously and had been stockpiling large quantities of medical supplies ever since.

There was little rest for some of the troops in Frankfurt as well. For nearly a week, the members of a transportation corps truck company had been working through the night. Backing up to the Reichsbank to load heavy wooden boxes labeled "Clay" and "Bird Dog," they had then been driving off under heavy guard to locations throughout the country.

Several of the soldiers thought that the operation related to events half a world away, in Palestine, where war had broken out between the Jews and the Arabs when the British pulled out.

"They can't fool me," one trucker said. "Know what we're carrying in them boxes? Ammunition for the Israelites!"

"It's ammo, all right," his coworker said, "but something tells me it's going to the A-rabs."[6] They were both wrong. The cases contained millions of freshly printed marks, which were being distributed in anticipation of the currency reform.

All across the city, Berliners rushed to buy the few remaining goods on the black market, driven by the swirl of rumors about devaluation of the currency. The price of a one-pound tin of coffee shot up to two thousand four hundred marks, up from two thousand just the day before. A single cigarette brought thirty marks to the seller. Shops across the city closed, and even the bars were empty.

Where people did gather, much of the talk was about one of the more notorious disappearances, that of journalist Dieter Friede. On November 2, 1947, Friede was summoned by a doctor to come and see a patient the doctor said he was treating. The writer arrived at the doctor's office and found no injured man. Instead, three NKVD officers were waiting. They drove off with Friede to the Soviet sector. His daughter Christine, a child of Berlin old beyond her ten years, said at the time, "I hope Papa had a chance to kill himself before they killed him."[7]

On November 7, the American military government requested an explanation, and General Kotikov had replied a week later that he would investigate. A month passed, and the Soviets issued a bland denial of any knowledge of the case, stating that they had taken no such individual into custody. Now, in June 1948, they reversed themselves, admitting that they seized Friede on November 2 and had been holding him ever since.[8] A copy of his signed confession to being a spy for the West accompanied the report in the Communist press. The story added to the tension, fear, and sense of disquiet in the city.

The people of the Western zones of Germany had been alerted that their military governments would be making an important announcement at 8:00 p.m. on Friday, June 18. Most of the country was tuned in when Robert Lochner, the American control officer at Radio Frankfurt, came on the air. Lochner had been fully briefed by General Clay on the currency reform plan, and in the moments before the broadcast, he had still been working over last-minute details of the translation with a financial expert on Clay's staff. Noting that one particular section didn't seem clear to him, he asked for an explanation, and the expert shot back, "I don't understand that part myself."[9]

Now Lochner began to explain to sixty-eight million anxious Germans that all old currency in the Western zones, except Berlin, would become invalid as of midnight on Sunday, June 20. Beginning at 7:00 a.m. on Monday, Germans would register their old currency at their food ration offices and would be entitled to receive sixty of the new blue-backed, deutsche marks in exchange for the first sixty of the old marks. Forty deutsche marks would be issued immediately and the other twenty would follow in two months. The fact that Berlin was not included in the reform plan was repeated several times during the broadcast.

Lochner's broadcast had barely concluded when General Ganeval, with the approval of the British and the active encouragement of a chastised Colonel Howley, delivered a note to Soviet general Kotikov calling for a special Saturday morning meeting of the Kommandatura to discuss the implications of the currency reform. By midnight, Kotikov's aide, Colonel Yelizarov, replied. The Soviets were unable to attend, due to the pressure of unspecified business.

One part of the business was the immediate imposition of new restrictions on travel into and within the city. All passenger travel in and out of the Soviet zone was prohibited, and vehicles from the West were barred from entering the East. While rail freight and barge traffic would be permitted to continue to enter Berlin, both the cargoes and the crews were subject to examination by the Soviets. They stated that these measures were necessary to prevent a flood of devalued currency from entering their zone.

Another part of the business was the issuance of a statement by the Soviet military governor, Marshal Sokolovsky, declaring importation of the new currency into the Soviet zone a crime. "Bank notes issued in the Western occupation zones of Germany are not being admitted for circulation in the Soviet occupation zone in Germany and in Berlin, which is part of the Soviet occupation zone," the announcement said.[10] The Soviets had made the claim that the city was theirs, and theirs alone.

That claim drew an immediate rejection from the Western powers. General Clay made a statement to the press, denouncing Sokolovsky's remarks and reiterating that Berlin was an international city. He promised to meet with his Western colleagues to determine what they could do to ease the new restrictions on travel.

Clay's statement did little to calm the fears of the Berliners, faced with a bald statement from the Soviet military governor that their city was a part of the Soviet zone. Many worried Germans stopped American personnel in the streets, asking if Marshal Sokolovsky's statement was correct.[11]

That evening, the city assembly met and listened while Acting Mayor Schroeder read a statement expressing regret that the Allies had not been able to agree on joint currency reform and appealing to all four powers to maintain the quadripartite nature of the city. She also attempted to reassure the public that the functions of city government would go on. The SED loudly objected to her statement, contending that the currency reform had split Germany and that Berliners should now act to tie their city to the Soviet authorities. Schroeder's statement was approved by the assembly; the SED members voted against it as a bloc.

The Sunday edition of the Soviet-licensed newspaper *Tägliche Rundschau* carried an article that hinted that negotiations might solve the currency difficulties, although Clay received a formal letter from the Soviet military governor the same day protesting the reforms and again asserting that Berlin was a part of the Soviet zone. Clay chose to respond by inviting Marshal Sokolovsky to a four-power discussion of the question of currency for Berlin at the Allied Control Council. To his surprise, the Soviet accepted, and the meeting was set for the evening of Tuesday, June 22. The question of a common currency for the remainder of Germany was now, however, a closed question. Even as they agreed to talks on the money that was to circulate in Berlin, the Soviets announced a currency reform plan of their own for their zone. The Soviet plan allowed the SED, various Soviet-controlled enterprises and Communist-dominated groups, and the officials of those groups as individuals, to exchange their old money for the new Soviet-sponsored marks at a one-to-one ratio. The general public got a much less favorable rate, and the regulations provided that no funds at all would be converted for "profiteers," "fascists," and some other groups. Those who had earned the disapproval of the Communists were to be deprived of their money.[12]

At the same time that he was corresponding with the Soviets, Clay assured the Berlin public through the press that United States forces were in the city to stay, even if land access was not available. The garrison could be supplied by air for an indefinite period, he said. Clay made no mention of attempting to supply the entire population of the city; that idea had been rejected as impossible in April, when options to counter the first Soviet traffic restrictions had been explored.

On Monday, June 21, Germans in the French, British, and American zones of the country stood patiently in long lines to exchange their old marks for the new currency. On Tuesday, they were amazed and euphoric at the appearance of products they had only been able to dream about and long for the previous day. Secretly hoarded goods appeared in abundance on store shelves. Butter, eggs, and vegetables suddenly became available. Bakeries produced not only bread, but pastries as well. Stockings, once available only on the black market, appeared and sold for four deutsche marks.

In Berlin, things were different and clouded with uncertainty. The price of a pound of coffee had risen to three thousand marks, and a single Chesterfield cigarette now commanded seventy-five. Both were hard to find.[13]

The special meeting of the financial experts of the four powers convened at the Allied Control Council headquarters in the old Prussian state court in the late afternoon on Tuesday. The head of the American delegation was Jackson Bennett, Clay's chief financial advisor. Bennett was dismayed to see that the Soviet delegation was led by Professor Paul Maletin, a hard-line Communist and uncompromising negotiator.[14] The French delegate managed to convince his allies that they should allow the new Soviet-sponsored currency to be the legal tender for the city, and the Americans and British agreed, provided that issuance and control of the money was under the Kommandatura rather than a single power. The Soviets balked at this, insisting that they must have sole control and repeating their recently adopted position that Berlin was an integral part of the Soviet zone of Germany.[15]

Even as the financial experts were meeting, a courier summoned Acting Mayor Louise Schroeder and her assistant, Deputy Mayor Ferdinand Friedensburg, to report to city hall. Schroeder and Friedensburg were used to calls such as this at unexpected times; it was a well-worn tactic of the Soviet liaison officers with the *Magistrat.* But they were unprepared for the demands that liaison officer Major Otschkin made on this occasion.

The Soviet handed them some documents and a handwritten note from General Lukjantschenko, the Soviet chief of staff in the city, and informed them that these were Marshal Sokolovsky's decree and the necessary orders to carry out currency reform in Berlin. Friedensburg looked at the documents and asked if the reform applied to all sectors of the city. When the Soviet answered that it did, the Germans pointed out that such a unilateral action was not permitted under the city constitution and that the *Magistrat* would be at a loss if the other occupying powers objected to the regulations and made other arrangements. Otschkin responded that he did not believe that the other Allies would object and demanded that Schroeder and Friedensburg act on the Soviet demand, bringing Marshal Sokolovsky's decree before the assembly on the following day.

The meeting of the financial experts at the Control Council building ended at 10:00 p.m., without reaching agreement. Just before it adjourned, Jackson Bennett noticed that a uniformed Soviet messenger entered and spoke with Professor Maletin. Bennett was close enough to hear the messenger tell the head Soviet delegate that the proclamation was ready and that the new financial regime would be announced in the morning.[16]

Western reaction to the Soviet declaration that only its new currency would be legal in the city of Berlin was swift. At Kaufbeuren Air Base outside of Munich several crews of the 39th Troop Carrier Squadron were assigned to fly to Rhein-Main, pick up a cargo, and transport it to Berlin. On leaving the operations office at Rhein-Main, where their ships were loaded with wooden crates marked "Bird Dog" and "Clay," the crews were issued hand grenades and ordered to blow up their airplanes if they were forced to land in the Soviet territory they would be flying over. On arrival at Tempelhof, the planes of the 39th were met by jeeps crowded with armed MPs, and the crews were ordered to stand clear of their aircraft while unloading took place. The new Western currency had arrived in the city, and the press releases announcing its introduction had been written. Berliners learned in their Wednesday morning newspapers that there would be two competing currencies in the city effective Friday, June 25.

Late on Wednesday afternoon, a few SDP members went to city hall, where the 130 members of the assembly were set to debate Marshal Sokolovsky's decree that only Soviet currency would be valid. Ruth Andreas-Friedrich and her daughter Karin were among them, and the scene she saw reminded her of accounts of the storming of the Bastille. Over 3,000 members of the SED packed the streets around Parochialstrasse and the red-brick building that housed the assembly. Red flags and banners fluttered above the crowd. The recorded voices of Walter Ulbricht and Otto Grotewohl boomed from loudspeaker trucks as the crowd chanted, "Down with the secessionists."[17] The assembly had called central police headquarters for additional men to control the crowd, but none had been sent, and it was becoming abusive and violent.

One of the SDP members of the assembly, Jeanette Wolff, a diminutive sixty-year-old grandmother who had spent six years in a Nazi concentration camp, was spat on by the demonstrators as she struggled through the crowd to enter the assembly chamber. The assembly speaker, Otto Suhr, was vainly calling for order and refusing to begin the meeting until the demonstrators had cleared out when Wolff managed to get inside. SED assemblyman Karl Mewis was standing on a bench, encouraging the demonstrators to remain. When Mewis saw Frau Wolff enter, he shouted at her, "Traitors are to stay outside." Unfazed by his threats, the gray-haired, five-foot lady strode over to his bench and toppled Mewis unceremoniously onto the floor.[18]

Acting Lord Mayor Schroeder was greeted with catcalls and jeers from the SED when she tried to gain order in the chamber. Only after she threatened to move the meeting to the American sector did Roman Chwalak, chairman of the Communist-organized trade union and SED assembly member, urge the crowd to leave the building.[19] "Comrades," he called out, "Wait outside. Our faction will keep you informed of the course of debate."[20] The demonstrators, singing the "Internationale," cleared the hall and the debate began.

Frau Schroeder explained to the assembly that it was the position of the *Magistrat* that Marshal Sokolovsky's Order 111, dealing with currency reform, could apply only in the Soviet sector and that the orders of the Western powers would apply in their sectors. SED members loudly protested that the *Magistrat* majority was following orders they had received from London and New York and that the action they were taking would split the city. One member also pointed out that the savings deposits and social insurance funds of the city were held in the Soviet sector and that these would be forfeited if the *Magistrat* action to honor both new currencies was upheld.[21]

In spite of these threats and the mob that was still gathered outside the building, the assembly voted solidly, 106 to 24, to back the *Magistrat*. Only members of the SED voted against the resolution. When the members of the assembly emerged, the mob was waiting. Those who had voted to back the *Magistrat* were viciously attacked, while the few police on duty stood by and watched. Some police officers even pointed out particular individuals to members of the mob.[22] Jeanette Wolff was badly beaten as she left the building, and several members of the assembly refused even to go outside until the crowd dispersed. A police official who helped them sneak out the back door of the building later that night was summarily dismissed by his superiors the following day.[23]

Berlin braced for the next move in the political game between the rival occupiers of the city. This seemed to belong to the Soviets, and reporters working the late shift at newspapers were the first to learn what it was. At eleven the usually quiet teletype machines of ADN, the Soviet news agency in Germany, began to clatter out a bulletin:

> The Transport Division of the Soviet Military Administration is compelled to halt all passenger and freight traffic to and from Berlin tomorrow at 0600 hours because of technical difficulties. . . . water traffic will also be suspended. . . . coal shipments to Berlin from the Soviet zone are also halted. . . . Soviet authorities have also ordered the central switching stations to stop the supply of electric power from the Soviet zone and Soviet sector to the Western sectors.[24]

The city of Berlin was under blockade.

# SEVENTEEN

# "TWO HOURS LEFT TO LIVE"

As military governor, Lucius Clay maintained his headquarters in Berlin; as commander of United States Forces in Europe his headquarters were in Heidelberg, and he and Robert Murphy had flown there on June 23, 1948, to make the necessary staff arrangements for a contingency plan that the general wanted to have in place. They met with Lieutenant General Clarence R. Huebner, whom Clay had specifically requested be reassigned from the United States as tactical military commander soon after he had taken over supreme command in Europe. Huebner was a tough disciplinarian who had entered the army as a cook and had risen from the enlisted ranks to be an outstanding combat leader. Clay's first directive to Huebner had been to reestablish the 1st Infantry Division, which he had commanded at the end of the war, as an effective fighting force. Now Clay had another task for his tactical commander—the organization of an armed convoy of six thousand men, consisting of a regimental combat team supported by armor and artillery, accompanied by a combat engineer battalion equipped with bridging equipment. General Clay wanted a column ready to roll down the autobahn from Helmstedt, straight through the Soviet zone to Berlin, when he gave the order.

Brigadier General Arthur Trudeau, the engineer who commanded the First Constabulary Brigade at Wiesbaden, was selected to command the proposed convoy, which was designated Task Force Trudeau.[1] Air Force general Curtis LeMay was instructed to be prepared to provide air support and was ready to launch a preemptive strike against Soviet fighter fields. "I think we would have cleaned them up pretty well, in no time at all," he later said.[2]

Clay and Murphy retired that night in Heidelberg, unaware of the Soviet announcement that all traffic into Berlin had been halted. They learned of it, along with the residents of the city, in the morning news reports on June 24.

Colonel Frank Howley was a busy man on what he described as "one of the most infamous days in history."[3] Soviet-controlled Radio Berlin was broadcasting a barrage of false rumors—that riots were going on in the city; that Western troops had fired on the mobs and that Germans lay dead in the streets; and that the Americans, British, and French were hastening to leave. One newscast even reported that Mrs. Howley was packing the family silver. Very early, Radio Berlin reported that the water supply would fail as a result of the power cuts, and the rumor almost fulfilled itself. Fearful Berliners rushed to fill every available container with water, and the gauges at the city's pumping stations fell at an alarming rate.

Howley contacted William Heimlich, head of Radio in the American Sector, which immediately began broadcasting a plea to Berliners to use all the water they wanted to—to give their babies baths and to take baths themselves, as there was plenty and no danger at all that the system would fail. The ploy worked, and the gauges at the water plants soon climbed back to their normal readings.[4]

Colonel Robert Willard, the United States troop commander in the city, called Colonel Howley to place his two battalions of troops at his disposal to assist in putting down the alleged riots. Howley had to assure Willard that the widespread reports were false. In many of Willard's units, the commanding officers called together their senior NCOs to brief them on the situation as they understood it. Jim O'Gorman was a nineteen-year-old corporal in Company K of the 16th Infantry Regiment, whose usual duty station was the autobahn courtesy patrol, an assignment that was now canceled. O'Gorman's company commander, a first lieutenant only a few years older than O'Gorman himself, concluded his briefing with words that sent a chill through the group.

"Gentlemen," he said. "You should know this. If the Russians decide to come in, we all have about two hours left to live."[5] It was a stunningly accurate appraisal of the situation. The three Western allies had a total of 6,500 troops stationed in Berlin. The Soviets had 18,000, there were an additional 300,000 massed in the Soviet zone of Germany that surrounded the city, and there were reports that "Stalin" heavy tanks were maneuvering near the suburbs.

Soviet announcements of restrictions continued through the day. Medical supplies from the Soviet zone were cut off, and it was proclaimed that fresh vegetables and milk brought into the city from that source would be distributed in the Soviet sector only. All deposits in the central bank, which was located in the Soviet sector, were frozen. Frank Howley knew that the nervous Berliners needed reassurance. Contacting William Heimlich at RIAS again, he arranged to make a radio broadcast at 2:00 p.m.

Without instructions from General Clay, who was still in Heidelberg, and without guidance from the State Department in Washington, Howley went on the air to promise that the Americans were not leaving Berlin and to assure Berliners that they would be supplied with food. Acknowledging that he couldn't tell them exactly how it would be done, Howley said, "this much I do know. The American people will not stand by and allow the German people to starve."

Then he concluded, "And now I will give the Russians something to chew on besides black bread. We have heard a lot about your military intentions. Well, this is all I have to say on the subject: If you do try to come into our sector you had better be well prepared. We are ready for you."[6]

The French foreign ministry announced that France intended to stay in Berlin, and General Herbert, the British sector commander, told the population that steps were being taken to meet the emergency. He did not specify what the steps were. In Heidelberg, Clay told reporters that the Soviets could not drive the United States out of Berlin by any steps short of war.[7] There was, for now, nothing but silence from the State Department in Washington.

At 5:30 in the afternoon, the SDP held a mass meeting because "Communism is trying to bring Berlin into its power by economic pressure." Berliners, the announcement said, could show that they would not take part in any arbitrary political act by attending the rally.[8] The eighty thousand people who jammed into the Herthaplatz sports stadium greeted Assemblywoman Jeanette Wolff and Acting Mayor Louise Schroeder with thunderous applause. Wolff, leaning on a cane because of the injuries she had received in the riot outside city hall, lived up to her nickname, "The Trumpet," which she had gained for her earlier tough, anti-Communist statements. "None of us can be kicked down for long," she said. "This is Berlin, not Prague. We shall not bend until our freedom is secure."[9]

How freedom for Berliners could be secured in the face of the blockade of fuel and food supplies for the city fell to the three Western military governors, whose responsibilities included supplying the city with its basic needs. However, Clay could find no support from his counterparts for his plan to ram an armored convoy down the autobahn. It was an idea that the British military governor, Sir Brian Robertson, found both foolhardy and appalling. "If you do that, it'll be war—it's as simple as that. In such an event," he told Clay, "I'm afraid my government could offer you no support, and I'm sure [French military governor] Koenig will feel the same."[10]

Robertson floated an alternative suggestion that had been developed by Air Commodore Reginald Waite, the Royal Air Force staff expert at the Control Council. Waite believed that Berlin could be supplied by air, a possibility that Clay had already briefly considered and dismissed. When he had returned to Berlin earlier, Clay had been greeted at Tempelhof by a clutch of reporters and repeated his statement that the Soviets could not drive the Western allies out of Berlin by any action short of war. Marguerite Higgins, aware that the earlier "Little Airlift" of supplies for the American garrison had been a success, asked the general if it was conceivable that the city could be supplied in the same way. "Absolutely impossible," Clay replied.[11] He knew that the strength of the United States air transport units in Europe consisted of the 60th and 61st Troop Carrier Squadrons and a few liaison airplanes—only about one hundred aged C-47s.[12]

Furthermore, at the time Robertson first made his suggestion, the RAF had only six Dakotas—the RAF designation for the C-47—flying courier runs from Wunstorf to Berlin. Its single transport unit on the continent, No. 30 Squadron, equipped with another nine Dakotas, was in the process of packing to return to England. Commanded by Squadron Leader A. M. Johnstone, No. 30 had been flying from an old Luftwaffe airfield in Schleswigland, on the Baltic in northern Germany, and the planes were configured to carry and drop paratroops, because they had been operating with the 16th Independent Parachute Brigade, recently withdrawn from Palestine.

General Clay spent most of the night of June 24 and early morning of the next day in the darkened underground communications center of his Berlin headquarters. There, telex messages sent over secure channels were boldly illuminated on huge, backlighted screens. Sipping from the uncountable cups of black coffee he consumed each day and chain-smoking Camels, Clay engaged in an electronic battle of wills with his superiors in the Pentagon and with the diplomats at the State Department. The army was universally opposed to the idea of an armed convoy to relieve the city. Secretary of the Army Kenneth Royall urged that the currency reform in Berlin be delayed, and Clay fired back that it had already begun and the people would regard any delay now as not only a betrayal but a sure indication that the West would soon leave the city. When Royall persisted, saying that he didn't think that the currency issue was one to go to war over, Clay hotly responded, "If the Soviets want war, it will not be because of Berlin currency issue but because they believe this the right time."[13]

Next, the secretary of the army returned to a suggestion he had been making since the Soviets began their threatening moves six weeks earlier—the evacuation of American dependents from the city. It seemed almost an obsession with Royall. The military governor was as adamant in his refusal to consider such a course, as he had been to the suggestion all along. He knew the effect such a move would have on the morale of the Berliners. "We should not destroy their confidence by any show of departure."[14]

In the messages that flashed to him across the Atlantic from the Overseas Communication Room on the fifth floor of the new State Department building, Clay found that his plan for an armed convoy was not just unsupported—it was disdained. Robert Lovett, the undersecretary with whom he had clashed in the past over aspects of the European Recovery Plan, openly derided the idea as "silly." Merely by demolishing a couple of bridges, Lovett contended, the Red Army could bring the effort to a standstill. "The Soviets would just sit up on the hillside and laugh," he said.[15]

Undersecretary Lovett had no better idea than Clay's armed convoy to offer; the experts at the State Department were debating the significance of the latest Soviet action and the possible effectiveness of such countermoves as barring Soviet ships from using the Panama Canal or blockading the Soviet port of Vladivostok. There was a reluctance on the part of official Washington to believe that the Soviets would actually condemn the two and one-half million Berliners in the Western sectors to slow death by starvation to further a political goal. The State Department offered no positive suggestions to the commander on the ground in Germany, and Lucius Clay, denied the ability to go ahead with Task Force Trudeau, was left to his own devices.

If the diplomats in Washington were reluctant to accept the facts on their face, there was a growing awareness in Berlin itself of what the Soviet plan was. Curt Reiss, a naturalized American who had returned to his native Berlin as a news correspondent, had built up a wide and varied set of contacts in the city, including some highly placed German Communists. One of these was Karl Schwarz, one of the chiefs of the ADN news agency. A dedicated member of the party since long before Hitler came to power, Schwarz was gradually becoming disillusioned with the Soviets and his German Communist fellows. Reiss and Schwarz met in an out-of-the-way cafe to talk of the blockade, and Schwarz told of a meeting he had had in March with the chief Soviet press officer, Major Faktorovich. His assistant, Shenya Katseva, a pretty young woman from Leningrad whose opinions were valued because it was rumored that she was General Kotikov's mistress, was there as well.

"The Western Powers no longer have the right to remain in Berlin," Faktorovich had told Schwarz. "Their presence here is a provocation."

"Your job, Herr Schwarz," Shenya Katseva cut in, "consists in explaining to the German public that it is to the interest of the Germans themselves for the Americans and British to get out of Berlin.

"And I tell you," she concluded, "the Americans will get out of the city."[16]

The Soviets could not imagine that the Americans, British, and French would allow the people of Berlin to starve to death and were certain that they would withdraw from the city before such a thing happened. The Communists reasoned that this would make the people of Berlin, and elsewhere, realize that the Americans could not protect even a single city once the Soviets had decided to take it over and that the German people and others in Europe would then flock to the

Communist party. The blockade seemed to them to be an action without risks and one that they were certain to benefit greatly from.

General Clay had had little contact with Ernst Reuter since the latter had been elected lord mayor and subsequently declared ineligible for the post by the Soviets; the military governor paid little attention to the day-to-day administration of the city of Berlin, preferring to leave that to Colonel Howley and the Kommandatura.[17] Clay devoted his attentions to the wider question of Germany. Now, however, he requested that the elected but unseated leader of the city visit him at his headquarters to discuss the problem of the blockade and the possibility of supplementing the city's supplies by air. Reuter arrived with his aide, Willi Brandt. The military governor and the political leader spoke in English, a language in which Reuter was fluent.

"Before I go ahead," Clay began, "I want you to know this: No matter what we may do, the Berliners are going to be short of fuel. They are going to be short of electricity. I don't believe they are going to be short of food. But I am sure there are going to be times when they are going to be very cold, and feel very miserable. Unless they are willing to take this and stay with us, we can't win this."

"General," Reuter answered without the least hesitation, "I can assure you, and do assure you, that the Berliners will take it."[18]

"There can be no question of where the Berliners stand. They will stand up for their freedom and be glad to accept any help they are offered," he added. Outside Clay's office, Reuter paused to remark to his aide that the general's proposal to supply Berlin by air was impossible, but that it was necessary for Berliners to resist the Communist takeover no matter what the cost.[19]

Sir Brian Robertson called on General Clay again later that afternoon, telling him that the Royal Air Force was going ahead with its plan to start bringing supplies into the city by air. While Robertson was in his office, Clay reached for the telephone. Without bothering to clear his action with either the State Department or his superiors at the Department of Defense, Clay contacted General LeMay at U.S. Air Forces Europe headquarters in Wiesbaden.

"Have you any planes there that can carry coal?" he asked.

"Carry what?"

"Coal."

"We must have a bad phone connection," LeMay responded. "It sounds as if you were asking if we have planes for carrying coal."

"Yes, that's what I said—coal," Clay repeated again.

"General, the Air Force can deliver anything," LeMay responded. "How much coal do you want us to haul?"

"All you can."[20]

Clay asked for neither permission nor approval from Washington before deciding to begin to supply Berlin by air, because he felt that the

Western rights in the air corridors into the city were clear. On the ground, had the Soviets thrown up guarded obstacles to a convoy, the United States forces would have had to initiate fighting to remove them. In the air, the onus of committing the first overt act of war would fall on the Soviets, because the only way they could stop the planes full of supplies would be to shoot them down. Clay remained convinced that the Soviets were not prepared to start a war.[21]

Royal Air Force Squadron Leader A. M. Johnstone led the nine Dakotas of No. 30 Squadron off the field at Schleswigland, flew a farewell circuit of the installation, and set a heading for the German isle of Sylt on the Baltic. During their stay on the continent, the officers and men of the unit had discovered that the resort was a popular gathering place for attractive young women, and "training flights" to the spa had become a part of their routine. Now they made two parting passes over Sylt, then pointed their noses across the North Sea to England.

Two hours later, No. 30 Squadron put down at RAF Oakington. Johnstone's aircraft had not even cleared the runway when his radio crackled.

"Squadron Leader Johnstone will report at once to the Station Commander."

Worried that he had violated some obscure air traffic regulation with the passes over Sylt, Johnstone presented himself at the Station Commander's office.

"How soon can you go back to Germany?" the commander asked.[22]

Number 30 Squadron had been reassigned to an operation given the code name "Carter-Paterson."

On Saturday, July 26, 1948, a motley collection of aging C-47s scraped together by Headquarters, USAF Europe, made thirty-four flights into Tempelhof, carrying a total of 80 tons of food and medicine. With the Soviet blockade of Berlin only a day old, the weapon that would break it was beginning to be forged.

# EIGHTEEN

# "WE STAY IN BERLIN— PERIOD"

The needs of an urban population of two and one-half million people are enormous, even on the meager rations that the people of Berlin were allotted in the summer of 1948. According to the calculations that were made by Colonel Howley's team of experts at OMGUS and by the *Magistrat*, Berlin needed 646 tons of wheat and flour each day, along with 125 tons of other cereal grains. The rations called for 109 tons of meat and fish to supply necessary protein, and 11 tons of coffee, regarded as an essential stimulant for a population on short rations, was also called for. Baking bread for a population as large as that in the Western sectors of the city required three tons of yeast each day, and the minimum requirement for as mundane an item as common salt was 38 tons. In all, the city required over 1,400 tons of food each day.

As important, in the long run, was fuel: Berlin required kerosene and heating oil in the thousands of gallons and coal by the ton, for coal was the universal fuel in the city. It heated homes, fired bakers' ovens, and powered the generators at the electric plants. Converted to gas at the municipal gasworks, it was the source of cooking fuel for the majority of Berliners.

The planners calculated a total of 4,500 tons of food and fuel as being necessary each day as the minimum amount required to sustain the city. No one had ever contemplated making such an effort by air before, even though the idea of air supply is nearly as old as powered flight itself. During World War I, the Royal Flying Corps used nine small biplanes in an effort to supply a garrison at Kut during the Mesopotamian Campaign. In spite of the 160 missions that were flown, the supply mission failed, and the garrison surrendered. The British had greater success with a mission to supply a group of French and Belgian troops in the Houthulst Forest by air in 1918. Between the first and the fourth of October, No. 82 and No. 218 Squadrons flew nearly 200 missions and dropped 60 boxes of ammunition and 1,220 sandbags packed with

18 pounds of rations each to the beleaguered troops. The supply drop was the key to the successful defense of the position.[1] During World War II, the Soviets had made unsuccessful attempts to supply the city of Leningrad by air, and Hermann Göring's boastful offer to have the Luftwaffe supply 300 tons of food and ammunition a day to the beleaguered German troops at Stalingrad ended in utter failure.[2]

The single successful large-scale supply mission in aviation history was the one conducted by the United States over "the Hump" of the Himalayas in the China-India-Burma theater during World War II. Commanded by Brigadier General William Tunner and operated to supply the needs of 60,000 American troops and the Chinese armies, the "Hump Airlift" had flown 72,000 tons from India to the troops in China during its best month. That was slightly more than half of the calculated minimum required per month for the city of Berlin.

General Clay, trained as an engineer at West Point and with a keen mind honed by years of experience on massive public works projects and on the problems of materiel procurement during the war, recognized the magnitude of the problem at once. Even using the most modern transport aircraft available, the C-54, with its cargo capacity of ten tons, an airlift to sustain Berlin would mean landing 450 aircraft per day in the city.[3] While he was still hopeful of convincing Washington that the armed convoy would succeed and that the aerial supply mission would be short-term, Clay wanted an all-out effort to supplement the modest stock of supplies that Colonel Howley's "Operation Counterpunch" had built up in Berlin.

In Wiesbaden, Curtis LeMay still had not grasped how consequential the airlift could become or how serious General Clay was about it.[4] LeMay had won a reputation as a hard-driving, hard-charging, hard-nosed combat leader as a bomber commander against both the Germans and the Japanese. Born in Columbus, Ohio, in 1906, he had not realized his boyhood ambition to be appointed to the Military Academy. He had instead studied engineering at Ohio State University and enrolled in the ROTC program there. Granted a commission in the Field Artillery Reserve in 1928, he went on active duty at Fort Knox and did not complete college until 1932, when he was again stationed in Ohio. But first, inspired by Lindbergh's trans-Atlantic flight, he took time to attend flight school and transferred to the Army Air Corps.

He was a captain in March 1941 and the rapid promotion of veteran flying officers made him a colonel by March 1942, when he was selected to command the 305th Bombardment Group and lead it to England as one of the first elements of the newly formed Eighth Air Force. He almost missed the trip. After a training flight in Muroc, California, shortly before the unit was to fly to Europe, he complained to the flight surgeon of numbness on the right side of his face. It was diagnosed as Bell's palsy. LeMay chose to reject treatment for the ailment rather than miss going overseas. While he partially recovered, the right side of his face never regained full mobility or feeling, and the trademark cigar that he often clamped in his teeth even on formal occasions masked the fact that the right side of his mouth drooped.

While flying in Europe, LeMay won a Distinguished Service Cross, Distinguished Service Medal, and Silver Star and was elevated to the rank of major general at the age of 37. Transferred to the China-India-Burma theater in 1944, he headed the 20th Bomber Command and later directed the 21st Bomber Command in the low-level incendiary raids that laid waste to most major Japanese cities. He was involved in the planning of the nuclear strikes against Hiroshima and Nagasaki that brought about the rapid end to the Pacific War.

When he returned to the United States after the Japanese surrender, the governor of Ohio offered him appointment to the United States Senate to replace Harold Burton, newly appointed to the Supreme Court. LeMay declined because he wanted to stay in the Air Force.[5] His assignment to command the U.S. Air Forces in Europe came after a tour as deputy chief of the air staff for research and development in Washington.

While only a few years earlier Curtis LeMay had commanded a force that could put over a thousand bombers in the air to obliterate a city, he now struggled to pull together a few outworn transports to sustain one. With Clay's approval, he cabled General Lauris Norstad, the Air Force deputy chief of staff for operations, requesting thirty C-54 transports.

In the city, the Communist press kept up the drumbeat of propaganda and rumor. It reported that the Berlin Electric Company had coal enough for only another ten days of power and that industries were grinding to a halt. It accurately reported that there was food for only thirty days in the Western portion of the city. SED leader Wilhelm Pieck told a press conference that the Berlin crisis could be settled only if the Western allies departed.[6] In the Soviet sector of the city, the first arrests of people found to be in possession of western deutsche marks were made. The charge filed against them was fraud and violation of Sokolovsky's Decree 111.[7]

In Washington, Secretary of Defense James Forrestal, Undersecretary of State Robert Lovett, and Army Secretary Kenneth Royall informed President Harry Truman on June 25 that no documents had been found in any of their records to confirm that the United States had legal rights to access to Berlin. While the matter had been discussed at various of the wartime conferences, the right of access had never been formalized. They also informed the president of Clay's initiation of the supply lift. On Saturday, June 26, Truman directed that the airlift be put on a full-scale, organized basis and that every available plane in the European

Command be pressed into service, in the hope that Berlin could be fed until the diplomatic deadlock could be broken.[8]

Lovett and Forrestal joined Secretary Royall in his office in the Pentagon at 2:45 on Sunday afternoon for an emergency meeting to discuss the Berlin situation. General of the Army Omar Bradley, General Norstad of the Air Force, and Secretary of the Navy John Sullivan also sat in. Even though the situation in Berlin had been deteriorating through the spring, this meeting was the first at which the question of a counterreaction to the Soviet pressure was faced at high levels in the American government. The meeting took place under the worst possible circumstances, with everyone talking at once about a complicated situation, but the choices eventually boiled down to three: The United States could either leave Berlin, a view supported by many; attempt to stay, hoping for a diplomatic solution; or expect to fight a major war with the Soviet Union.

General Bradley, Clay's immediate superior as army chief of staff, did not think highly of the idea of an armed convoy. He had said of Clay's cabled proposal to place armed guards on the trains to Berlin earlier in the year, "If I had enough hair on my head to react, this cable would probably have stood it on end," and Clay's views on the current situation came to be known in the discussion group as the "shoot our way into Berlin" policy.[9] Knowing the weak state of American armed forces, Bradley urged extreme caution in any possible confrontation with the Soviets, fearing that it might lead to an all-out war. He suggested that armed convoys should not be considered except as a last resort.

The question of supplying Berlin by air did not even come up, and while the meeting didn't end until 7:00 p.m., very little was settled. All that was decided was that Forrestal, Lovett, and Royall would meet with the president the following day and present the major issues, with the departments of State and Army having short statements of the alternative courses available, along with pro and con arguments for each.[10]

There was no such indecision in London. The same day as the emergency meeting in the Pentagon, Foreign Secretary Bevin announced to a group of six Americans gathered in his office that the full British cabinet had just agreed that under no circumstances would Great Britain pull out of Berlin. The news came as a shock to Major General Albert Wedemeyer, the United States Army director of plans and operations. He had been sent to Europe on an emergency mission by General Bradley to sound out British intentions in the crisis and to prepare for the evacuation of Berlin. That was the course both Bradley and Wedemeyer favored, given the indefensibility of the city against a Soviet attack. Bradley had also by this time arranged for a personal evacuation from the city. His daughter, Lee, and two grandchildren were in the city, where their father was on duty with the air force. Bradley felt that the loss of his own family members if the Soviets overran the city might incapacitate him for his duties as chief of staff, so he requested that the air force reassign his son-in-law. He was soon back in Washington at a new job on the Air Staff at the Pentagon.[11]

In Germany, in response to the presidential order to place the airlift on an organized basis, LeMay put his headquarters commander in Wiesbaden, Brigadier General Joseph Smith, a gruff forty-seven-year-old, in charge. Telling Smith that it was a short-term effort of a couple of weeks, LeMay asked him what he thought he needed to do the job. Smith requested a couple of operations officers and a few mechanics, without being specific.

An air force public relations man, thinking to capitalize on the potential drama of the operation, suggested to General Smith that the operation be given the code name "Operation Lifeline."

"Hell's fire," Smith responded. "We're hauling grub. Call it 'Operation Vittles.'"[12]

The British had by now begun hauling a daily load of sixty tons of food into Berlin, and Squadron Leader Johnstone's No. 30 Squadron was back in Germany. The RAF Station at Wunstorf, designed by the Luftwaffe with barracks to accommodate 700, was expecting the arrival of 1,600 personnel within days. The hastily chosen code name for the British effort, Operation Carter-Paterson, was becoming troublesome, however. Carter-Paterson happened to be the name of the largest furniture moving firm in Great Britain, and the Communists, seizing on this, loudly proclaimed that it was just another indication that the English intended to scuttle and run from the city. The name was quickly changed to one that indulged the British fascination with puns—Operation Plain Fare.

At the White House on Monday, June 28, 1948, Harry S Truman listened intently as Robert Lovett outlined the details of the previous day's meeting in the Pentagon. When Lovett reached the possible alternatives, beginning with the abandonment of the city, Truman cut in sharply to say something that startled everyone in the room.

"There is no discussion on that point. We stay in Berlin—period."

Army Secretary Royall, thinking the president's reaction too swift and unconsidered, protested.

"Mr. President, have you thought this through?" he asked, going on to point out that the United States might be committing itself to a position where it might have to fight its way into the city.

"We will have to deal with the situation as it develops," Truman shot back, "but the essential position is that we are in Berlin by terms of an agreement and that the Russians have no right to get us out by either direct or indirect pressure."[13]

At the moment he made the commitment that the United States would stay in Berlin, the president was at the beginning of a domestic political campaign that not even his closest friends or advisors thought he had a chance of winning. On the same day that the Soviets had clamped the blockade on Berlin, the Republican party had nominated Governor Thomas E. Dewey of New York for president. Most political observers in the country expected that Dewey would be elected in a landslide in November. Truman did not consult his White House political staff on the initial decision about Berlin, nor, during the months that followed, did he ever ask them for input on how his handling of the crisis would make him look or if it was to his political advantage. The president simply stated his intention to stay in the city and let no one doubt that he meant what he had said.[14]

That night, Robert Lovett, who had strongly advocated evacuating the city, cabled the American ambassador in London to notify him of the U.S. intention to stay. General LeMay received an urgent cable as well. This one came from the Air Force chief of staff and said:

> Approximately 39 C-54 Skymasters, passenger and cargo carrying acft [aircraft], from the Alaskan, Caribbean and Tactical Air Commands of the USAF have been ordered to the Frankfurt area of Germany at the request of the Theater Commander, Gen. Lucius Clay, for increased air facilities to supply Berlin. The airplanes will begin leaving their bases within 24 hours, singly or otherwise as they become operationally ready for the mission.[15]

Until the Skymasters arrived, however, the vital supplies for Berlin would have to be hauled three tons at a time in the available C-47s in Europe. A twin-engine plane originally designed for passenger use by the Douglas Aircraft Corporation in 1934, the C-47 had been a mainstay in every theater of the war, hauling cargo and troops and making parachute drops. Most of the available C-47s in Europe were battle-worn veterans, some still painted with the black-and-white underwing stripes they had worn during the Normandy invasion in 1944. Others were an incongruous dusty-rose color that gave witness to their service in the desert campaign in North Africa in 1943. By requisitioning every available plane in the theater, LeMay brought together 110 C-47s for the Berlin run.

Crews were pulled together by ordering anyone with a set of wings on his chest and a few hours of multiengine time in their logbooks into the air. In many cases, the fliers remained responsible for their primary jobs as well, meaning that they would work at them for eight hours, then put in an additional eight hours or more of flying. Operations officers, public relations specialists, and others in staff positions suddenly found themselves making two flights a day into Berlin. General LeMay himself made several flights hauling supplies.

Among the first men sucked into the vortex of the fledgling airlift was 2d Lieutenant Robert Wilcox, a liaison pilot with the headquarters of the Fifth Supply Wing at Erding Air Force Depot in central Germany. Wilcox was given a set of orders that pulled him out of his desk job and placed him on a forty-five day temporary duty assignment to fly in the airlift. His commanding officer, a major, erupted in anger and said that he would have the orders canceled in ten minutes, but this didn't work. Wilcox canceled his own plans for a leave in Switzerland and flew off to Wiesbaden. On his first flight into Berlin in a C-47, he carried 6,000 pounds of canned crushed pineapple; on the second flight, his load was three tons of flour. Wilcox and his fellow pilot, "Nick" Nicholson, got back to Wiesbaden from their second flight at 10:00 p.m. At the end of their debriefing, the operations officer told them that their first flight the next day was scheduled for 2:15 in the morning. They had a scant three hours to get some sleep.[16]

Teletypes were clattering out orders in the headquarters buildings of air force units around the world. In Anchorage, Alaska, the wingtips and tails of the C-54s of the 54th Troop Carrier Squadron were painted a bright orange-red so that if one of them went down in the Arctic it would be easier to spot from the air. The officers and men of the flight crews were issued snowshoes as emergency gear. At 6:00 p.m. they were called together by their commanding officer, Lieutenant Colonel James Sammons, who said to them, "Gentlemen, this is what we've been waiting for."

One of the pilots muttered, "Maybe you have, but we haven't."[17] Nearly half of the men had wives and families who would be left behind in Alaska. By 9:30 the next morning, the 54th was on its way to Europe. Not knowing what else to do with them, they had packed their snowshoes along with the rest of their gear.

The 20th Troop Carrier Squadron left from the Panama Canal Zone on equally short notice, and the 19th flew out of Hickam Field in Hawaii the next day. The men of the 19th left no wives and families behind them. They flew over their relatives halfway between Hawaii and California. Their dependents were on an army transport ship, sailing to join them at what they believed would be their new base. By the time the ship docked, the husbands and fathers they expected to meet were already half a world away.

A gathering of eagles was beginning in Germany.

# NINETEEN

# LEMAY COAL AND FEED COMPANY

As the flights of C-54s headed for Europe, Brigadier General Joseph Smith called a meeting of his small staff to assess the airlift effort. When it came time to make a forecast of potential performance, he called on Major Edward Willerford, who had been engaged in working out plans for the operation, even though he was a combat flier who did not even know the carrying capacity of a C-47 when he was given the assignment.[1]

Willerford stood up and said, "I estimate that by July 20 we'll be flying in 1,500 tons every 24 hours." On the previous day, the airlift had carried only 384 tons into the city, and all of the other officers in the meeting stared at him with consternation. To the young air cargo officer, their expressions seemed to say, "Get the strait jacket. Poor old Willerford is tetched in the head."[2]

On the flight lines, air crews began to put up makeshift signs and scrawl in chalk on the sides of their ships, "LeMay Coal and Feed Company—Round-the-clock service—Delivery guaranteed." The operation began in the best tradition of seat-of-the-pants flying. The confusion that Lieutenant Robert Wilcox and his partner, Lieutenant "Nick" Nicholson, encountered and the hours that they put in were typical of the early days of the airlift. Told that the first flight of their second day on the job would be a bare three hours after they had landed, they grabbed one hour of sleep and dutifully reported to operations at 2:15 a.m., only to be informed that something was wrong with their plane and that they should report back at 12:30. That flight did not go far, as the left engine began to misfire badly soon after takeoff, and they were forced to return to their base.

They were then told that their first flight on the next morning would be at 1:15 a.m. Just before midnight, the time of that flight was changed to 6:15 a.m. Wilcox confided to his diary that evening, "It's getting so that we're living on such a confused schedule that we can hardly tell what day it is."[3]

In the middle of the night, the headquarters orderly informed Nicholson and Wilcox that all takeoffs had been postponed until 7:00 a.m., due to the weather. When the pilots checked with Operations, they discovered that their flight wasn't due off until 2:30 in the afternoon. Just before going to lunch, however, they checked again because of the continuing confusion, to learn that their takeoff time had been moved up to 12:30 p.m., and no one had bothered to inform them. Skipping lunch, they dashed down to the flight line—and sat in their plane until 4:15 p.m., when it was finally loaded and they were cleared to take off. The following day, the two pilots hung around on the field until 5:40 p.m. before they got off, but an apparently pleasant surprise was waiting for them when they landed.

As Nicholson and Wilcox came dragging into Operations just before midnight, they noticed that a coffee and donut shop had been set up. Wilcox thought that someone was finally giving some thought to taking care of the troops, but when he asked for a donut, he got a shock. The girl behind the counter sweetly informed him that they were for sale. It was a concession stand. Wilcox was disgusted.[4]

There are two red lines, each one-inch wide, in the green carpet of the House of Commons. They run in front of the benches of the opposing parties, and it is a rule of the House that no debater may step across the red line in front of his or her bench. The lines are there out of a tradition that grew from a practical purpose, for they are just far enough apart that a man with a drawn sword cannot strike someone on the opposing side.

There were no swords, real or verbal, drawn on June 30, 1948, when Commons took up the question of the Labor government's position on Berlin. Ernest Bevin rose from his bench to state, "We cannot abandon those stouthearted Berlin democrats who are refusing to bow to Soviet pressure." Acknowledging that "a grave situation" might arise, Bevin concluded, "His Majesty's Government and our western allies can see no alternative between that and surrender, and none of us can accept surrender." The cheers that greeted the statement came from both sides of the House.

Summing up for the Tory opposition, Harold Macmillan said, "We must, if we are frank with ourselves . . . face the risk of war. The alternative policy—to shrink from the issue—involves not merely the risk, but the certainty of war."[5] That grave pronouncement drew more cheers. When the roll was called, the entire House, with the exception of the single Communist member, voted to support the position of the government.[6] The British lion had roared its indignation over the Soviet actions in Berlin.

The British air operation, however, was getting off to as shaky a start as the American one. Group Captain Noel Hyde was sent to Germany by RAF Transport Command Headquarters in England to coordinate the British effort. He found out on arrival at the RAF station at Wunstorf that the headquarters of British Air Forces Overseas—the European RAF command—had given identical orders to Group Captain Wally Bigger, who had reached Wunstorf the same day. The "clarifying" orders that followed did little to help, stating that the BAFO officer at Wunstorf would exercise operational control over transport aircraft allotted to him by BAFO, but that he would do it through the RAF station commander, who would get his orders from the Transport Command.[7] It took several weeks after that confusing order to iron out the organizational details of Operation Plain Fare, but it was eventually agreed that the task should fall to Transport Command, as BAFO had no experience whatever in mounting a complex airlift effort.

While the administrators haggled, Dakotas began to accumulate at the base at Wunstorf, and it became heavily congested. In addition to Squadron Leader Johnstone's No. 30, the planes of Squadrons 46, 53, 77, and 238 crowded onto the field, and a further squadron of four-engine York aircraft was expected in a week. Wunstorf was a small airport, originally built by the Luftwaffe as part of its 1934 expansion, and a single Luftwaffe bomber group had used it as a base for raids against England in 1940. It had then been relegated to a training role, although a few fighters had been based there in the last stages of the war. Equipped only with two concrete runways and a perimeter track, there were no hard stands for parking or unloading aircraft. The rest of the field was sod, except for the aprons in front of the hangers. From this meager facility, with accommodations for 700 men now jammed with 1,600, the RAF was ordered to make 161 Dakota sorties per day, carrying a total of 400 tons, plus an additional 6 trips on the normal, scheduled Dakota service into the city.[8] The day after the order arrived, it began to rain, and the aircraft and trucks churned the unpaved portions of the field into a sea of mud.

At the Pentagon, Major General William H. Tunner, the recently appointed deputy commander of the Military Air Transport Service, began to follow the developments in Germany closely, even though his MATS unit was not directly involved. The C-54s speedily deployed to Germany after the president's order had been taken from the Troop Carrier Command, which had nearly three hundred of the ten-ton-capacity aircraft. MATS had nearly three hundred more, but its resources had not been tapped as yet. Tunner, the only man in the world who had ever run a large-scale aerial supply operation, felt strongly that this was a mistake and that MATS should be immediately involved in the Berlin operation.

Forty-two years old, Tunner was the fourth child of Austrian emigrant parents. He learned in a high school civics class that the United States maintained a military academy at West Point where a boy could get a free college education. His family had already put his older sister through teachers college, and his two older brothers were attending college, so the financial strain on the family was large. His congressman informed Tunner that he made appointments from his district on a competitive basis, so Tunner crammed for the examination, achieved the highest mark, and entered West Point at age seventeen. By the time he emerged as a second lieutenant, he had fallen in love with flying. During his senior year at the academy, the cadets had been posted to Mitchell Field on Long Island for a week to learn about the Air Corps. There, Tunner flew as a passenger in five different aircraft and had no further questions about the branch of service he would choose on graduation: it would be the Air Corps. He entered and completed flight school and had been flying for a year before he told his parents of his choice. He hadn't wanted to worry them.

Tunner trained initially as a bomber pilot, but soon moved into transport flying. Assigned first to Rockwell Field in California, he later was an instructor at Randolph Field and served in the Panama Canal Zone. He got his first command, that of the Memphis Air Corps Detachment, when he was a captain with eleven years of service. He was the only officer in a detachment consisting of a sergeant, fifteen enlisted men, and a civilian secretary. The duties consisted of building up a flying reserve corps by enticing civilians with an interest in flying to accept reserve commissions and ensuring that military planes stopping in Memphis received prompt and efficient service.

In the middle of 1939, Air Corps major Victor Blau arrived from Washington to inspect the Memphis Detachment. Impressed with what he saw, Blau turned to Tunner toward the end of the inspection and said, "Say, Bill, how'd you like to come to Washington?" Tunner was characteristically blunt. "Frankly, sir," he said, "there's nothing I'd hate more."[9]

His transfer came through less than a month later. He was assigned to the operation that would grow into the Ferrying Command, the unit responsible for delivering new airplanes from factories to combat units and to Allied air forces. When a history of the Ferrying Command was written, the historian offered a portrait of William Tunner:

> An unusually handsome man, cold in his manner except with a few intimates, somewhat arrogant, brilliant, competent. He was the kind of

officer whom a junior officer is well advised to salute when approaching his desk. His loyalty to the organization he commanded was notable, and so was his ability to maintain the morale of his men.

Air Transport Command Headquarters came to look upon him with a mixture of exasperation, admiration, and reliance. They wished he would mend his ways, be less independent, more willing to conform. Action to realize this wish was baffled by the frequency with which the non-conformist proved to be in the right.[10]

From the Ferrying Command, Tunner was assigned to the China-India-Burma theater and placed in charge of airlifting supplies over the Himalayas—the Hump—from bases in India to operational areas in China. His China-India Division of the 10th Air Force kept sixty thousand American soldiers and nineteen Chinese armies supplied so that they could continue to tie down over a million and a half Japanese soldiers. Over a million tons of supplies, including food, ammunition, and gasoline, and four entire Chinese armies had been airlifted over the forbidding Himalayan mountain barrier by Tunner's command. The India-China Division earned commendations from the highest echelons of the Army and the Army Air Forces. When it launched an all-out effort on Army Air Forces Day in 1944, its planes flew 1,118 round trips over the mountains, delivering 5,327 tons of supplies with an accident rate of zero that earned a cable from General Albert C. Wedemeyer, commander of U.S. forces in the China theater: "The achievements of your command . . . will go down in history as one of the outstanding records of the war."[11] William H. Tunner had written the book on air transportation of supplies and knew more about running an airlift than anyone in any air force in the world. Yet no one had asked him a thing about the growing Berlin operation.[12]

Elsewhere, the potential to supply the city by air was gaining attention. At the State Department, Clay's oft-time foe, Robert Lovett, was studying the question. A flier himself, Lovett had won the Navy Cross during World War I by leading a daring Hadley-Page bomber raid against German submarines bases at Bruges, Belgium, while his unit was attached to the Royal Naval Air Service.[13] Later, Lovett had served as Assistant Secretary of War and had concentrated on the Air Corps.

Now he began informally to sound out acquaintances from those times and became convinced that the city could at least be fed, if not supplied with coal, by air. He conveyed that conviction to Defense Secretary Forrestal on June 30.[14]

Army chief of plans General Albert Wedemeyer, who had been the recipient of the supplies Tunner had airlifted over the Hump during the war, was also thinking about a large air-supply operation to Berlin. While in London, he had dined with Air Marshal Sir Charles Portal, now retired from the RAF and working on Britain's nuclear program. They discussed the potential of an airlift, Portal voicing his conviction that one could succeed. Later, in Berlin, Wedemeyer reviewed the matter with Clay, who still regarded the airlift as a temporary measure designed to stretch out the existing stock of supplies in the city until a diplomatic solution was found or until he could gain approval for his armed convoy.

The city itself was beginning to take on the same look it had had during the first horrible summer after the war. At night, the uncleared rubble from the bombing and shelling again became seemingly endless caverns of dark and menacing ruins as street lighting was cut 75 percent. Both the members of the occupation and the Berliners, crowded into damaged but usable buildings, were reduced to a few hours of electricity per day. Entertaining by the Allied families virtually ceased, and one Berlin nightclub operator complained about having to use candles: "At other times this might provide an intimate atmosphere, but how can you be intimate when there is no crowd?"[15]

There were unseen dangers in the rubble and the ruins as well. Thousands of unexploded bombs and shells lurked there, and demolition disposal units were constantly being dispatched around the city to cordon off blocks and disarm them. Even the occupiers of the city sometimes encountered such ordnance in relatively undamaged sections of the city. On one occasion, Colonel Howley's oldest son, Dennis, and one of his friends came on an unexploded bomb on the banks of a canal not far from the Howley home at Geldfertstrasse 2123. With the disdain of twelve-year-olds for danger, they enlisted Dennis's younger brother Peter, eight, in an effort to try to explode the bomb by pitching rocks at it. Luckily unsuccessful in their efforts, the Howley boys mentioned their adventure to their parents that evening. The bomb squad arrived on the scene soon after.[16]

The streetcars and the subways in the city stopped running at 6:00 p.m., and the citizens could not even listen to radios for news, because of the power cuts. Colonel Howley quickly realized that this would allow rumors to gain a foothold and pressed the ingenious radio men of RIAS into developing a method of broadcasting news to thousands of homes without power. RIAS sent out a fleet of sound trucks to roam the city, stopping at street corners and switching on their loudspeakers for news programs. Crowds rapidly gathered around them wherever they stopped.

The problem of dual currencies continued to plague the people and the government of the city. Cut off from funds by the Soviets, the *Magistrat* was supported by the Western powers, and the police and other municipal workers demanded to be paid in Western marks rather than those of the East. On the black market, the exchange rate was thirty Eastern for one Western mark, and the permutations of purchasing the simplest of goods were bewildering because different commodities required payment in different ways. Ruth Andreas-Friedrich's daughter, Karin, complained, "Are we mathematical acrobats, or what? Matches, only Western money. Onions, half East and half West. Raisin allotment, Western money. Sugar coupons, Eastern money. A small bunch of chives, half and half. Soap, Eastern currency. The matching soaking agents, Western currency."[17]

It was equally confusing for the publishing house where Ruth Andreas-Friedrich now worked. The publisher informed her that magazines could be paid for only in Eastern money, but that the printer demanded to be paid in Western marks. The employees demanded at least 25 percent of their pay in Western currency, but all of the income was in marks from the East.[18]

The drone of the planes in the sky, landing in Berlin at a rate of one every eight minutes, was somewhat reassuring, but Andreas-Friedrich and her daughter had both heard one of the most widely circulated stories in the city about Soviet plans—the parable of the wart.[19] It was one that remained current throughout the blockade, told over and over in various versions.

The story went that a German-speaking Western intelligence officer wearing civilian clothes somehow found himself seated between two Russian officers on a bus, or a subway, or in some other place.

"The Americans seem to be making out all right with their airlift," the first Russian commented, and the second replied, "Yes, but this morning I was talking to Alexander Gregorovitch—"

"Who?"

"You know, the General. Alexander Gregorovitch says we'll give the Americans the wart treatment."

"What's the wart treatment?"

"Well, when you have a wart on your finger, you tie a string around it tight, and keep tightening it. Then, you wait until the wart falls off."[20]

As the Berliners worried about what would happen next, the twin-engine C-47s that LeMay and Smith had scraped together from all across Europe continued their flights into the city, and the larger C-54s from across the globe began to arrive at Rhein-Main. The first of the ten-ton-capacity planes landed at 9:30 on the morning of June 30. By 7:36 p.m., it had taken off on its first run to Berlin with a full load of flour.

## TWENTY

# TEETHING PROBLEMS

As a countermeasure against the harassment of Western personnel who entered the Soviet sector, General Clay had ordered the enforcement of a traffic safety program in the American sector, knowing that it would mean the arrest of high-ranking Soviet officers. Driving at high speeds in cars that they had confiscated from Germans, many of them passed through the American sector each day en route between their homes in Potsdam and the Eastern portion of the city.[1] The blockade had barely begun when one of the American safety patrols gave chase to a limousine that was "going to beat hell," in the words of one of the American MPs who managed to pull it over after a two-mile pursuit down the Potsdamer Chaussee.[2] Armed bodyguards who had been following the limousine caught up, leaped out of their car, and brandished machine guns, while the driver of the limo shouted, "Marshal! Marshal!" The MPs, unfazed by the shouting and the weapons, shoved a tommy gun in the pit of the limousine passenger's stomach, and the sergeant in charge of the traffic patrol sent for his lieutenant. The lieutenant called a colonel, who took an hour to show up. When he did, he recognized the passenger as Marshal Vassily Danilovich Sokolovsky, the Soviet military governor.[3] The marshal was allowed to proceed with a warning not to break the speed limit again.

At the time General Clay felt bad about the incident, as he and Sokolovsky had once been what Clay considered friends. The American military governor called on the Soviet marshal the same day as the incident, expecting that Sokolovsky would treat it in his usual humorous way. Instead, the Soviet was cold, hostile, and indignant, saying that the arrest had been a deliberate plot to humiliate him.[4]

Consequently, Clay did not know exactly what to expect when he and the two other Western military governors called on Marshal Sokolovsky on July 3, in an effort to exhaust all possibilities of resolving the current crisis locally. The Western generals proceeded separately to Soviet headquarters in Potsdam, in the company of Soviet escort officers. When they were ushered together into Sokolovsky's office, the marshal was waiting with three other officers whom Clay had never seen before.

General Brian Robertson, the British commander, acted as the Western spokesman and expressed concern over the deterioration of relations, explaining that they wished to discuss an agreement on the currency issue that would allow the resumption of normal traffic into and out of Berlin. Sokolovsky was again cold and unreceptive. He interrupted Robertson's presentation to state—blandly, in Clay's account of the meeting—that the "technical difficulties" that had halted traffic would continue to exist until the West had abandoned its plans for a separate West German government.[5] Sokolovsky's statement was the first one from an official source that named the plans for establishment of a government in the West as the real reason behind the Soviet blockade. Sokolovsky didn't even wish to discuss the currency question with his counterparts. It was evident to Clay that Sokolovsky was confident that the West would soon be forced out of Berlin. It was not a remarkable conclusion on the Soviet's part, as the Allied airlift was off to a shaky start.

At the RAF base at Wunstorf, it had rained for eighteen hours straight, and twenty-six of the Dakotas assigned to Operation Plain Fare were out of commission with electrical problems. The mud was a foot deep, and the only way the pilots of the larger, heavier Yorks that had recently arrived could get their planes out of it was to rev all four engines at half speed and churn their way to the runway. When they hit the hard surface, they had to cut their throttles immediately and apply their brakes fully. If they did not, the plane shot across the pavement and mired in the mud on the other side.

When the rain finally stopped, the mud dried into hard ridges and troughs, and the station commander had to call in bulldozers to flatten them. That reduced the surface to a fine, powdery dust, and every time someone started an engine on one of the aircraft, the flight line would disappear from view in a dun-colored haze. In addition to the problems it created with the engines, the dust settled on and clung to the windshields of the airplanes. As the planes rose through the clouds on their flights, the dust turned back into mud again. When the pilots turned on their wipers so that they could see, the fine particles scratched the Plexiglas of the windshields. On night flights, the scratches acted as tiny prisms, turning the flare paths and landing lights of their airfields into blinding rainbow displays of light. Many of the pilots refused to carry out any night flights until the windshields were replaced, and replacements were scarce.[6]

The land-based British planes were not the only ones with difficulties, for the RAF Coastal Command had thrown the ten Sunderland flying boats of Nos. 201 and 230 Squadrons into the effort. Hastily reassigned from their base at Lough Erne, Northern Ireland, on June 5 they flew to Finkenwerder, on the Elbe River near Hamburg. There, they were expected to operate from the old Blohm and Voss shipyard basin. Fragile-skinned aircraft, the Sunderlands were required to tie up not to their usual bright-red rubber mooring buoys, but to ancient cast-iron ones, where battleships had once moored. Refueling had to be accomplished by hand pumping fuel from fifty-five gallon drums on barges into the enormous flying boats.

Squadron Leader Tony Payne, commander of No. 230, flew the first load down the Hamburg corridor from Finkenwerder. He was amazed at the number of Soviet planes he encountered en route. Yaks, MiGs, and small spotter planes from which the observer snapped photographs of the giant flying boat, rose from every field along the route. Even more surprising was the reception he got when he touched down on Lake Havel in Berlin with his 6,500-pound load of Spam. A flotilla of paddleboats, canoes, and rowboats, filled with Berliners bearing garlands of summer flowers, rushed from the shore to greet him, looking for all the world like some Hawaiian welcoming party.[7]

Some of the British air crew members assigned to the new duty of flying supplies to the beleaguered Germans found the job an odd reversal of what they were accustomed to. As he watched a German crew unloading his plane after his seventeenth flight into the city, Royal Air Force Signalman Jack Euston, a Londoner, noted that this was really his twenty-second trip to Berlin. The first five had been made as a radioman on planes that had bombed the city. "It still seems a bit strange to me and my buddies," he said, "but we take it as part of our job."[8]

On the American operation, things were equally hectic and disorganized at the outset. No one impressed the urgency of the airlift on the air traffic controllers at the Frankfurt Air Traffic Center, and they continued to insist on maintaining the normal standard of requiring a twenty-five minute interval between takeoffs. General LeMay summarily placed all air traffic control directly under General Smith's command, bluntly directing that planes would leave at five-minute intervals. In Berlin, it was little better, as the operations office insisted that all pilots report to the weather office for a full briefing before each flight and that the Air Traffic Center across town on Potsdamer Strasse get full details of every proposed flight before it departed.

The solution to the problem of supplying the city with even a small amount of the coal necessary for its existence was proving elusive. General LeMay's staff believed at first that it could simply be done in a series of low-level drops from B-29 bombers, and the RAF believed that such a scheme was practical as well. Air Commodore R. N. Waite, the British military government's air chief, told reporters that he envisioned a system in which coal would be shot directly out of the bomb bays of heavy bombers, such as B-29s and the British Lancasters, using

wooden or canvas chutes and without bothering with bags or containers. A full load, Waite said, could be dropped into open fields by low
flying bombers in a matter of seconds.[9] The first experiment in this
method, attended by a group of high-ranking observers, proved to be a
disaster. The soft bituminous coal, raining from the planes and gaining
speed as it fell, shattered on impact and instantly pulverized into fine
dust that rose from the target area in a dark and mushrooming black-
brown cloud. The wind was blowing toward the observers, so the dust
settled back to the ground across them, begriming their tan summer
uniforms. The concept of air-dropping coal clearly wasn't practical, but
it had received so much attention in the press that the Air Force felt
compelled to put a brave face on the fiasco. Colonel Malcolm Stewart,
commander of the Furstenfeldbruch base where the drop had been attempted, announced that the experiment had been a success, but that
B-29s would not be used to deliver coal to the city unless it became
absolutely necessary. He gave as the reasons the fact that the bombers
were expensive to operate and that "there might be a wastage of coal
in dropping it."[10] Meanwhile, a call went out for all of the surplus GI
duffel bags on the continent. One hundred pounds of coal could be
packed into each one and transported into the city that way, in the
cargo spaces of C-54s, not the bomb bays of B-29s. The first duffel bags
of coal arrived in the city on July 7.

As the coal was soft, dust remained a problem, even when the coal
was packed in bags. The dust seeped through the bags, covering its
handlers and the insides of the aircraft with a dark, sooty grime that
penetrated everywhere. It fouled instruments, shorted electrical cir-
cuits, and abraded the airplane's control wires. The loading and unloading crews perpetually looked like Silesian miners, and the flying
personnels' uniforms were soon black with it.

The dust from the flour was nearly as bad as that from the coal, except that it was white, and everyone involved in handling it took on a
ghostly appearance. When the flour dust became wet, as it often did in
the leaky old C-47s, it formed a slick, slippery paste on the floors of the
aircraft. Several crew members were injured when they fell because
of it.

Worst of all, the dust from both swirled about in the planes while
they were in flight, and both were explosive at certain concentrations.
Before long, an ingenious flight engineer jury-rigged a piece of surplus
hose that, when thrust out one of the windows into the slipstream of
the moving airplane, created a suction that vacuumed the dust out of
the air inside.

American aircraft were going off line with maintenance problems
at a rate equal to that encountered by the British, and the rainy, over-
cast weather hampered their operations just as much. On July 5, returning from Berlin to Wiesbaden with Nick Nicholson at the controls,

Lieutenant Robert Wilcox came as close to crashing as he ever had. Stacked in a holding pattern over the Wiesbaden radio beacon, their aircraft was gradually let down to 4,000 feet, although it took over an hour before they were cleared for a ground-controlled approach (GCA) to the field. Nicholson missed his landing pass, and they were diverted to Rhein-Main. By the time they got there, both of their main fuel tanks had run dry, and the fuel gauge for the left auxiliary tank showed ten gallons—enough fuel for fifteen minutes' flying. The right auxiliary tank showed only slightly more. Informing the tower of their position, they were cleared to land but lost sight of the field in the murk. Then the GCA operator told them to proceed to another radio beacon and hold at 3,000 feet.

"We don't have enough gas to reach the Offenbach beacon," Wilcox said as calmly as he could into the microphone. "We are going to continue our approach and we would appreciate it very much if you could help us in."

"Roger, 198, continue on pattern," the tower responded.

As the plane dropped lower through the clouds, Wilcox held his hands on the fuel selector switches, ready to flip them the instant the left engine sputtered, so that both engines could draw from the rapidly emptying right auxiliary tank. When they passed through 300 feet, they were still in gray murk and could see no sign of the landing lights of the field. Glancing over, Wilcox could see that sweat was pouring off Nicholson's face.

At just 200 feet, the plane suddenly burst through the cloud layer, and they picked out the lights lining the runway. Nicholson cut back the throttles, Wilcox dumped the flaps, and they touched down. The tower couldn't decide where to park them, and Wilcox urged by radio that they be given the first hardstand, before they ran out of gas.

While Nicholson and Wilcox slept in the transient barracks, waiting for the fog to lift so that they could fly the ship back to their home base, a ground crew lieutenant tried to taxi their plane to a different hardstand. The right engine coughed to a start but sputtered out when he tried to start the left one. When the lieutenant had the plane gassed up, he was amazed that it swallowed 814 gallons. The normal full fuel load for a C-47 is 804.[11]

On June 6, in London, Washington, and Paris, notes from the governments of Great Britain, the United States, and France were delivered to the Soviet embassies. Aside from the fact that the note to the embassy in Paris omitted any reference to the Truman-Stalin discussions about Berlin in 1945 and the withdrawal of Allied troops to allow Soviet occupation of their designated zone of Germany, the notes were identical.[12] They stated categorically that the Western allies had an absolute right to be in Berlin and that each country viewed the blockade as "a clear violation of existing agreements concerning the administration of

Berlin by the four occupying powers."[13] They stressed that the West was willing to enter into negotiations about any disagreement about the administration of the city but made it clear that any such negotiations could take place only after the blockade was lifted.

On the day the notes were delivered, there was heavy Soviet fighter activity in the air corridors into the city. United States and British authorities warned their fliers to take care not to stray from the corridors and to maintain their altitude above 5,000 feet. The Soviets filed a formal protest, complaining to the British that Lake Havel was under Soviet control and its use by the Sunderland flying boats was illegal. Later in the day, four Soviet officers arrived at the Berlin air traffic safety center to protest that the American supply planes were rupturing the air traffic regulations.

As the crisis continued to develop, General Clay tried to maintain the same routine he had adopted when he first came to Germany. He rose at 6:30 a.m. and ate a light breakfast, during which he passed out crackers to his Scottish terrier, George, and a recently acquired spaniel, Sambo. He was at his large walnut desk at headquarters by 8:00 a.m. and spent the first hour there reading top-secret reports, teletype news, and intelligence reports. Now his routine often had to be adjusted to include briefings for high-level visitors, such as Undersecretary of the Army William J. Draper and Lieutenant General Albert Wedemeyer, who were both in Berlin during the first week in July. For two and one-half hours, Clay and his staff reviewed for them the basic needs of the city and what Clay felt would be necessary to supply them. It was during this visit that Wedemeyer attempted to convince Clay that Berlin could be supplied by air. The military governor remained doubtful, still thinking of the operation as one to supplement the existing stocks in the city. He was still hopeful that his proposed armed convoy would be approved.

Normally, General Clay ate a light lunch in half an hour and spent another two at his desk before inviting Robert Murphy into his office for a talk and their customary brief game of gin rummy. After that, the general worked until 8:00 p.m., went home for dinner with his wife, Marjorie, and then returned to headquarters at 11:00 p.m. to file reports and hold teleconferences with the War Department.[14] It was during one of these, shortly after General Wedemeyer had left the city, that Clay was informed that the armed convoy he kept proposing would not be approved. The day before he got that word, the Soviets made a formal announcement that all water traffic into the city would also cease.[15] There was no way in or out of the city except by air.

The flying conditions in Germany remained bad. First Lieutenants George B. Smith and Lelan V. Williams, both of whom had been assigned to the base at Erding before the airlift, were not as lucky in dealing with them as their friends Lieutenants Nicholson and Wilcox. On the night of June 8, 1948, their C-47 crashed into a mountain just west of Wiesbaden and burned. Both were killed, as was Karl V. Hagen, a Department of Defense civilian employee flying as their passenger. The airlift had claimed its first casualties.

☆　☆　☆

The airlift continued pulling in personnel from around the globe. Gail Halvorsen, a lanky, prematurely bald first lieutenant from Bear River Valley, Utah, had recently been reassigned from a C-54 squadron to one that flew the newer and larger C-74, but his plane was out of service for maintenance. A flight he was scheduled to make from his base at Brookley Air Force Base in Alabama to Ramey Field in Puerto Rico had been canceled, and Halvorsen decided to sit in on an emergency briefing that the group commander, Colonel George Cassidy, called on July 10.

Cassidy informed his men that four of their C-54s and twelve crews would be moving to Germany almost immediately. Halvorsen, a bachelor, was not assigned to the mission, but his good friend Pete Sowa was, and Pete wasn't at the briefing. He was flying a mission to Panama and wasn't even aware that orders had come down that would separate him from his young wife and newborn twins. After a quick telephone conversation with Pete's wife, Halvorsen asked his commanding officer if he could switch assignments with Sowa.

"It's all right with me, but you'll have to take the replacement issue up with Sowa's commander," Halvorsen's boss said. "I'll transfer you if he'll agree to the switch." [16]

James Haun, the lieutenant colonel in command of Sowa's squadron, had no problem with the transfer. Halvorsen and several other pilots were stowing gear in one of the Germany-bound C-54s when Sowa returned from his Panama mission and asked what was going on.

Halvorsen and his group arrived at Rhein-Main airfield on July 11 and were greeted by a harried-looking lieutenant whose first words were, "Welcome to Rhein-Main. Who will be the first crew to Berlin?" [17] Within an hour and fifteen minutes, Captain John Kelly and his crew were in the air, their C-54 loaded with coal for the blockaded city. The remainder of the crews from Brookley found billets in an abandoned barn in Zeppelinheim, just across the now-deserted autobahn from the airfield, having rejected quarters in a set of vermin-infested tar-paper shacks recently vacated by a group of displaced persons. Halvorsen flew copilot to Captain John Pickering on a flight to Berlin at 1:00 p.m. the following day, carrying 138 sacks of flour, which came close to the C-54's ten-ton weight limit.

At Tempelhof, Halvorsen and the crew scurried off to the snack bar in the sprawling terminal building while their plane was being unloaded. When they returned, they found the plane empty and an operations officer looking for them so that they could be sent back to Rhein-Main for another load.

The second load for the day was soft coal from the Ruhr, packed in GI duffel bags, and there was another load after that. It was 3:00 the next morning before Halvorsen and his crew got back to the barn they were now living in.

☆　☆　☆

Just after the war, William Tunner had passed up a lucrative business opportunity in order to remain in the Air Force. Retired general H. H. "Hap" Arnold had asked Tunner to serve as president of a new company, World Air Freight, at a salary several times his brigadier general's pay. Tunner initially agreed but then turned the deal down at the last minute. His beloved wife was terminally ill and comatose, and he was acting as both father and mother to his two sons, Bill and Joe. More important, he found after deep reflection that he simply didn't want to leave the Air Force, even though he fully expected to lose his star and be set back to his permanent rank of colonel in the wave of reductions and consolidations that occurred with demobilization. Thus, it had come as a surprise when, instead of a demotion, he received the second star of a major general and the assignment as deputy for operations at the Military Air Transport Service under Major General Laurence S. Kuter. The task of building an effective organization out of the Air Force personnel from the old Air Transport Command, which had been combined with several Naval Air Transport Squadrons to form MATS, was a rewarding one, and it had kept his mind off his personal sorrow. Now, the fact that MATS was not getting involved in the events in Germany began to trouble him severely. He could tell from the reports that came across his Pentagon desk that the airlift there could use significant improvement.[18]

When something bothered William H. Tunner, he always did something about it. In this case, he wrote a memo to General Kuter, the MATS commander, strongly urging that they recommend to the Joint Chiefs of Staff that MATS become involved in the airlift immediately. After Kuter read the memo, he calmly told his deputy to relax.

"That's not the way to do it, Bill," Kuter said. "Let's just sit tight and see what happens."[19]

**1** As the Soviets impose their blockade of Berlin, convoys back up on the Helmstat-Berlin autobahn. *USAF Museum*

**2** The early workhorses of the airlift, C-47s (here in a variety of paint schemes), unload at Tempelhof Airfield in Berlin. They were scrounged from throughout Europe. *USAF Museum*

**3** Tempelhof Airfield, in the center of the American sector of Berlin. *USAF Museum*

**4** The airlift soon claimed casualties. This C-47, crewed by lieutenants Robert W. Stuber and Charles H. King, crashed on July 25, 1948, into an apartment building in Kaiserplatz, three blocks from the Tempelhof runway, killing them both. It was the first airlift crash in the city. *Louis N. Wagner Collection*

**5** The airlift became an endless parade of C-54 Globemasters. Here they are shown unloading at Tempelhof and preparing to taxi out. *USAF Museum*

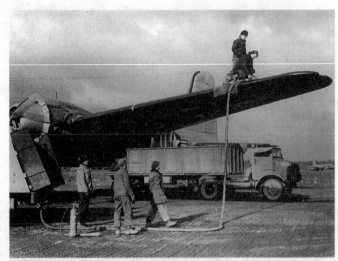

**6** While crews rush to unload a Globemaster, it is refueled. Between July 1948 and April 1949, the U.S. Navy sea-lifted 2,638,000 barrels of aviation fuel to the port of Bremerhaven for the planes of the airlift. *USAF Museum*

**7** At the British base at Fassberg, a Tommy directs a coal truck into position to load an American plane bound for Berlin. *USAF Museum*

**8** Reserves of coal were kept at each of the airfields. This is a stockpile of 1,400 tons, an average day's lift, at Celle. *USAF Museum*

**9** Loading was done by crews of Displaced Persons supervised by U.S. Army personnel. The supervisors here are members of the "Circle C Cowboys"—the U.S. Army Constabulary. *USAF Museum*

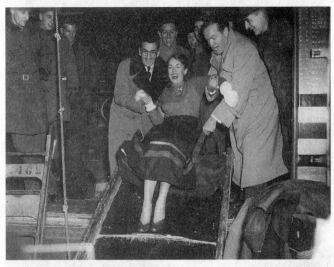

**10** During their Christmas 1948 entertainment tour, Bob Hope and Irving Berlin clown around aboard a C-54 at Tempelhof, sliding troupe member Jinx Falkenberg down a coal chute while the unloading crew looks on. *Louis N. Wagner Collection*

**11** When the cargoes were sacks of flour, the work crews were covered with it. *USAF Museum*

12 A C-54 flies over AN/CPN-4 ground radar trailers installed at Tempelhof to facilitate bad weather landings. *USAF Museum*

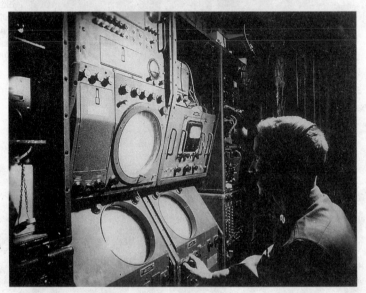

13 Inside a radar trailer, ground control operators carefully track each aircraft. *Louis N. Wagner Collection*

**14** Brig. Gen. Alexander, USAF, commander of Tempelhof, and Col. S. Wrey, USAF, Tempelhof operations officer, greet the mixed Navy/Air Force crew of the Globemaster that carried the two millionth ton into Tempelhof on July 2, 1949. Left to right: General Alexander; 1st Lieutenant Korbal, USAF; Ensign Case, USN; Tech. Sergeant McMillen, USAF; Colonel Wrey. *USAF Museum*

**15** This crash of a C-54 occurred during the extremely foggy weather of November 1948. *Louis N. Wagner Collection*

**16** In addition to goods, the airlift also carried people. Here a group of children—some of the approximately 72,000 Germans flown out of Berlin—await take-off in a C-47. *USAF Museum*

**17** Among the dignitaries to visit Berlin during the airlift was British foreign minister Ernest Bevin. Here (from the right) Maj. Gen. William Tunner, Bevin, and Gen. Lucius Clay speak to unidentified airlift crewmen, who are accompanied by Colonel Barr of the Tempelhof base. *Louis N. Wagner Collection*

**18** General Alexander greets the crew of the last flight of Operation Vittles to touch down in Berlin on September 30, 1949. *USAF Museum*

**19** On September 30, 1952, a huge crowd gathers in Kaiserplatz—sight of the first crash in the city and renamed Luftbrücke (Airbridge) Platz—for the dedication of the Airlift Memorial. *USAF Museum*

# TWENTY-ONE

## FULL WARTIME FOOTING

After the frenzy and confusion of the first three weeks, Operation Vittles began to take on the appearance of a determined military operation, with the aim of ensuring that a planeload of supplies landed in Berlin every four minutes. To maintain that steady, relentless beat, thousands of soldiers, airmen, and civilians across the continent had to be organized. The historic pattern of handling heavy freight had been from ship to railhead and then to a trucking point. Because of the integration of airplanes into the movement of heavy freight into Berlin, an entirely new pattern had to be developed that moved freight to the airfields in Germany from which it was flown, and away from the airports where it was landed in Berlin.

The daily needs of the American sector of the city were determined in Berlin itself by Colonel Howley's Military Government Office, which dealt with the needs of the French sector as well. Aside from a former Luftwaffe Fokker, which ground-looped—spinning and flipping and wrecking on the runway at Tempelhof—shortly after the blockade was imposed, the French had no aircraft available to contribute to the effort in Europe. They had committed all of their resources to the growing war they were fighting in Indochina. The responsibility to supply their sector and the French garrison was assumed by the Americans.

The primary organizer of the army's supply operation was Brigadier General Williston B. Palmer, the stocky former artillery commander of VII Corps. One of the few bachelor general officers in the army, Palmer had a jutting chin, a growling impatience with inefficiency of any kind, and a temperament to match that of General Curtis LeMay.

As soon as he learned that the modest early effort to supply the military garrisons in the city was to be expanded to feed the entire population of the Western sectors, Palmer ordered the Army Quartermaster Corps depot at Giessen to move 300 tons of assorted foodstuffs to Rhein-Main so that food shipments could begin immediately. Then he

contacted General LeMay, who announced his intention to begin sending air freight into Berlin at maximum capacity, twenty-four hours a
day, seven days a week.

"We'll be on a full wartime footing," LeMay growled.[1]

Palmer quickly established liaison with the Air Force logistics staff,
placing Lieutenant Colonel M. N. Stone in LeMay's headquarters. Next
he ordered the establishment of supply traffic control offices at both
Rhein-Main and Wiesbaden and established a rail regulating and re-
consignment point at the Frankfurt rail yards. To accommodate the additional personnel who would be working on the airlift, Palmer ordered the commander of the Frankfurt military post to find facilities to
quarter eight hundred officers and men in barracks, with meals available twenty-four hours a day, and to arrange bus transportation to and
from the air bases.[2]

When the city's requirements were transmitted to the headquarters
of the Office of the Chief of Transportation, European Command, in
Frankfurt, Army Transportation Corps specialists from the 7795th Traffic Regulating Detachment matched the requests against the inventories
in the warehouses in the port of Bremen and other locations in the
north of Germany. The goods were then shipped to the marshaling
yards in Frankfurt, where they were loaded for shipment by rail to the
American air bases at Rhein-Main and Wiesbaden. At the railheads
near the bases there was no warehouse space, and whatever goods had
been ordered remained stored either under tarpaulins or in one of the
284 ten-ton trailers—a size roughly corresponding to the cargo capacity of a C-54—that the Transportation Corps had available until the
goods were ready to be loaded onto the planes. Enlisted personnel of
the Transportation Corps drove the tractors hauling the trailers and supervised the loading crews, but the actual work of loading was performed by gangs of displaced persons, known within the military as DPs.

The army had already organized its work gangs of DPs at the airfields
in Germany into quasimilitary labor service units, which had been set
up along national lines after early experience indicated that mixing
nationalities often led to conflicts. The 4060th Labor Company (Lithua-
nian) served at Rhein-Main, while the 8958th Labor Service Company
(Polish) was based at Wiesbaden. When the airlift started, both of these
were expanded, and there were soon 384 DPs working at each shift at
Rhein-Main. At Wiesbaden, 170 worked on each shift, moving the
cargo to feed the city of Berlin. When the operation started, both the
loaders and the Transportation Corps personnel were working twenty-
four-hour days, just to keep the shipments moving. After the first three
weeks, they went on twelve-hour shifts as the operation took on a set
routine.[3]

For a small wage, the loaders had a standard set work rate that
required that each man move one ton an hour when loading trucks

from boxcars or planes. The laborers were entitled to a daily ration amounting to 2,900 calories, which was served to them in the mess halls at their camps, and they were served one hot U.S. Army meal while they were at work.[4] There was never a shortage of men willing to do the job.

The Transportation Corps began to develop time- and labor-saving methods, based on the experience they were gaining. Where there was a mixed cargo, such as food, items were "married" in such a way that each plane carried nearly its full capacity. For example, a load of pasta would occupy the entire cargo space of a C-54 but weighed in at two tons less than what the plane could carry. The Transportation Corps experts would mix the load so that some of the macaroni was replaced by sacks of sugar, so that the plane carried a full ten tons. Marrying the cargo was performed at the railhead, so that each of the trailers arriving at the air base carried exactly a ten-ton load. In that way, only one trailer ever had to pull up to a plane to make sure that it was loaded to full capacity.[5]

Some of the mixed cargoes contained distinctly odd items. Most of the fruit brought into the city was of the dried variety in order to conserve weight, but there was one weekly shipment of five bunches of bananas, intended for nineteen-month-old Peter Bucher. The child suffered from a rare intestinal disorder that made the assimilation of anything but bananas difficult, and the airlift planners committed themselves to maintaining his special diet.[6]

One of the special food needs of the French garrison nearly sparked a revolt among the American pilots. When they discovered that they were flying in large quantities of red wine for the French military contingent, at a time when they were hard pressed to find a bottle of Coca-Cola at their bases, they protested loudly. It had to be carefully explained to them that *vin ordinare* was as much a staple of the French diet as milk was of an American one.

At Rhein-Main, the major Operation Vittles base, the Transportation Corps headquarters was in a converted trailer, the walls of which were adorned with charts. Some gave the locations of all of the field's hardstands. Others showed the numbers of each airplane assigned to the operation, along with the weight that that particular aircraft could carry. "Each plane has its own idiosyncrasies," Lieutenant Colonel R. L. Ford, the officer in charge, would explain when asked about this. "Some will take a few hundred pounds less than others."[7]

The flight operations, like those on the ground, were also beginning to take on a routine. Aircraft assigned to Operation Vittles were divided into three groups. Group A, based at Wiesbaden, consisted entirely of C-47s. So did the small Group B, which was based at Rhein-Main and was chiefly responsible for ferrying supplies for the United States and French military personnel in the city. Group C was a provisional squadron, made up entirely of the C-54s that had been called to duty on the airlift from bases around the world. It was also based at Rhein-Main.

The three groups operated on a block system, with the first C-47 leaving Wiesbaden at 7:00 a.m., and the sixty remaining planes of Group A following at four-minute intervals. At 11:00 a.m., when the last C-47 left Wiesbaden, the first of the fifteen planes in Group B took off from Rhein-Main, with the final plane of that group off the ground by noon. The first C-54 of Group C didn't take off until twenty minutes later, as the larger planes cruised at 180 miles per hour—30 miles per hour faster than the C-47s. When the last of the C-47s of Group B reached Berlin, the first C-54—having made up time and closed distance on it—was only four minutes behind, maintaining the steady beat of the airlift.

By the time the last C-54 of Group C left its Rhein-Main base, the C-47s of Group A had already returned to Wiesbaden, refueled, and reloaded, and the first had taken off again. Each individual mission to Berlin took eight hours, including the time on the ground in the city, and each group flew three missions each day. The aircraft crews were assigned to a schedule where they would fly two missions—a sixteen-hour stretch—and then have the next sixteen hours off.

Once the airlifted cargo reached Berlin, it was speedily unloaded by crews of Germans—over two hundred were employed by the first week of operations—who were supervised by American enlisted men. Very few of the American supervisors were Transportation Corps personnel, as that branch was stretched thin by the airlift. Most were ordinary GIs, pressed into service for the crisis. Jim O'Gorman, the 16th Infantry corporal who had been startled when his commanding officer had told his assembled NCOs that they had two hours to live if the Soviets were to mount an attack on the American sector of Berlin, was one of these. He and his fellow GI supervisors noted that when the incoming cargoes were powdered eggs, the mouths of their German workers soon became rimmed with yellow. The hungry laborers were eating the spillage from the sacks as they were unloading them.

That habit created problems when the cargo was dried potatoes, because the small dehydrated flakes expanded enormously in the workers' stomachs, causing painful cramps and crippling distress. After the third time he was forced to call an ambulance for one of the Germans on his crew, O'Gorman laid out a simple rule for the men: "Put the stuff in your pockets and we won't bother you. But, for God's sake, don't eat it uncooked. We need you on the work gang, not in the hospital."[8]

The British effort, Plain Fare, was also beginning to take on the shape of a regular operation. Because of bad weather and maintenance problems, the original target of 160 Dakota sorties per day was never reached until the larger York aircraft came into use, but the RAF did manage to raise its deliveries to Berlin from 474 tons on July 6 to 995 tons on July 18.[9]

The British had begun by operating their Dakotas at intervals of six minutes during the day and fifteen at night before the arrival of the Yorks, as that was as fast a pace as the servicing and loading parties could initially achieve. When the faster Yorks arrived, the RAF encountered the same problem with speed disparity that the Americans had and solved it in a similar manner. They dispatched the planes in blocks so that one arrived in Berlin every four minutes, the same rate the Americans achieved. The base at Wunstorf was, however, becoming far too crowded for the growing operation, so the RAF began the rehabilitation of the old Luftwaffe field at Fassburg in anticipation of transferring the Dakotas there.

Throughout Germany, communities held rallies to collect food to be sent to the people of Berlin. In Melsungen, an old walled town in Hesse, twenty-two miles from the border of the Soviet zone and directly under the flight path of the planes flying out of Rhein-Main, the citizens rose early one day to attend a rally in the town square. They saw the local SDP leader, Ernst Spars, point to the sky and say, "Up there, the American people are showing their faith in the cause of our Berlin brothers every hour of every day. Now we must act. There is not much food for us here, but let us share with those brave Berliners what little we do have." The square resounded with a "Ja!" from the crowd. The people of Melsungen agreed to pledge four freight cars of grain, dried fish, and fresh vegetables to Berlin.[10] It was the same in other cities and provinces of western Germany; the local governments in Hamburg, Lower Saxony, and Bremen all pledged a full day's rations to their Berlin brethren.

Frank Howley hadn't been able to visualize how 920,000 Berlin families could be supplied with the necessities of life by an airlift but, after visiting Tempelhof and watching the planes arrive and depart in their regular rhythm, he realized that this was the beginning of something wonderful—a way to break the blockade. He returned to his office almost breathless with elation, as one who had made a great discovery and could not hide his joy.[11] He immediately set to work with a staff of experts drawn from the three Western military government organizations to try to cut the basic requirements of the city to the bare minimum. That way they could help to ensure that the city could survive on the amount of goods that the airlift could transport. Reductions in the weight of items flown in became a priority. His planners found that if meat was boned before it was flown in, the weight was reduced by one quarter. After that, all fresh meat entering the city as air cargo was shipped without bones. Calculations revealed that one third of the weight of bread consisted of water and that the shipment of yeast and flour into the city to bake bread there would be more efficient than flying in bread itself, even though it meant that more coal would have to be brought in to fire the baking ovens.

As all of these efforts were going on, British commandant Edwin Herbert remained pessimistic, adhering to the gloomy prediction he had made when Howley had showed him the basic Assumption Plan before the blockade began. Herbert expected that the Western allies would be driven from the city by October, and said so. "By that time, the people of Berlin will be so fed up with starvation rations that they'll start rioting."[12]

That was not a sentiment shared by most other members of the British administration. On July 13, Sir Arthur Henderson, the British secretary of state for air, told a press conference that the airlift to Berlin would "steadily mount, to resist this deliberate attempt to starve two million men, women, and children," and that Britain would use "all the air resources that can usefully be brought to bear."[13]

To that end, the British government had already begun to contract with civilian air charter companies to augment the RAF activities on the airlift. The RAF planners knew, from their experience on the earlier operation that had supplied the needs of the British garrison in May, that transportation of liquid fuel by air was a difficult and dangerous business. The cargo had to be carried in drums, which wasted space, were heavy, and were difficult to secure in place on the planes. Some of the fuels, like gasoline and aviation gasoline, were highly volatile as well, creating an explosion hazard. Unfortunately, no aircraft specifically designed for fuel transport were in service with any air force in the world. However, aerial, or in-flight, tankers did exist.

Aerial refueling had been born as a stunt in America, but an English civil aviation pioneer, Sir Alan Cobham, was making a business of it. In May 1945, he had acquired some surplus Lancaster bombers and converted them to tankers. By May 1948, after trials that had lasted since the end of the war, Cobham's Flight Refueling Services, Ltd., was about to begin in-flight refueling operations for the British Overseas Airways Corporation. Just then the airlift to Berlin started. Sir Alan immediately offered his aerial tankers and their crews to the government. The offer was accepted, and arrangements were made to base these and other civilian aircraft at fields in Germany. The air ministry clearly did not believe that the airlift would be a short-term effort.

General Herbert's sour assessment of the attitude of the Berliners was far off the mark as well. Rallies to denounce the Soviet blockade and the German Communists who supported it were being held on a nearly daily basis. Acting Mayor Schroeder, addressing a large rally at which speakers assailed the Soviet Union's "new totalitarianism" and Communist attempts "to sell Germany into slavery through force, terror, and tyranny," said of the struggle, "Berlin fights for the world."

She was wildly cheered.[14] Colonel Howley spoke often to the people of Berlin over RIAS, honestly telling them that they faced shortages, but adding, "We only ask . . . that you cheerfully stand up to these privations and that you bear in mind that freedom and democracy have always been purchased only by struggle."[15]

In spite of the attitude of the Berliners and the regularity of the operations of the airlift, there was ample reason for General Herbert's pessimism. The airlift was encountering serious problems. The initial shortage of windshield wiper blades was minor compared with engine, tire, and propeller supply problems. There was less than a two-day supply of these items, and emergency flights from the United States were being made to keep up with the demand. The airlift was swallowing up so much gasoline that three tankers already at sea had to be diverted from their original destinations to supply it.[16] Worst of all, the runways at both Gatow and Tempelhof were near collapse. Colonel Henry Dorr, Tempelhof's commander, informed General Smith that he did not expect the single runway there to last out the month of July, and construction of a new runway was being delayed by the absence of heavy equipment in the city. Only six bulldozers and a single scraper were available to work on the project.[17]

Most of the American fliers saw little more of the city they were supplying than Tempelhof airport. Gail Halvorsen was an exception. He delighted in taking home movies with his spring-wound, eight-millimeter Revere camera and was determined to get some pictures of Berlin. Hopping a flight into Tempelhof during his off-duty time, he began by filming the aircraft operations there, concentrating on the planes coming in low over the barbed wire fence at the end of the runway. Then he noticed that the area behind the fence was crowded with children watching the planes. He made his way over to them.

They talked for twenty minutes in a mixture of Halvorsen's halting, limited German, with four of the children translating in rudimentary, schoolbook English. As Halvorsen turned to join the sergeant who was waiting with a jeep to give him a tour of the city, he realized that there was something odd about the children. Everywhere else he had been in the world—South America, Africa—children had regarded Americans as fair game, begging for candy or gum, and the GIs were willing participants, reaching into pockets and producing treats for the beggars. Not one of the German children he had been talking to at the fence had asked for anything, Halvorsen suddenly realized. Reaching into his pockets, he found that he had only two sticks of Wrigley's Doublemint gum with him. He turned back, tore the two sticks in half, and parceled them out to the children who had served as his interpreters. Then, on an impulse, he promised that he would drop candy to them from his plane on his next flight to Tempelhof if they would promise to share it equally.

The children shouted, "*Jawohl!*" Then one of the interpreters, a little blue-eyed girl in oversized boy's trousers, asked how they would know which plane was his.

"When I get overhead, I'll wiggle the wings of the big airplane back and forth several times," he responded.[18]

As the steady beat of the airlift went on, the Soviets responded to the Western note with a resounding "*Nyet.*" In their reply, the Soviets claimed that the situation had come about because of the West's currency reform and the moves toward the creation of a separate West German state. It also said, "Berlin lies in the center of the Soviet zone and is a part of that zone."[19] In Berlin, the Soviet propaganda campaign in the press continued, Red Air Force fighters buzzed dangerously close to airlift planes in the corridors, Markgraf's police staged brutal raids on the black market in the Potsdamer Platz, and the harassment of Western allied personnel continued. John J. Sims, an official of the British military administration responsible for barge traffic, had been dealing with the Soviets since 1946. He arranged with them to visit forty barge crews marooned in the city because of the blockade so that he could make sure that provisions had been made for barge men to be able to draw rations. When he reached the Soviet checkpoint at Wittenberg, the officials that he knew well from his dealings in the past asked to see his papers. Then they accused him of being a spy and threw him into a jail cell, where he was held for three days.[20] American civilian engineer R. F. Goff got much the same treatment, as did MP Privates First Class George Hunt and Elwood Dwinnel, who were yanked from their jeep by the Soviets after they had inadvertently entered the Soviet sector of the city.[21]

The blunt refusal of the Soviets to negotiate, coupled with the provocative Soviet actions in the city, led President Truman to order General Clay and Robert Murphy to Washington to meet with him and the National Security Council to discuss the crisis. They flew out of the bustling Tempelhof airport on July 19. At the end of the runway there were crowds of children, eagerly waving to each airplane that passed over their heads, as if to thank them.

At Rhein-Main, Lieutenant Gail Halvorsen had talked the other two members of his regular crew into joining him in his plan to drop candy and gum to the children near the Tempelhof runway. Captain John Pickering and Sergeant Herschel C. Elkins even contributed their candy rations to the effort, even though both of them had doubts about the wisdom of the undertaking. Pickering spoke for both when he said, "You're going to get us in a big mess of trouble."[22]

When they approached Berlin on their second flight of the day, Halvorsen and the crew could see the children waiting near the end of the runway. Halvorsen wiggled the wings of the C-54, and Elkins shoved three packages out of the flare chute at the flight engineer's station in the plane. Attached to each package was a small parachute, fashioned out of a handkerchief, which Halvorsen hoped would break its fall. When they took off for the return flight to Rhein-Main, they saw the crowd of children again. They were all waving to each plane that took off, unable to tell which of them had dropped such a precious treasure to them.[23]

President Truman was as blunt with the National Security Council as the Soviet reply to the Western notes had been. The position of the United States was precarious, and a show of strength had to be made in Berlin. When the president called on General Clay, the military governor echoed that sentiment, stating that the abandonment of Berlin would have a disastrous effect on plans for West Germany and for general European recovery. The United States, Clay asserted, had to stay in Berlin.[24]

Clay reported that the attitude of the people of Berlin was remarkable and that they were determined to resist Soviet pressure, adding that they could do so without undergoing hardship so extreme that it might break their will if the airlift could carry a minimum of 4,500 tons of supplies into the city each day. He noted that the airlift was now hauling an average of 2,500 tons per day, an amount that ensured adequate food but that did not allow enough fuel.

The president turned to General Hoyt Vandenberg, the Air Force chief of staff, to inquire what supplying the planes necessary to bolster the airlift would entail. He was told that any such action would disrupt military transport throughout the world and would necessitate the construction of a new airport in already crowded Berlin and the establishment of a major maintenance depot in Europe. The Air Force chief added that the allocation of additional planes to the airlift would risk their being destroyed at once in the event of hostilities with the Soviets, adversely affecting the ability of the United States to wage a strategic war.

Turning to Clay's suggestion of an armed convoy, the president and his advisors discussed the dangers that the Soviets would resist such a move with force. Clay alone had faith that the convoy would succeed. The rest of the president's advisors were convinced that it would not, so the group turned again to discussion of the potential of the airlift. Vandenberg reiterated his point that concentrating aircraft in Germany to fly supplies into Berlin would mean reducing air strength elsewhere and would create a dangerous weakness.

Truman, who had spent most of the meeting listening rather than talking, now broke in to disagree sharply with his Air Force chief. He pointedly asked Vandenberg if he would prefer the United States to make an attempt to drive the armored convoy into the city, pointing out that if the Soviets did meet it with armed resistance, the Air Force would certainly find itself involved in a general war. Not waiting for an answer from the general, Truman provided his own. An airlift involved fewer risks than armed road convoys, so the United States would pursue the airlift. Truman directed that the Air Force furnish the fullest possible support to Operation Vittles.

Vandenberg, still reluctant, again pointed out that additional landing facilities in the city would be required, but Clay quickly responded that he had already selected a site for a new airfield in the city. Construction could begin immediately. Vandenberg promised his complete cooperation with the effort to supply Berlin.[25]

A sealed envelope came to General William Tunner from the Air Force chief of staff. It contained a highly classified document addressed to General Vandenberg from Army Lieutenant General Albert Wedemeyer. In it, Wedemeyer stated his belief that the airlift could either break the blockade of Berlin outright or, at the very least, sustain the city while negotiations were going on. Citing the success of the Hump airlift in Asia, Wedemeyer recommended to the Air Force chief that Tunner be sent to Germany to run the Berlin operation. There was no note from Vandenberg with the copy of Wedemeyer's recommendation, and there were no orders shipping Tunner to Germany either. That was mystifying and annoying to the air transport expert, who was well aware of the problems that the airlift was beginning to encounter.

Orders did go out from the Pentagon to units of Tunner's command, however, as the Air Force began to draw the resources of the Military Air Transport Service into the Berlin operation. The 11th and 12th Air Transport Squadrons from Westover Field in Massachusetts were sent, and the 22d and 23d from Fairfield, California, were alerted to be ready to follow soon after.

Several days after the confidential memorandum arrived, Vandenberg called Tunner into his office and said, "O.K., Bill, it's yours. When can you leave for Berlin?"

"Right away," Tunner replied, taking advantage of the moment to ask permission to take a few officers he knew with him as a staff.

"Go ahead, but be reasonable," Vandenberg told him. "Tell personnel the names of the people you want, and their orders will be cut right along with yours."[26] The man who was called "Willy the Whip" by his staff was on his way to Germany.

## TWENTY-TWO

# WILLY THE WHIP

General Clay's plane from Washington landed in Berlin at 1:00 a.m. on July 25, 1948, and the military governor had to be carried off in a chair. He had contracted a severe cold in his neck and was in such extreme pain that any movement on his own was impossible. He was embarrassed to be seen in that condition by the throng of reporters who greeted him at the terminal. Clay had been accompanied on the trip back to Berlin by Chip Bohlen of the State Department, and the reporters knew that the American ambassadors to Moscow and London were expected to arrive in the city later in the day. Clay promised the newsmen that he would hold a press conference that evening, in spite of his condition.[1]

As the military governor and his guest were en route to the general's quarters on Im Dol, the airlift claimed its latest casualties, the first to occur in the city itself. A C-47, inbound to Tempelhof with a load of flour and yeast, plunged into Kaiserplatz in the Fredenau section, three blocks from the end of the Tempelhof runway. Cutting down several trees as it descended, it crashed into the front of an apartment building and burst into flames. The pilots, First Lieutenant Robert W. Stuber and First Lieutenant Charles H. King, died instantly.[2] No one in the building was injured, and the arriving rescue crews were surprised to discover that one family was still in the basement after the crash, calmly cutting up odd pieces of wood they had gathered to use as fuel.

General Clay's condition did not deter him from holding the promised news conference at his home that evening. Dressed in a robe and slippers, the military governor told the reporters gathered in his dining room, "The U.S. does not want to go to war. We intend to stay in Berlin, however, as we have stated we would do." Going on, Clay told the gathering that the Western allies were willing to negotiate with the Soviets but would not do so "under duress." Clay also disclosed to the reporters that the airlift would not only continue, but was soon to be enlarged with the addition of more C-54s.[3] Three days later, U.S. Air

Forces in Europe (USAFE) issued a terse bulletin announcing that Major General William H. Tunner had been "made available by the air staff to head air lift operations to Berlin."[4]

In the city, the split between East and West was becoming even more evident. The *Magistrat,* long dissatisfied with the performance of police president Paul Markgraf and the apparent complicity of the force in Communist kidnappings, became alarmed that a purge was going on. Between July 12 and 25, 1948, 590 high-ranking police officials had been summarily dismissed by Markgraf. All were non-Communists. The chief refused even to discuss the matter with the city administration, which had no power under the city constitution to fire the head of the police department without four-power approval. The *Magistrat* could, however, suspend Markgraf from duty. It took that step on July 26, appointing Assistant Police President Johannes Stumm to take over.

Soviet military governor Kotikov immediately issued an order reprimanding the government and ordering Acting Mayor Schroeder to dismiss Doctor Stumm. Kotikov signed the order "Military Commandant of the City of Berlin," implying that the Western powers no longer had any authority in the city. When the Western commandants rejected Kotikov's order as unilateral and invalid, Doctor Stumm set up his headquarters in the huge administration building at Tempelhof and invited members of the Berlin police force to report to him. Well over half did, splitting the force into two opposing groups. From now on, the city would have two separate police forces, each claiming to represent the legal authority, with neither recognizing the other as legitimate.[5]

Most of the men that Tunner requested be assigned to accompany him to Germany were veterans of the Hump. For chief of operations, he picked Colonel "Red" Forman, whom he had first met in Memphis when Forman was a civilian who flew on weekends. He had met Orval O. MacMahon in Memphis as well. Now a lieutenant colonel, MacMahon had been the staff sergeant in charge of maintenance then. He had later been commissioned and had served with Tunner in the Ferrying Command. Lieutenant Colonel Kenneth Swallwell was picked as the head of airfield construction, as Tunner respected his ability and knew that new airfields would be required on the airlift.

Communications would be handled by Lieutenant Colonel Manuel Fernandez. Known universally as "Pete," Fernandez had earned a reputation as the Air Force's premier scrounger, making scarce supplies and materials appear as if from nowhere. Raymond Towne, a captain and former B-26 pilot, was picked as public relations officer, and

Robert Hogg, another captain, was tapped as administrative officer. Hogg, who had a habit of pointedly informing people that his name was pronounced "hoag," the Scottish word for "unshorn lamb," was an example of the kind of priority Tunner had gotten from the Pentagon. Hogg was stationed at Westover Air Force Base in Massachusetts, and Tunner flew to Europe by way of Westover just to pick him up. In all, the staff Tunner assembled numbered twenty officers and his secretary, Staff Sergeant Katie Gibson.[6]

Wiesbaden Air Force Base was busy during the late afternoon of July 29, with Polish and German displaced persons working in gangs to load flour for Berlin onto C-47s and C-54s. They didn't even pause in their work when yet another Skymaster, this one bearing the yellow tail number 5549, landed and taxied to a hardstand.

Number 5549 carried twenty-two people. The single woman aboard debarked carrying her own typewriter. The rest of the passengers were men in army uniforms but wearing fliers' crushed caps and Air Force insignia. Uniform regulations require that the insignia of an individual's current unit be worn as a patch at the shoulder of the left sleeve; the patch of a unit a person has served with in combat may be worn on the right sleeve. The right sleeves of most of the men debarking from 5549 bore a patch rarely seen in Europe—the Star of India and the symbolic sun of China in white on blue above a set of red and white stripes signifying the United States—the insignia of the China-Burma-India theater. "Willie the Whip" and his staff had arrived in Germany. The greeting party at the airfield was small and was headed by General Alfred Kissner, LeMay's chief of staff.[7] Tunner's first stop was at General LeMay's quarters to report to his new commanding officer.

General Curtis LeMay and his wife were quartered in a 102-room mansion in Wiesbaden once owned by the Heinkel family, which had made its fortune selling champagne. It was unrelated to the family of the same name that manufactured aircraft for the Luftwaffe. One of the champagne-Heinkel daughters had been married to Hitler's foreign minister, Joachim von Ribbentrop, who had once been a salesman for the firm.[8] The house, with its elaborate furnishings and a staff of fifteen servants, made a deep impression on William Tunner when he reported to the commander of USAFE on the evening of his arrival.

In his characteristically terse manner, LeMay told Tunner, "I expect you to produce." Tunner's reply was just as brief. "I intend to," he said.

He departed to locate the quarters he had been assigned. They turned out to be a single room on the third floor of the once luxurious, now decrepit Schwartzer Bock Hotel, overlooking a block of bomb-ruined buildings. The hotel elevator no longer worked, so Tunner had to climb the stairs. When he opened the door, Tunner found that he was looking into a bathroom—the only way he could enter his room was to squeeze between the sink and the commode. It was obvious to him that he was in Germany because General Vandenburg had ordered it, not because his presence there had been requested by LeMay or anyone else at USAFE headquarters.[9]

Tunner and his staff were in for an even greater shock the next morning when they got their first look at the apartment house that had been requisitioned for their use as headquarters. It was badly beaten up and filled with debris, and the floors and walls were filthy. There were no desks, chairs, or telephones, and Colonels MacMahon and Fernandez were sent off to try to scrounge some. Just about then, a fresh-faced airman from the adjutant's office appeared to announce that the group could stop by that afternoon to pick up their PX and commissary cards. Tunner took the opportunity to vent to his staff his feelings about the relatively easy life of the personnel regularly assigned to Air Forces Europe: "Look, we came here to work. We didn't come to Germany to go shopping at the PX or commissary, so I think we can just skip that little ceremony this afternoon. Inasmuch as we don't have chairs, desks, or phones, I'll expect every one of you to go to the air bases we will operate from and start learning this business."[10]

Tunner didn't like what he found on his own tour of the bases. Just as he had anticipated, the airlift was functioning as what he called "a real cowboy operation."[11] Few of the personnel involved had any real idea what they would be doing the next day, neither the flight nor the ground crews knew how long their temporary duty assignments to the operation would last, and no one had any solid idea as to what schedule he was working.[12] Constant hustle, bustle, and excitement reigned, and the last place Tunner wanted to find that was on an airlift operation. To William Tunner, the operation of a successful airlift was about as glamorous as drops of water on stone.[13]

On his first trip to Tempelhof, Tunner strolled around the field, noting the confusion evident everywhere. A dozen pilots and copilots milled around in the operations room, waiting for clearances; the crowd in the snack bar next door was larger. A quick check of the records indicated that very few planes were getting off at their scheduled times.[14] The hastily instituted modifications to the peacetime system that Smith had put in place in response to LeMay's directives clearly would not be enough to deal with the demands of a full-scale airlift.

Tunner knew that Red Forman, his chief of operations, was going to have plenty of headaches on his new assignment. On the Hump airlift there had been thirteen bases in India, feeding supplies into six bases in China, and the planes had had all of southeast Asia to maneuver in. In Berlin, there were only the two airfields, Gatow and Tempelhof, accessible from three narrow corridors. In addition, they were surrounded by a checkerboard of Soviet airfields just outside the city. The reports Tunner got from the other members of his staff indicated more problems.

Maintenance was the first, as all aircraft require constant care and attention to keep them flying. Routine maintenance checks are required after every twenty-five hours of flight time, up to two hundred hours. At that point, planes undergo a major inspection. At one thousand hours, a comprehensive overhaul is needed.

With the airlift squadrons crowded into existing facilities, a serious shortage of tools and spare parts in Europe, and many of the squadrons short of mechanics, the schedules were impossible to maintain, and aircraft were constantly being taken out of service for maintenance or repair work or because they were no longer airworthy.

Then there was the condition of the existing Berlin airfields themselves. With the runway of pierced steel planking on a base of rubble at Tempelhof going to pieces under the pounding it was taking in the landings, a slapdash expedient had been devised to keep it usable while construction of the new runway went slowly ahead with inadequate equipment.

A force of over two hundred German laborers had been organized by the Tempelhof base engineers. Lining the runway and equipped with supplies of sand, asphalt, and extra steel planking, the German laborers would dash out onto the runway as soon as a plane had passed, quickly making what patchwork repairs they could, then dash to safety as the next plane roared in, four minutes later.

"We've got to have two additional runways there," Ken Swallwell said. One was to handle the additional traffic he was sure would come. The other was for emergency use when either of the first two was closed for repairs.[15]

Tunner knew that there were other problems as well, but the solutions would take time to develop. Some things could be changed quickly, however, and "Willy the Whip" began to issue orders.

There was consternation and a great deal of griping among the air crews when they read the order that he issued on July 31, after only three days in Germany. Henceforth, no crew member could leave the site of his airplane when it was in Berlin. That meant there could be no more visits to Operations and Weather, and the crews wondered how they would get their flight information. It also meant no more visits to the snack bar for coffee, donuts, and conversations with the fräuleins, and there was a great deal of grumbling about that. The fliers didn't know the transformation in the system that Tunner's staff had already put in place.

When a plane landed in Berlin, a truck with an unloading crew now pulled up just as the pilot was cutting his engines after taxiing to the unloading ramp. A jeep driven by an operations officer pulled up as the crew was getting out to stretch; the officer handed the pilot his clearance slip for the return flight and passed on any information the pilot needed to know about flying conditions. Then the operations officer threw his jeep into gear and roared off to meet the next plane. He had barely left when another jeep, driven by a weather officer, arrived, and the crew was filled in on weather conditions for the return flight.

The next jeep that arrived was fitted out as a mobile canteen with hot coffee, donuts, and hot dogs. Tunner's staff had enlisted the support of the German Red Cross, and the refreshment jeeps were staffed by some of the most attractive girls they could find. The griping about the order to stay with the planes stopped.[16]

Candy and gum were available for fliers to purchase in a weekly ration. Gail Halvorsen, John Pickering, and Herschel Elkins pooled theirs and continued to drop it by parachute to the growing crowd of children at the end of the Tempelhof runway. On a flight soon after their third drop and just before Tunner's new rules went into effect, Halvorsen's crew was forced to rely on instruments to get into Tempelhof, as a dense fog bank had blanketed all of Central Europe. No flights were taking off, and Halvorsen wandered over to Base Operations to see how long a delay they could expect.

In the corner of the room was a large table, stacked high with what looked like mail. Curious, Halvorsen looked at it and was startled to find that the stacks were letters addressed to *Onkel Wackelflügel* (Uncle Wiggly Wings) and *Der Schokoladen Flieger* (The Chocolate Flier), Tempelhof Central Airport, Berlin.

Shaken by the attention that his unorthodox and totally unauthorized acts of charity were getting, Halvorsen hurried back to his C-54 and told his fellow crew members, "There's a whole post office full of mail in there for us."[17] The three fliers decided, then and there, to stop their parachute drops before the Air Force disciplined them for improper procedure.

When the Western envoys in Moscow attempted to arrange a meeting with Soviet Premier Joseph Stalin and Foreign Minister Vyacheslav Molotov, they were told by deputy minister Valerin Zorin that the situation had not changed so there was no need for further talks. Besides, Zorin added, Molotov had just started his vacation and could not see them. The Soviets were clearly in no hurry to open negotiations on the question of Berlin. General W. Bedell Smith, the American ambassador, had to remind Zorin that Stalin had told him earlier that he would meet with him at any time, that the present situation was the most dangerous he had seen since becoming ambassador, and that the American government believed that an informal exchange of views would improve prospects for a solution.[18]

Still, it was not until July 31, 1948, that Molotov returned from his rambling summer dacha in the forests west of Moscow to meet the envoys in the foreign ministry, across a square from the KGB's forbidding

Lubyanka Prison.[19] A meeting with Generalissimo Stalin was arranged for August 2, and General Smith served as the chief spokesman for the West. The Soviet dictator appeared to be in a happy mood and began the discussions by reiterating the earlier Soviet position that suspension of discussions of a West German government was a precondition to the lifting of the blockade. After much discussion, Stalin proposed a meeting for the following day, but this suggestion was not well received by his guests. Then he suddenly proposed a solution to the problem of Berlin. The Soviet zone mark, he demanded, should be introduced throughout the city as the sole currency. With this, all transportation restrictions would be removed. Stalin dropped the demand that the London discussions about the establishment of a West German state be discontinued, stating that he merely wished it recorded that it was the insistent wish of his government that they not go forward. It seemed that a breakthrough had been achieved. The details of the proposed agreement were to be left for the Western envoys to work out with Minister Molotov.

While the meetings in Moscow went on, the British were building up their airlift effort with the addition of civilian planes and pilots from a number of companies. Crowding into the already jammed facilities at Wunstorf, they began flights to Berlin. A civilian Halton of Bond Air Services, piloted by Captain Treen, made the first flight on August 5, touching down in the city at 1:30 a.m. Captain Treen made four more flights that day, part of the civilian total of thirty-three sorties. The operation did not get off to a smooth start, however. The radios of the civilian aircraft were not set up to receive signals from the RAF and had to be hastily reequipped with the appropriate crystals. When the Dakotas of the civil airlines came to be loaded, it became apparent that they could not carry the same standard loads as similar RAF planes were carrying, because the Certificates of Airworthiness issued by the British Air Ministry rated them as safe only with smaller loads. Applications to amend the certificates were filed immediately.[20]

General Tunner and his staff continued to try to transform the American operation into a smooth one. When the new rules for flying into Berlin had been in effect for several days and the pilots were familiar with them, Tunner called a meeting of thirty of the line pilots. Neither squadron nor group leaders were invited, and the young fliers did not know what to expect when they trooped into the ballroom of the Schwartzer Bock Hotel at 10:00 a.m. What they found was a keg of German beer, a table full of food, and a general who wanted to hear their gripes. There was little hesitancy on the part of the fliers in voicing their complaints. Tunner and his staff took it all in, sometimes making changes on the spot, frequently promising that changes would be made as soon as possible.

Many complained that more marker beacons were needed for effective operations, a complaint that Tunner knew made sense. The general looked over at Pete Fernandez, his communications chief, and saw that he was taking notes and making calculations. They all knew that setting up marker beacons was a process that normally took several months to accomplish.

The session went on, and the beer and the food dwindled, as the men turned their complaints to the living conditions. The food was poor, the mess halls were crowded, and the barracks were even worse. With people coming and going all of the time, it was hard for exhausted air crews to get any sleep.

The meeting didn't break up until after 7:00 p.m., when a young lieutenant asked what many considered the most intelligent question of the day: "How about getting the Red Cross or somebody to send over a couple of hundred beautiful American girls?" With a dead-serious expression and the cold logic of a trained engineer, Ken Swallwell replied, "We don't have enough housing as it is. Where would they sleep?" The entire gathering gave him the answer, and the meeting broke up with laughter.

Forty-eight hours later, having worked out an ingenious system of mounting the new marker beacons on trucks, Pete Fernandez had them in place and operating.[21]

A derelict Luftwaffe base at Oberpfaffenhofen, near Munich, was requisitioned and opened as a maintenance facility to perform two-hundred-hour checks on the aircraft until a more adequate installation could be established. The mechanics and technicians assigned there immediately dubbed it "Ober-huffen-puffen."[22]

At Tegel, in the French sector of Berlin, ground was broken on the site of a new airport, and work on the new runway at Tempelhof moved ahead. On both projects, gangs of German laborers, many of them women working in brief swimsuits in the heat of summer, labored by hand to perform tasks normally done by heavy machinery. There were no airplanes in Europe large enough to fly in construction equipment.

Then, an anonymous member of Tunner's staff recalled an incident that had occurred when Brazil had declared war on the Axis powers and made sites available to the Allies for the construction of airfields for antisubmarine patrols over the South Atlantic. The locations were in the jungles along the Amazon, where it had been impossible either to drive or to airlift heavy construction equipment to the sites. A clever civilian employee of the army had found the solution in his oxyacetylene torch. He had deftly cut up bulldozers, rock-crushers, and graders into transportable pieces, rode with them on small planes into the jungle, and then calmly welded them back into operating condition after they landed. A call went out through military channels to find a welder named H. P. Lacomb, wherever he was. Located by the FBI working on an obscure job at an airfield in the American Midwest, Lacomb was put on a priority flight to Europe to again practice his unique artistry.[23]

By Thursday, August 12, the British civilian aircraft, the RAF, and the USAF were able to make a total of 707 flights into Berlin. The 4,742 tons of cargo they carried exceeded the minimum daily requirement of the city for the first time since the airlift began.

# TWENTY-THREE

## BLACK FRIDAY

A driving rain fell from black, scudding clouds as General Tunner's C-47 took off from Wiesbaden on Friday, August 13, 1948. Lieutenant Colonel Stu Bettinger was in the lefthand seat and Red Forman was flying as copilot. Tunner sat in the jump seat behind the pilots, peering out the windscreen at the dark gray nothing that the skies had become. Tunner was on his way to Berlin for a ceremony honoring Lieutenant James Lykins, a twenty-five-year-old from Brownsville, Texas. Lykins had flown the most missions of the airlift so far—forty-six round-trips in forty-two days—and was to be given an antique gold watch that a German had insisted on donating as "a little token from an old and grateful heart," and the ceremony that was planned was impressive. The Honor Guard of the 3d Battalion of the 16th Infantry was to be there, and music was to be provided by the 298th Army Band and the Berlin Military Post Fife and Drum Corps.[1]

But the weather in Berlin was worse than at Wiesbaden. The ceiling had fallen to zero, and a cloudburst so heavy that the men in the Tempelhof tower couldn't see the runway was drenching the field. The radar screens were registering nothing except the clutter from the falling rain. At 10:22 a.m., C-54 pilot Lieutenant Henry T. Fulton, who had been waiting over Tempelhof for forty-five minutes for radar guidance, thought he glimpsed the runway in a break in the clouds and attempted a visual approach. What he had seen was the new runway under construction. Fulton brought his plane down into eighteen inches of crushed rubble, badly damaging the aircraft. Seven minutes later, Lieutenant Francis Adams badly overshot on his approach, touching down on the last third of the primary runway. His plane piled into a fence, and the left gas tank exploded, engulfing the ship in flames. Adams and his crew escaped without injury.[2] A third pilot, seeing the fire as he was landing, braked too hard and blew both tires, stranding the plane in the center of the strip. By the time Tunner's aircraft arrived over the city, ground control had begun to stack the planes over the field, where they circled at altitudes of between 3,000 and 12,000 feet. Nothing was landing, and because of the danger of collisions with the circling planes, nothing was taking off either.

"This is a hell of a way to run a railroad," Tunner snarled.

Then he snapped up the microphone on the control panel and raised the control tower.

"This is 5549, Tunner talking, and you listen. Send every plane in the stack back to its home base."

The tower operator was nonplussed. "Please repeat," crackled in Tunner's earphones.

"I said: Send everybody in the stack above and below me home."

"Roger, sir," replied the tower operator, recognizing the caller and regaining his composure.

Turning to Bettinger and Forman, Tunner barked, "And as for you two, I want you to stay in Berlin until you've figured out a way to eliminate any possibility of this mess ever happening again—ever! I don't care if it takes you two hours or two weeks, that's your job."[3]

On the ground, after the ceremony, Tunner offered his two aides further guidance on their assignment. Knowing that weather was a fickle and ever-changing element of flight operations, the general directed that all aircraft under his command would fly by instrument flight rules at all times, night and day, good weather or bad. Even if the pilots could see perfectly, each flight would take place as if the visibility were zero. That would provide a single, constant standard for operations. Second, if any plane missed its approach in Berlin for any reason, it was to be immediately directed back to its home base. There would be no stacking over the city.[4]

Making certain that the airlift remained effective in supplying the city was critical, because the talks that had begun on such a hopeful note in Moscow had now bogged down through the Soviet foreign minister's intransigence. Molotov insisted on acceptance of the East marks in the city, with no Western control of monetary policy. Further, while Stalin had not made the suspension of West German government plans an absolute condition for removal of the blockade, Molotov made it clear that it was the main Soviet condition. Ambassador Smith knowingly referred to the maneuver as "the typical Soviet tactic of trying to sell the same horse twice."[5]

Secretary of State Marshall maintained that there should be no weakening or compromise of the Western position. He instructed the ambassador to remind the Soviets again that the West was in Berlin as a matter of right under treaties and to tell them that the United States could accept no currency arrangement that would give the Soviets unilateral control. Further, the United States would accept no restrictions on plans for a government in non-Soviet Germany.

Following reports on the talks over which they had no control but that had so great an impact on their lives, Berliners vacillated between hope and despair. Ruth Andreas-Friedrich noted in her diary the strain of being in the position where "one isn't the dog fighting over the bone, but the bone the dogs are fighting for."[6]

Any hope that remained for an agreement through discussions with Molotov withered after a lengthy session on August 16. The American team concluded that the Soviet foreign minister was playing for time, hoping that the approaching bad weather of autumn and worsening economic conditions in Berlin would force the West into concessions. Smith suggested to the secretary of state that it was time for another meeting with Stalin. Marshall agreed.

While the envoys talked in Moscow, Soviet pressure in the city of Berlin increased. General Kotikov informed Frau Schroeder by letter that he considered the city assembly's recent recognition of the Independent Trade Union Organization an illegal act, demanding that it be rescinded and that the assembly recognize the Soviet Central Labor Office instead. The Western commandants rejected Kotikov's demand, and the labor movement in the city was split into Communist and anti-Communist camps. On August 12, there was an ugly incident when Soviet sector police were stoned after chasing fugitives into the British and American sectors. The Western commandants formally warned the Eastern police to stay out of the Western sectors. A week later, Soviet sector police president Markgraf announced that boundaries between the various sectors "must not be an obstacle" to actions by the police force he controlled, and Frank Howley's staff at OMGUS predicted that the announcement would be used as a pretext for further raids into the West by Markgraf's forces.[7]

They were right. Two days later, a massive raid was conducted by Soviet sector police on the black market that thrived in the Potsdamer Platz. When the black marketers began to throw stones at the police, they responded by firing into the crowd, wounding at least six and setting off an even more violent reaction during which the crowd seized and overturned a Soviet vehicle. British and American military police units rushed to the scene, as did reinforcements from the Soviet army, and soldiers from the East and the West were soon tensely facing each other across the plaza. Lieutenant Vincent Spaccarotello of the American MPs attempted to explain to his Soviet counterpart, a major, that his men were in the plaza to maintain order.

The Soviet officer offered the opinion that no one had been hurt by the police action, and when shown a pool of blood on the cobblestones, he ventured that one of the black market operators had fallen as he fled and injured himself. By 10:00 p.m. both of the military groups had withdrawn, and the black marketers were back in business.[8]

The next day, Markgraf's police staged three more raids. Two were in the Potsdamer Platz, and the third took place on Bethaniendam, a street that formed the boundary between the Soviet and U.S. sectors. In that raid, Western police precinct captain August Hoppe and four of his officers were seized by Soviets at gunpoint and marched off into the Eastern sector. In all, 2,500 Berliners were arrested, and the Soviet sector police refused to speculate on when, or if, any of them would be released. Police president Markgraf announced that the raids had been carried out against "organized Fascist groups" that had been carrying out "provocations" in the raided areas.[9]

Colonel Howley's public reaction to the raids was immediate and sharp. He issued a statement condemning the raids, the shooting, and the abduction of the Western police officers, adding that the Soviets had themselves to blame for the increase in black market activity, as it had come about as a result of the blockade.[10] Privately, he determined to meet Soviet force with a show of strength.

When a force of 400 Soviets and 260 of Markgraf's police arrived on the Potsdamer Platz the following afternoon, they found themselves facing a full battalion of American military police, armed with carbines and submachine guns. Where the British sector abutted the plaza, barricades had been erected, and British soldiers stood at arms. One of the Soviet officers approached American MP Col. E. M. Kelly to ask for his cooperation in raiding the black market and was curtly informed that there would not be "any sorties or any seizures" by the Soviets in the American sector. The Soviet forces retreated to their section of the plaza and glared at the barricades.[11]

Things were not as calm in other areas of the city. In the British sector, two members of the police force were kidnapped by Markgraf's men. In Kreuzberg, where one of the earlier raids had taken place, one American sector policeman was stabbed and another was clubbed senseless before both were dragged into the Soviet sector. The Markgraf police had also taken into custody Dr. Curt Mueckenberger, the *Magistrat*'s chief of coal distribution, after having informed him that he was being dismissed from his post. The Western commandants sent a note to Kotikov, demanding an explanation for both actions, but not expecting an answer on either.

The citizens of the city had, in the meantime, found that yet another commodity would be available only on the black market. Berlin had long been a center of pet breeding, and many Berliners had managed to nurture pedigreed animals through the worst years of the war. Those animals had been given ration cards after the war ended, as breeding was considered an enterprise of commercial value. The cards entitled the smallest of dogs to two pounds of horsemeat a week and the largest to as much as seven. That meat had come from the Soviet zone. Now, the ration cards for all but the 2,785 dogs belonging to the blind or the police were canceled.[12]

☆　☆　☆

Overhead, with the weather having cleared, the airlift droned on.

The resolve of Halvorsen's crew not to risk court-martial to satisfy the cravings of the children for candy lasted for two weeks, during which they noticed that the crowd of kids at the end of the runway grew larger every day. Finally, Elkins asked the others, "What are you guys doing with your rations these days?"[13] All three had been saving them, so they determined that they would make one last candy drop. It took six parachutes to handle the pooled goodies.

The day after the drop their plane was met on one of its returns to Rhein-Main by an officer in a jeep. The squadron commander wanted to see the pilot, and Gail Halvorsen was soon in the office of Colonel James R. Haun.

"Halvorsen, what in the world have you been doing?" the colonel began.

"Flying like mad, sir," was the best Halvorsen could muster.

"I'm not stupid. What else have you been doing?"

Halvorsen owned up to the candy drops.

"Didn't they teach you in ROTC at Utah State to keep your boss informed?" Haun whipped a copy of the newspaper *Frankfurter Zeitung* from under his desk and invited Halvorsen to look at it.

"You almost hit a reporter on the head with a candy bar in Berlin yesterday. He's spread the story all over Europe. The General called me with congratulations and I didn't know anything about it. General Tunner wants to see you and there is an international press conference set up for you in Frankfurt. Fit them into your schedule. And, Lieutenant, keep flying, keep dropping, and keep me informed."[14] On their next trip into Berlin, Halvorsen and his crew picked up the mail that had been piling up in base operations, knowing that they were not in line for a reprimand after all.

The new procedures that Tunner's team of Bettinger and Forman worked out for operating the airlift were as uncomplicated as possible under the circumstances. While negotiations were going on with the British to base American planes at their fields in northern and central Germany, only one corridor—the southern one—was available to the Americans. There were also three times as many American planes based at Rhein-Main than at Wiesbaden, so Rhein-Main was made the American control center. Planes from that base were dispatched at regular intervals, and those from Wiesbaden were fitted in with the steady stream flying from the larger base.

Each pilot was given the numbers of the three planes immediately ahead of him and of the two that would take off just after him, and he carefully noted and reported the exact time when he took off. The moment a pilot entered the corridor, he was required to broadcast the identification number of his plane and the precise time, so that the planes ahead and behind could check the intervals between it and themselves and make necessary adjustments. In this way, the stream of aircraft winging toward the city was operating on a steady, rhythmical cadence of an airplane every three minutes. Had all of the airplanes on the airlift been ten-ton-capacity C-54s at the time Tunner's new rules were adopted, Berlin's minimum daily requirement could theoretically have been met. There are 1,440 minutes in each day, allowing time for 480 flights at three-minute intervals. An all-Skymaster airlift with sufficient aircraft could theoretically carry 4,800 tons a day into Tempelhof alone.

The pilots flying into Tempelhof were now given orders that they would land if the ceiling was over four hundred feet and the visibility was one mile; if it was less, they were to abort the mission and return to their base. Tunner let it be known that he would court-martial and reduce to copilot any pilot who broke that rule.[15]

The shortage of replacement parts eased somewhat as well. On August 14, a Douglas C-74 Globemaster, piloted by Capt. Brady Cole of MATS, arrived at Rhein-Main from the United States. The flight was characterized as a training mission, but the ship carried eighteen replacement engines and other parts for the airlift's C-54s in her elevator-equipped hold. When the engines had been unloaded, the giant aircraft took on twenty tons of flour and carried that into the city in a demonstration. That flight was one of only a few that it made before returning to the States. It made a spectacular show, but the runway at Tempelhof could not take constant landings by such a large craft, and the Globemaster was urgently needed by MATS for other duties. The Air Force had only three operational C-74s in its entire fleet, and two were engaged in MATS operations in other parts of the world.[16] The airlift was beginning to adversely affect MATS operations worldwide, as General Vandenburg had predicted it would. Within the United States, transcontinental and feeder routes operated by MATS were reduced by 20 percent, and C-47s were substituted for the C-54s that had previously flown the coast-to-coast run. In the Pacific, all but five regular runs were canceled entirely.[17]

The British, operating from their bases in northern Germany, were making moves toward better organization as well, but progress was slow. The overcrowding of the airfield at Wunstorf with RAF Dakotas and Yorks and a growing number of planes of the civilian companies became unworkable. All of the twin-engine Dakotas, military and civilian, transferred operations to a decrepit former Luftwaffe bombing school at Fassberg. Royal Air Force Group Captain Wally Bigger was put in charge of the work of converting the weedy field to an operational base for Operation Plain Fare. Remembering the muck and mire of Wunstorf, Bigger placed a high priority on the installation of adequate hardstands for parking and loading the airplanes, and 3.6 million square feet of pierced steel planking was laid in just seven days. The British fliers did not get to use it for long, however. By August 22, General Tunner had worked out an arrangement with the RAF to transfer a squadron of C-54s to Fassberg, from which they could use the northern corridor to fly into Gatow. Because Fassberg was an RAF facility, Group Captain Wally Bigger stayed on as station commander when the British aircraft from Fassberg transferred to Lübeck, another former Luftwaffe base—this one barely two miles from the border of the Soviet zone. This field, added to the existing facilities of Wunstorf, Fassberg, and Finkenwerder made a total of four air bases in the British zone feeding into Gatow and Lake Havel in Berlin.[18]

The use of civilian planes by the British was also slowly building up. Many of the charter operators, following the news of the Moscow negotiations, expected that the need for the airlift would soon end and that any charters they arranged would be canceled. They were therefore reluctant to make a major commitment of resources. The initial civilian efforts were disorganized as well.

The first flight that Tom Marks, a pilot for Flight Refueling, made in one of the Lancaster Tankers was no more confused than most. Taking off from England, Marks tried to follow the instructions he had been given by his company. He had been told to put the plane on the ground at Gatow, and someone would unload it. Then he was to fly it back out to wherever they sent the previous Flight Refueling crew. The instructions continued that on the next day Marks was to trade aircraft with the other crew and fly its plane back to England.

Marks, knowing nothing of either diplomacy or air corridors, flew by the straightest route possible into Berlin. Luckily, he was unmolested by Soviet fighters. On landing, he asked if anyone had seen another of Flight Refueling's tankers and was told that one had been there, unloaded, and flown out to Wunstorf. As soon as his plane was drained, Marks followed, again taking the quickest route, and again he was unmolested. He could find no sign of his company's other plane when he arrived. No one at RAF Wunstorf even knew that civilians were flying fuel into Berlin. They suggested he try the airport at Bückeburg. Marks did. The other plane was there, but its crew was nowhere to be seen. After driving around the surrounding countryside for hours in a borrowed RAF truck looking for the other crew, Marks returned to the airfield—to find them drinking in the officers' mess.

The next morning, Marks discovered that no one at Wunstorf knew anything about the part of his instructions that concerned his flying the other plane back to England. The air ministry wanted two Lancasters available to ferry fuel into Berlin, so Marks spent the next six weeks flying two sorties a day into the city. He hadn't even brought a change of clothes with him on his flight from England, so he flew all of his sorties to Berlin in the same shirt and pants he had worn on the first. Finally briefed on procedures, he did manage to stay in the corridors.[19]

Edwin P. Whitfield, the chief of British European Airways in Germany, had been asked to head the civilian portion of the operation the day before the first civilian planes arrived at Wunstorf. He found that no clear instructions had been given to the RAF about what, if any, operational support and maintenance they should give the civilians, and that no accommodation, hangar, or workshop facilities had been allocated to them as a result. Further, none of the charter companies had dispatched any administrative personnel to Germany, somehow expecting that such work would be handled by the chief pilot when he was not flying or by someone else.

Worst of all, no one at the air ministry had bothered to inform the charter companies that Whitfield was in charge of running the civilian side of the airlift, so most of the air crews regarded his organizational efforts as nothing more than meddling. It was not a good beginning, but the airlift droned on while the diplomats in Moscow continued to thrash out the details of a possible agreement to end the blockade.

On August 24, the United States' effort set a new record of 3,020 tons flown into the city in one day, but it did so at a price. Military police privates Richard Whitesell and Edward Clemmons of the detachment of the 528th MP Company stationed at Ravolzhausen, north of Frankfurt, had grown used to the roar of planes overhead by now. Their patrol area was directly under the route the planes took in and out of the base at Wiesbaden.

When the two privates saw a column of smoke rising from a field near the village, they did not at first associate it with the airlift. They thought it was a house on fire, and drove toward it to investigate. As they got closer, they saw another, larger, puff of smoke about a mile away. When they reached the first, they found a crashed and burning C-47. The second pillar of smoke was another C-47. The two had collided in midair. Army rescue teams from the 15th General Dispensary and the Hanau Signal Depot rushed to the scene, but there were no survivors. All four crew members were dead.[20]

# TWENTY-FOUR

# "GENTLEMEN, I HAVE A NEW PLAN"

The initial burst of enthusiasm of the airlift crews for their job was beginning to fade as the work settled into the rigorous routine that General Tunner established. The morale-sapping effects of being away from their wives and families on temporary duty (TDY) began to work on the married men, and "Dear John" letters began to arrive for the bachelors. The men of the 54th Troop Carrier Squadron hung a curious reminder of what they had left behind on the walls of their new operations room in Wiesbaden. Finding no use for them in the mud of west-central Germany, the crews decorated the room with the snowshoes they had brought from Alaska.

General Tunner knew that there was nothing that he could do immediately about the TDY situation, as no one could predict when the crisis might end. He could try to boost morale, however, and did so by fostering competition between units. Tunner believed that if Americans have the spur of healthy competition, they can accomplish almost anything. Daily quotas for each unit were set up and posted on "howgozit" boards at each base. Tunner then proposed that the daily tonnage figures be published in the newspaper, the *Task Force Times,* he was setting up. That led him into a major conflict with the headquarters at USAFE.

Security officers on LeMay's staff argued that the figures of the daily tonnage carried into Berlin must remain a military secret, to be released by USAFE when, and if, it was considered appropriate. The Soviets, the intelligence men argued, could not be allowed to learn what the airlift was accomplishing. Tunner wanted to advertise the figures on a daily basis and post them openly at his airfields, as a morale and propaganda tool. The position of the security men didn't make any sense to Tunner, for a number of reasons.

He reasoned that a C-54 is not something that can sneak into a city. The Soviets could, and did, monitor the incoming flights, and they received data on them from the air safety center in Berlin. It was a matter of simple mathematics for them to calculate the tonnage being carried. Therefore, the figures couldn't be kept secret, even if it was a good idea to do so. And it was not, Tunner argued. If the world saw that the airlift was achieving success, it would be a tremendous propaganda victory.[1] He took his arguments all the way to the top of USAFE. General LeMay agreed with him, and the figures were published each day in the *Task Force Times* and were soon reproduced in the world press, including newspapers in Berlin where the morale of the citizens also needed bolstering.

Since the talks in Moscow began, hope among Berliners in the Western sectors that the blockade would be lifted had alternated with fears the Western allies would desert the city as the price to be paid to accomplish that end. Berliners, along with the rest of the world, knew little of what was happening in Moscow; the participants were keeping the details of the talks secret until they concluded. The people of Berlin and the world did know that, when the talks had appeared to be faltering, the Western envoys had held a second meeting with Premier Stalin, and a proposal had been made to shift the discussions back to the military governors in Berlin. General Clay and General Robertson, the British military governor, had canceled a planned inspection tour of the Ruhr to await instructions, and discussions between the West and Stalin's foreign minister on this possibility continued in Moscow.[2]

When the Western diplomats met Stalin for the second time, on August 23, 1948, they came prepared with the draft of a document that they hoped would break the deadlock. They wanted to agree on a directive to be sent to the four military governors, ordering them to work out concrete proposals about the transport restrictions and currency, along lines that had first been agreed to by Stalin, but on which Molotov was now hedging.

The Soviet dictator was smiling and greeted the delegation in a friendly fashion, saying, "Gentlemen, I have a new plan." Told by Ambassador W. Bedell Smith that the West had one as well, Stalin replied, "Good, we can compare them."[3]

The Soviet dictator seemed very accommodating. The question of exactly what travel restrictions were to be lifted had been a sticking point in the discussions with Molotov, who again stated that only those imposed since June 18 would be rescinded. Stalin interrupted him to suggest that it might be better if they referred only to restrictions that had been imposed lately, without specifying a date. With regard to the currency question, Stalin agreed in principle to have it controlled by a four-power financial commission. Then he turned to the question of the formation of a West German government, suggesting language that stated that any decision on this matter would be deferred until the next meeting of the Council of Foreign Ministers. Smith expressed his doubts that the United States would accept such wording, but the French and British were ready to accept in order to resolve the crisis. On that note, the meeting with Stalin ended, with the Western envoys expected to continue their discussions with Molotov.

Ambassador Smith's evaluation of his government's reaction was correct. Secretary Marshall set forth in unmistakable terms, in a cable to Smith, the basic American requirements for agreement. They were a clear statement of the four powers' coequal rights to be in Berlin; no abandonment of the United States' commitment to the formation of a West German government; complete lifting of the blockade; and adequate quadripartite control of currency in the city.[4] This response bitterly disappointed Molotov, but discussions on a joint communiqué and a set of directions to the military governors went slowly forward. The spirit of accommodation was not evident in the city itself, however. There, Wilhelm Pieck, co-chairman of the SED, declared, "The only way that the suffering of the Berlin population can be eased is if the Western allies decide soon to leave Berlin."[5]

On August 26, a mob of over 6,000, singing the "Internationale" and carrying red flags and placards demanding that the Western powers leave the city, converged on city hall where a meeting of the city assembly was scheduled for 12:30 p.m. The chairman of the council, Dr. Otto Suhr, recalling the events of June 23, abruptly canceled the meeting "to avoid bloodshed."[6] The mob was unfazed by the cancellation, breaking into the building and swarming upstairs to the second floor council chamber. There, Karl Litke, chairman of the SED, took the podium to make a speech in which he denounced the current *Magistrat* as "agents of the imperialistic Western powers" and demanded that they resign immediately. To replace them, Litke proposed an eighteen-man "action committee" be appointed.

It was announced to the cheering crowd that Ferdinand Friedensburg, acting as mayor because Louise Schroeder was ill, had agreed to see a delegation. Ten men, including former deputy mayor Karl Marion, were chosen. They demanded of the acting mayor that the Western marks be withdrawn from the city and that the police force be reunited under the leadership of Paul Markgraf. They also denounced the *Magistrat,* saying that it had caused chaos in the city. Friedensburg listened politely to the delegation, then pointed out that the only way to legally effect a change in the administration of the city was by municipal elections. They were not happy at the conclusion of the interview.[7]

That evening, over 30,000 Berliners gathered on three hours' notice at a rally held in front of the Reichstag. The meeting was jointly sponsored by the three democratic parties. The crowd listened to their leaders declare that the city would not surrender to Communism and that, if a putsch was attempted, it would be met by force. Ernst Reuter drew loud cheers when he said, "We Berliners have said 'no' to communism, and we will fight it with all our might as long as there is breath in us."[8] The city assembly announced that it would attempt to meet the following day and that assurances that the Eastern sector police would provide protection would be sought. General Clay had been close-mouthed about the delicate negotiations going on in the Soviet capital. However, on learning of the riot at city hall, Clay told reporters frankly, "No action committees are going to take over the millions of people we are responsible for."[9]

In Moscow, Frank Roberts, the British delegate to the talks, complained bitterly to Molotov about the social disorders that were occurring in Berlin at this critical juncture in the negotiations. He suggested that Moscow order Marshal Sokolovsky to take measures to preserve calm in the city, in light of the fact that the four military governors were soon to be asked to meet and resolve the conflict. Molotov gruffly responded that Marshal Sokolovsky already had his instructions from Moscow and refused to be drawn into further discussion of the matter.[10]

Doctor Otto Suhr called the Berlin city assembly to order at 10:00 a.m. on August 27, even though there was a mob of over 2,000 outside the building, waving their red banners and chanting slogans. After eight minutes, Suhr announced that it would be necessary to adjourn the session indefinitely, until the assembly could be guaranteed police protection. The assembly members departed by the rear door of the building to avoid assaults like the ones that had occurred a month earlier. As they left, members of the mob clambered over the iron gates at the front and pounded on the glass of the main doors, which were locked. One of the Soviet liaison officers in the building appeared inside the main entrance, demanding that the ushers let him out. When the doorkeepers asked that he use the side door so that the crowd would not seize the opportunity to enter, he refused, renewing his demand that the front door be opened. When it was, the crowd surged forward into the building and rushed up the stairs to the assembly chamber. There the leaders harangued the crowd, declaring that, unless the current city administration was ousted, millions of Berliners would die of starvation in the coming winter. The speakers disparaged the Allied airlift, stating that it could not bring in enough supplies to save them. After an hour, the crowd drifted away. Many chanted as they left, "We'll be back."[11]

That evening a Lend-Lease jeep carrying four armed Soviet soldiers roared through the American sector under the command of a red-bearded lieutenant colonel. When an American military policeman on a motorcycle tried to stop them, they ran him off the road, breaking his arm. Other pursuing MPs fired on the Soviet vehicle, wounding one of the soldiers. Faced with gunfire, the Soviets careened through roadblocks and barricades, heading back into their own sector. The pursuing Americans gave up the chase eight hundred yards inside the Eastern sector.

During the investigation of the incident, the Soviet lieutenant colonel told American liaison officers, "I didn't want to be stopped and fall into the hands of an uncivilized animal-like people who shoot without any provocation." The formal protest that the Americans filed with the Soviets noted that the shots were fired only as a last resort. The Soviet counterprotest charged the Americans with violating Soviet jurisdiction by entering their sector.[12]

Doctor Suhr petitioned the Soviet commandant of the city, General Kotikov, asking that he either establish a four-square-mile neutral zone around city hall or guarantee that the Soviet sector police would give the city assembly protection from the mobs that were disrupting meetings. Kotikov's response was sarcastic. "We do not clearly understand what the Assembly Speaker wishes from the Soviet authorities," he wrote, asking if Suhr wanted demonstrations banned throughout the city or just where the *Magistrat* building was located. Why didn't Suhr ask the police directly, Kotikov asked, and did he desire the Soviets to forbid meetings of people who were opposed to the current city administration?[13]

The text of Kotikov's response was released by the city administration. When reporters showed up at city hall to obtain it, several were arrested. They included an American, John Meehan of United Press, and three Germans. Four American soldiers in various parts of the city were also arrested that day by the Soviets. Released after being held for twenty-four hours, the reporters said that they had been treated "all right—by Russian prison standards."[14]

The Soviets further riled the Americans by demanding the forced repatriation of a fourteen-year-old orphan who was hospitalized in the U.S. sector awaiting an operation. Born in the Ukraine, Helena Korelenko had come to Germany as a refugee during the war. She had contracted infantile paralysis and was now unable to walk. Doctors in the American sector sought permission from Soviet officials to operate on her, because it was presumed that she was a Soviet national. What they received instead was a visit from an officer and a sergeant in an ambulance, prepared to transport the girl to the Soviet zone. Howard Studd of OMGUS sent the Soviets away, saying that it was against United States policy to release a displaced person without approval of the International Refugee Organization and expressing doubts that the girl was in fact a Soviet national.[15]

Whatever instructions Marshal Sokolovsky had gotten from Moscow, it was clear to the people of Berlin and to the Western military government officials in the city that they had little to do with maintaining an atmosphere of calm.

The diplomats from the three Western powers continued to meet with Molotov in Moscow, wrangling over the instructions that were to be sent to the four military governors. Given the differences in the American and Soviet positions, no agreement was reached on the text of a joint communiqué to be released to the press, but directives were sent to the military governors to begin discussions in Berlin of technical details about the simultaneous lifting of the blockade and introduction of Soviet currency under four-power supervision. The Berlin discussions were expected to be concluded in seven days, and the military governors were directed to issue a report to their respective governments at the end of that time. The Western envoys spent the evening of August 31 in Moscow relaxing together in the press department of the British embassy, watching a movie in which Vivian Leigh played the title role of Anna Karenina.[16]

General Clay was unhappy with the instructions that he received as a result of the Moscow talks. He was convinced that the Soviet moves were nothing more than a delaying tactic and that the only agreement they were likely to be able to reach would be one that resulted in turning the city over to the Soviets.[17] His attitude was so truculent and bellicose that his superiors worried that he might abort the conference. Defense Secretary James Forrestal even suggested that Army Secretary Kenneth Royall go to Germany to assist Clay in the discussions. Robert Lovett, who was also gravely concerned about Clay's attitude, thought that this approach was impractical, as it would indicate that the government had no confidence in its military governor. Royall agreed with Lovett's view.

Learning of these concerns during a teleconference with Washington on August 30, Clay said, "I am not going to be the warmonger which plunges defenseless France and U.K. as well as U.S. into war. On the other hand, I have no hope of reaching a solid agreement. It is not Soviet custom to give more in the field than in Moscow."[18] With his opinion of the probable outcome of the talks well known to his superiors and fellow Western military governors, Clay now set about to carry out his job in the most effective way possible. He was a good soldier who would follow the orders that were given to him. It was Clay who suggested at the first meeting that working committees of staff experts be set up to deal with specific technical matters. The meetings were closed and took place in great secrecy, with reporters unable to discover from the guards even where the various parties sat during the discussions. At the close of the first meeting, Clay's only comment to the crowd of reporters waiting outside the Allied Control Council building was that there would be another meeting the next day. Western traffic control experts, speaking off the record, let it be known that they had already set up a schedule for incoming freight and that trains were loaded and waiting at the border, ready to roll into the city.[19]

Ruth Andreas-Friedrich greeted that news with unbridled pleasure. "No more dehydrated potatoes and canned meat," she wrote in her diary the next day. "No more power cuts. No more tiresome conversion gymnastics between East marks and West marks. Most important, no more enmity and unrestrained hatred between Berliners."[20]

Marshal Sokolovsky was proving intransigent in his opposition to most Western proposals made at the talks. It was almost as if he had not received the same instructions from Moscow that the others had, as he refused even to discuss lifting the blockade until the question of currency was settled. The East Berlin Communists continued to take actions indicating they expected the government of the city to fall in the near future. At a meeting on September 3, they set up a bloc system of political representation designed to take over all the functions of municipal government and announced that this new creation was the "true voice of Berliners."[21]

☆　☆　☆

General Tunner had more immediate problems than those that confronted the military governors. If the governors were successful in their talks, Tunner's operation could be shut down. If they were not, it would go on, and maintaining the airlift meant maintaining the planes that flew it. His most acute problem was the shortage of trained men to perform the necessary maintenance, and that problem was complicated by his chain of command. General Tunner knew what the technical solution was—to employ former Luftwaffe mechanics—but permission to use Germans in such a capacity could come only from General Clay, and Tunner's operating orders from USAFE did not allow him to communicate directly with the military governor. He was required to handle things through proper military channels, and Tunner's channel was through Headquarters, USAFE, not the military governor. Tunner's requests to arrange to hire Germans, made through those channels, had gone unheeded, and his maintenance problems kept growing more acute.

One day, when Tunner was at Tempelhof checking on a routine turnaround problem, General Clay passed through the airport on his way to a plane. Seeing Tunner, he walked over and asked, "Any problems?" It was all the opening Tunner needed to tell the military governor about the maintenance problem.

"But I think I can lick it," Tunner added, "if you will allow me to hire some skilled German mechanics."

"Go ahead and do it," Clay responded. "Tell Curt I said it's O.K."

Tunner put his own people to work finding a qualified German to run the program after reporting the conversation to LeMay's personnel people. He knew that USAFE could not turn the plan down in light of Clay's approval, but it was not something that endeared him to the people in headquarters.[22]

The man whom Tunner's staff found to head the German mechanic operation was a former Luftwaffe general, Hans Detlev von Rohden, who had served in air transport during the war and was fluent in English. Translating U.S. Air Force maintenance manuals into German as he went, von Rohden quickly organized a force of mechanics who grew so proficient that there were, eventually, more German mechanics assigned to each squadron than there were Americans.[23]

The German mechanics, Tunner wryly noted, even had one advantage on the Americans. They were able to pronounce "Oberpfaffenhofen." That base, with the jawbreaking name, was another of Tunner's concerns. It had worked well as an expedient maintenance facility in the summer and early autumn. However, if the airlift were to go on into the winter, Oberpfaffenhofen was totally unsuited for its function. It had insufficient indoor areas in which to work on aircraft, and indoor work space was essential in winter. Looking about Europe, Tunner's staff came on the RAF base at Burtonwood, just north of Liverpool. A huge depot, it had a perimeter of over seventy miles and had, during the war, housed 30,000 British and American airmen. Now it was nearly deserted and used only for "pickling" obsolete RAF planes—the British equivalent of the U.S. Air Force's "boneyard" in the Arizona desert, where aircraft were parked while awaiting destruction. Most of the windows on the base were broken, the roofs sagged and leaked, and much of the equipment had been ruined through neglect. However, Burtonwood offered enclosures where the water used to clean the airlift planes would not freeze and where the maintenance crews could work in relative comfort while they carried out the vital two-hundred-hour inspections.

By the time the military governors met in Berlin for the second time since the Moscow talks, the base at Burtonwood had been reactivated. Twenty-five hundred airmen, most drawn from Griffiss Air Force Base in Rome, New York, were on their way to England to man it. Even this number of mechanics and technicians would not be enough to handle the maintenance demands of the two-hundred-hour checks on airlift craft. Tunner was forced to detail mechanics from his own squadrons to fill out the complement at Burtonwood. In return, he received a promise that the new maintenance depot would perform the required work at a rate of seven planes per day once it became fully operational.[24]

☆    ☆    ☆

The members of Berlin's three democratic parties knew that it was imperative that the city assembly hold a meeting in spite of the continuing Communist promises to disrupt any such gathering. At the same time they issued their threats, the Communists were condemning the assembly as ineffective and defunct because it was not holding meetings. The assembly was worried about the possible outcome of the conferences going on between the military governors and anxious to present their views to that body. Further, the Soviet military government had been instrumental in the dismissal of nearly 25 percent of the municipal employees in the Soviet sector, all anti-Communists, on charges of sabotage or criminal attitude. A protest against this action was on the agenda of the assembly.

On September 4, Acting Mayor Friedensburg disclosed to the press that defense squads of municipal employees had been recruited to try to prevent riotous disruption of assembly proceedings such as had occurred in late August. Therefore, the city assembly was scheduled to meet on Monday, September 6, 1948, in spite of the refusal of the Eastern sector police to ensure protection. Hans Seidel, the deputy chief of that force, publicly announced that his men would in no way interfere with Communist demonstrators.[25] In a Sunday radio broadcast, Dr. Otto Suhr made an appeal to Berliners in general, and the Communists in particular, not to allow another riot at city hall. He asked for a political truce, so that law and order could prevail, at least during the critical negotiations that were going on at the Allied Control Council. His speech made it clear that Berliners would judge the sincerity of the Soviets by the actions of the Berlin Communists, who were known for their strict adherence to the instructions they got from their Soviet masters.

## TWENTY-FIVE

# "WE ARE VERY CLOSE TO WAR"

Forty-six Western sector police officers volunteered to stand by in city hall when the assembly came together for its meeting on September 6, even though they knew that the Eastern police had threatened to arrest them. They wore civilian clothes and special armbands to identify themselves, but were unarmed.

The Communist mob began to gather at 10:00 a.m., even though the meeting was not scheduled to begin until noon. By 11:00, over 2,000 men, mostly young and mostly burly youths, had gathered in front of the building, shouting slogans. The Soviet zone police stood idly outside their station, just across the street, making it clear that they intended to do nothing to try to control the mob. Officials in city hall ordered the front door closed, which provoked members of the mob to kick in the glass and knock down two of the guards. They then seized a wooden bulletin board and used it as a battering ram to smash down what was left of the door.[1] The rest of the crowd surged into the building, driving the city assembly out. While the leaders of the mob shouted more slogans to the followers gathered in the chamber from which the assembly had just fled, Eastern sector police also rushed in and began to scour the building for their Western counterparts. Forcing their way into the suite of the American liaison officer, Major John E. Davisson, at gunpoint, they seized nineteen of the Western police who had taken refuge there.[2] These officers were dragged off in handcuffs and chains to the police station across the street. Associated Press photographer Henry Burroughs was attempting to photograph the riot when the police grabbed his camera and smashed it. Ernest Leiser of the Overseas News Agency came to Burroughs's aid, and the police began to beat him. When Joe Evans of the *Wall Street Journal* tried to intervene, he was thrown down the flight of stairs leading to the assembly chamber. Unable to force their way into the British and French liaison offices where the remainder of the Western police had taken refuge, Markgraf's forces threw a cordon around the building. Adolph Wagner, chief of the uniformed Eastern sector police, first announced that no one could enter or leave the building. Then he changed the order, saying that those in the building could leave, but no one could enter.

Frank Howley made a prompt protest to the Soviet commandant but was rebuffed. Colonel William Babcock, Howley's deputy commandant, arrived on the scene and, protesting loudly, was taken into custody by the police and transported to Soviet headquarters, only to be released an hour later. The police cordon around the building was reinforced by Soviet troops, who refused entry to anyone. Inside, the officers of the French liaison group burned their confidential papers. The non-Communist members of the city assembly convened the scheduled meeting—in an unfurnished hall at the Technical University in the British sector. Now, the legislative body of the city was split between East and West.

Major General Jean Ganeval, the French commandant, was a small, gray-haired man who maintained his headquarters in a former SS facility, now renamed the Jeanne d'Arc Barracks, in Frohnau. He rarely showed his feelings and had once told a reporter, "Be careful when you write up your interviews with me. I don't want you putting any idiotic statements in my mouth. And above all, don't have me saying anything clever."[3]

Ganeval's superior, the French military governor, General Joseph-Pierre Koenig, had strongly protested to Marshal Sokolovsky about the treatment the liaison officers were receiving at city hall and had appealed to him to find a solution to the impasse. The Soviet had suggested that the French and Soviet commandants in the city work out details of how to settle the crisis at city hall.[4] Ganeval arranged with Soviet commandant Kotikov to remove the Western police from the building under French escort and transport them back to the Western part of the city. The two French military trucks carrying the men were only three blocks from city hall when they were flagged down at a roadblock of two Soviet jeeps at the Schloss bridge. As the trucks stopped, twenty Soviet zone police poured out of an adjacent building, and four jeeploads of Soviet soldiers, armed with submachine guns, raced in behind. The jeeps were followed immediately by a truck with sixty-five more Soviet soldiers, who formed an armed cordon around the small convoy.

"Those who have papers may go on," the Soviet officer in charge said. "Those who don't will have to come with us."[5] The nineteen policemen who were being escorted away from city hall by the French were handcuffed and driven away.

All three of the Western commandants lodged protests with the Soviets. General Ganeval's was the most bitter. "In the course of a telephone conversation," he wrote to General Kotikov, "you and I reached an agreement. I did not doubt your word for a moment and issued my orders accordingly. I still cannot believe that an agreement personally guaranteed by you could have been violated in so flagrant a form."[6]

Kotikov responded to Ganeval by accusing the French liaison officers of being drunk. Howley's protest was answered with an admonition to the Americans "not to interfere in matters which don't concern them."[7] The Soviet commandant even denied that a mob had broken into city hall, describing what had happened as an appeal by the working people of the city to take measures for the coming winter. He again signed his notes, "Military Commandant of the City of Berlin."[8] By the time those harsh responses had been read in the West, the talks between the military governors had broken down on Sokolovsky's obstinence, and Harry Truman had called together the National Security Council to review the status of the crisis.

Through it all, the airlift kept increasing its pace, in spite of the increasing frequency of Soviet fighter flights in the air corridors. The airlift was still drawing in pilots on TDY from their normal duties to fill its ranks. Kenneth Slaker was one of them. Twenty-eight years old, Slaker had flown fifty bombing missions against Germany during the war but had left the military to study engineering at the University of Washington at Seattle. Offered a regular commission late in 1947, he had accepted, had completed a training course for engineers at Fort Belvoir, Virginia, and had just been assigned as Base Operations Officer at Fürstenfeldbruck Air Base, twenty-five miles west of Munich. On September 8, 1948, he received orders to report for temporary duty as a pilot with the 62d Troop Carrier Group at Wiesbaden.

Slaker attended a briefing on airlift flight procedures the following day and what the operations officer said at the end of the briefing was very disturbing to him:

> The Russians say they will shoot down any aircraft that strays out of the Berlin airlift corridor, and that captured pilots will be treated as spies. This is a serious threat to our pilots and if you should find yourself down in the Soviet Zone, we cannot say that you should turn yourselves in, or that you should try to escape. There is no published or firm policy on this.[9]

Slaker had hoped that he would be assigned to a daylight flying schedule, so that he could visually orient himself to the corridor and Tempelhof, but he was not. His first flight, on September 10, was at night, and two of his next three were made in bad weather as well, requiring ground-controlled approaches in Berlin. On his fifth flight, on September 14, First Lieutenant Clarence Steber, an experienced 62d Troop Carrier flier, was assigned as Slaker's copilot. They drew an ancient C-47 that still bore the dusty pink paint that marked it as a veteran of the campaign in North Africa, early in the war. Slaker and Steber were scheduled to make two flights that evening. On the first, the cargo was 55-gallon drums of gasoline, and the airplane reeked of it. In spite of the driving rain, they took off and flew with the side windows of the cockpit open to bleed off the pungent, volatile fumes. During the entire flight, Ken Slaker had visions of the C-47 erupting in a ball of flame. He was happy to find, on his return to Wiesbaden, that the cargo for the second flight was flour, not gasoline. As they boarded, Slaker noticed that Steber unclipped his parachute from his harness and laid it by the rear cargo door. It was a habit many transport pilots had, knowing that they would have to use that door in an emergency and wanting to avoid the discomfort of wearing the parachute during flight. Slaker, schooled in bombers, kept his parachute on his six-foot-three frame at all times in flight.[10]

☆ ☆ ☆

The dangers of flying gasoline in drums would soon be addressed by eliminating that method completely and making the aerial tankers of the British civilian line, Flight Refueling, responsible for all such shipments. The British civil airlift was continuing to grow in size and was now attracting some formidable characters. One was Air Vice Marshal Donald Bennett.

Bennett was a driven man, and that drive had much more to do with personal and professional vindication than cash, although he believed that money would also come out of his firm's participation in the airlift. Air Freight, Bennett's newly formed charter company, was equipped with Avro Tudors, four-engine civil planes whose performance Bennett had championed. His faith in the Tudor had cost him a lucrative job as chief of British South American Airways. It had also badly damaged the reputation of a flier who was an aviation legend. Bennett's twelve-year-old textbook, *The Complete Air Navigator,* was the standard for the flying industry, and he still held the world long-distance seaplane record, set in the autumn of 1938 on a flight from Scotland to Alexandria Bay, South Africa. During the war, Bennett had ferried American and Canadian planes to Britain. Then, transferred to combat operations, he was shot down in an attack on the German battleship *Tirpitz,* evading capture and escaping through occupied Norway. Later in the war, Bennett led the swift squadrons of twin-engine, wooden Mosquito bombers that had illuminated German cities with incendiary bombs to mark targets for the waves of Lancasters that had followed.

He had piloted an Avro Tudor on its 16,200-mile test flight from London to Chile and back and had convinced British South American Airways to buy a fleet of them when he was appointed its managing director and chief executive officer at the end of the war.

On January 29, 1948, however, disaster struck B.S.A.A. One of its fleet of sleek new Tudors, with twenty-six passengers and a crew of six, vanished without a trace on a flight from the Azores to Kindley Field in Bermuda. The Civil Air Ministry promptly grounded all Tudors until suspicions about its airworthiness could be addressed. Bennett's sharp, stinging diatribe against the ministry's action led the board of directors of B.S.A.A. to give him £4,500 in severance pay and show him the door. He used the money to buy two Tudors and establish Air Freight as a charter company.

On September 3, 1948, Air Freight's Avro Tudor II, Registration G-AGRY, lifted off from Wunstorf on its initial flight into Berlin with Air Vice Marshal Donald Bennett at the controls and a rather frightened Royal Army Service Corps major as a passenger. Not long after takeoff the major noticed that the outer starboard engine was belching flames and pointed it out to Bennett.

"Don't worry about it," Bennett said. "The wind will blow it out." It did, and Bennett was able to give his passenger an unauthorized flying tour of the city of Berlin, contrary to all regulations, pointing out to him the sites he had fire-bombed during the war to provide blazing beacons for the RAF.[11]

The British were also bringing in military aircrews to supplement the modest resources of the RAF from locations that would give the airlift effort a more international character. In mid September, thirty volunteer pilots from the Royal Australian Air Force arrived in Germany. They were assigned to and integrated with the RAF squadrons and began flying duties as soon as they arrived.

With the breakdown of the talks among the military governors, dialogue shifted to Moscow and to the streets of the besieged city of Berlin. In the Soviet capital, the three Western envoys requested yet another meeting with Premier Stalin, only to be informed that the Soviet leader was now on vacation and was not available to meet with them. If they wished to talk, it would have to be with Foreign Minister Molotov.

In Berlin, the free parties scheduled a rally in the Platz der Republik in the British sector. It was in front of the Reichstag ruins, a block from the Soviet war memorial and the Brandenburg Gate, over which floated a giant Soviet flag. The British commandant, General Herbert, tried to prohibit the meeting, knowing that it had a great potential to turn ugly and could be provocative to the Soviets. Herbert was overruled by General Robertson, the British military governor, who shared the former's reservations but believed that banning the gathering would have a disastrous effect on the morale of the people of the city and would be interpreted by the Soviets as a major retreat. General Herbert had to be content with stationing a battalion of the Royal Norfolk Regiment under Lieutenant Colonel George Turner-Cain out of sight in the ruins of the Reichstag, ready to deploy at the first sign of trouble.

General Clay believed that the demonstration had the potential for trouble as well, but he did not prohibit the RIAS mobile newscasters from spreading word throughout the Western sectors that it was scheduled. By 5:00 in the afternoon, over a quarter of a million people had jammed into the square. It was a larger gathering than had occurred even during the reign of the Nazis, when attendance at rallies was compulsory. They heard speakers denounce the Eastern sector police for their actions at city hall. Doctor Suhr, president of the displaced assembly, said, "Today the Russian general gets the answer to his behavior from the masses of assembled Berliners." Ernst Reuter told them, "What Russian promises are really worth is proven by the broken promises of General Kotikov."[12]

When the meeting ended at 6:30 p.m., a delegation headed off with yet another petition for the military governors. The rest headed toward their homes. Thousands were passing through the towering Doric arches of the Brandenburg Gate on their way back into the Soviet sector when they spotted a truck full of Markgraf's police and began to jeer at them. Several of the police dismounted and pointed their weapons at the crowd. At that moment, a Soviet jeep carrying the relief guards for the soldiers pacing their posts in front of the Soviet war memorial roared into the square, only to be greeted with a shower of stones.

Henry Burroughs, the AP photographer, had gotten a new camera to replace the one that had been smashed in city hall. He was snapping pictures of the crowd booing and laughing at the three Soviet soldiers in their jeep when he noticed the even larger crowd milling around the Brandenburg Gate. He made his way there just as a series of shots rang out.[13] Fifteen-year-old Wolfgang Scheunemann, who was trying to shield a woman behind him in the crowd, fell with a wound to the groin. Most of the crowd took shelter behind the columns of the gate or in buildings, but a lone unarmed German youth tussled briefly with the Eastern sector police, shouting, "Traitors! Communist swine!" Then he too was shot.[14]

Several of the demonstrators tried to climb to the top of the gate in order to tear down the red flag fluttering there, but fire from the police drove them off. A second try, at 7:10, was successful, and the flag and pole crashed to the ground as the crowd shouted "Burn it!" A practical twelve-year-old seized a large section of the wooden pole, dragging it through the crowd and saying to those who tried to stop him, "I'm taking it to my Uncle. We need fuel for the stove."[15]

The Soviet guards from the war memorial, seeing the flag torn down and burning, rushed to the scene and pointed their machine guns menacingly at the crowd. Major Frank Stokes of the British military police advanced on the cordon of Soviets, armed only with his holstered pistol and a swagger stick. Speaking softly and tapping their gun barrels down with his stick, Stokes convinced the Soviet soldiers to withdraw.

They were doing so when British reinforcements arrived and the crowd began to drift away.

When the casualties were counted, twenty-two Germans had been wounded.[16] Wolfgang Scheunemann was dead.

The following day, the Soviet press in Berlin claimed that the demonstration had been touched off by anti-Soviet speeches made by leading political figures at the rally. Police president Markgraf singled out acting mayor Friedensburg for blame and warned that the appearance of city officials "in such a riotous Fascist mob may lead to serious consequences." Squadrons of Yaks still buzzed about in the air corridors, and in the air traffic center in Berlin, Soviet Captain Korchenko presented a letter to his American counterpart, Captain Vincent H. Gookin. The text read:

> You are requested to guarantee to submit to me beforehand not later than one hour before take-off to or from Berlin the following information: Type of aircraft, pilot's name, route of flight, height of flight along route, take-off time from air field, radio details, object of flight.[17]

The request was immediately rejected, but the Western allies worried that it was the first Soviet move to close the air corridors.

☆　☆　☆

President Truman had been following the developments in Berlin closely, even though the election campaign against Thomas Dewey was taking up an enormous amount of his time. On September 9, 1948, he convened an extraordinary session of the National Security Council only hours after returning from a campaign trip to Michigan. Few people in official Washington felt that the current negotiations in Moscow would be successful in light of the recent events in Berlin. Most favored referring the matter to the United Nations in hope of a resolution.

Other questions required resolution as well. Since the beginning of the crisis, Secretary of Defense Forrestal had been pressing for an answer to whether the United States would use the atomic bomb in the event of a war with the Soviet Union. When the airlift began, three squadrons of B-29 bombers had been flown to Britain under hastily arranged pacts to allow them to be based there. While these planes were not equipped to drop the atomic bomb, the defense secretary now asked again for an answer to his question and for permission to build storage facilities in Great Britain for atomic weapons. He got both.

At a cabinet meeting on September 13, the question of the use of atomic weapons came up. Harry Truman said that, while he prayed that he would not have to make that decision, there should be no doubt about what it would be.[18] That evening, the president confided to his diary, "I have a terrible feeling that we are very close to war. I hope not." [19]

The following evening, Phillip Graham, publisher of the *Washington Post,* hosted a dinner at which he and the publishers of nineteen other influential newspapers listened while Secretary of State George Marshall, Undersecretary of State Robert Lovett, General Omar Bradley, and Secretary of Defense James Forrestal discussed the Berlin crisis. Among the guests was John Foster Dulles, advisor to presidential candidate Thomas Dewey and the man everyone expected would succeed Marshall when Truman went down to defeat.

When the question of the use of the atomic bomb arose, the unanimous opinion of the guests was that the country would fully expect it. "The American people would crucify you if you did not use the bomb," Dulles said. [20]

☆　☆　☆

Lieutenant Steber and Captain Slaker usually shared the piloting of their C-47; Steber flew the lefthand seat—pilot—on the leg into Berlin, and Slaker took that spot for the return flight. On the night of September 14, their "Gooney Bird" had passed over the Fulda beacon, had turned into the south corridor into Berlin, and was twenty minutes into the Soviet zone when both of the engines quit at once. Slaker, who was stretched back in his seat, eyes closed, pitched forward with the sudden loss of power.

"What's wrong," he shouted over the loud drumming of the rain on the fuselage.

"I don't know."

The fuel pressure and temperature gauges were all in the green and there was plenty of fuel in the main tanks, but Slaker and Steber switched to the auxiliaries anyway, attempting to restart the engines. It didn't work. The props continued to windmill in the airstream, but the engines didn't catch.

"What's the highest terrain in this part of the corridor, Slaker?" Steber shouted, and Slaker told him: "4,200 feet."

The altimeter read 5,000 feet.

Steber ordered, "Go back and open the cargo door and lay out my parachute while I go through the emergency procedures again."

Slaker made his way to the rear cargo door, yanked the emergency release, and watched the door whoosh away into the blackness of the night. Then he laid Steber's parachute out on top of the flour sacks and made his way back to the cockpit just as Steber completed his third try at restarting the engines. The altimeter read 4,300 feet.

"We'll have to bail out at 4,000 unless these engines start," Steber said as he began his fourth desperate run through the emergency restarting procedures. When he was done, with the propellers still windmilling powerlessly, Steber shouted, "Let's go," and the two men scrambled back through the plane to the open door.

Slaker went out headfirst, yanking at his ripcord the instant his left foot exited the door. He watched for Steber to come out of the plane but did not see him in the few seconds of his descent. Then he landed hard on his back, saw a thousand lights flash through his head, and blacked out.

Clarence Steber was fastening his chute to his harness as Ken Slaker went out the cargo door. Just then, the engines caught, and Steber made his way back to the cockpit and slid into the lefthand seat. He had just managed to get off a "Mayday" message on the emergency channel when both engines died again, so he scrambled back through the plane and went out the door. His parachute had barely opened when he hit the ground, badly injuring his shoulder. Both pilots were down, deep inside the Soviet zone of Germany.[21]

# TWENTY-SIX

# AIR FORCE DAY 1948

When Ken Slaker recovered consciousness, he was lying in the mud of a potato field, with the rain beating down on his face. He was shaking uncontrollably, and he couldn't move his legs at first, but he could hear the steady roar of aircraft in the sky above him, and the words of the operations officer at the initial briefing came back to him: "We cannot say that you should turn yourselves in, or that you should try to escape." Slaker had no desire to be arrested as a spy and decided that, if he could walk, he was going to try to make it back to the West, which he estimated was not more than 45 miles away. Not having seen Steber bail out, he presumed his fellow flier was dead. Actually, Steber was lying miles away, even deeper in the Soviet zone, his shoulder badly injured from his jump from the plane.[1]

On the day Slaker went down in the Soviet zone, the three Western envoys in Moscow delivered identical notes to the Kremlin and the Foreign Ministry. The notes reviewed the basic points at issue in Berlin and indicated that the Soviet military governor had deviated from the understandings reached on each point in Moscow when he had discussed them with his counterparts in Berlin.

With Stalin still on vacation, Molotov was in no great hurry to reply to the notes and said that he was in favor of referring the questions back to the military governors again. That was a course the West would not accept, so Molotov reluctantly agreed to present the matter to Stalin. Ambassador Smith left the meeting convinced that the Soviet foreign minister was playing for time.

Ken Slaker managed to get to his feet, even though a wave of nausea swept over him from the pain in his back. He dragged his wet parachute to a patch of weeds and scraped mud over it with his feet. It was nearing dawn, and he could see shapes moving in the potato fields. The farmers in the area were beginning their day. Ken Slaker faced a decision. With his coal-begrimed flight coveralls now muddy, what he was wearing bore little resemblance to an American military uniform. Slaker turned his leather flight jacket inside out, so that his rank insignia and the embossed silver wings would not show, and he began to walk painfully down a country lane, away from the farmers. When he found a worn road, riddled with potholes, he paused for a moment, in great pain from his back. Then he turned west toward freedom and started down the road, determined to try to get back to his base.

He had been on the road for only a few moments when he spotted a Soviet soldier on a bicycle, headed right toward him. Slaker had no choice but to continue walking down the road and was shocked when the soldier suddenly veered straight toward him. Then it dawned on him that the soldier was just going to force him off the road to remind him to respect the Soviet military. He stepped to the shoulder, eyes cast down, as the soldier pedaled past.

Now uncomfortable walking on an open road, he sought cover in a wooded copse but kept heading west, picking up a stout stick to help him walk and to use as a club if he needed to defend himself. Suddenly, and without warning, he came on a man walking in the opposite direction.

"*Guten morgen,*" Slaker said as they passed, knowing that if the other man was suspicious, he would stop. The man did, and Slaker turned to confront him, ready to use his club if necessary.

"I am an American pilot," Slaker said in English. "Which way to Fulda?"

"Fulda *nicht gut,*" the man replied, shaking his head from side to side. Slaker was ready to hit him when he went on.

"*Ich* American prisoner of war." The man dug a set of papers out of his pocket and thrust them at Slaker. They were his discharge papers from an American POW camp.

"Americans good to me," the man said, pulling up his pant leg to reveal a badly scarred and mangled leg.

"American tank did that to me. I go to Deutsch hospital, doctor say, 'cut off leg.' I say, '*nein.*' Soon Americans capture me, save my leg."

The German, Rudolf Schnabel, had been in the woods foraging for food for his family. Now, he agreed to help Slaker make his way back to the West.

The journey began with a trek through the woods to the home of a farmer Schnabel knew. There, Slaker exchanged his flight overalls and leather jacket for old clothes that the farmer produced. Schnabel and Slaker then took the railroad to Eisenach, the village near the border where Schnabel lived. Slaker was reluctant to ride the train, but Schnabel convinced him.

If they could reach the town of Eisenach, Schnabel explained in his halting English, friends of his could arrange for Slaker to go through the border that night. The longer it took Slaker to get to the border, Schnabel went on, the less chance he would have to escape the Soviets.

When they reached the city, Schnabel took Slaker to his apartment and introduced the American flier to his wife and small child. When Schnabel left to arrange for the border crossing, Kenneth Slaker stretched out on the sofa at one end of the single, large room and wondered what had happened to his fellow pilot.

Though Slaker did not know it, Lieutenant Clarence Steber had been quickly apprehended by Soviet troops. Taken by car to a headquarters, Steber was confined to a small room and interrogated by a team of officers he could not see because of the lights they directed at his face. He knew from the sound of her voice that one was a young woman, and she spoke very good English. After several hours of interrogation, Steber was finally moved to an East German hospital and given medical treatment. A guard stood outside his door.

When Rudolf Schnabel returned to his apartment, he bid Slaker come with him to a meeting with the men who would help him across the border. Slaker gave the men most of the West German money he had with him—five hundred marks—when they explained that they would need it to bribe the East German policeman who stood guard on the bridge at the Werra River, close to the border. They were to cross the bridge between 8:00 and 8:30 that night, when the bribed guard would be the only one on duty, then lie in wait in a cabbage field about a hundred yards away until they were joined by two others who were also trying to sneak into the West. The actual border crossing was scheduled for midnight. Rudolf Schnabel would accompany and guide the group across the border, then return to the East the following day. It would be easy, he said. He had papers and could, therefore, return by commercial bus. It was only leaving the Eastern zone that was difficult.

The two who joined Slaker and Schnabel in the field at dusk were a young German veteran and his eighteen-year-old girlfriend. They lay there together, looking toward the border in the gathering dusk. On a hill several hundred yards away, clearly outlined by the light of the setting sun, was their destination—a police border station on top of a hill in the West. Between them and its safety were cabbage fields, then a row of barbed wire fencing, with Soviet sentry boxes to the left and right of the path they would take. Beyond that was an open area, more barbed wire, and then the hill.

The lights of the sentry boxes, directed into the cabbage fields, came on even before it was fully dark. Worse, a bright, three-quarter moon rose, illuminating the fields. The escape party continued to wait and watched hopefully as the sky clouded over. At 11:00 p.m., with the moon fully obscured, they began to crawl slowly through the fields toward the fence, keeping as low as possible. Kenneth Slaker remembered the warning he had received from the men early that afternoon: the guards will shoot first and investigate later.

Once they were past the cabbage field and the sentry shacks, the group paused, then rose and began to run toward freedom. Slaker, his legs numb from the long crawl and his back still painful from the shock of his parachute landing, became entangled in the barbed wire of the second fence. While he desperately struggled to free himself, he heard shouting, then automatic gunfire. Breaking clear of the fence, he raced for the hill, aware that bullets were bouncing off rocks around him. Nearly to the top, Slaker stumbled, tumbling backward. The girl shouted that he had fallen, and his three companions formed a human chain to drag him back up the slope. Together, they ran for the Western police shack. There, gasping for breath, Slaker showed the guard his military identification card. Schnabel, asked for his papers, discovered that he had somehow lost them in the dash for freedom. His carefree plan of returning to the East by bus was shattered, and if the Soviets found the papers, his family would be in trouble.

Five minutes after the border guard called his headquarters to report on the events, the field telephone on his desk rang. Answering, he motioned Slaker to take the call. A colonel from American counterintelligence in Hersfeld was on the line. He told Slaker that he would arrive at the police post in twenty minutes.[2]

☆  ☆  ☆

While the Soviets contemplated the notes from the Western powers, the attention of the world was riveted on the events in Berlin and Germany.

On the day the envoys met with Molotov, General Clay gave a ninety-minute interview to a group of visiting newsmen. He predicted a long siege and a large increase in the number of aircraft employed in the airlift during the coming winter but added, "I certainly don't believe war is around the corner."[3] In Washington, the Air Force announced that forty additional C-54s would be withdrawn from service in various parts of the world and assigned to the Berlin airlift.[4]

George Marshall was pessimistic about the situation when he spoke to reporters in Washington the following day. He told his press conference that he would not comment on the latest meeting in Moscow or on the possibility of future meetings, while fending off most other questions on Berlin. One of the reporters asked him to comment on a story that Anthony Eden had said in London that the international situation was going from bad to worse. The secretary of state refused to comment directly but observed that he had not had any periods of great relief in the past ten days and would welcome a little encouragement.[5]

In Berlin, Colonel Howley dealt with a recent protest from the Soviet commandant, who demanded the return of five tons of food American military police had seized a month earlier from Soviet trucks that were stopped in the American sector. Howley assured General Kotikov the food had not been wasted and that an equivalent amount would be returned "when the Soviet blockade of Berlin is lifted."[6]

Some of Howley's dealings with the Soviets that month were less pleasant. Because the United States was still adhering to other four-power agreements in spite of the Soviet blockade, Howley had been forced to turn over fourteen-year-old Helena Korlenko, the Ukrainian girl who had been in a U.S. sector hospital, to the Soviets.[7] While there were expressions of dismay in the press, there was nothing that could have been done to prevent the girl's return, as it was clearly required under the agreements still in force.

The situation in the city was tense as 10,000 Berliners attended the funeral of Wolfgang Scheunemann, the youth killed by the Soviets at the Brandenburg Gate demonstration. Eastern sector police and Soviet troops were out in force, and the Soviets made several jeep incursions into the American sector, shoving a gun into the stomach of an American military policeman at one point. In the Potsdamer Platz, Soviet troops fired several shots into the American sector at a German who was fleeing with a sack of potatoes.[8]

Kenneth Slaker, his back injuries treated by an army doctor, was flown from Hersfeld to Wiesbaden in a single-engine liaison plane for a meeting with General Tunner. He left Rudolf Schnabel behind, in the care of Army Counterintelligence. In Wiesbaden, Slaker was delighted when he was reunited with Clarence Steber, who he thought had died when their plane crashed. Steber had his own tale of Cold War derring-do to relate.

The morning after Steber had been moved to the German hospital, two American officers—members of the Potsdam Liaison Committee with diplomatic status—arrived to see him. Once inside Steber's first-floor room, they asked him if he thought he could make it out the window. He said yes. The three of them clambered out and sped off toward Berlin in the liaison team's car. As they neared the city, Steber crawled into the trunk of the diplomatic vehicle, and they passed through the Soviet checkpoints with the two officers flashing their diplomatic passes. From Berlin, Steber was put on one of the planes of the airlift that was returning to Wiesbaden. There he was reunited with Slaker. They posed for photographs for waiting and eager newsmen, and the USAFE public relations office issued a brief press release on the event. A lid of security had been clamped on the entire affair, and no mention was made of the help Slaker had received while making his way back to the West. The Soviets had already protested that the escaped flier had been on a spy mission, and there was no desire by the Americans to create yet another international incident in the midst of the crisis over the blockade. Steber's rescue from the Soviet zone hospital was characterized as a return "through channels."[9]

From his headquarters in Wiesbaden, General LeMay had a proclamation of his own to issue the following day. The first anniversary of the establishment of the United States Air Force as an independent service would occur on September 18, and the celebration of "Air Force Day 1948" was scheduled for that date. LeMay announced that his command would celebrate the new holiday by flying between four thousand and five thousand tons of coal into Berlin. As the airlift recorded tonnage per twenty-four hour period on a noon-to-noon basis, the celebratory flights were going on even as LeMay's announcement was made.

Colonel Howley announced that the coal would be distributed as a special ration and that all families with two or more children under ten would receive one hundred pounds. Twenty-five pounds each were to be distributed to other families and to individuals.[10]

The airfields at Wiesbaden and Rhein-Main were opened to the public in celebration of Air Force Day, and thousands of Germans and Americans thronged to them to watch as planes took off with clockwork regularity. The crowds were undeterred by the heavy clouds and occasional rain squalls that swept the fields, and the airlift personnel did not let the weather bother them, either. By noon on September 18, a new tonnage record had been set. In 651 flights, the Americans had carried 5,572.7 tons of coal into the city. The British had carried an additional 1,700 tons. General LeMay, not noted for effusive praise, congratulated General Tunner for "the splendid performance conducted in spite of the unsatisfactory weather conditions."[11]

☆   ☆   ☆

On September 18, as the airlift was in the process of setting a new daily record, Foreign Minister Molotov called the Western envoys to his office to deliver the Soviet response to their earlier identical notes. The meeting lasted one and a half hours. Ambassador Smith had little to offer to the reporters who crowded around him when he arrived back at the United States embassy from the meeting.

"I have no comment," he said. Pressed on whether the talks would continue, he repeated, "I have no comment." Asked if the talks were at an end, Smith again said, "I have no comment."[12]

There was in fact very little to comment on. During the meeting, the Soviet foreign minister had flatly denied that Marshal Sokolovsky had deviated from the agreements reached in Moscow and went on to state that the reason that the military governors had not been able to reach an agreement was that the Western generals had given new interpretations to the Moscow directives. During the discussions of the Soviet note, Molotov gave lengthy explanations, all of which confused rather than clarified what the Soviet position really was. All three of the Western envoys concluded that the Soviets were no longer interested in meaningful negotiations on the Berlin question. This belief was reported to their governments.[13]

The president and secretary of state agreed that further negotiations with the Soviet Union about Berlin were useless. They favored immediate referral of the matter to the United Nations, which was scheduled to begin a meeting in Paris on September 23. Both the British and the French, however, urged one final attempt to resolve the crisis by negotiation. Meeting in Paris with the British foreign minister, Ernest Bevin, and the French foreign minister, Robert Schuman, Secretary of State George Marshall agreed to the last-ditch effort, provided that it was understood the matter would go to the U.N. immediately if the Soviet reply was unsatisfactory.[14] Another set of identical notes was delivered to the Soviet embassies in the three Western capitals on September 22.

The opening session of the U.N. General Assembly took place the following day in the converted theater of the Palais de Chaillot. The delegates and visitors passed between ranks of blue-coated *Gardes républicaines* to enter the building, where the flags of the fifty-eight nations that made up the body were boldly displayed behind the dais. The delegates sat at desks covered with green felt, and some were easily identifiable to members of the crowd. The Swedish delegation wore mourning bands on their sleeves in memory of Count Folke Bernadotte, recently assassinated by the radical Zionist guerrilla group Irgun, while in Palestine on a U.N. peace mission. British foreign minister Bevin looked weary; he was in very ill health. Secretary Marshall sat quietly at his desk, dressed in a blue serge suit, and Eleanor Roosevelt, named to the delegation by President Truman, sat nearby. Everyone rose with a burst of applause when France's president, Vincent Auriol, arrived to convey the official greeting of the host country to the assembly. When he left, the atmosphere became more sober. Members of the crowd began to fidget or retreated to the corridors of the palace to gather in small groups. Everyone was aware of the notes the West had sent to the Soviet Union. There was general fear the Soviets might walk out of the world body if the West attempted to bring the matter of Berlin before it.[15] Everyone at the session was waiting for the Soviet reply to the latest Western notes.

The reply came on September 25. It was as sharp and pointed as the bayonets of the Red Army at a May Day parade. The Soviets reiterated their position that the Berlin problem had arisen as a result of the Western currency reform and went on to accuse the Western powers of an attempt to dislocate the economy of the East in order to force a Soviet withdrawal from Germany. The Soviet note repeated the demand that all avenues of traffic into Berlin, specifically including the air corridors, be subject to their control. The next day, a long story from TASS appeared. It repeated the line contained in the notes and reproached Western spokesmen for not giving an accurate picture of the Berlin negotiations.

Western reaction was swift. The U.S. State Department quickly released a 24,000-word white paper detailing the entire course of the negotiations, including Marshal Sokolovsky's deviations from the points to which Stalin had appeared to agree. In Paris, Marshall and the British and French foreign ministers quickly came to agreement on the text of a note to the secretary-general of the United Nations. The note flatly accused the Soviet Union of a clear violation of the United Nations charter for its actions in Berlin, saying it was using illegal and coercive measures to achieve political objectives it was not entitled to and could not gain by peaceful means. Stating that "the Soviet Government has taken upon itself sole responsibility for creating a situation which constitutes a threat to international peace and security," the note declared "the United States, the United Kingdom, and France, therefore, find themselves obligated to refer the action to the Security Council."[16]

The diplomats of the world would debate about Berlin. While they did, the airlift would have to go on supplying the desperate city.

# TWENTY-SEVEN

## "BLOKADA NYET"

Soon after the West rejected the Soviet version of the negotiations and decided to bring the matter of Berlin before the United Nations, Joe Fleming of *Stars and Stripes* toured the city. His taxi driver spoke to him about the faith of Berliners in the Allies.

"Sure we lost our faith at first," the man said. "We thought the West would pull out. Now we have it back again." Over their heads was the steady drone of aircraft—one every three minutes—flying into the city.

"Ah, there. You hear?" the driver asked. "There is another plane. And there another. Our faith, Mister, doesn't come from our hearts or our brains anymore. It comes through the ears."[1]

The vast majority of the citizens seemed to feel like the taxi driver, and they showed their appreciation for the airmen's efforts in constant small gestures. Berliners were continually turning up at Tempelhof with flowers that they pressed on fliers who would almost invariably be greeted with the question, "Getting married?" when they returned to their base operations rooms. Captain Edward Hensch once received a fairly typical gift package, along with a note that began, in German, "To an unseen Blockade Flier." The package contained a porcelain snail, a few flowers, and a toy walrus made of rat fur.[2]

The feeling that Berlin could be sustained by the airlift was not universal, however. Jo Thaler, Ruth Andreas-Friedrich's friend and fellow underground fighter against Hitler, left the city in October. "It's pointless to stay here," he said on parting. "Berlin is lost."[3] Ruth contemplated leaving as well, but she was writing again for a monthly magazine and the editor had figured out an ingenious way to continue publishing in spite of the blockade. The magazine was written and the typesetting was performed in Berlin. Then the typeset matrixes were flown by the airlift to southern Germany, where the printing was performed. Then, in the fourth step of the process, completed copies were returned by the mail train, which was the single overland conveyance that the Soviets had not stopped. Told of the process by the editor, Ruth pessimistically remarked, "However inspired, you seem to forget that your fourth step requires the cooperation of the Soviets."[4]

The cooperation of the Soviets was something that was lacking in the air corridors. Red Air Force fighter planes regularly rose from their fields to buzz incoming transports. Flak frequently dotted the sky near where the C-54s were flying, as the Soviets held antiaircraft exercises. At night, high-powered searchlights swept the air in the flight paths of the American and British fliers. Many of the pilots took to taping old maps and newspapers to the insides of their cockpit windows so they wouldn't be temporarily blinded by the bright lights. As all flights into Berlin were made on instrument flight rules, being able to see out the windows was not necessary until it was time to land.

On October 2, the Soviets announced that fighter aircraft of the Red Air Force would hold live-fire exercises in the corridors and Marshal Sokolovsky issued a detailed statement charging the West with "using the Berlin problem as an excuse to build up an aggressive Western bloc directed against the Soviet Union." He denied that the blockade existed.[5]

On October 3, Sokolovsky's deputy, Lieutenant General Dratvin, accused the Americans and British of having committed 656 violations of flight rules since August 20 and asked for "immediate measures to remedy this abuse."[6]

Some of the American pilots took small retaliatory measures such as flying close enough to the single-engine Soviet target-towing planes to buffet them in the powerful prop wash of the C-54's four Wasp radial engines. Most others shrugged the Soviet harassment off. During the flight when Captain Hensch received the rat's-fur walrus, the plane he was piloting struck a bird on its way back to Rhein-Main. He and the copilot, First Lieutenant William Baker, walked around their craft when they landed, looking to see whether it had sustained any damage. They found none. As Baker went off to file his routine report to intelligence, Hensch yelled after him, "Hey! Better tell them the Russians sent a bird up after us."[7]

The Soviet tactics in the air were a real danger, however. On October 4, Air Vice Marshal Don Bennett was approaching Berlin down the northern corridor when a Soviet Yak fighter made a tactical pass at his Avro Tudor. The Yak buzzed by less than two hundred feet from the transport.[8]

☆   ☆   ☆

The American complaint against the Soviet Union was formally filed with the United Nations in a note Ambassador Warren Austen handed to Secretary-General Trygve Lie on September 29, 1948. The actual handling of the matter before the Security Council was a job delegated to Dr. Phillip Jessip, the American deputy representative. "Chip"

Bohlen was asked to assist Jessip. The Security Council was composed of five permanent members—Great Britain, France, China, the Soviet Union, and the United States—and six smaller nations serving on a rotating basis. When the council began debate on the procedural question of whether it should even consider the matter, the speeches of Andrei Vyshinsky, the Soviet representative, were peppered with the phrase "*Blokada nyet.*" "There is no blockade," he repeated time and again, shouting across the green-covered table at Jessip. "There is no threat to peace. Only the Allied Control Council and the Foreign Ministers Council may correctly deal with the problem of Germany."[9]

The histrionics did him little good. The question of placing the matter on the agenda was procedural and not subject to a veto. When the roll was called, only the Russian and Ukrainian representatives on the council voted against including the item on the agenda. The body would debate an issue in which three of its permanent members accused a fourth of creating a threat to peace.

The debate was one-sided, as Moscow had directed Vyshinsky to take no part whatsoever in it. When other members of the council began to speak on the question, Vyshinsky took a few notes. Then he pulled off the earphones that provided delegates with simultaneous translations of what speakers were saying and threw them down on his desk. Looking bored, he picked up a French socialist newspaper and began to read.

When he again began to listen, Phillip Jessip was denouncing the actions of the Soviet Union in Berlin and in the negotiations about it. "The Soviet Government has revealed the weakness of its position by adopting what I may refer to as grasshopper tactics," Jessip said. "Each leap ends on a blade of grass which turns out to be a flimsy pretext requiring a jump to a new but equally unstable position." It was plain, Jessip concluded, that good faith, "that prerequisite to settlement, was absent from the Soviet mind."[10]

As the United Nations debated the events swirling around their city, the Berliners were involved in their own politics, and it was deeply influenced by the attitudes of the occupying powers. The city constitution that had been adopted in 1946 called for new elections to the municipal government to be held in 1948. The city leaders in the West were determined to go ahead with the election and scheduled it for November 14. The Soviet military government threw every roadblock it could in their path.

The constitution provided that election lists, candidates, and regulations be published in the official *City Gazette,* a document printed at a plant in the Soviet sector. When they were presented with the required texts, the Soviets refused to allow them to be printed, canceling the October issue of the *Gazette.*[11]

On October 8, the Berlin City Assembly, meeting in the British sector and still boycotted by the Communist members, voted to hold the elections without the cooperation of the Soviet military government. December 5 was selected as the date. At the same meeting, the assembly voted to remove the chief of the Labor Department, Waldemar Schmidt, from his post. Schmidt, a Communist, was dismissed for refusing to recognize wage contracts that had been negotiated with a non-Communist union.[12] He vowed that he would not leave the *Magistrat,* which still held its meetings in its headquarters in the Soviet sector. The Soviet military government denounced Schmidt's removal as illegal.

The neutral members of the United Nations Security Council—China, Syria, Canada, Belgium, Colombia, and Argentina—attempted to work out a compromise on the Berlin question under the leadership of Dr. Juan Bramuglia, the Argentinian foreign minister, who was sitting as president of the Security Council. Initially, they backed one of the primary positions adopted by the Western allies, holding that the blockade itself must end before negotiations on the broader questions commenced. Ultimately, they softened even on this, coming up with a solution that called for the travel restrictions to be eased gradually as talks on the currency issue went forward. The West was not inclined to accept this, and the Soviets made it plain that they would not, either.

On October 25, a carefully worded resolution was put before the Security Council. It took only two minutes to read the document, which proposed that all restrictions on travel and trade in Berlin be lifted immediately, that the four military governors arrange for withdrawal of the Western marks in favor of four-power sponsorship of the Eastern mark, and that the Council of Foreign Ministers meet within ten days for negotiations on the entire German question. Diplomatically, the resolution made no reference to a "blockade," did not name the Soviet Union as responsible, and omitted any mention of a "threat to peace."

Debate on the resolution proceeded around the crescent-shaped table at which the council sat. At precisely 6:18 p.m., Soviet foreign minister Vyshinsky stated bluntly, "The Soviet Union will veto this resolution."[13] Any hope that the United Nations could resolve the crisis was dead. The United States continued to build up its airlift efforts.

☆　☆　☆

The United States Air Force base at Great Falls, Montana, lies on the desolate and wind-swept reaches of the high plains, eighty miles east of the continental divide and only 120 miles south of the Canadian border. Great Falls, swollen by servicemen and their families to a population of 30,000, was the second largest city in the second least populous state in the union. The nearest "civilian" city, Helena (population

20,000) was eighty miles south, down the twists and turns of Route 15. There was no civilian air traffic to interfere with military maneuvers at Great Falls. It was far from any commercial airway. The summers were short and cool, and even in the best of weather, flying conditions at Great Falls were difficult. Fogs were frequent and dense, and icing was a problem most of the year. For those very reasons, in October 1948, Great Falls, Montana, became an imitation Berlin for airmen training as replacements for airlift crews.

On the plains around the base, radio beacons broadcasting on the frequencies of those around Berlin were erected and activated. Ground control approach radar operators, set up in the control tower, worked by the same guidelines as the teams on duty in the city under siege. C-54s, packed with ten-ton cargoes of sandbags, wheeled in the sky on courses that duplicated flights down the corridors in central Germany. With pilots operating on instrument flight rules, they approached Great Falls on the same magnetic heading as those that approached Tempelhof, then landed on a runway marked out to duplicate the length of the one in Germany.

The course, officially known as the Replacement Training Unit for Operation Vittles, was twenty-one days long. Each student received 133 hours of instruction during his stay on the high plains. Forty-eight hours were spent on preflight instruction and twenty were spent in the air. Pilots attended a supplementary ground school for the fifty-five hours when flight engineers were engaged in engine and systems training. It was expected that the school would produce twenty-nine complete air crews each week when in full operation.[14]

Some of the first crews were made up of civilian reservists recalled to active military service to fill the manpower needs generated by the airlift. Many of the pilots and copilots of civilian airlines had experience with C-54s, and many faced layoffs during the winter months, when civilian operators frequently curtailed flights. In an agreement reached between the Air Force and the civilian carriers, between one hundred and two hundred of these experienced pilots were recalled and assigned directly to the Airlift Task Force, with the understanding that they would be released from duty in the spring, at the end of the seasonal slump in air travel in the United States.[15]

In Europe, General Tunner had solved many of the supply problems that had plagued the airlift in its early days. As the commander of the Airlift Task Force, Tunner was operating under a letter of instruction issued by Headquarters, USAFE, that spelled out his responsibilities and the chain of command he was required to follow. He was authorized to command and coordinate with the personnel assigned to the airlift and with various base commanders, but the letter was silent on coordination with such Air Force organizations as the Air Materiel Command and MATS. Tunner took that silence to mean that he was not forbidden to communicate directly with them, so he did, with General LeMay's full awareness. Those lines of communication helped smooth the flow of supplies and spare parts to the airlift.[16]

USAFE's difficulty in obtaining enough aircraft for the crews to fly and to sustain the airlift effort through the winter remained, however. General Clay was by now completely convinced that the airlift could continue to supply the city indefinitely, provided it was given the required support and equipment. He had cabled the War Department on September 10 and September 13, requesting that 116 additional C-54s be allocated to the airlift. Fifty were dispatched within a week but no more followed. By October 4, seriously disturbed that no decision had been reached on the allocation of the remaining sixty-six, Clay cabled Washington again, triggering a special staff study by the Army Plans and Operations Division. They recommended that the planes be provided.

The staff study was, however, part of a much larger picture. The National Security Council was in the process of a full reappraisal of American policy, and both the Department of State and the Joint Chiefs of Staff had been requested to prepare a report on what should be done in light of the failure of the four-power talks on Berlin and the anticipated referral of the matter to the United Nations.

The report submitted to Secretary Marshall by George Kennan concluded that the United States should be prepared to allow the UN to open the entire question of West German sovereignty as a possible avenue to a solution to the blockade. That advice was contrary to the policy that Marshall had been pursuing—and wished to continue to pursue—and was quietly ignored by him. The view expressed by the Joint Chiefs was far more devastating.

As their considered opinion, the Joint Chiefs of Staff presented the view that "our present military power cannot effectively support the supply of Berlin by airlift on an indefinite basis without such diversion of military effort as has affected and will continue progressively to affect seriously and adversely the ability of the National Military Establishment to meet its primary national security obligations."[17] Translated out of jargon, the Joint Chiefs had proclaimed that continued support of the Berlin airlift was making it difficult for the military to protect the United States against potential enemy action.

The papers filed by the Joint Chiefs also sharply criticized the policy of staying in Berlin in any event, pleading that either the possibility of all-out war be recognized and prepared for, or that plans be made for withdrawal from the city. There was no doubt where the Joint Chiefs stood, as they stated that risking war "in our present state of readiness and for the Berlin issue is neither militarily prudent nor strategically sound."[18]

It was a recommendation that the National Security Council reacted to immediately and indignantly. The council convened in the absence of the president, who was campaigning in the West. Robert Lovett noted that the Joint Chiefs appeared to have a case of the jitters. Both he and Secretary of the Army Royall reminded the council at a meeting on October 14 that the decision to stay in Berlin had already been made, in full knowledge of the military weakness of the United States. Neither Royall nor Lovett could, however, provide an answer to the question of whether the United States would go to war in order to remain. When Truman learned of the report of the Joint Chiefs and the deliberations of the National Security Council, he directed that General Clay and Ambassador Murphy be ordered to return to the United States for the next meeting of the council on October 21.

On an operational level, it had been obvious to General Tunner and his team that the airlift operation would function more smoothly and efficiently if the British and American operations were combined into a unified command. For one thing, the weather in the British zone in northern Germany was better for flying. More important, the consolidation and coordination of flights into Berlin would be safer than two parallel operations, and the bases in the British sector were closer by one-third to the city than the American ones. Two planes based at Fassberg, for example, could carry the same amount of cargo into the city in the same time as three based in Wiesbaden, and Tunner had sent a squadron of C-54s to that base for just that reason. Hoping to send more planes to the British bases, Tunner approached LeMay with his proposal for a combined airlift task force. LeMay had been very supportive of Tunner, and the commander of USAFE saw the advantages of Tunner's proposal for a combined command at once. He immediately broached the subject with his British counterpart, Air Marshal Sir Arthur Saunders.

While agreeing in principle, Sir Arthur disagreed on the details. Opposing the American plan that one person be named to command the operation, Air Marshal Saunders argued that the operation be directed by a coordinating committee. The British, knowing they were carrying only one-third of the cargo into Berlin, rightly assumed if the American proposal was accepted, the overall commander would be an American.

Conference after conference was held, during which Sir Arthur spoke eloquently in defense of the British position, while Tunner and LeMay listened. His mind already firmly made up, LeMay sat quietly and puffed on his large cigar while Saunders talked, but he never gave an inch. He had been selected to return to the United States to take over the Strategic Air Command and was due to leave soon, and he seemed determined to leave the airlift operation on the best possible footing. Tunner observed that Sir Arthur might just as well have been

talking to the cigar alone, for all the good his well-thought-out arguments did him.[19] Sir Arthur finally capitulated on the day before General LeMay was scheduled to turn over command of USAFE to Lieutenant General Joseph Cannon. On October 14, a joint directive signed by
LeMay and Saunders set up the Combined Air Lift Task Force (CALTF),
with Tunner in command and Air Commodore J. W. F. Merer of the
RAF as his deputy.

As important as merging the efforts into a smooth and coordinated
effort, the directive changed the overall concept as well. Until now, the
airlift had been assigned a minimum amount of cargo that had to be
transported. With the creation of CALTF, the goal became the maximum tonnage possible consistent with the combined resources of
equipment and personnel available. The sky was now the limit, and
General Tunner was happy at the prospect.

Tunner was at the airport at Wiesbaden when the usually taciturn
General LeMay departed for his new command. Taking Tunner's hand,
LeMay said, "Thanks, Bill," adding "You're doing a good job anyway,
but this [CALTF] agreement's going to help." Tunner was anxious to
brief the new commander, General Cannon, on the operations of the
airlift.[20]

# TWENTY-EIGHT
## TUNNER'S TROUBLES

General Joseph K. Cannon was a widely respected aviation pioneer who had led bombers from England during the war and who had served on the continent of Europe before. It was General Cannon who had originally requisitioned the 102-room Heinkel mansion as the quarters of the USAFE commander, taking it over in the immediate wake of the departing ground soldiers. Finding that many of the furnishings had been stripped, Cannon had created a tremendous row, threatening courts-martial and other punishments, until many of the opulent items had been returned.[1] Now, he was back among the priceless objets d'art of the Heinkels and in command of the United States Air Force on the continent.

Early in his career, Tunner had been posted to Kelly Field for bomber training, and Joseph K. Cannon was there at the time as a fighter check pilot, but their paths had not crossed. Tunner knew Cannon only by his reputation for being tough but fair. He was totally unprepared for the greeting he received from the new commander when he reported on October 17 to brief Cannon on the operations of the airlift.

"What in hell is this, Tunner?" Cannon roared with rage, waving a copy of the order setting up the combined airlift task force. "What are you trying to do to me?"[2]

The sparks from the first meeting never cooled. General Tunner was issued a new letter of instruction from headquarters in which he was specifically forbidden to coordinate his efforts with MATS, the Air Materiel Command, or any other Air Force agency. All contact with other commands was to be made exclusively through USAFE Headquarters. Tunner was not only issued specific orders not to deal directly with MATS, but was also verbally reminded not to take up any matters with them.

☆ ☆ ☆

Harry Truman presided at the October 21 meeting of the National Security Council. After General Clay had made his presentation, arguing the case that the airlift could succeed only if he were given the additional aircraft he had requested, the president went around the table, polling the members on their views. No one supported Clay's request, and the general believed the fight was lost. As he and Robert Murphy rose to leave at the end of the meeting, Truman said, "Come on in my office." Turning to Royall, Truman said, "You come too."

When they joined the president in the Oval Office, he directed his remarks to Clay: "I'm afraid you're very unhappy, General," he said. "Don't be. You're going to get them." Harry Truman ordered the sixty-six additional C-54s be allocated to the airlift at once.[3]

Clay was scheduled to make a speech that evening. On a visit to Berlin on the previous Christmas, Francis Spellman, the Roman Catholic cardinal of New York, had asked Clay to speak at the annual Al Smith dinner. Clay had agreed, not knowing at the time that he would be in the midst of a crisis. Now, he asked the president for permission to use the dinner as an occasion to announce that additional airplanes would be allotted to the airlift. Harry Truman agreed.

That evening, with Truman's opponent in the presidential election, Thomas Dewey, seated on his left, Clay made the announcement about the additional aircraft. Governor Dewey, when questioned about Berlin, had heartily supported the Truman administration's tough policy. Now Dewey led the applause that followed the announcement about the airplanes. Unrestricted support for Berlin was not then, nor would it ever become, an issue in the presidential election campaign. The Soviet Union could expect no change in policy from a Dewey administration, which almost everyone expected would take office in January.

☆　☆　☆

With the majority of the personnel flying on the airlift on temporary duty assignments, morale was bound to be low. General Tunner had no control over that under the letter of instruction from General Cannon that limited his authority; transfers in and out of Europe were the sole responsibility of General Cannon's command. Tunner and his staff were themselves on temporary duty. The general had placed his oldest son in a boarding school and left the younger one in the care of the wife of Red Forman, his chief of operations, when he had reported to Europe.[4]

The TDY arrangement was particularly awkward. Airlift personnel lived and worked side by side with personnel who were on permanent assignment to Europe, and the contrast was stark. Airlift personnel were housed in temporary quarters that were squalid compared to those enjoyed by the occupation forces, who lived regally by contrast.

Tunner believed the command of any large, vital operation should include control of personnel, replacement, promotions, and even the awarding of medals. The CALTF had none of this control and was dependent on USAFE for things as mundane as bus transportation between their spartan barracks and the airfields—and Cannon's command could not even get the buses to run on time.[5]

There were other, much more serious problems as well. When the maintenance depot at Burtonwood had been activated for the purpose of performing two-hundred-hour inspections, Tunner had been assured that he could count on it completing seven each day, provided CALTF could produce additional personnel to augment those who had been assigned by General Cannon's command. Tunner provided the personnel and permitted the transfer of two-hundred-hour checks from Oberhuffen-puffen, as it was familiarly known, which was under Tunner's direct control, to Burtonwood, which fell under USAFE. After a reasonable start, the rate of inspections at Burtonwood dropped to less than two a day, and General Tunner was faced with a shortage of 35 planes a week on operations in and out of Berlin. It was an unacceptable situation. Tunner and his staff made numerous visits to the maintenance center in England, identifying problems and suggesting solutions. With no authority to take the problems up with the Air Materiel Command, whose expertise could have helped, Tunner was reduced to listening to excuses and empty promises.

Tunner was not alone in his concern about the maintenance performed at Burtonwood. Navy fliers operated under different maintenance arrangements from the Air Force, and naval squadron mechanics were trained to perform two-hundred-hour checks. When naval squadrons VR-6 and VR-8 joined the airlift, they were directed that their mechanics could no longer do so. Navy R-5Ds, like the Air Force C-54s, would go to Burtonwood for maintenance work. When the first one returned, the sailors found that it had so many uncorrected defects that they issued a new order of their own. Any Navy plane sent to Burtonwood would be accompanied by the aircraft commander, who would oversee the maintenance work and ensure that it was done correctly.

Tunner knew that he could not accept a situation where the airlift would be short 35 planes each week because of slow maintenance at Burtonwood. He did the only thing that he could. Until the problems at Burtonwood could be solved, he followed the example of Navy practice and transferred responsibility for the two-hundred-hour maintenance checks back to the squadrons. As he had earlier stripped off mechanics to provide personnel for Burtonwood, that meant that the mechanics on the line in Germany would be putting in twelve-hour days. Tunner had no other choice if he wanted to maintain the pace of the airlift.[6]

There were bright spots in the operation as well. The new airport in Berlin was one. The best available site for a third airport in Berlin was a rolling field located in the French sector. Eight hundred yards by five hundred yards, it had once been used as a training ground for the

antiaircraft gunners of Göring's Luftwaffe. It was located close to rail
and road facilities, and with the exception of a pair of transmission
towers for Radio Berlin, the surrounding terrain was unobstructed,
allowing for a shallow approach for the heavily loaded aircraft of the
airlift. The French quickly agreed to let the Americans construct an
airport on the site for use by American planes. The French would
maintain the field and unload the planes.

The plans called for a 150-foot-wide runway, 5,500 feet long, with
500-foot overruns at either end. The rest of the facility was planned for
maximum efficiency. The taxiways were designed to feed directly to
loading docks that were six feet high, so that goods from the planes
could be sent down chutes to increase the speed of unloading. The
living quarters and operations rooms were clustered near the central
aprons rather than scattered as at many other airlift bases.

Under ordinary conditions, the construction of an airfield like Tegel
would have been a straightforward, routine job. In Berlin, however,
nothing was routine. The runway specifications called for a base course
a minimum of two feet thick. Because of the rolling terrain, in some
places material five feet thick had to be laid down to achieve the level
required. This material would ordinarily be concrete, an item unavailable in the city and far too heavy to bring in efficiently by plane in the
required quantities. The solution was found in the rubble of the city
itself. Bricks from bombed-out buildings were crushed in six-inch lay-
ers until the required depth was built up. The bulldozers, graders, and
rollers were among the items cut up, then reassembled in the city by
L. C. Lacomb and the crew of technicians he was now training in his
craft. The labor force consisted of 15 American officers and 150 enlisted men, who ran the heavy equipment, plus 17,000 Germans who
worked for one mark, twenty pfennigs an hour and one hot meal a day.
Forty percent of the workers were women.

The wearing surface of the runway, subject to the repeated shocks
of C-54 landings, was proposed to be of crushed rock bound together
with asphalt. Again, the ruins of the city provided the raw material.
The cobbles from disused streets were torn up and crushed, as was
ballast from disused railroads. Because the Soviets maintained that
they were in charge of the operation of all of the railroads in the city,
they protested strongly. They were ignored. When the project started
in September, the estimated completion date was January 1, 1949. That
was later revised to a target of December 15.[7]

Another bright spot was the favorable coverage the airlift was getting
in the world press outside the Communist sphere. General Tunner
knew how to take advantage of a public relations bonanza, and he
knew that Lieutenant Gail Halvorsen's "Operation Little Vittles" was
exactly that. With the secret of the "Chocolate Flier" out, Gail Hal-

vorsen often found his bunk in the old barn at Zeppelinheim stacked high with candy bars and packages of gum when he returned from his scheduled flights into Berlin. GIs and airmen were sending him goods that could have bought many fine German cameras and other things on the black market. Halvorsen soon began to run out of handkerchiefs and started to cut up old shirts, using the sleeves for candy sacks and the tails for parachutes. He wondered what he would do when he ran out of shirts.

That problem solved itself when a half sack of mail for him arrived from the States, and he found that each envelope contained a handkerchief. The wire services had picked up on the European reports of what he and his crew were doing. Radio stations across the country were playing requests if the listener would promise to send a handkerchief to what had come to be known as "Operation Little Vittles." The *Weekly Reader,* a publication for elementary school children, ran a story about Little Vittles, and letters poured in. In Chicopee, Massachusetts, an old fire station was converted into a 24-hour assembly station for Little Vittles donations from 22 schools in the area, and it processed 2,000 sheets to be cut into parachutes, 3,000 individual handkerchiefs, and 18 tons of candy. At the peak of its operation, the Chicopee committee using the erstwhile fire station was shipping 800 pounds every other day.

Halvorsen was soon relieved of routine flying duties and allowed to rove the city of Berlin, making unscheduled drops at schools and playgrounds. In response to many letters, he began dropping candy over Communist-controlled East Berlin during his approaches to Tempelhof, but that didn't last long. Returning from one such flight, he was again greeted by an officer in a jeep on landing.

The officer asked what they had been doing, flying over East Berlin, and Halvorsen told him that they were dropping candy to some children there who had written them letters.

"You can't do that," the officer said. The Soviets had filed a strong diplomatic protest against the flights over their sector of the city, which they denounced as a capitalistic trick to influence the minds of young people. Drops over East Berlin were ordered to cease at once.[8]

A few days later an operations officer handed Halvorsen a note. It was signed by General Tunner and said, "I want to see you as soon as possible."[9]

The summons was not, as Halvorsen feared, a prelude to the termination of Operation Little Vittles because of the Soviet complaints. General Tunner sent Halvorsen on a whirlwind trip back to the States for a series of radio and television appearances and newspaper interviews. Toward the end of the tour Halvorsen was invited to lunch with John S. Swersey, the president of Huyler's Candy Company and a prominent member of the American Confectioners Association. Swersey promised his support of Operation Little Vittles, without bothering to specify what form that support would take.

Ken Slaker, who had escaped from the Soviet zone with the help of Rudolf Schnabel, was growing concerned about what had happened to the German he now regarded as a friend. Slaker, pulled off the airlift and returned to his normal duties at Fürstenfeldbruck, had been attempting to locate Schnabel through Air Force channels. For three weeks, every attempt he made resulted in evasive answers. Finally, in desperation, he contacted an old friend, Colonel Sig Young, the commander of the Wiesbaden base, and asked him to help.

Two days later, Young called back, asking Slaker to fly up to Wiesbaden the following day. Schnabel would be there when he arrived. When Slaker reported, he was amazed when Young informed him that it had taken a great deal of work to get Schnabel released from the Army to the custody of the Air Force. His amazement became astonishment when Schnabel was escorted into Young's office and, with tears in his eyes, told Slaker, "Kenneth, Army police put me in jail and they beat me with rubber hose."

Slaker looked over to Young for confirmation, and the colonel nodded, adding that the Army could not really be blamed for being paranoid about Rudolf Schnabel. He was an East German, he had no papers, and he had admitted that his brother was a member of the Communist party. The Army, disregarding the fact that Schnabel had assisted Slaker in his escape, suspected that he was a Communist plant. Now in the custody of the Air Force, Rudolf Schnabel was cleared of that suspicion, and Colonel Young promised that he would try to get him settled into a job in the West.[10]

The United States Navy had suggested as early as mid summer that some of its air transport resources could be allotted to Operation Vittles.[11] By the beginning of October, the Military Air Transport Service had no further reserves of C-54s, and the Navy offer was accepted. Two squadrons that operated with the R-5D, the naval version of the C-54, from bases in the Pacific were assigned to Berlin. The orders gave squadrons VR-6 in Guam and VR-8 in Honolulu only hours to close down operations and begin the move to Moffett Field in California. Most of the R-5Ds were fitted out with passenger accommodations because they had been assigned to moving personnel across the wide expanses of the Pacific.

At Guam, nineteen-year-old Tom Flowers of VR-6 was working at the passenger assignment desk when he got the word that the squadron was going to Europe. Within minutes, he was dealing with an irate officer—a four-striper who was scheduled to fly to Pearl Harbor to take command of a ship that was under orders to sail the following day.

The captain knew that the ship would sail whether he was on board or not, and he was in no mood to listen while Flowers tried to explain that orders are orders and VR-6 had just gotten its set. They read Berlin, not Pearl Harbor. The effect of the Berlin airlift on United States military operations worldwide was spreading.[12]

When the squadrons reached Moffett Field, the aircraft were either modified by removal of all passenger seating and accessories or swapped completely for aircraft from other squadrons that were already configured for carrying cargo. They flew to the naval air station at Jacksonville, Florida, where extra radio and radar equipment was installed. As the work on each aircraft was completed, it flew individually to Germany.

General Tunner made it a point to meet the first of the Navy planes to arrive at Rhein-Main. The weather was terrible. It had been raining for several days, and the hardstand at which the first R-5D was to park was knee-deep in water. The Navy plane came in, splashing spray high into the air as it landed. Then it rolled to the hardstand, and the cargo door opened to reveal a crew in dress blues and highly shined shoes. The first thing they saw was a two-star general, attempting to look dignified while standing in water that came up to his knees. It was only a moment before both the general and the Navy men were laughing. Given the situation, there was little else to do.

One of the Navy officers said, "General, sir. Just tell me one thing— are we on land or at sea?"

"We ordered this just for you," Tunner replied. "We wanted the navy to feel at home."[13]

The Americans were not the only ones to call on their Navy to aid in the airlift. The RAF was short of air traffic controllers at Gatow, and those it had were strained from working long shifts. The Royal Navy offered four men, two ground control approach operators and two for general air traffic control duties. The GCA men did not measure up to the standards of the RAF and were soon sent back to England. The ATC men, Lieutenant Douglas Farge and Lieutenant John Gall, who told everyone to pronounce his name as if he were "divided into three parts," were fitted into the working rosters at the Gatow control center. The British Commonwealth also continued to contribute to the effort. In early November, the pilots of a Royal New Zealand Air Force squadron arrived for duty in Germany. A few weeks later, a contingent of pilots from the Royal South African Air Force arrived as well.

The British were also tapping other military resources for pilots. The British Army had formed a Glider Pilot Regiment in 1942, which had earned high distinction during the war. One of the many honors the regiment carried on its standard was one for the assault on the bridges in Holland in 1944, an effort that had resulted in debilitating casualties. By 1948, however, the British Army was in the process of reorganization, and the concept of assault by glider-borne troops was being questioned. A number of the men of the regiment were qualified as enlisted pilots of the planes that towed gliders into battle. With the Berlin airlift in full operation and their own unit in the process of being disbanded, several volunteered for service in Germany.

The airfield at Tegel was open on November 5. The first plane to land was a C-54 of the 19th Troop Carrier Squadron, piloted by Captain Charles Ludwig. The plane carried ten tons of cheese and two very important passengers—Lieutenant General Joseph Cannon and Major General William Tunner. They were greeted by over 2,000 cheering Berliners and a French honor guard and band, which played "The Star-Spangled Banner," "God Save the King," and the "*Marseillaise.*" It was quietly announced to the press, after the ceremony, that "normal flight operations" would not commence until the completion of various additional work on the field.[14] On November 18, Squadron Leader Johnstone of No. 30 Squadron was ordered to fly into Tegel from the British base at Lübeck to determine whether the airport was ready to receive planes on a regular basis. Asking whether he was to carry cargo, Johnstone was told that no one flew into Berlin in an empty plane. He took off in a Dakota crammed with a mixed load of cooking fats, tractor tires, and condensed milk. He flew into Tegel to find that it had opened, but it had a nonoperational control tower, no ground approach radar equipment, no telephone lines to the air safety center, no arrangements for meals, and no latrines. Met by a French officer who disappeared immediately after blurting out a greeting, Johnstone was unable to find anyone who would unload and take charge of his cargo. He had to fly it all back to Lübeck.[15]

The towers of Radio Berlin also remained as an obstruction in the flight path that complicated landing patterns, adding to the danger of landings. General Ganeval made a formal request to the director of the station, Heinz Schmidt, that the towers be removed. The French commandant did not bother to inform the Soviet military government of the request. Although Soviet liaison and press officers continued to control the programming, the Soviets had announced months earlier that they had officially turned direction of the radio station back to the Berlin City Assembly. Ganeval therefore felt no duty to inform the Soviet military government about his concern with the antennas. The directors of the station ignored the French commandant's first request, as well as his second, in which he stated his intention to remove the towers himself if the request was not heeded.

The mechanical efficiency that the airlift had developed under General Tunner's direction was in keeping with his clockwork standards. The Abilene Flour Mills of Kansas had been sending goods to Germany since immediately after the end of the war. Now, the sacks no longer carried the vengeful message, "We come as conquerors, not liberators," that had been stenciled on them three years earlier.

At 10:07 p.m. on a typical airlift night, a load of flour from the Abilene Mills arrived at a railroad siding in Zeppelinheim. There, it was loaded onto a ten-ton trailer driven by a soldier of the 63d Truck Company by a team of DPs working under the orders of an Army Transportation Corps private. By 10:31 the truck held 212 sacks, exactly the amount that a C-54 could safely carry. The truck headed for Rhein-Main, where the driver, Private Earl Windom, uncoupled his trailer in Bay 27 on the transfer strip at the airfield. Then, Windom headed back for another load.

While the load of flour was en route to Rhein-Main, the crew of the airplane that would carry it was receiving up-to-date information on their flight path and being briefed on current Soviet activity in the corridor, alternate landing sites, and any new navigational procedures. Then they proceeded to their plane, a C-54 bearing the number 5540. Captain Douglas A. Graham slid into the pilot's seat for this leg of the trip; his copilot, Captain Harold Klopp, would fly the right-hand seat.

The trailer Windom had left had been on the field for only twenty-one minutes before the control tower called the Air Force van at the transfer strip to let the men there know that aircraft number 5540 would be ready for a load in four minutes. Another 63d Truck Company tractor hitched up to the trailer and pulled the Abilene Mills flour out to the loading area of the field. By 11:00, another crew of DPs was heaving the sacks onto the waiting Skymaster. By 11:21 that work was complete, the flour sacks were strapped down, and the line mechanics were completing their servicing of the plane.

At 12:21 a.m., Skymaster 5540 lifted off from Rhein-Main and began a climb to nine hundred feet while maintaining its takeoff heading. Then, turning and climbing at a rate of three hundred feet per minute, Graham headed for the Darmstadt radio beacon. There he turned again and, in the next twenty-two miles, continued to ascend so that he was at his assigned altitude when the plane was over the Aschaffenburg beacon. There, Skymaster 5540 turned for Fulda.

The old city of Fulda is a Baroque masterpiece, largely untouched by the destructive bombing raids of the war. One of Germany's oldest churches, that of Saint Michael, was built there in the ninth century. Pilgrims from across the country have come for years to worship in the magnificent eighteenth-century cathedral, where the remains of Saint Boniface, the martyred "Apostle of the Germans," lie in a crypt beneath the altar.

To Graham and Klopp, the church and cathedral were lost in the dark landscape five thousand feet below them. Fulda was nothing more than a monotonous radio voice in the ether, broadcasting a cryptic refrain at 265 kilocycles. "Dit, dit, dah, dit; dah, dit, dit," the Morse code signals for *F* and *D*, was the endlessly repeated, and vital, message of the Fulda radio beacon that came through their earphones. Those letters marked that point in the sky where the airmen changed course again. When the needle on their radio compass spun 180 degrees, indicating that the beacon was now behind them, they made a turn of 23 degrees. That put them on the heading of 57 degrees magnetic that pointed straight down the southern air corridor to the city of Berlin.

When the compass needle flipped, Klopp called in the exact time, so that the ship just behind could adjust its speed to reach the Fulda beacon a precise interval later, maintaining the steady stream of aircraft. By 12:56 a.m., Skymaster 5540 had entered the airspace above the Soviet zone. Exactly forty minutes after they had passed over Fulda, copilot Klopp called into Tempelhof radio control for clearance to begin to descend to two thousand feet on their initial approach to Berlin. Over the Wedding beacon, the plane turned again, slowed to 140 miles per hour, and began to lose another 500 feet of altitude. Two turns later, the plane was on its final approach. At 2:05 a.m. the wheels touched the runway at Tempelhof. As it slowed, a jeep with a large "Follow Me" sign in the rear appeared to lead number 5540 to its unloading station.

Two minutes later the plane was stopped on its hardstand, and by 2:09, the first sack of flour was being heaved down a chute off the plane. The crew of DPs doing the unloading was supervised by Donald Chase, a young private assigned to the 26th Infantry but pressed into airlift duty.

By 2:27, all 212 sacks of flour had been placed on the back of a truck and were headed to a transfer station ramp. Within twenty-two minutes the load was transferred to a diesel truck supplied by the *Magistrat* of the city of Berlin. At 3:00 a.m., Martin Bromer, a Berliner, chugged away with it. By 3:13, it had been delivered to the Schluterbrotfabrik, the Schluter Bread Factory. There, three shifts working around the clock produced 60,000 loaves of bread a day.

By 7:30 in the morning, the sacks of flour from the Abilene Mills had been converted to bread that was in vans on their way to be delivered to shops throughout the city.[16] The airlift was feeding the city. There was no alternative that anyone in the West could see, now that diplomatic efforts to resolve the crisis had failed.

There is a pair of photographs of the American delegation to the United Nations meeting in Paris, listening to the results of the 1948 presidential election on the radio. In the first, John Foster Dulles looks elated as Governor Dewey leads in the early returns. Secretary of State

Marshall appears thoughtful. In the second photograph, it is apparent from Dulles's face that he knows that he will not be the new Secretary of State. Contrary to all predictions, Harry Truman was reelected. Marshall appears thoughtful in the second photograph as well.[17]

With his business at the United Nations completed, George Marshall reached a decision. Like many Americans, Marshall had doubted that President Truman would be reelected, and he had been prepared to resign from his post when the new president took office. While his resignation was not now required, he informed President Truman of his intention to resign anyway. He had been informed by his doctors in June that he had a large cyst on his right kidney but had postponed surgery so that he could follow through on the efforts to resolve the Berlin crisis. Truman reluctantly accepted Marshall's decision. The secretary entered Walter Reed Hospital, and his right kidney was removed on December 7, 1948. Although Marshall wished to be home for Christmas, the doctors would not release him until just before the beginning of new year. Once there, he drafted his resignation, timing it to coincide with Truman's inauguration. His successor in the post of secretary of state was Dean Acheson.[18]

# TWENTY-NINE

# THE BLEAK NOVEMBER

While General Tunner justifiably felt that his ability to control the airlift was hobbled by the command arrangements in Europe, the demands that the nature of his command placed on the resources of the Air Force were far-reaching. With the establishment of the school for replacement pilots at Great Falls, the long arm of the airlift swept the globe in search of more pilots.

Fain Pool, a captain, fell in love with flying in 1928 when he was ten and a pilot from the 2d Air Observation Squadron at Post Field, Fort Sill, Oklahoma, took him up for a ride. As soon as he was old enough, Pool began flying lessons, earning a civilian license before being accepted as an Air Corps cadet. During the war, he flew thirty-five missions over Europe in a B-17. Once, he had limped home from a raid on Berlin with his number-three engine destroyed by flak.

Late in 1948, Pool received orders to report for an assignment with the Pacific Air Forces. He checked in at Hamilton Field, north of San Francisco, for processing and assignment to transportation. When he did, the clerk asked him how much time he had on four-engine aircraft.

"About 1,700 hours," Pool said, without even looking at his log book.

"Good. You're going to the Berlin airlift."

"No, I'm not," Fain replied, unaware of the priority the airlift had. "I've got orders for the Pacific."

"That's what you think," said the clerk, rubber-stamping Pool's orders with a large, black "CANCELED." The clerk told Fain that new orders would be issued "forthwith." They were. Captain Fain Pool was in the first class of replacement pilots to train at Great Falls.[1]

By the middle of December, Great Falls was operating at full capacity and expected to graduate its seventh class. It had already furnished 79 pilots, 195 copilots, and 91 aerial engineers to the airlift from its first five classes, and the men from the sixth class were in transit to Germany. Of the candidates training to be pilots, only 20 percent failed their final checks, and, because of a policy that men failing to qualify to fly in the left-hand seat automatically reverted to copilot status, only fourteen fliers had washed out completely.

Most of the pilots were recalled Air Force reservists, including the civil airline personnel taken on during the winter slack period. Many of these had been flying as copilots on civilian airlines, and most were glad to be back in the service. One spoke for the majority when he said, "There's more pulling rank on the airlines than there ever was in the service."[2]

The minimum requirement for pilots to enter Great Falls was 1,200 hours of time on four-engine aircraft, but the average for those entering was 1,800 hours. One, Robert Dyer, a former bomber and civilian airline pilot, had 9,800 hours in his log book. He was quickly pulled out of training and made an instructor.[3]

The need for pilots was so great that recruitment was not restricted to the Air Force Reserve. It even netted a few men who had once worn the Navy's golden aviator's wings. Three former Navy fliers—Howard Hoover, Joseph Gerrity, and R. J. DeSomer—and two former Marines— Robert Steck and Charles Schroder—all still held reserve commissions in the sea services when they were given the chance to switch to the Air Force and serve on the airlift. They jumped at it and, immediately after completing the course at Great Falls, pinned on silver Air Force wings.[4]

As bad as the weather at Great Falls was, it could not quite match the conditions over Central Europe at the time. There was nothing that anyone on the CALTF could do about the fact that the weather in which the crews flew was bad and subject to rapid changes. They could, however, set up a weather forecast system that made it possible to foresee and prepare for the worst that the area had to offer. Because the weather in Germany is determined by systems that generally travel from west to east, observation stations in the United States and the Arctic and on weather ships in the Atlantic contributed data to the development of long-range forecasts. So did weather reconnaissance flights by RAF planes flying out of England, Scotland, Northern Ireland, and Gibraltar. Four converted U.S. B-29s operating from a base west of London and ranging over the Atlantic as far as Iceland also contributed data, as did weather observation points as far away as the North Cape of Norway and Casablanca in French Morocco. Funneled into Airweather Central at Rhein-Main, the data were analyzed by the meteorologists under Lieutenant Colonel Nicholas Chavasse. In addition to long-range forecasting, Airweather Central provided four-day forecasts, regular twenty-four-hour forecasts, and emergency updates to the airlift crews.

November, notorious as the worst flying month of the year in Europe, began with rain and fogs that slowed the pace of the airlift. Then, on November 13, 1948, the worst fog in years settled over all of Europe in a cold, yellowish blanket a thousand feet thick. Colonel Chavasse, reviewing the data from his hundreds of weather stations, informed General Tunner that the conditions might last for weeks. In Berlin, there was less than fifty days' supply of coal.

Tunner reached a decision. Henceforth, if the ceiling was below 2,500 feet, planes would be spaced five minutes apart rather than three. If the ceiling fell to below 250 feet, the planes would sit on the runway, waiting for the fog to lift. In practice, many of the operations officers and pilots pared away at the minimums, just to keep the airlift in operation. At Rhein-Main, C-54s took off on nights when the fog was so bad that even the buses in nearby Frankfurt had stopped running. Many nights the fog was so thick that pilots were unable to pick out the beams of the flashlights of the ground crew members guiding them to their hardstands. An anonymous ingenious flight-line technician found that by gluing Plexiglas cylinders to the flashlight lenses he could create a wand of light that the pilots could see in the fog. His invention was soon in use at all of the fog-shrouded airlift bases and came to be a standard piece of equipment at civilian airfields in the United States as well. The loading crews worked in human chains, like bucket brigades, each man with his feet firmly planted against those of the men next to him, who could barely be seen in the fog. Truck convoys from the railheads to the airfields were guided by men walking ahead with flashlights, and the drivers stayed on the roads only by following the glowing red taillights of the truck ahead of them.

Landing minimums were reduced to a two-hundred-foot ceiling and four hundred yards visibility, but many planes landed when the operators in the tower couldn't even make out the runway lights and were certain that the pilots could not either. November brought problems with icing as well. On some takeoffs it was such a problem that planes could barely lift off the runway. Another anonymous ground crewman devised a solution, mounting spare jet engines on the back of trucks and using the hot exhaust gases to warm the wings, props, and control surfaces of the idling C-54s.

In the first half of November, the average daily tonnage flown into the city dropped to 2,635 tons. The stock of coal in the city was down to forty-four days' supply but the airlift spokesmen tried to put a bright face on it. They said that there was no cause for alarm about shortages in the stockpiles and expressed confidence that the airlift could make up its losses and boost tonnages later in the year. With colder weather, they said, the flying conditions would actually improve. Further, now that the British and American efforts had been combined in one command, there were plans to move even more C-54s to bases in the British zone, where the flying distance to Berlin was shorter. There were already fifty Skymasters operating from the British base at Fassberg, and a base at Celle was scheduled to open in mid-December. Fifty more C-54s would operate from that base.[5]

With the Soviets harping daily in their controlled press and over Radio Berlin that the airlift was a failure, it was necessary to put on a brave show even as the stockpiles dwindled further. On November 27, the airlift was shut down for a full fifteen hours. The fog was so thick that no planes at all flew from midnight until three o'clock in the afternoon. The next day, General Lucius Clay announced that he was ordering a special distribution of coal to Berlin households in celebration of the fact that the airlift had beaten the worst flying weather that Germany could offer. Each family was to receive fifty pounds of coal, with extra allotments going to families with children. "We are deliberately depleting our stockpiles," the general said. "We have done so well this month—the worst weather month of the year—we are confident the airlift can continue to grow and be maintained indefinitely. And we intend to keep it up indefinitely if that is necessary," he added for the benefit of the Soviets.[6]

However, the airlift had its worst day on November 30. During that twenty-four-hour period, only ten planes reached Berlin from the West. The beginning of December brought no relief, and stocks of food and fuel in the city continued to dwindle. There was nothing that brave talk about beating the weather could do about that.

General Clay experienced the perils of the dense fog at first hand. He was at his headquarters in Frankfurt but was determined to return to the beleaguered city of Berlin on the day preceding the municipal elections. No planes were flying, but General Cannon promised to inform him immediately if there was a break in the weather. The break came at two o'clock in the afternoon, and Clay, his wife, and several aides rushed to Rhein-Main, where their staff car was guided through the fog by a jeep to a C-54. A ground crew was scraping ice off the wings as Clay's party boarded.

Missus Clay rode in the jump seat in the cockpit, just behind the pilots. There was heat in that area of the plane, and both the general and his wife appreciated the courtesy. Clay and the rest of the group sat in the canvas bucket seats in the cargo area, and the general tried to doze while Robert Murphy and one of the others in the party played a particularly rowdy game of gin rummy.

When they reached Berlin, both Tegel and Gatow were completely socked in by fog, and the conditions at Tempelhof were far below minimums. When the pilot finally managed to get the plane down, the visibility was so poor that they could not see the "Follow Me" jeep that had come out to meet them and had to be guided to the unloading ramp by two men with flashlights walking just ahead of the wings.[7]

The elections for which Clay was so anxious to be in the city were a reflection of the continuing problems that the civil government in Berlin faced. For example, when the *Magistrat* dismissed Waldemar

Schmidt, the head of the city labor department, he had refused to accept the decision. Shortly after his dismissal, Schmidt had appeared at a meeting of the *Magistrat,* taking his usual seat in the chamber. Acting Mayor Friedensberg, committed to uphold the decision, said to Schmidt, "I call upon you to leave the meeting. You are no longer a member of the council. You have no right to be here."

Schmidt delivered a brief speech denouncing his dismissal and resumed his seat. As he did, Friedensberg adjourned the meeting, "since Herr Schmidt, who apparently feels sure of support from certain quarters, does not obey my request." An hour later, the *Magistrat* reconvened in the British sector. It never returned to its headquarters in the Soviet sector. The split in the government of Berlin was complete.[8]

Not long after the *Magistrat* moved, indications reached Western intelligence officers of an attempted coup by the SED in the Western sectors of the city. The plan, it was said, involved the infiltration of SED operatives armed with pistols into the West. There they would mix with crowds and, at an arranged time, begin to shoot at members of the Western sector police. It was assumed that this would lead to the Western police being reinforced by soldiers and that this in turn would lead to more shooting. In response, "spontaneous" protest demonstrations in the East would call for the liberation of the West Berliners from their "imperialist oppressors," and the East German police would move across the border to occupy government buildings in the West. If the allies tried to bring in reinforcements by road, the Soviet army would blow up the bridges to make this impossible. The plan might have worked, but Western intelligence leaked details of it to the press, which gave it wide coverage. Convinced that the world would not now accept the idea of a "spontaneous" uprising, the Soviets canceled the operation.[9]

By November 30, it was evident to all observers that the election was going to result in a resounding defeat for the SED, so the Soviet military government took further action. Marshal Sokolovsky informed the Western military governors that the USSR would boycott the scheduled election. Residents in the Soviet sector were prohibited from voting in the December 5 election, and members of the SED in the Western sectors were directed by their party to stay away from the polls.

The Soviets then issued orders to the twenty-six Communist members of the assembly who had been elected during the earlier debacle in 1946, when the SED polled only 20 percent of the vote. The Communists were to meet in convention with a group of handpicked delegates from the Communist trade unions and elect a new city government.

The meeting was held in the Admiralspalast, a theater that normally served as the site of light opera productions. All of the delegates had been given white cards to wave as they raised their hands to vote. The leader of the convention opened by proposing that the "undemocratic, reactionary city administration be dismissed," and all hands in the room went up, creating a sea of waving white cards.

Then a candidate for mayor was proposed. He was Friedrick Ebert, Jr., whose father had been the first president of the Weimar Republic and had squelched the Communist uprising of 1918. The younger Ebert, known as Fritz, was a drunkard and a weakling who had gone from initial resistance to the Nazis to running a publishing house for them. Again, the white cards fluttered in a unanimous vote. The newly elected "mayor" noted that his was a provisional government, stating that there would be "free" elections as soon as "self-evident suppositions" could be established. Everyone in the West knew that to mean: as soon as the Western allies abandoned the city. The convention broke up after only ninety minutes, and the staff of the Admiralspalast went back to preparations for the evening's performance. The scheduled production was Rimsky-Korsakov's *The Czar's Bride*.[10] The West Berliners, with their sense of humor still intact in spite of the blockade, immediately took to calling the Ebert government "the operetta council."[11]

Colonel Howley wasted no time in denouncing the sham election in the Soviet sector. In a press release on the day it was held, he bluntly characterized it as "an arrogant action—in flagrant violation of the existing constitution of Berlin and of all quadripartite agreements pertaining to the city."[12]

The following day, Colonel Howley joined a group of city officials and American playwright Thornton Wilder, who was on a visit to the city, in a pleasant duty. While lectures in law, history, and philosophy had begun on November 15, the Free University of Berlin, set up in the British sector, had not held an official opening. Now it did, and Frank Howley was there to give a speech on the value of freedom.

Then the American commandant returned to his office to face the other problems relative to the forthcoming election in the West. The Communists had pulled out all stops in their campaign to disrupt the process. Riders on the *S-Bahn* were showered with leaflets urging them, "Stay away from the polls. Don't endanger your future."[13] A whispering campaign reminiscent of the 1946 tactics started. It suggested that the polling lists would fall into Soviet hands after the Western allies left the city, and voters would be punished. Reports circulated that Communist gangs would march into the Western sectors and attack voters at the polls. Howley let it be known that if they did, they wouldn't run into frightened, unarmed civilians, but the United States Army. Force would be met with force.[14] The Communist government issued orders to the 150,000 Western sector residents who worked in the East to report to work at 8:00 a.m. on election day, the hour the polls opened, and to work an extra hour, so they could not make it to the polls before they closed. The transport workers responded by calling a strike from 6:00 a.m. to 10:00 a.m., allowing those voters to get to the polls before work.[15]

On election day, 10,000 Western sector police, reinforced by American, French, and British troops, patrolled the streets as long lines of Germans stood before polling places. Those Berliners who were old or crippled were brought to vote by their friends. Of all those eligible to vote, 86.3 percent cast their ballots on December 5. The Social Democrats led, with 64.5 percent of the total. Ernst Reuter was named lord mayor of the city of Berlin.[16]

☆　☆　☆

At 9:00 a.m. on December 16, 1948, a squad of French military police cordoned off Tegel airport. Jack Fellman, a nineteen-year-old U.S. Air Force tower operator was on duty talking airplanes in and was mystified when a French officer entered the control tower and told him to shut down operations and evacuate the area. Incoming airplanes were diverted, with no reason given, to the two other airports in the city.[17]

There were a number of Soviet technicians in a small building near the radio towers, and they tried to telephone for instructions and assistance when the French military police arrived, but the telephone wires had been cut. The technicians were taken into custody, and French demolition engineers began to set charges at the bases of the towers. By 11:45 a.m. the work was done, and, with a roar that could be heard as far away as the center of the city, the towers crumpled in a twisted heap. The control tower personnel were allowed to go back to work and happily announced to incoming aircraft that the field's lone obstruction no longer existed.

Colonel Sergei Tulpanov, the head of the Soviet Information Section and member of the NKVD, flew into a rage so violent at the news that it triggered a gallstone attack. A doctor had to administer morphine to ease his pain while he dictated a dispatch ordering all Soviet and Communist officials to say nothing at all about the demolition of the towers. The Soviet commandant, General Kotikov, had been suffering from heart pains for a week and was confined to bed. Tulpanov, holding the power of the Soviet secret police, virtually ordered Kotikov to call on Ganeval at once to protest.

Kotikov, so ill that he looked as though he might collapse at any moment, raged at his French counterpart at a pace the interpreter could barely follow. Then, calming, he said, "Why didn't you get in touch with me? We would surely have been able to reach an agreement?"

General Ganeval smiled, remembering the affair of the kidnapped policemen at city hall. "I don't think that would have been possible. Not after you broke your promise to me."[18]

☆　☆　☆

When the fog had begun impairing airlift operations in November, Ruth Andreas-Friedrich's magazine was forced to suspend publication, and she grew more despondent each day. Her daughter, Karin, urged her to leave the city that held so many dark memories, and her friend, Frank, had few words on the subject. "Hurry up and get out," was all he said. Berlin was a dreary city in the winter of the blockade.

With the modest coal ration, people shivered in the cold if they remained at home. Electric power was off except for a few hours each day, sometimes at night, and people rose at odd times to do the household chores that required it. Gas, which most families used for cooking, was also shut off at specified times, and the newspapers reported deaths by gas poisoning every week. People would accidentally leave gas jets on when the supply was cut off and be overcome when it came back on and they failed to light the burners.

Most of the people of Berlin endured and even tried to find humor in their bleak situation. One restaurant waiter said to an American writer, "From morning to night I'm a hero now. I wish I could relax."[19] By far the most common joke was one that said, Things could be worse: imagine what life would be like if the Americans were running the blockade and the Soviets were attempting to supply us.

To Ruth Andreas-Friedrich, wandering in the cemetery where her lover, Leo Borchard, was buried, the tombstones looked like ghosts in the fog. She could find no solace in her memories or in attempts at humor. She made reservations on Overseas Airways to leave the city on a flight on December 29, consoling herself that a reservation wasn't really a decision to leave.[20]

THIRTY

# THE CHRISTMAS SHOW

By the second week in December, the strain of operating for long hours in weather conditions that were less than marginal, coupled with the poor living conditions the airlift personnel had to endure, began to lead to personnel breakdowns. At Rhein-Main, several of the pilots refused point-blank to fly anymore and were sent home, although no other disciplinary action was taken against them. Morale was even lower at the British bases to which American personnel were assigned. At both Fassberg and Celle, which had just opened, Americans subsisted on British rations, which were both meager and deficient by American standards. The English food was definitely not to the U.S. airmen's tastes. Dinner was usually thin slices of overcooked beef, accompanied by brussels sprouts. General Tunner noted on one of his frequent inspection visits to the base that the biggest complaint he got from the men was that there was too much roast beef. It was not just dinner that irked the fliers. Creamed kidney and kippered herring were not the average American's idea of a hearty breakfast, and no butter whatsoever was available in the British messes.

At Fassberg there were often incidents between the Americans and the small RAF contingent that ran the base. On one notable occasion, a group of pilots took over the officers mess for a drinking party, and the mess piano ended up as a casualty. The front, back, sides, keys, and strings were all removed piece by piece and scattered around the room.[1] Tensions rose so high that the RAF station commander, Wally Bigger, requested that either he or the commander of the American contingent be removed. CALTF Headquarters decided that the problems of trying to have the RAF operate what was essentially an American base were not worth the effort. Both Bigger and the American commander were removed, and Colonel John Coulter of the U.S. Air Force was appointed commander of Fassberg.

Coulter brought his wife with him to the base, and she created quite a sensation, because she was a famous American movie star, Constance

Bennet. Between trips to Hollywood, London, and Rome, Miss Bennet found time to visit the mess halls and clubs on the base, where she was always trailed by news cameras. She even managed to star in several productions at the camp theater.

Not all of the base personnel were taken with the vivacious Miss Bennett, however. On one occasion, she was leaving the PX with a large package. Seeing an officer passing by, she called to him, "Captain, would you mind carrying this to my car?"

The flier stopped, looked at the movie star, and said in a deep drawl, "Ma'am, I'm an Air Force pilot and I'm going to carry coal to Berlin. But I ain't due to be a grocer's boy." Then he calmly walked away.[2]

Binges of drinking among the fliers, both military and civilian, became frequent during the fogbound weeks of early winter. The contract fliers of the British civil airlift were among the heaviest of the drinkers. Flight Refueling, Ltd., responsible for hauling most of the liquid fuel into the city, had grown from a company with four flight crews and thirty-five maintenance men to one that employed a thousand mechanics just to keep its tankers in the air. It also found it necessary to have 150 aircrews on hand, just to insure that 32 would be sober and sensible enough to fly on any given day.[3] One rowdy group of charter fliers, anxious to get back to their airfield, armed themselves with shovels and hijacked the Stockholm-Lübeck express train. Another, carousing in Hamburg, came on a store of tools used by the work gang that maintained the city's streetcar tracks. Using oxyacetylene torches, they welded a series of switches into the closed position. The following day, most of the streetcars ended up in one section of the city, and their operators found that they could not return because of the sealed switches. That airlift crew was dismissed and sent back to England.

The one notable exception to hard-drinking habits of the civil pilots and crews was Air Vice Marshal Bennett's operation. Bennett's men were forbidden to drink for forty-eight hours before any scheduled flight. Given their schedule, that meant that they were forbidden to drink at all, and the air marshal rigidly enforced his rule.

He also worked his men, and himself, nearly to the breaking point. Bennett was the only pilot in his company qualified for night flights into the city, so he carried the entire load of twice-nightly flights for two months, until his chief pilot, Captain Clarence Utting, became qualified for flying at night. During the days, Bennett worked alongside his mechanics, overhauling the engines of the Tudors. He was doing the job of two people but expected that the burden would ease now that Utting could assume some of the flying duties.

At 2:22 a.m. on December 8, Captain Clarence Utting was walking across the tarmac at Wunstorf toward Avro Tudor G-AKBY to commence his first night flight into Berlin. His radio officer, John Kilburn, and the copilot were lagging slightly behind Utting, and they clearly saw the heavy Bedford truck that raced out of the darkness, headlights out, hitting Utting. The pilot went down on the asphalt. The truck raced away without stopping.

Utting died the following morning. The investigation failed to find or identify the truck or the driver. As no truck had been scheduled to be at that location on the field at that time and it was apparent that the driver could easily have swerved to avoid the walking man, suspicions rose that the Soviets were behind the death. For two months, the only person who had crossed the tarmac at that precise time had been Air Vice Marshal Bennett, a leading figure of the airlift.

At dusk that evening, Bennett rolled down the Wunstorf runway at the controls of G-AKBY, leading the evening wave into Berlin.

Many among the Americans on the airlift were frankly fed up with the duty. One veteran pilot confided to John Thompson of *Newsweek,* "What I try to do now is to fly one flight a day instead of two. That way I beat those bastards in Berlin out of 10,000 pounds of coal a day." Another told Thompson, "I've had enough. I want to go home. I've got enough problems of my own without worrying about the ones the Germans have. They asked for it, didn't they?"[4] General Tunner frankly admitted to his public relations officers that pilots completing between 300 and 500 flights into the city required a continuous selling job on the value of the operation. Constant stories in the world press and in the *Task Force Times* helped. Right now, that newspaper and the European edition of *Stars and Stripes* were filled with items about the anticipated arrival of Bob Hope and an entertainment troupe in Germany and others about the continuing goodwill flights of the Chocolate Flier.

On a return flight to Rhein-Main in early December, Gail Halvorsen's plane was once again met by an officer in a jeep.

"I wonder what little surprise he has for us today," Halvorsen's copilot, John Pickering, said.[5]

The officer hustled Halvorsen into the jeep and drove to a railroad siding where a boxcar, guarded by two MPs, was sitting.

"There are 3,500 pounds of chocolate candy bars and gum in that car for your operation," the officer said. "Almost enough stuff to buy King Ludwig's castle on the black market."

"Where did it come from?" Halvorsen asked.

"Some guy named Swersey in New York. It came by ship to Bremerhaven."[6]

That shipment from the American Confectioners Association, and one of nearly equal size a week later, was flown into Berlin by pilots of the airlift in 100-pound increments and stored in a jailhouse near the flightline. The Air Force and the German Youth Organization organized a series of parties throughout free Berlin on Christmas Eve, staggering them to occur when power was on in the various neighborhoods.

☆  ☆  ☆

Every member of the airlift was looking forward to the Bob Hope Christmas show. It had been ballyhooed for weeks in the service newspapers, and everyone on the lift was hoping for the opportunity to get to one of the shows. When General Tunner saw the schedule that USAFE had worked out for the Hope troupe, he was furious. Every show was scheduled for a location where it would be almost impossible for airlift personnel to attend, although the sites were very convenient for permanent USAFE personnel. The Christmas Eve performance, for example, was scheduled for downtown Wiesbaden, close to USAFE headquarters but miles from the base from which the planes of the airlift operated. And USAFE still had not set up an efficient bus service at that base.

The official minutes of the staff meeting of the Combined Air Lift Task Force for the day Tunner learned of the Hope troupe's schedule state that "General Tunner expressed his extreme displeasure over the Bob Hope show."[7] It was a diplomatic, bureaucratic understatement on the part of the meeting recorder.

His patience was exhausted. "Willy the Whip" did much more than express his displeasure to his staff. While he could make no formal or official protest because of the limits in General Cannon's letter of instruction, Tunner let the USAFE headquarters know exactly how he felt. He demanded that, unless Hope's schedule was changed to include more appearances at airlift facilities, all mention of the airlift be dropped from the show's advance billings. He also hinted that it would be impossible to conceal such a juicy story from the avid press. Reporters were sure to learn of the scheduling snafu, particularly in light of the fact that much of the early publicity had emphasized that Hope was coming to Germany specifically to entertain Berlin airlift personnel. Several additional stops were quickly added to the troupe's schedule, including ones at the airlift bases at Celle, Fassberg, and Rhein-Main.

When the Bob Hope show arrived for Christmas, Air Force Secretary Stuart Symington was with the group. Tunner had the opportunity, on Christmas Eve, to brief the secretary on routine airlift operations. Given such an opportunity, Tunner took full advantage of it, speaking freely to Symington about the many problems he had with an effort he considered to be vital to the security of the United States.

The following day, Tunner and General Joe Cannon joined Symington for a tour of the air base at Rhein-Main. Symington covered virtually every working area, shaking hands and talking to the men while they were working, then asking them questions about the operation. He heard firsthand about the unpleasant living conditions and other things that were troubling the airmen. Stopping by a grease-covered mechanic laboring over an engine in the maintenance hangar, the secretary said, "I'm Stu Symington. Just wanted to see how you're getting along with that engine."

"Oh, I'm going to get it fixed all right, sir," the mechanic said, "but I could do it better if I had better tools."

"What's the matter with your tools?" Symington asked.

"See these?" the mechanic said, holding up pliers, a screwdriver, and a wrench in his grimy hands. "Well, I bought 'em myself right here in Germany, and they're all I got, and I can't get any more, and they ain't worth a good god-damn."

After a long silence, the Air Force secretary looked at Tunner and said, "That's what you've been telling me." Joseph Cannon turned bright red. Tunner said nothing. By the time the tour of Rhein-Main was completed, Symington had heard the same complaints from many more of the men. He directly ordered Tunner to furnish him with a report detailing the most serious problems and promised that action to solve them would be initiated immediately. Tunner could not have asked for a better Christmas present. By December 27, after having worked his staff for thirty-six hours straight, he was able to hand the secretary a long report titled "Supply and Maintenance Problems— First Airlift Task Force." It laid out, in detail, each of the problems the airlift had, followed by a set of solutions suggested by Tunner's staff. General Cannon's staff at Headquarters USAFE was given the courtesy of a carbon copy.[8]

☆ ☆ ☆

At the Bob Hope Christmas show at the Titania Palace, the two front rows were filled with VIPs. Ambassador Smith and his wife were visiting from Moscow and were guests of General Clay and his wife. A party from Washington included the secretary of the Air Force Stuart Symington, and the Secretary of the Army Kenneth Royall. After the performance, Royall announced the issuance of the Berlin Airlift device, a miniature silver C-54 to be worn on the ribbon of the Army Occupation Medal, and gave awards to two sergeants.

The day after the show, Secretary Royall called on Colonel Howley in his office for an informal briefing on the situation in the city.

Howley began by asking the secretary how much time he had, and Royall replied, "Enough."

Launching into a history of Berlin, Howley found the secretary cutting him off.

"I know all about that," the secretary said, and he stopped Howley again when the colonel began to talk about the operation of the Kommandatura.

Starting a third time, outlining how the Soviets had started the blockade, Howley was cut off again by Royall, who said, "I have all that material back in my office. And I don't want to see any more charts, either. I've seen hundreds of them."

"Well," Howley asked with his typical bluntness, "What in hell do you want?"

Royall grinned at Howley's impertinence, then said he wanted to know things that currently applied, not ancient history.

"For instance," the secretary asked, "what would have happened if we had brought an armored convoy into Berlin when the blockade started last June?"

"We would have gotten our asses shot off," Howley responded with his usual candor.

"Then what would happen if we brought one in this month or at some future date?"

"We'd have a better chance," Howley assured the Army secretary, adding that the Soviet decision would be based solely on their estimation of their ability to win. "Our chances will increase as the willingness of the American people to fight increases, and as our rearmament progresses," he concluded.[9] Royall listened intently to Howley's presentation, deeply impressed by the reserve colonel's forthright and honest appraisal.

Mrs. Howley wasn't in Berlin to enjoy the Christmas show with her husband and their three children. She had flown back to Philadelphia to visit for the first time since she and the family had joined the commandant in June 1948. While at home, she spoke of the privations of the German people in the city. "The German people haven't been warm since the war," she said. "They usually have one room they can heat." She shied away from political questions, which she said she always left to her husband, and focused on her primary purpose, buying winter clothes for the children. "I'm doing the Christmas shopping, too," she said, "because there isn't anything to get them in Berlin." Among her planned purchases were Boy Scout uniforms for every member of her eldest son's troop.[10]

☆ ☆ ☆

The troupe that Bob Hope had brought with him to Germany was tired by the time they did their second show of Christmas Day in Berlin. The tour had begun on December 22, and they had made six appearances at Wiesbaden that very first day. The day after that, they did three shows at the Frankfurt Military Post and were back in Wiesbaden again on Christmas Eve. Then they flew into Berlin.

Captain Antonio T. Criscuolo, a former C-47 navigator now assigned as a special service officer for Tempelhof Air Field, stood in the wings near Bob Hope and Jinx Falkenberg, watching as Vice President Alben Barkley told the audience of the great appreciation the country had for their day-and-night efforts. Criscuolo had been with the troupe since they arrived, and he marveled at the amount of work they put into each performance. The entertainers started each day with a morning rehearsal, then did their shows. Each show was scheduled to be two hours in length, but every one stretched out by encore after encore. Criscuolo likened the drain that such a regimen puts on the performers to that of Air Force crew members flying long, complex missions. His knowledge of how the performers must be feeling at this point in the tour made his task much more difficult.

At Tempelhof, many of the airlift personnel had been on duty during the entire day and had missed the show that had been done there. The Air Force men had been busy keeping their own "big show" going, maintaining the pace of the airlift. Criscuolo had promised these men that he would attempt to bring some of the Hope troupe back to the airfield after the final scheduled show of the evening. Near midnight, riding to Harnack House where the troupe was billeted, Criscuolo knew just how much he would be asking of the weary performers.

In the hotel's lounge, he approached Bob Hope and told him of the problem. Hope looked to him, at that moment, "like a doctor just come home on a winter night from a difficult call being told that another emergency is waiting for him on the far side of town."

Just as Criscuolo finished his pitch, a younger member of the troupe who was sitting where he had heard every word, blurted, "He wants us to go out to the airport and do it all over? What do those people mean to us?"

Hope glared at the younger man but said nothing. His mind was made up.

Ten minutes later, Criscuolo was in the back seat of the first of three cars that were carrying the troupe back to the airfield. Irving Berlin was on one side of him. Bob Hope was on the other.[11]

When the Hope troupe reached Fassberg on December 26, Bob Hope wanted to introduce a new skit as an opener. He asked Bruce Kates, the public affairs officer of the 313th Wing, to supply several cartons of cigarettes to be used in the sketch. With cigarettes a major form of currency in Germany and closely rationed, Kates had to pledge everything but his car to the PX officer in order to get the cartons that Hope needed.

Sitting near the front of the base theater, waiting for the curtain to rise and the show to begin on the stage, Kates was surprised when the back door burst open and Bob Hope raced in, dragging an open parachute and being chased by two MPs in full gear. He was yelling that he had just bailed out over Berlin and had to get rid of the evidence before he was arrested for dealing in the black market. Kates's heart sank as Hope began to throw the cartons of cigarettes into the audience as he sped down the aisle toward the stage. Every carton disappeared into eager hands.[12]

Then he opened with a joke he had used in every show thus far. It related to the fog that still blanketed Europe. "Soup I can take—but this stuff has noodles in it." The air crews in the audience roared with laughter.

There was little laughter in the city as the Western commandants studied their stocks of food and coal. The RAF began a regular series of flights carrying passengers out of the city. Each Dakota that left removed twenty hungry mouths; over 50,000 adults and 17,000 children quit Berlin that way. At the insistence of the British commandant, those who were despondent about the city's survival got the highest priority in leaving. He reasoned that one nervous individual could affect a hundred others with his or her pessimism.

So, as the Bob Hope troupe was leaving Berlin, Ruth Andreas-Friedrich was, as well. She carried the allotted twenty kilograms of luggage as she boarded the flight for Frankfurt. As she sat and fastened her seatbelt, the passenger next to her said, "Toward freedom." When Andreas-Friedrich tried to answer, the words stuck in her throat.

As the plane left the runway, the Berlin she had known as a battleground for so long disappeared in the fog below her.[13]

☆   ☆   ☆

The American commandant in Berlin often let his temper show, but many of his barbed jibes at the Soviets were kept out of print by American correspondents, with whom he was very popular. Just after Christmas, however, Howley let loose a blast that was not suppressed. Learning that one of the American officials of OMGUS had invited a Soviet to his quarters for New Year's dinner, the commandant exploded, "None of my men are going to play footsie-wootsie with the Russians. While American and British fliers are dying I do not want my men to be mixing socially with them. They can damn well eat their own shank bones of German cattle." The colonel's anger was characteristic, and understandable to many in the beleaguered city. When he heard about his subordinate's indiscretion Howley had just finished reading a letter he had received from the pregnant widow of one of the airman recently killed on the airlift.[14] By the time the new year began, seventeen Americans had died in the airlift effort. Seventeen Britons were dead as well, eight of them civilians.

Howley's temper wasn't improved by the fact that the weather was still bad for flying. It looked as though the airlift might fail after all. In an effort to save coal, the Allied commandants put the most stringent energy cuts so far into effect. They cut the hours that electricity was available to a new low. The people at OMGUS all prayed for a break in the weather.

At the headquarters of CALTF, staff members prayed for the same thing and made arrangements for what they would do when it came. It was decided there, and by the British government, that Operation Plain Fare had to be regarded as a long-term commitment that would last a minimum of two more years. New, more efficient flight plans and schedules were drawn up and circulated to the RAF commanders and the civilian operators. The Air Ministry in London began making plans to support the long-term effort with continuing supplies of men and material.

The Americans continued to improve their efforts as well. It was recognized that landings could be made easier and safer if high-intensity approach lights were installed to guide the pilots down the glide path to the runway at all of the airlift fields. At Tempelhof, however, the final approach was over the Neukölln Thomas Cemetery, which gave many of the landing fliers feelings of foreboding. Permission had to be obtained from the city assembly to move several graves, and it not only gladly gave it, but urged that the work begin immediately. As a ring of five- and six-story apartment buildings lay just beyond the cemetery, the height of the approach lights had to be graduated. The one nearest the runway was planned to be at ground level; the one closest to the apartments was intended to be mounted seventy-five feet high on a tower.

As building materials in the city were scarce, the engineers fabricated the towers for the lights out of an expedient material—pieces of pierced-steel runway mats welded together into the tall masts. While they were being fabricated in one of the massive hangars on the field, gangs of German workers began digging the cable trenches and excavating for the tower foundations. The Soviets seized on this as a propaganda tool.

Headlines in Soviet-sponsored newspapers and magazines screamed, "Cold war does not leave the dead alone." The stories went on to say that heavy damage had already been done to the cemetery by "hundreds of children chasing after candies dropped by American pilots," and the erection of the lights was a further desecration. "Americans behave in Berlin like troops engaged in a war in an enemy country," they concluded.[15]

Improvements like the new approach lights helped, but Tunner and his staff knew that better flying weather, as well as the improvements they had recommended to the secretary of the Air Force, were what would make the airlift a success.

# THIRTY-ONE

# A CHRISTMAS BONUS

General Tunner was amazed at the response that his memorandum to the secretary of the Air Force generated. He concluded that Stuart Symington must have gone directly from the airport to his office when he returned to Washington and there had begun to push bureaucratic buttons to make things happen.[1]

Orders came through immediately for USAFE to requisition better housing and to begin the construction of emergency barracks for airlift personnel. The maintenance depot at Burtonwood received a complete shake-up, along the lines that Tunner and his staff had been suggesting. It increased the number of inspections it was performing almost at once, although the Navy continued to send each plane's commander to the depot to ensure that the inspections and repairs were performed correctly.

A system of personnel rotation was established to relieve the TDY situation. Conditions for the fliers on the airlift began to improve almost overnight.[2] One of the earliest fliers to leave Germany under the new rotation policy was Lieutenant Gail Halvorsen. In January 1949, he went back to his old squadron in the United States. Operation Little Vittles carried on even after Halvorsen left. It was taken over by Captain Larry Caskey and, when Caskey also rotated home, by Captain Eugene Williams.

Several months before Halvorsen left, he had been approached at Tempelhof by a little girl clutching a tattered brown teddy bear. The fuzz was completely worn off the bear's elbows. The girl did not know that she was talking to Uncle Wiggly Wings, the Chocolate Flyer. She had come to the airport, like so many other Berliners, to give a gift to any one of the fliers who were sustaining them. To her, Gail Halvorsen just happened to be one of those fliers, standing by his airplane.

The bear, the little girl explained, had been her constant companion in her cellar during the bombing raids and during the Soviet assault on the city.

"Please take my teddy bear," she stammered, eyes filling with tears. "Good luck he will bring you and your friends on your flights to Berlin."[3] The worn, fuzzy Berlin bear was in Halvorsen's B-4 bag as he boarded the airplane to go home.

Not all of the problems evaporated, however. Some mundane things essential to the operation of the American airplanes remained in short supply. One of those was a simple item—one-inch cotter pins. They were used extensively on the C-54s and R-5Ds, and neither the supply officers at Rhein-Main nor the depot at Erding could seem to find enough.

When the two Navy squadrons had arrived, they had brought with them a stock of spare parts, but their supply officer, Lieutenant Courtney Smith, had been forced to relinquish them to the Air Force central supply, very much against his will. It had taken a direct order from the secretary of the Navy to get him to part with the precious material.

He had retained, however, a three-month supply of the vital cotter pins and had been doling them out one at a time to the entire contingent at Rhein-Main. When the supply was finally exhausted, he contacted the supply base at Erding once again, only to be told that there were no one-inch pins in stock.

Desperate, as cotter pins are essential to hold connections together in heavily vibrating airplanes in flight, Smith inquired whether the supply depot had any one and one-quarter inch pins. He was assured by the clerk that there were plenty in stock. It had occurred to no one that the shortage could have been quickly corrected by shipping longer pins and instructions to nip them off with diagonal cutters.[4]

Some of the physical improvements fell short of perfection, as well. At the base at Rhein-Main, construction of a new loading bay got under way. Since the airlift started, the trucks of freight had been coming down to the hardstands so that planes could be loaded while they were refueling, and the complicated traffic pattern was considered to be a danger. A rail spur was installed, as were an approach-way and taxiway to the new loading bay, to relieve the congestion. It was only when the bay was completed that it was discovered that, while it was fine for the trucks, the entrance and exit doors were too small for the wings of a C-54 to clear, and it had to be rebuilt. The laughs that the pilots got at the expense of the base engineers did, however, improve the fliers' morale a bit.

The flying remained a dangerous business. The United States Navy suffered its only fatality of the airlift in a crash in the Taunus Mountains, north and east of Rhein-Main. Machinist's Mate Harry Crites, Jr., the crew chief, was killed. The Navy had close calls on other flights. One R-5D, loaded with sugar, burst a tire on takeoff from Rhein-Main and, although the pilot was able to raise the landing gear and fly to

Berlin, the gear would not come down when he got there. Ordered to divert to Erding, the airplane rained ten tons of sugar across the Soviet zone as the crew tried to lighten the plane for an emergency landing. It was a success, with no injuries to the crew, although all of the propellers on the plane were bent and the flaps were worn completely off.[5]

Air Force Captain Franklin Crawford saved the life of his copilot after their C-54 crashed and burst into flames just east of Celle after losing three of its four engines just after takeoff. The copilot, Charles Weaver, was unconscious and hopelessly entangled in his seat harness. Crawford somehow managed to wrench the seat itself free and drag both it and the flier still strapped to it through the window of the cockpit.[6]

Others were not so lucky. The airlift claimed ten American servicemen during the month of January—six died in one crash as the plane they were in was landing in England for maintenance. Three ground engineers of the British civilian lift also died that month.

The month of January 1949 brought good news for Frank Howley, and it was totally unexpected. In spite of the dire predictions he had heard about his prospects, he was named a brigadier general. Army Secretary Royall, deeply impressed by Howley's straight-from-the-shoulder answers to his questions during the Christmas visit, had been instrumental in the promotion.[7]

Howley made it a point, particularly in light of his order banning fraternization, of having only official contacts with the Soviets during the blockade. On only one occasion was he compelled to eat with General Kotikov, and that was during a working luncheon. The Soviet general made the mistake of complaining that the chicken that Howley's staff had served was tough, and the American commandant snapped back, "It ought to be. It had to fly all the way from Frankfurt."[8] Therefore, he was surprised and suspicious when, shortly after his promotion was announced, he received a visit from Kotikov's chief of staff, Colonel Kalinin. The Soviet commandant was indisposed with an attack of ulcers, Kalinin explained, but wanted to extend his congratulations to Howley.

Knowing that things were rarely what they seemed in dealing with the Soviets, Howley said, "Thank you. But what do you really want?"

"Well," answered Kalinin after a brief hesitation, "we are building a large war memorial in Pankow and much of the material for it is tied up in the American sector. You have 110 tons of bronze wreaths and statues and things we need and we wondered if you would permit the factory to deliver them to us."[9]

Howley picked up his telephone and called the OMGUS economics department. While the personnel there confirmed Kalinin's story, they added a fact that he had failed to mention—the Soviets had not paid for the bronze castings. Since the work had been performed in the American sector, the foundry demanded payment of its 186,000 mark fee in Western currency.

Howley ordered release of the statuary but told his Soviet visitor to inform his commanding officer that he was doing so "simply out of respect for the Russian soldiers who fought as our allies during the war. As for the rest of you," Howley added, "it is my personal guess that unless you put a stop to your current policies you are going to need a lot more war memorials."

The Soviet chief of staff winced, saluted, and departed, saying, "I will report to General Kotikov." [10]

☆  ☆  ☆

The RAF Dakota KP491, with Pilot Officer E. J. Eddy at the controls, landed at Gatow at 4:30 on the afternoon of January 24 and the women cleaners swept the plane as clean as they could get it after the sacks of coal were unloaded. Not only was the coal dust valuable, but KP491 was to carry a load of twenty-two passengers out of the city that afternoon.

Eddy's plane spent only half an hour on the ground; at 5:00 p.m., in the gathering darkness, it took off again for Lübeck, into a looming cloudbank. The air was turbulent, and several of the passengers became airsick. Most of the children on board were crying.

At 6:20 p.m. Pilot Officer Eddy began a gradual descent through the turbulence, following the instructions from the air traffic controller at Lübeck. A moment later there was a jolt and a series of loud noises from the fuselage, and the plane crashed into a forest and burst into flames. The plane's radioman and seven of the passengers died in the worst crash of the month. The Soviets and East Germans made a propaganda bonanza of the disaster, spreading photographs of the wreck across the front pages of the East zone newspapers under headlines reading "Airbridge—Deathbridge" and "One Dakota Less—One Lesson More." [11]

Berliners had begun referring to the airlift as *die Luftbrücke*—the air bridge—and it dominated their lives.

Juergen Werner was three years old. He spent his days staring out the window of the single room that he and his family shared at 32 Fraenkelufer in Kreuzberg, on the bank of the Landwehr Kanal. Juergen amused himself by watching the American planes swooping down to land at Tempelhof and dreaming of becoming a pilot and flying away to America.

"At first the noise of the planes kept us awake at night," his mother, Charlotte, told a reporter. "But now we sleep through it all. It's only when it's quiet that we wake up—afraid the *Luftbrücke* has stopped.

Every bite of food we get is flown in by those planes, and now even Kurt's job is part of the airlift."

Juergen's father, Kurt, worked at Tempelhof, on the gangs unloading cargo from the planes. A Wehrmacht veteran who had been wounded only a day before the war ended, Werner returned to his wife in Berlin to find her living in a room that had been shattered by a shell that had fallen in the courtyard outside. The woman living in the next apartment had been killed, but Charlotte Werner, who was pregnant with Juergen at the time, had been in a shelter with Wolfgang and Ines, the Werners' older children. They fixed the apartment as best they could and Kurt Werner had found work as a presser in one of Berlin's largest clothing factories. That job, like 90,000 others, had ended when the blockade began, and Werner and his family lived on 28 marks a week from the city. In November, he found work at Tempelhof.

"It's a good job," Charlotte Werner said, "even if Kurt's suit is ruined." The single set of clothing Werner had to wear was a blue pinstriped suit that had the appearance of having been dipped in cement.

"When it rains, dust from the coal and flour sacks makes a thick paste over it. I've tried to get it out, but it's in there forever now."

With the job at Tempelhof, Werner earned fifty-five marks a week, one third of which was paid in West marks. Those the Werners hoarded for "luxury items," such as a few articles of used clothes. The less valuable East marks were used to pay the rent and to buy rationed food in the besieged city. Breakfast for the Westerners was bread smeared with part of their fat ration. Lunch for Charlotte Werner and the children was a stew of potatoes, noodles, or beans and whatever meat they had. Kurt Werner got a hot meal at noon at work at the airport. Dinner was bread again, and coffee. Power in the apartment was on for only four hours each day, two hours at a time, and chores had to be arranged around those periods.

In spite of the hardships of the blockade, the Werners remained hopeful and defiant. "The Western Allies must not leave," Frau Werner told the reporter. "I will not give up my hope that everything will work out. After all, that is all I have."[12]

There was reason for that hope at the end of January 1949. The weather had cleared, and the pace of the airlift had quickened. It was obvious to the West, and was becoming obvious to the Soviet Union as well, that the Soviet blockade of Berlin was a failure. The airlift was successfully supplying the city of Berlin with the necessities of life, and nothing short of armed force, in the form of attacks on the transport planes, could stop it. That, the Soviets now knew, would mean full-scale war.

At the beginning of 1949, talks among the major Western powers aimed at the establishment of a comprehensive defensive military alliance had progressed to the point that a treaty was being drawn up. Condemnation of the concept by the Soviet press and government had been harsh, and as Norwegian foreign minister Halvard Lange arrived in Washington for the treaty talks, the Soviet government was delivering an official note to Oslo, calling for a Norwegian-Soviet nonaggression pact and pointing out that Norway's participation in NATO could involve it "in a policy of far-reaching aggressive aims."[13]

In spite of Soviet pressure, NATO was becoming a reality, and any attack on the aircraft supplying Berlin would invite war with a united Europe. The options available to the Soviet Union were dwindling, and the Western allies were tightening the counterblockade that had been imposed shortly after the Soviets began their transport restrictions. General Clay had noted as early as November 23 that the effects of their blockade were costing them money. More than twelve million marks worth of material that the Soviets were due from the Western zones under long-standing trade agreements had been withheld from them.[14] Now the counter-restrictions against the Soviets, which had been partial and sporadically enforced, were made more stringent. Until now, anyone could enter the Western sectors, buy goods, and transport them back to the East. For the first time, vehicles bound to or from the East were forbidden to cross the American or British zones of Germany, and shipments of goods to the Soviet zone were halted entirely. Before long, factories in the East were laying off workers and cutting back on hours.

The next time the Soviet deputy commandant called on Colonel Howley, it was to arrange the release of a large bronze head of Lenin that had been cast in a West Berlin foundry. That, too, was destined for the planned memorial, and the foundry was holding the casting while it waited for payment. This time, Howley refused to help. The Soviets were required to pay, in West marks, before he ordered the likeness of the Communist hero released.[15]

In Washington, diplomats at the State Department wondered whether the failure of the Soviet effort would lead to new initiatives for a settlement. George Kennan, who had been so instrumental in developing the policy of containment of Soviet expansion, was beginning to have serious second thoughts about what had come about. Speaking to a private meeting of the Council on Foreign Relations, he said, "We must refrain as much as possible from making the present East-West line a hard and fast one, and should continually engage in negotiations with the Russians."[16] Further, Kennan began to press Secretary of State Acheson to consider an idea he had taken to calling "Plan A." Coming from the man who had first said that a divided Germany was inevitable and that the Western portion should be strengthened as a bulwark against Soviet expansion, the plan was stunning. Kennan called for negotiations aimed at the mutual withdrawal of all troops from Germany and its conversion into a reunified, demilitarized state. General Clay dismissed the plan as "suicidal to our objectives" and accused Kennan of trying to lose the war that the United States was beginning to win in Berlin. Chip Bohlen took a more practical view than Kennan, believing that the Soviets would soon send a signal that they were ready to talk about Berlin again.[17]

Reporters from the West were constantly sounding the Soviets out about their position on world peace. Joseph Stalin gave information to the free-world press only when he thought it would be to his advantage, and he rarely granted interviews. The usual practice of reporters seeking information was to submit a list of questions for the generalissimo to the Soviet Foreign Office. Occasionally, the questions would generate a response; most often they did not.

Kingsbury Smith, the European general manager of Hearst's International News Service, followed the usual practice in January 1949. He submitted a list of four questions relating to world affairs in general and Germany in particular and was surprised when the answers came on January 31, only four days later. The answers caused a sensation in the Western press, where they were regarded as the beginning of a Soviet "peace offensive," directed at heading off the formation of NATO. One of the questions had dealt with Berlin, the focal point of so much East-West tension. Asked about the conditions under which the Soviet Union would end the blockade, Stalin had made no mention of the issue of Germany currency—the officially stated Soviet reason for it. Bohlen was convinced that this was the subtle signal he was hoping for—Stalin wanted to negotiate again. He went to Acheson and convinced his superior that something was happening inside the Kremlin that was worth exploring. Acheson consulted with President Truman about a suitable response to the reported peace offensive and to the particular question about Berlin.

Truman had developed a great respect for Dean Acheson's ability since the elegant, urbane graduate of Groton and Yale had first briefed him on the State Department's view of the world shortly after Roosevelt died. The president's respect had grown since Acheson had taken over the State Department from General Marshall just ten days earlier. He listened to Acheson's presentation, and they jointly developed a response.

It was decided that Acheson would hold a low-key press conference in the middle of the week, so that it would appear to have little significance. As planned, the secretary's remarks appeared extemporaneous but were in fact well thought out. He confessed puzzlement, both at Smith's first question and at Stalin's response. Smith had asked whether the Soviet Union would join the United States in declaring that the two nations did not intend to go to war with each other, and Stalin had replied that he would consider issuing such a joint declaration. Stalin's willingness to repeat what was already stated in the charter of the United Nations that bound both countries was certainly not news, Acheson pointed out.

The Soviet dictator had said that he would "naturally" consider disarmament talks with the United States. Acheson reviewed the long history of Soviet obstructionism in Europe as an indication of what the Soviet Union apparently felt was "natural."

Asked if he would be willing to confer with President Truman personally, Stalin had replied affirmatively. Acheson noted that Truman had invited the generalissimo to the United States on many occasions but had been refused, and that American presidents had journeyed halfway around the world to meet with Stalin three times.

In Stalin's response about Berlin, he had omitted the currency question and stated that the blockade could be ended if the plans for a West German government were dropped and the West lifted the counterblockade. Acheson made short work of the second point. It was a given that countermeasures would end as soon as the blockade did. Then Acheson delivered the subtle diplomatic message that he wanted to convey to the Soviets.

"There are many ways in which a serious proposal by the Soviet Government could be made," he said. "I hope you [the press] will not take it amiss if I point out that . . . I would chose some other channel than the channel of a press interview."[18]

Artfully avoiding expansion of the answer during the question-and-answer session that followed, Acheson gave the public impression that the thought of new negotiations on Berlin, under the terms that the Soviets had previously insisted on, was a dead issue. In actuality, Acheson's remarks opened the door just a crack for the Soviets.

Phillip Jessip, the United States ambassador to the United Nations, was called to Washington to meet with Acheson and Chip Bohlen. During the meeting, he was instructed to casually approach the Soviet U.N. ambassador, Yakov Malik. Jessip was to ask, as a matter of personal curiosity, whether there was any significance to Stalin's omission of the currency issue in his responses to Kingsbury Smith's questions. A few days later, in the delegates lounge at the United Nations, Jessip met with Malik, and they chatted for a moment about the weather. Then Jessip asked his casual question. The Soviet ambassador was noncommittal but said that he would inquire of his government and get back to him.

# THIRTY-TWO

## EASTER
## PARADE

Yakov Malik's telephone call of March 14, 1949, came as a surprise to Ambassador Phillip Jessip. Even the most optimistic of the diplomats at the State Department were beginning to doubt that there had been any hidden meaning in Stalin's failure to mention the currency question in his January response to Kingsbury Smith. It had been over a month since Jessip had mentioned it to Malik, and he had heard nothing from the Soviet envoy. Now, the Soviet ambassador invited Jessip to meet with him at his office on Park Avenue.

Stalin had, indeed, been sending a signal in January. The currency question was important, Malik related, but it could be discussed at a meeting of the Council of Foreign Ministers.

Jessip asked whether that meant that the blockade could be lifted if such a meeting were scheduled. Malik replied that he had not asked that question of the Kremlin but would do so at once. While the United States waited for a reply, the three Western allies took a bold step in Berlin itself. They outlawed the East mark in the Western sectors of the city. While not making possession of the East marks illegal, as the Soviets had done with West marks in their sector, the Western allies proclaimed that no one in the West was required to accept them in payment for any goods or services. The Western allies said that they took the action "only after every possibility of agreeing on a Four-power controlled currency had been exhausted."[1] At the same time that the announcement of the new currency regulations were made, General Howley was telling a news conference, "It must be obvious to even the most dense Communist that their tactics have failed. Neither the blockade at the Elbe nor the ice of winter stopped the airlift."[2]

The reply from Moscow to the question Jessip had put to Malik came on March 21. It was short and simple: if a date could be set for the foreign ministers to meet, the blockade would be lifted before the meeting took place.

Now it was Malik's turn to pose a question: Would the West defer preparations for a West German government until the council met? The response was an unequivocal "No."[3]

British foreign minister Ernest Bevin and Robert Schuman, the foreign minister of France, were due in Washington in two weeks for the signing of the NATO treaty and for talks about Germany. President Truman, who had followed the developments closely and had been delighted at this demonstration of the United States' resolve, directed that Jessip inform his British and French counterparts at the United Nations of the developments. While leaks to the Soviets from the French foreign service were frequent and well known, in this case it was felt that these could only give the Soviets more assurance of Western sincerity. Aside from this presumed leak, the American feeler to the Kremlin was kept a close secret.[4]

Bevin, Schuman, and Acheson agreed that the Malik-Jessip talks were the best possible channel through which to seek a solution to the problem of Berlin. Jessip transmitted a message to Malik on April 5 that the three foreign ministers understood that there were only two points under discussion—lifting the blockade and setting a date for the meeting of the Council of Foreign Ministers. Malik referred the question to Moscow, which responded on April 10 that it understood that no West German government would be set up until after the council meeting. Jessip again emphatically responded that nothing of the sort was intended, and the three Western foreign ministers backed him in a strong message. Then they settled back to await the Soviet response.

While the diplomats waited, spring finally came to Germany. The airlift was back in full swing and operating well. Over 150 British planes of assorted types were assigned to the effort. The Americans were operating 225 C-54s, with an additional 75 either undergoing maintenance or in use at the training school at Great Falls. The problems at Burtonwood had been solved, and the maintenance base was now meeting its quotas for two-hundred-hour checks. Morale was high, both because of the pride the men had in the job they were doing and because the problems of food, living accommodations, and being on TDY had been addressed. Everything was going so well that General Tunner felt uneasy, fearing that complacency might set in. Remembering the record tonnage of Air Force Day, Tunner looked at the calendar and noted that Easter was only a few days away. He began to form a plan.

He sounded out Red Forman, who was now the base commander at Wiesbaden. When Forman indicated that he liked Tunner's idea, they reviewed it with the rest of the staff, which was equally enthusiastic. The Combined Air Lift Task Force was going to give the people of Berlin an Easter parade such as they had never witnessed before. They set a goal of carrying ten thousand tons—50 percent more than their previous record daily total—into the city during the twenty-four-hour period beginning at noon on Holy Saturday. Because it is more efficient to load planes with a single type of cargo, the staff decided to focus on carrying coal. There was a stockpile of much more than ten thousand tons available in Transportation Corps storage areas. Because they knew if they announced a high goal and did not attain it the Soviets would score a propaganda victory, CALTF tried to keep the plan a secret. The organization of such an effort is hard to hide, however, and word filtered out that something big was coming up. Rumors abounded.

General Cannon was in the United States, but Tunner received an urgent call from Major General Robert Douglas, Cannon's chief of staff.

"I don't want to discourage you," Douglas said, "But even if you have a lot of tonnage and then drop way off the next day, Joe's going to raise hell."

"We're not going to drop off the next day,"[5] Tunner responded. He knew that while the figures would fall somewhat after the big push, the level they fell to would be higher than the levels the airlift had previously been obtaining. It had worked that way on the Hump, and it had happened after the Air Force Day effort in September. Tunner was certain it would work that way again. The momentum of the big push would carry over.

Squadron operations officers were alerted to ensure that the maximum number of planes were available and on the line for Easter. They were not told why, but they could tell that something big was in the air. Exactly what the secret was became evident to the airlift crews the moment the operations sergeants posted the daily quotas on the "howgozit" boards just before noon on Saturday. The men crowded around, looked at the figures, and whistled in amazement. Because there were so many bases involved in the overall effort, no one except the members of Tunner's staff could yet figure out how high the goal for the day was, but they all knew that this Easter was scheduled to be the biggest day ever on the airlift.

Soon after the "Easter Parade" began, General Tunner flew into Berlin himself to watch the planes as they landed. Listening as the pilots called in to the tower, he could catch the enthusiasm in their voices. The pilot of Skymaster 77, who often identified himself on approach by calling "Here comes 77, the bundle from heaven," added to his doggerel on Easter, "with a load of coal, for the daily goal."[6]

Leaving Berlin, the airlift commander went to Celle and found that the base was running 12 percent ahead of its quota. Long past midnight, Tunner arrived at Fassberg, where Colonel Jack Coulter told him proudly that his men were exceeding their goal by 10 percent.

"That's fine," Tunner said, "but of course it's not up to what they're doing at Celle. They're really on the ball over there."[7]

Coulter's grin vanished. He hurried off to the flight line to speed up operations while Tunner, grinning himself, flew back to his headquarters in Wiesbaden. Unable to sleep, he went to the mess hall for breakfast as dawn was breaking. It was there that he learned that they had already passed the ten-thousand-ton mark. By midmorning, the word on what was going on was out. No one could hide the fact that planes were landing in Berlin at a rate nearly three times the usual. CALTF had no desire to keep the secret anymore.

General Clay called Tunner with congratulations on what he was doing. Then he asked exactly what it was that he was doing. When he was told, he notified the press corps, and they descended on Tunner's headquarters in droves. In the city, everyone was aware that a record was being set. A reception party was quickly put together and was waiting at Tempelhof well before noon.

☆ ☆ ☆

First Lieutenant Brian Herrin pulled back on the yoke to lift Skymaster 108 from the runway at Rhein-Main a few minutes before noon on Easter Sunday. While in flight to Berlin, Herrin's radio crackled with the news that his was the 1,383 trip since noon of the preceding day and that his cargo of coal would bring that day's total of supplies airlifted into the city up to 12,849 tons in the past twenty-four hours. His was not the final flight of the Easter Parade. That one was behind him, with the legend "TONS: 12,941, FLIGHTS: 1,398," slathered on the side in red paint. But there was a reception committee waiting in the city, and Herrin had been picked to meet it. Landing at Tempelhof, Herrin and his crew were greeted by a crowd of photographers, reporters, and officers, including Generals Frank Howley and Courtney Hodges, who was there from Washington on an inspection tour. While the dignitaries and reporters gathered at the aircraft, the teams of German workers hurried about their task of unloading, even though they were tired after their exceptional exertions of this special day.

In remarks that were nearly drowned out by the roaring engines, Howley spoke of the gratefulness of the free world for the efforts of the airlift, what the supplies that were being brought in meant to the city, and how continuing the airlift would help to prevent a war.

"Thanks, General," Herrin replied. "I believe we are all very glad to be able to help."

Later, after the press and the brass had departed, so did Skymaster 108. Herrin boosted power on the engines, released the brakes, and howled down the runway, lifting off from Berlin after a run of 200 meters. As his plane rose, Herrin swung it to the right, on course for the central air corridor, to pick up another load for the return trip to Berlin. The record day was over. There are 1,440 minutes in each day. On Easter 1949, CALTF fell only two sorties short of landing a plane a minute in the city.

At the base at Wiesbaden, Army Transportation Corps Colonel William Bunker thought of the effort with a mind-set more attuned to traditional methods of delivering coal. "Have you ever seen a fifty-car coal train?" he asked Tunner's assembled staff. "Well, you've just equaled twelve of them."[8]

☆    ☆    ☆

A few more weeks of Soviet maneuver took place after the firm Western response to Vishinsky's attempt to tie once again lifting the blockade to the issue of a West German government, but Acheson and his colleagues held fast. On May 4, 1949, a four-power communiqué was issued. It announced that all restrictions imposed on the city since March 1, 1948, would be lifted on May 12. On May 23, the Council of Foreign Ministers would meet in Paris to consider questions relating to Germany and problems arising out of the situation in Berlin.

The people of the city had doubts that their ordeal was about to end. "I won't believe it until I see it," a bricklayer told one of his companions.

"If the blockade is lifted, then something worse will happen," said one woman. "This is just another Russian maneuver and nobody knows what's behind it."

In the Soviet sector, an old woman in a food line complained bitterly, "If only we could be liberated from this Russian plague. Unfortunately, where vermin have once firmly settled, they don't move so fast again."[9]

☆    ☆    ☆

First Lieutenant William R. Frost, 3d Battalion, 16th Infantry, sat in a jeep that had wide white sign reading "Autobahn Courtesy Patrol" under the windshield. It had not been used for that purpose for nearly a year. Frost was clutching a bouquet of lilacs that Johanna Kraapz had handed him as he and his driver, Private Horace Scites, waited for the white-and-black-striped barrier in front of their vehicle to be lifted. At exactly one minute past midnight Corporal Victor Cluff, Jr., and Private John Bean, both clad in the sharp-pressed khaki uniforms of the Berlin Constabulary, leaned on the counterweight of the barrier, and it swung upward. The road from Berlin to the West was open for the first time in 328 days.

Private Scites gunned the jeep forward toward the Soviet checkpoint at Nowawas. Several hundred spectators by the American barricade, many dressed in tattered evening clothes, cheered. At the Soviet post, a battered white shack, there were about twenty soldiers waiting, including a full colonel. As the jeeps pulled up, they were waved through. The caravan of cars that followed were treated in the same fashion. The Soviets did not even bother to check the papers of the occupants.[10]

Two minutes after the convoy of jeeps, trucks, buses, and passenger cars left the city, Captain Allen Hutchinson of the Royal Horse Guards presented his papers to a smiling Soviet captain at the Soviet barrier at the boundary of the British and Soviet zones, 105 miles west of Berlin. The Soviet glanced at the papers and handed them back, waving the jeep through. The next vehicle in the convoy, a heavy Royal Army signal truck, pulled up.

"How many persons," the Soviet guard asked.

The driver held up four fingers and was waved on.[11]

The autobahn route to Berlin was open again.

At 1:23 that morning a British military train with two cars of singing Tommies left the station in the British zone, heading east to Berlin. The rail lines to the city were open as well.

In Berlin the street lights were on again, and so were the lights in the shops and homes; the Soviets were supplying electricity again. In the U.S. sector the streets were quiet. Late shift workers hurrying home noticed that the lights were on but hurried on anyway, out of force of habit. Above the quiet streets was the constant drone of aircraft engines. The airlift carried on.

☆   ☆   ☆

The party should have been a festive one; it was the general's fifty-second birthday. Instead, it was a bitter-sweet occasion for Margaret Allen, Edna Shelley, and the rest of the members of General Clay's small staff, because it was the beginning of the general's leave-taking. They knew that Clay had submitted his resignation; his service in Germany would soon end. After he cut his birthday cake, Lucius Clay raised his glass in a toast to those who had gathered to celebrate with him. "To those who made me happiest," he said.[12]

Ten days later, after President Truman accepted his resignation, Clay reviewed 10,000 troops of the 1st Infantry Division and the Constabulary at Grafenwöhr. On the following Sunday, he attended his last retreat ceremony in front of the massive military government headquarters on Kronprinzen Allee in Berlin. Thousands of residents of the city appeared to cheer the man they regarded as their savior. Then the general and Mrs. Clay boarded a plane at Tempelhof. It was only when the plane landed at Newfoundland to refuel that Clay learned that he was scheduled to address a joint session of Congress the following day.

Clay made the brief address without notes. He said:

For two years, the United States had tried desperately to make four-power agreement work. We failed because one of the four powers had but two objectives in Germany: the one to exact the maximum in reparations and the other to establish the type and kind of government which could be controlled or at least exploited to the full by a police state.

I saw in Berlin the spirit and soul of a people reborn. Two and one half million Germans had a second opportunity to choose freedom. They had forgone their first opportunity, they did not forgo their second opportunity.[13]

The relentless drone of the airlift continued, even though the blockade had been lifted. By the time the Council of Foreign Ministers held a final meeting in Paris on May 23, 1949, to discuss the future of Germany, British and American planes were on their way to delivering a total of 250,818 tons of food, coal, and other material to the city for that month.

Dean Acheson, the secretary of state, represented the United States at the Paris meeting; Andrei Vishinsky was there for the Soviet Union. The site was the Palais Rose, once the residence of the American-born Duchesse de Talleyrand and the wartime headquarters of General Otto von Stuelpnagel, the Nazi commandant of Paris who had heroically disregarded Hitler's hysterical orders to burn the city during the last days of the occupation. The council meetings took place in the Grand Salon where, Acheson observed, "satyrs pursued nymphs through clouds without gaining on them even through the double translation of Vishinsky's longest speeches."[14]

Although the conference lasted a month, the Soviets accomplished nothing. At the second session, Vishinsky proposed that the four-power control council for Germany be reconstituted, that the Berlin Kommandatura and a *Magistrat* representing the entire city be reestablished, and that the Soviets be given a share in the administration of the Ruhr. Acheson's reply was succinct: the United States would not accept such regressive proposals. The Soviets and East Germans should instead adopt the progressive and democratic institutions of West Germany in their zone, Acheson suggested. Too much had changed for the clock to be turned back to the arrangements that had been made under the Potsdam declaration.

The Parliamentary Council of West Germany had adopted a constitution, and a West German government, overseen by Allied high commissioners rather than military governors, was being formed. General Clay, the last military governor, had already returned to private life. Even while the foreign ministers were meeting, the Foreign Relations Committee of the United States Senate unanimously recommended approval of the NATO pact. The battle lines of the Cold War had been drawn in Europe, and they split Germany. Berlin, the country's once-proud capital, still lay 120 miles behind the Iron Curtain that Winston Churchill had so prophetically seen descending.

By the end of July 1949, the Western powers felt that there was a large enough stockpile of food and coal in Berlin to resist any attempt by the Soviets to reinstitute the blockade. On July 30, it was announced that the Combined Air Lift Task Force would be disbanded at the end of October, and operations began to phase it out during August and September.

On August 16, a Halton of the Eagle Aviation Corporation landed at Gatow at 1:45 in the morning. It was carrying 14,400 pounds of flour and was the last of the British civil aircraft to sortie into the city. A total of twenty-three companies had participated in the civil airlift, using 103 different airplanes. In slightly over a year, they had flown 21,921 missions into Berlin, carrying a total of 146,980 tons, including most of the liquid fuel the city required. The total tonnage they had carried was almost double that of all freight and mail carried by all British civil airlines on scheduled services between 1924 and 1947.[15] Twenty-one civilian personnel had died in the effort.

The Navy squadrons, VR-6 and VR-8, departed, returning to their previous postings with MATS. Many of the C-54s were returned to the United States, and the bases at Wunstorf, Celle, and Fassberg were closed down. On September 1, the personnel from the British dominions—Australia, New Zealand, and South Africa—who had flown on the airlift were returned to the United Kingdom on their way home.

The final RAF flight from the base at Lübeck was the twin-engine Dakota KN652. It landed at Gatow at 7:22 p.m. on September 23. One of the ground crew at Lübeck had chalked on the nose, "Positively the last load from Lübeck, 73,705 tons—Psalm 21, Verse 11." To those who bothered to look it up, the biblical reference seemed appropriate. "For they intended great evil against us; they imagined a mischievous device, which they are not able to perform."[16]

An American C-54, with the legend "Last Vittles Flight—17,835,727 Tons Airlifted to Berlin" painted on the fuselage just behind the pilot's side window, landed at Tempelhof on September 30, 1949. The airlift phase of the battle for Berlin had ended, and the warriors who fought it were departing.

Brigadier General Frank A. Howley had been in Berlin quite long enough. His thick thatch of dark brown hair had gone completely gray since the day, more than four years before, when he had ridden into the city with the 37 officers, 50 vehicles, and 175 men that the Soviets had allowed. In September 1949, he applied for retirement, and his request was granted.

In one of his last official duties before leaving, Howley presided over a meeting of the Kommandatura and, as chairman in rotation, acted as host at the buffet that followed. The Soviet-controlled radio had been gleeful at the news of Howley's departure, inexplicably referring to the Philadelphian as "the roughrider from Texas" to the accompaniment of cowboy music. General Kotikov had used a major portion of the meeting complaining about a variety of things, including Howley's rudeness, but the Soviet warmed up at the buffet, offering to toast Howley on his departure. He announced, however, that he wanted a weak drink, as his ulcers were bothering him.

"Champagne?" someone suggested as a waiter stood by with a tray.

The Soviet puffed out his cheeks. "Makes me belch," he said.

"Have a Martini," Howley suggested.

"What is Martini?" Kotikov asked, and Howley handed him one from the tray.

"To a successful journey to the United States," Kotikov proclaimed and, as Howley sipped from his glass of champagne, the Soviet gulped down the entire martini, olive and all.

Seeing the look of pained astonishment on Kotikov's face, Howley seized the moment to press another martini into his hand and propose another toast. A third and a fourth followed in rapid succession.

Offering the suffering Soviet general yet another martini, Howley was met with a gasped "nyet," and had to steer the Soviet commandant of Berlin to a table.

Running his hand through the gray hair Kotikov had given him, he felt they were even.[17]

The departing commandant also found time for interviews with the press. Speaking to a reporter for a newspaper in his home town, Philadelphia, he said, "There is no simple solution for Berlin and all the difficulties that were created when we allowed ourselves to take our stand on an island in a sea of Soviet power." While admitting to the reporter that it remained to be seen how it could be brought about, Howley then looked forward to a day when there would again be a free and united Germany. "Berlin will, and must, some day be the capital of a united Germany," he concluded.[18]

Recognition for the participants in the airlift was somewhat grudging. In Great Britain an effort to award them a medal was scotched by an Air Ministry memo that pointed out that such an award would give the airlift a "military, and perhaps even an aggressive character."[19] The best that could be arranged was a ceremonial review by the King George VI of selected RAF participants in the forecourt of Buckingham Palace, followed by a march down the Mall and the Strand and a lunch at the Guildhall. General Tunner was individually honored by the British. Air Marshal Sir Arthur Tedder, acting on behalf of the king, invested Tunner as a companion of the Order of the Bath in recognition of his direction of the airlift.[20]

Goaded by a campaign by New York *Daily Mirror* gossip columnist Walter Winchell that the tiny silver C-54 on the ribbon of the Occupation Medal was insufficient recognition for participants in the airlift, Congress directed that the Department of Defense authorize the issuance of the Medal for Humane Action. It was intended for Americans who had served on the airlift for 120 days or more.[21] The medal bore a C-54 on the obverse, surrounded by a wreath of wheat, above the coat of arms of the city of Berlin, and was inscribed on the reverse, "For Humane Action to supply necessities of life to the people of Berlin." In a unique decision, the Defense Department authorized award of the medal to members of foreign forces and to civilians, and a number of these were issued on individual recommendations.[22]

General Tunner was also individually honored by his own country, and it was General Joseph Cannon who conducted the awards ceremony. Tunner received his third Distinguished Service Medal.[23] It was a well-deserved honor, for William Tunner had directed an effort that had delivered 2,325,509 tons of goods to a blockaded city by air. While the United States had carried 77 percent of that total and lost thirty-three men in the effort, the safety record was impressive. While it was in operation, flights on the Berlin airlift accounted for 5 percent of all Air Force operations in all theaters, and only 2 percent of the major accidents that occurred in that period.

The people of the city expressed their appreciation by the erection of a monument near Tempelhof airport, in the square where Lieutenants Stuber and King died when their C-47 crashed into an apartment building. The monument is in the shape of the base of an arch that terminates in three prongs that point skyward and to the west. At the base at Rhein-Main a duplicate monument was erected, with prongs facing east toward Berlin. The sky, and the memory of those brave airmen who rescued a city under siege, connects the two monuments.

# THIRTY-THREE
## "MISSION ACCOMPLISHED"

With the formation of the Federal Republic of Germany in the West on September 15, 1949, the Soviets and the German Communists in the East felt compelled to make a countermove. The German Democratic Republic was established in October, with its capital in the Soviet sector of Berlin, and that section was increasingly integrated into the new state, a clear violation of the Four-Power agreements. In West Berlin, the struggle to rebuild and recover began again after the ruinous blockade. Deprived of its status as capital, over 175,000 public service jobs no longer existed in the city, and institutions of finance, banking, and insurance, as well as the stock market and other enterprises normally associated with a capital, established themselves in Bonn, in the Federal Republic. Even with a reduced population, there were 300,000 unemployed in West Berlin as the decade of the 1950s began.[1]

As West German economic recovery, spurred by Marshall Plan aid, experienced what came to be known as the economic miracle in the early 1950s, West Berlin was declared an emergency zone, and the city enjoyed massive infusions of money for rebuilding its buildings and its economy. By 1952, the number of unemployed in the western sectors of the city had fallen to 25,000.[2]

The economy in the East faltered: workers saw their living conditions stagnate, their wages fall, and the demands on them for increased production rise. On June 16, 1953, faced with a mandated increase of 10 percent in their production quotas with no raise in pay, East German workers in Berlin dropped their tools. They marched on the House of Ministers to demand a reversal of the quota increase, free elections, the release of political prisoners, and a lower cost of living. By the following day, the strike had spread to 272 other cities and towns, and 50,000 workers rallied in Berlin. Some mounted the Brandenburg Gate, tore down the Red flag, and replaced it with the black-gold-red banner of the Federal Republic.

The Soviets, sensing that their East German allies were losing control of the situation, declared martial law and sent an entire armored division into their sector of the divided city. By nine o'clock that evening, the streets had been cleared. Western estimates were that over three hundred had been killed. Nineteen arrested "ring leaders" were swiftly tried and shot. The workers' revolt had been crushed within two days of its beginning.[3] The recently elected Eisenhower administration, still embroiled in a war in Korea, had no desire for a second military conflict. While deploring the events, the State Department and the president made it clear that the policy of the United States remained the containment of Communism, not its rollback. At a city assembly memorial service for the victims of the Soviet suppression, only the American liaison officer, Major Karl Maitre, was present. The West German president, Konrad Adenauer, appeared, but the Western commandants did not. Even the seats of the British and French liaison officers were vacant.[4] East Berlin would remain a gray and dreary "workers' paradise," while the western portion of the city blossomed in the wake of the economic miracle in the Federal Republic.

On November 27, 1958, having consolidated his hold on the reins of power in the Soviet Union after the death of Joseph Stalin and buoyed by the recent success of the Soviet satellite *Sputnik,* Nikita Khrushchev delivered an ultimatum to the West. Declaring the Four Power Agreement of 1944 null and void, he demanded that the Allies leave Berlin within six months. The level of harassment on the Western access routes to the city was increased. An American plane in one of the corridors was buzzed by a Soviet fighter, trucks passing down the Helmstadt autobahn were stopped for long periods of time, and barge traffic was delayed. In February 1961, the Soviets delivered an aide-mémoire to the Bonn government, stating that the need for a German treaty was critical and that the Western allies would have to leave Berlin. The newly elected U.S. president, John F. Kennedy, who had taken office the previous month, called for advice from an old hand in dealing with Berlin and with the Soviets. Dean Acheson was asked to form a special "Review Group" to study available options for the city. The Acheson recommendations were pugnacious, and as a British diplomatic delegation invited to hear them observed, skipped over most possible diplomatic and economic measures to focus on purely military ones, including sending a full armored division by autobahn to reinforce the city. The British were horrified by the prospect, and the new president's closest advisors were deeply divided, with a majority favoring a very soft line with the Soviets. A similar division was present at the Department of State. Secretary of State Dean Rusk was so noncommittal that no one could discern where he stood on the question.[5]

At a summit meeting in Vienna on June 3 and 5, Khrushchev repeated his Berlin ultimatum and even posed the threat of nuclear war to President Kennedy, who was still reeling from the botched invasion of Cuba at the Bay of Pigs. The president again called on Dean Acheson for advice. What he got from the elder statesman was an analysis titled "The Berlin Crisis," which argued that the crisis was not about Berlin at all—Khrushchev was testing America's will to resist and any sign of willingness to negotiate would be regarded as a sign of weakness to be avoided. Acheson urged that there be a rapid buildup of American forces, with three new divisions to be sent to West Germany, an increase in reserve military forces, and a declaration of a national emergency by the president. Soft-liners on the president's staff ferociously attacked the Acheson paper. By July 14, Acheson was thoroughly disgusted, since he felt that the new administration should be "acting now to bring home to Khrushchev that we are in deadly earnest about Berlin, which is only a symbol of our world position."[6] "I find to my surprise a weakness at the top," he wrote to his former boss and old friend, Harry Truman.[7]

On July 25, John F. Kennedy gave his response to Khrushchev's ultimatum in a speech that set out what Kennedy regarded as essential in Berlin: the right of free access, the continued presence of the Western powers, and freedom and security for Berliners. Throughout the speech, the president referred to West Berlin only; the tacit omission of the eastern part of the city seemed to cede that portion to Walter Ulbricht and the German Democratic Republic. In words that General Maxwell Taylor suggested, even though the general was one of his advisors urging extreme caution,[8] the president went on, "I hear it said that West Berlin is militarily untenable. And so was Bastogne. And so, in fact, was Stalingrad. Any dangerous position is tenable if men—brave men—will make it so."[9] It had a heroic ring.

To back up the words, President Kennedy extended the enlistments of all military personnel then serving for an indefinite period and called an additional 133,000 reservists to active duty, but there was no declaration of national emergency and no reinforcement of the garrison in Berlin or in West Germany. The Soviet reaction was quick and harsh.

John McCloy, former high commissioner in Germany, had been called back into government service as a disarmament negotiator and was visiting Khrushchev at the premier's villa at Sochi on the Black Sea when the Soviet leader reviewed the text of Kennedy's speech. In an emotional tirade, the Soviet dictator declared that the speech was a "preliminary declaration of war," that the Soviet Union could never accept such an ultimatum, and that if the Western allies tried to force their way into the city there would be a thermonuclear war. John Kennedy, the Soviet leader said, would be the last president of the United States, and he would have no successor.[10]

Khrushchev even posed his scenario for the outbreak of the conflict. The continuing mass exodus of East Germans to the West might spark a revolt similar to the one in 1953, he said, and the West German army, headed by "Nazi" generals, might invade the East. Somehow, Khrushchev said, the flow of refugees would have to be stopped.[11]

The problem to the Democratic Republic of refugees escaping to the West was, in fact, enormous. Between 1949 and the beginning of August 1961, nearly 2.7 million East Germans had fled, and 1.65 million of them had done so through Berlin.[12] As early as March 1961, Walter Ulbricht had proposed to the Soviets and other members of the Warsaw Pact that the border between East and West be sealed. The Soviet premier had vetoed the idea at the time but at a Warsaw Pact meeting on August 5, 1961, he approved the Ulbricht proposal. Just before that meeting, Ulbricht had announced at a press conference that he feared that the Federal Republic was preparing to attack the East. If the attack came, the leader of the Democratic Republic said, East German troops would defend the country, while East German workers would be sent east to the USSR to work in Soviet factories, freeing Soviet workers to be drafted into the Red Army. That pronouncement turned the hemorrhage of refugees from the Democratic Republic into a flood. In the first twelve days of August 1961, 21,282 East Germans arrived in West Berlin.

☆    ☆    ☆

At 1:54 on the morning of Sunday, August 13, West Berlin police Lieutenant Hermann Beck slipped out of his trousers, readying himself for a nap. In charge of the central police communication center for the city, which was housed in one of the massive wings of Tempelhof Airport, Beck knew from experience that early Sunday morning was normally a quiet time. Then the telephone rang.

The caller, the duty officer at the Spandau police headquarters, reported that the elevated train on the main east-west line had been stopped at the last station in the Soviet sector. Passengers were ordered off the train, which then rumbled back to the East. The station loudspeakers were now announcing that all train service would be interrupted until further notice. One minute later another duty officer reported a similar event at stations near the French sector, and a third call brought yet another report of train interruptions. At 2:07 a.m., the police station in the Tiergarten reported that East German trucks full of police had just driven toward the Brandenburg Gate and that twenty-three East German troop carriers were clustered behind it. Beck called Erich Duensing, chief of the West Berlin police, to report that something major was clearly under way.

East German troops and police moved in to completely seal off the boundary between East Berlin and the Western sectors with a human barrier of armed guards. Then East German Army engineers began stringing barbed wire barricades and tearing up paving stones all along the border. Radio announcements ordered East Berliners who held jobs in the West to report to their last place of employment in the East or to a State Labor Office to be assigned a new job. East German troops and police guarded every street entering into the West, and auto, bicycle, and foot traffic was stopped.

The East German move took everyone in the West by surprise, but Colonel Roy Murray, the American chief of staff, had the presence of mind to call U.S. Army Europe Headquarters to ask that they send him thirty-three bulldozer blades that would fit on the thirty-three U.S. tanks that were in the city. If the order came to tear up the wire, Murray wanted to be ready.[13]

Orders from higher authority were slow in coming, as the East Germans planned their coup for a weekend. President Kennedy was sailing off Hyannis Port, and the British prime minister, Harold Macmillan, was in the Scottish highlands on a grouse-shooting holiday. Even the mayor of Berlin, Willi Brandt, was out of town. The Social Democratic candidate for chancellor in the upcoming election, he was on a campaign train somewhere between Nuremberg and Kiel.

Brigadier General Frederick O. Hartel commented later, "We got stunning silence [from Washington] for a while."[14] The Allied garrisons in the city were put on alert, but the troops remained in their barracks. It was seventeen hours before the American State Department issued a weakly worded statement, citing the East German action as a sign of desperation in having to lock up the country's citizens. Mayor Brandt, hastening back to the city from his campaign trip, urged the Americans and their allies to knock down the barricades with their tanks, but none of the Western allies had orders from their governments. The troops remained in their barracks.

The day after the barricades went up, the East Germans cut all telephone communications with West Germany, closed the Brandenburg Gate, and reduced the number of border crossing points to twelve. That afternoon, 300,000 demonstrators gathered in the plaza in front of city hall in Schöneberg, in West Berlin, and listened while Mayor Brandt assured them that the city was still supported by the West. He spoke those encouraging words without knowing whether they were true or not, as no one had given him any assurance that the Western allies would remain in the city. It was not until the following day that a protest was filed with the Soviet military headquarters. The note, delivered by a messenger rather than the Western military governors themselves, made no demands; it merely protested the border closing.

Another crowd huddled under umbrellas in a driving rainstorm in the plaza the following afternoon. Soggy signs reading "Ninety Hours and No Action," "Kennedy to Berlin," and "Munich 1938–Berlin 1961," dotted the plaza, and the crowd took up a rhythmic chant, *"Howley soll her!"*—"Howley should come here!"—calling for the return of General Frank Howley to the city. Then Mayor Brandt began to address them. The mayor had spent most of the previous day drafting a letter to President Kennedy, begging for a stern response from a president who was already scrambling to develop an effective policy to deal with the unexpected developments in Berlin. Most of the senior State Department officials—Secretary of State Dean Rusk, Chip Bohlen, Chester Bowles, and Adlai Stevenson—were hoping to take the heat out of the crisis by sitting tight and waiting for it to subside.[15] Others were urging a firm stand.

Among them was Frank Howley. Now vice-chancellor of his alma mater, New York University, Howley was invited by columnist Westbrook Pegler to offer his opinion on the crisis in a series of newspaper articles. Howley reviewed the history of Berlin in the years since the end of the war and concluded, "I'm hopeful that the new President, now that he has seen the face of the enemy in Vienna, will start issuing ultimatums and demanding that our rights be respected. . . ."[16]

Edward R. Murrow, recently appointed by the president to head the U.S. Information Service, was on a visit to Berlin when the crisis broke. He also weighed in with a strong plea for action to bolster the flagging morale of the Berliners. Some old "Berlin hands"—experts on Germany—both inside and outside of the government were urging the same, and the oldest Berlin hand of all, General Lucius Clay, had offered to return to the city on behalf of the government.

Clay, just recovering from an ulcer operation that had cost him most of his stomach, seemed an unlikely volunteer to serve a young and inexperienced Democratic president. Following his retirement from the Army, Clay had become chairman of Continental Can Company and an important Republican party member. Clay had been instrumental in persuading Dwight Eisenhower to run for president in 1952 and had raised significant funds for the Eisenhower campaign. The double tug of duty and of the city of Berlin proved far greater than mere party considerations, however. Contacted by his old friend, Marguerite Higgins, Clay told her that he was thinking of volunteering to go back to Berlin "in Howley's old job"—a retired four-star general was thinking of taking up a brigadier's post.

Higgins contacted another old friend, Attorney General Robert Kennedy. His brother accepted the general's offer to help, sending Clay to Berlin as his special envoy, in the company of Vice President Lyndon Johnson. While they were there, a full battle group of 1,500 men was to be sent up the autobahn to reinforce the Berlin garrison as a demonstration of America's will to remain in the city. There was a growing political need for such a demonstration, although any action against the East German barricades was seen as impractical, as well as provocative and dangerous. The barricades had been erected just inside East Berlin, not on the very border itself. Any action by the Western allies to remove them would involve intrusion into the Soviet sector, and the East Germans could simply withdraw and reerect the barricades a few yards further back. If the West was determined to rip them down, there would surely come a time when the Soviets would intervene to resist intrusion into their territory. Forceful removal of the barriers was not an option that was even given serious consideration.

Vice President Lyndon Johnson was reluctant to undertake the role that the president assigned him, and it took all of House Speaker Sam Rayburn's eloquence to convince Johnson that his place was in Berlin.[17] When first informed by President Kennedy that he was to visit Berlin to bolster morale in the city, Johnson resisted. Told later that his visit would coincide with the arrival of the 1,500 reinforcements, the vice president complained, "There'll be a lot of shooting and I'll be in the middle of it. Why me?"[18] However grudgingly, he took on the assignment to demonstrate America's commitment to Berlin by his presence there.

Air Force Two, the Boeing 707 that flew the American party to Germany, arrived at Bonn-Cologne airport at 9:30 a.m. on August 19. By the middle of the afternoon, Clay and the vice president had changed planes and flown into Berlin. The motorcade carrying them to a symbolic visit to the barricades on the Potsdamer Platz was slowed by crowds of Berliners who, recognizing Clay's hawklike profile, took up the chant *"Der Clay ist hier."* Johnson became annoyed at the attention the general was getting. Ignoring the pleas of his Secret Service bodyguards, the vice president got out of the Cadillac to wade into the crowd, shaking hands, patting dogs, and kissing babies. The visit raised morale but had no effect on the barricades. Apparently convinced that the Allies would do nothing to risk war over them, the East Germans began to set the barriers separating the city in concrete on August 18. By August 22, 1961, the wall was nearly complete. A solid concrete barrier, one foot thick, six feet high, and twenty-eight miles long, snaked through the city.

On August 30, the White House announced that General Clay would return to Berlin on a formal basis as a retired four-star advisor to the two-star commander of the garrison, Major General Albert Watson II.

Tensions in the city remained high, but the Soviets maintained a public posture that there was nothing that they could do about the situation. The erection of the wall had been undertaken by the legitimate East German government. That government now demanded that Western allied vehicles passing into the Eastern sector stop so that the passengers' identification papers could be examined. A State Department vehicle was stopped by the East German police on October 22 on this pretext. The passengers refused to comply. The next time the East Germans tried to stop a State Department car, it contained Allan Lightner, a senior official who had volunteered for a special mission Clay set up.

As soon as Lightner's car was stopped, MPs arrived in several jeeps with machine guns mounted, and a platoon of American infantry with fixed bayonets appeared as if from nowhere. The East Germans allowed Lightner's car to pass.

On October 27, after the Americans had staged another such probe by a diplomatic vehicle into the East, the fiction that the Soviets were not involved came to an end. A company of Soviet heavy tanks suddenly rolled up just to the east of Checkpoint Charlie on Friedrichstrasse to face a company of U.S. tanks just to the west. The armored columns remained gun barrel to gun barrel for sixteen hours, while diplomats worried and talked. Then the gun tubes of the Soviet tanks elevated to a nonhostile position. The moment of deepest crisis passed. Gradually, both sides grew accustomed to the new status quo.

The seriousness of the nature of the service of troops in Berlin during that period of high tension in Berlin was tacitly recognized by Executive Order 10977 of December 4, 1961, establishing a new medal for members of the United States military forces. Designed by the Army Institute of Heraldry, it showed an eagle with outstretched wings standing on a sword unsheathed from its scabbard and was designated the Armed Forces Expeditionary Medal. It was intended to be given to any member of the armed forces who participated in a military operation for which no other campaign medal has been authorized. The first awards of the new medal were made to the soldiers of the Berlin Brigade and the reinforcements who had joined them at the height of the crisis. For members of the brigade, it joined a medal which they, by virtue of their assignment, were uniquely entitled to earn. Anyone assigned to Berlin was, by the nature of the duty, a member of the American army of occupation and was therefore eligible for the red, black, and white ribboned Army of Occupation Medal. Hundreds of thousands of the AOM had been awarded in the immediate postwar era, when American troops occupied Germany, Austria, Japan, Korea, and Italy. In 1961, only those soldiers stationed in Berlin were still, technically, on occupation duty in a conquered foreign land, and the ribbon on their uniforms was a visual reminder of that fact.

In 1963, President Kennedy himself came to Berlin and visited the wall. While there, he said, "Two thousand years ago, the proudest boast was, 'cives Romanus sum' [I am a Roman citizen.] Today, in the world of freedom, the proudest boast is '*Ich bin ein Berliner.*'" The crowd went wild with adulation when he concluded, "All free men, wherever they live, are citizens of Berlin and, therefore, as a free man, I take pride in the words, '*Ich bin ein Berliner.*'" [19]

By the time Soviet leader Mikhail Gorbachev came to Berlin to help celebrate the fortieth anniversary of the German Democratic Republic on October 7, 1989, much had changed in Europe. In Poland, the Communist government of General Wojciech Jaruzelski had been forced into negotiations and free elections by Lech Walesa's Solidarity movement. The Communist government of Hungary had given up power and had opened the barbed-wire barrier along the Austro-Hungarian border. Gorbachev was in the midst of reforms in the Soviet Union, and he cautioned East German president Erich Honecker that it was time for change in Germany as well, pointing out, "Life punishes those who come too late."[20] Honecker refused to listen, stating that perestroika and glasnost might be fine for the Soviet Union but that they were irrelevant in East Germany. He was wrong, and the SED forced him into retirement in the fall of 1989. By that time, East Germans were pouring out of the country into the West by a circuitous route that took them to Hungary, then across the open border to Austria. In a three-week period, 40,000 took that route, and demonstrations within East Germany for greater access to the West increased in strength, focusing on Berlin. Fifty thousand, then one hundred thousand, then two hundred thousand demonstrators gathered in the Alexanderplatz, chanting for freedom. On the night of November 4, the crowd numbered five hundred thousand.

Five days later, Günter Schabowski, one of the SED leaders, told a press conference that the government was going to ease travel restrictions. Asked when it would happen, Schabowski absentmindedly said, "Now, I suppose."[21]

Hearing the news, crowds of East Berliners hurried to the wall, demanding to know of the guards at the checkpoints why they were still on duty when it had just been announced that the wall was open. The guards, many sympathetic to the crowds, stepped aside. Within a week, the wall was gone. In less than a year, East Germany itself had disappeared. Negotiations on the future of Germany resulted in a treaty, signed in Moscow on September 12, 1990, by the four victors of World War II and the two Germanys the Cold War that followed had created. The terms of the treaty created a unified Germany and, for the Allies, ended "all rights and responsibilities in Berlin and Germany as a whole," on midnight, October 3, 1990. While it would take some time to wind things up, the occupation of Berlin was ending.

The last Soviet soldier left Germany on August 31, 1994, and the very last of the Allied troops pulled out of Berlin the following month. The United States Army's Berlin Brigade was deactivated at McNair Barracks by President Bill Clinton on July 12, 1994. He concluded his speech at the ceremony where the colors of the brigade were cased forever by saying, "Thank you for a job well done. America salutes you. Mission accomplished."[22]

There had been a parade on June 18, nearly a month before the president presided over the small, sad, final ceremony. The Berlin garrisons of the Western allies held their final march down the broad Strasse des 17. Juni, and the Berliners turned out to cheer them and bid them farewell.

The French contingent led, dressed in crisp khaki and their distinctive kepis. Next came the British, marching to the skirl of Highland bagpipes. American troops in modern battledress fatigues followed, and a squadron of helicopters swooped over the line of march.

At the very end of the parade a C-47 lumbered by in the air above the crowd, twin engines droning and filling the sky with a sound that had marked the heartbeat of the city forty-five years earlier. Most of the Berliners cheered. A few of the older ones cried, in remembrance of those days when their lives had depended on the strength and courage of a few brave airmen, and the will of the free world to sustain them through a siege.

# EPILOGUE

### Ruth Andreas-Friedrich
After leaving Berlin on December 29, 1948, Ruth Andreas-Friedrich moved to Munich and continued to work as a journalist. In 1955 she married Professor Walter Seitz, the director of the university hospital in that city. She died in Munich on October 12, 1977. In an obituary in *Israel Nachrichten,* Albert Frankenstein wrote, "She is one of those just Germans who saved the reputation of her people during its worst time. May her memory be blessed."

### Donald Clifford Tyndall Bennett
Immediately after the airlift, the erratic British airman founded a new company, Fairflight, carrying out charter flights to the Mid and Far East. He stood for Parliament as a Liberal party candidate on a number of occasions, but broke with the party in 1962 over its position in favor of the European Economic Community. In 1963 he founded a splinter movement known as the Association of Political Independents, which supported, among other things, forced repatriation of immigrants. His book, *The Complete Air Navigator,* remained in print until 1967. He died on September 15, 1986.

### Ernest Bevin
Bevin flew into Berlin to consult with Social Democratic party members prior to the meeting of the Council of Foreign Ministers that followed the lifting of the blockade, visiting the city he had helped to save. Tired from his continuing efforts and increasingly ill, he remained foreign secretary until March 1951, when his health caused him to resign. He died the following month.

### James Francis Byrnes
Byrnes dropped out of public life for a period after his resignation, then began to attack Truman's domestic policies late in 1949. In 1950, he was elected governor of South Carolina, retiring in 1955. During the 1952 election campaign, he endorsed the Republican candidate, Dwight D. Eisenhower, for president and never again endorsed a Democrat. He died in Columbia, South Carolina, on April 9, 1972.

### Lucius DuBignon Clay

General Clay retired from the United States Army on May 26, 1949, and returned to America. He became the chief executive officer and chairman of the board of the Continental Can Company in 1949, positions from which he retired in 1962. He was instrumental in convincing Dwight D. Eisenhower to run for president in 1952. When the Soviets constructed the Berlin Wall in 1961, bisecting that tortured city, Clay was called back to government service by President John F. Kennedy to act as the president's personal representative in the city. Following the abortive invasion of Cuba at the Bay of Pigs, General Clay helped to raise nearly $2 million to ransom the prisoners who had been captured there. After his retirement from Continental Can, General Clay remained active as a senior partner of Lehman Brothers and as a director of other companies. He died on April 16, 1978, one week before his eighty-first birthday, and was buried at the United States Military Academy at West Point, New York. At the foot of his grave is a small marble marker installed by the citizens of Berlin and inscribed *Wir danken den Bewahrer unserer Freiheit*—We thank the defender of our freedom.

### Gail S. Halvorsen

Gail married Alta Jolley, the young woman he was courting by mail while he served on the airlift. He continued his career in the United States Air Force, rising to the rank of colonel and returning to Berlin as commander of Tempelhof Airport. While there, he arranged to have a C-54 that was scheduled to be scrapped diverted from the "bone yard" and installed at Tempelhof as a memorial to the airlift. On retirement, he and Alta returned to Utah. An elder of the Church of Jesus Christ of the Latter Day Saints, Colonel Halvorsen and his wife were in St. Petersburg, in the former Soviet Union, on a teaching mission for their church, as this book was being written.

### Frank L. Howley

General Howley joined the advertising agency of Aitkin-Kynett when he returned to Philadelphia, and he lectured widely on his experiences in Berlin. He received many awards and honors, including the Distinguished Service Medal from President Harry S Truman and an honorary degree of Doctor of Laws from New York University. The one of which he was most proud, however, was the honorary degree of Doctor of Medicine awarded by the Free University of Berlin in recognition of his humanitarian efforts during the blockade. In 1952, he was appointed vice-chancellor of his alma mater, New York University, and he served in that post until joining Bache and Company as a vice president in 1967. General Howley traveled widely and wrote and lectured on the subject of the Cold War. In the end, it was General Howley—not General Kotikov—who lived to see the end of the class struggle. By the time Frank Howley died in 1993, the Soviet Union had ceased to exist. The Berlin Wall had fallen and the city was once again free and united, and the capital of a free and united Germany.

### George F. Kennan

Kennan left the State Department in 1950, taking up an academic post at Princeton University, but he returned to the Foreign Service as ambassador to the Soviet Union in 1952. He was recalled to Washington at the beginning of the Eisenhower presidency and straightforwardly informed that there was no place for him in the new administration. He returned to Princeton. One of his scholarly works, *Russia Leaves the War,* won a Pulitzer Prize. He remained active in public affairs, taking up the cause of disarmament and warning early and often about American involvement in Vietnam. He is retired and lives on a farm near Princeton, New Jersey.

### Alexander Kotikov

Recalled from Berlin in 1949, General Kotikov apparently fell from favor with the Stalin regime. Along with some 20 million of his fellow Soviet citizens, he became what was euphemistically described as a "nonperson." The man who was so prominent a figure in the life of Berlin at the beginning of the Cold War disappeared from public view, and all references to him in the press ceased. He does not appear even as a minor entry in the comprehensive *Great Soviet Encyclopedia* of 1986. The date and place of his death are unknown.

### Curtis E. LeMay

Ordered back to the United States in October 1948, LeMay took over the Strategic Air Command, where he instituted realistic training exercises and expanded the number of planes and men available. He was responsible for the integration of intercontinental ballistic missiles into the defense of the United States and, in October 1951, he became the youngest four-star general since Ulysses S. Grant. As chief of staff of the Air Force, he frequently argued with the decisions of the secretary of defense, Robert S. McNamara, during the early 1960s. Retiring in February 1965, he entered private business and ran for vice president with George Wallace in 1968. He died on October 1, 1990.

### George C. Marshall

Recovered from his operation, George C. Marshall served as president of the American Red Cross until September 1950, when he accepted President Truman's offer to make him secretary of defense. In that role, he strengthened the army, argued for the implementation of universal military training, and supported his commander in chief's decision to relieve Douglas MacArthur of command in Korea. In 1953 he became the only professional soldier to be awarded the Nobel Peace Prize. He died on October 16, 1959.

### Vyacheslav Michailovich Molotov
Molotov disappeared from Soviet politics in March 1949, and it was announced five months later that he had been relieved of his post, although he remained a member of the Politburo. Reappointed foreign minister by Nikita Khruschchev after the death of Joseph Stalin, Molotov formed a coalition with several others in the Politburo to challenge the new leader. In June 1957, the group unsuccessfully demanded Khruschchev's removal and were themselves removed. Banished to an obscure job in the east of the Soviet Union, Molotov was officially rehabilitated in 1980 and died in 1986.

### Jim O'Gorman
After his service in beleaguered Berlin, O'Gorman transferred back to the infantry and earned a Silver Star in combat in Korea. Back in Berlin for another tour, he again joined U.S. Forces Radio, then left the army to attend the University of Detroit, where he majored in communications. He retired after a career in production with NBC and lives in Deerfield Park, Florida.

### Ernst Reuter
Ernst Reuter was elected and reelected lord mayor of Berlin. In 1950, when the Communists threatened to stage a May Day rally to cow West Berliners into joining with East Germany, he organized a demonstration of 500,000 beforehand. The Communist demonstration fizzled. When East Germany broke out in riots in 1952, Reuter played an active role in the distribution of food packages to the East. On September 28, 1953, Reuter complained of having a slight cold. The following morning he delivered his usual Sunday radio address to the Eastern sector of his beloved city, a place he characterized as "where the shoe pinches." Shortly after the broadcast he suffered a massive heart attack. A second one, at 7:00 p.m., killed him.

### Rudolf Schnabel
The man who assisted Kenneth Slaker to escape to the West settled in Wiesbaden after Colonel Sig Young helped arrange a job for him with the German Post Office there. His wife and young daughter joined him from the East, and he and his wife had two more children. Now retired from *Deutsche Post,* he enjoys the occasional visits he has from his old friend, Kenneth Slaker.

### Louise Schroeder
Although she remained single and childless all her life, Frau Schroeder was revered by her fellow citizens as the "Mother of Berlin." Recovered from the illness that forced her to hand over her duties to her deputy, Louise Schroeder was elected to the newly established Bundestag of the Federal Republic of Germany in 1949. She was named by the Bun-

destag as a representative to the Council of Europe and continued to serve on both bodies until her death in 1957.

### Kenneth Slaker

Soon after his escape back to the West, Kenneth Slaker was transferred to California, even though he had eighteen months of his tour in Germany remaining. He was told that the Soviets had asked that he be turned over to them for trial as a spy. He remained in the Air Force, eventually gaining the rank of lieutenant colonel, and he earned a degree in history from Washburn University. He and Rudolf Schnabel remain in contact, having been reunited when Slaker was reassigned to Germany in 1962.

### Vassily D. Sokolovsky

Sokolovsky's relief from command in Berlin in March 1949 was clearly a reward and not a rebuke. He was elevated to the post of first deputy minister of the Soviet armed forces. In May 1949, shortly after the announcement of the end of the blockade, Sokolovsky aggressively and uncompromisingly attacked the Western allies in a long article in *Pravda.* In 1953 Marshal Sokolovsky succeeded General Sergei Shtemenko as chief of staff of the Soviet armed forces and attained full membership in the Central Committee of the Communist Party. He retired as chief of staff in 1960 and died in Moscow on May 10, 1968.

### William H. Tunner

Not long after the effort in Berlin ended, General Tunner was again in command of an airlift. This one, the Combat Cargo Command, supplied the United Nations forces fighting in Korea. For the most dramatic of its exploits—the parachute drop of a sixteen-ton bridge that enabled American infantrymen surrounded by the Chinese to span a ravine and escape with their equipment—Tunner was awarded the Distinguished Service Cross. He married a former Women's Air Service pilot, Margaret Ann Hamilton, in June 1951. Following the Korean War, he served as commander in chief, USAFEurope from 1953 to 1957, then took over as commander of MATS. Because of a heart problem, he left the Air Force in June 1960. The West German government named him a Knight Commander of the Order of Merit, and a street in Berlin was named for him. "Willy the Whip" died on April 6, 1983.

### Robert D. Wilcox

His near-crash early in the airlift did not deter Robert Wilcox from flying. Following his assignment back to Erding, he studied at the Air Force Institute of Technology and ended his military career twenty-one years later, serving as chief of Internal Information of the U.S. Air Force. He is now retired from his second career as advertising manager for Armstrong World Industries and lives in Lancaster, Pennsylvania.

## Georgi K. Zhukov

Recalled to Moscow in 1946, the conqueror of Berlin was first appointed deputy minister of defense, then suddenly transferred to an obscure command in Odessa, not to reemerge until 1955. In that year, the new Soviet premier, Nikita Khruschchev, appointed him minister of defense. During the Hungarian uprising of 1956, it was Zhukov who personally signed the order sending Soviet tanks into Budapest. A supporter of Khruschchev in the leadership crisis of 1957, Zhukov was the first military man appointed to the Presidium, but he was unceremoniously removed from all of his posts in October of that year and was pensioned off in March 1958. Officially rehabilitated by the Communist party in 1964, he did not return to a position of power, and he died in Moscow on June 18, 1974.

# APPENDIX

## *In Memoriam*

### ROYAL AIR FORCE

Flt. Lt. H. W. Thompson
Sig. II S. M. L. Towersey
Flt. Lt. J. G. Wilkins
Pilot II E. J. Eddy
Fg. Off. K. A. Reeves
Nav. I W. G. Page

Flt. Lt. G. Kell
Eng. II E. W. Watson
Sig. III P. A. Lough
Nav. II L. Senior
Flg. Off. I. R. Donaldson
Sig. II A. Dunsire

Nav. L. E. H. Gilbert
Pilot I F. I. Trevona
Sgt. F. Dowling
Sig. II L. E. Grout
M. Sig. A. Penny
Eng. II R. R. Gibbs

### BRITISH ARMY—GLIDER PILOT REGIMENT

Sgt. J. Toal

### ROYAL AUSTRALIAN AIR FORCE

Flt. Lt. M. J. Quinn

### UNITED STATES ARMY

Cpl. George S. Burns

### UNITED STATES AIR FORCE

1st Lt. George B. Smith
1st Lt. Robert W. Stuber
Capt. Joel M. Devolentine
Capt. James A. Vaughn
Capt. Billy E. Phelps
Capt. William A. Rathgeber
1st Lt. Richard M. Wurgel
1st Lt. Ralph H. Boyd
1st Lt. Robert C. VonLuehrte
2nd Lt. Donald Leemon

1st Lt. Lelan V. Williams
Capt. William R. Howard
1st Lt. William T. Lucas
1st Lt. Eugene S. Erickson
1st Lt. Willis F. Hargis
1st Lt. Lowell A. Wheaton, Jr.
Sgt. Bernard J. Watkins
TSgt. Charles L. Putnam
1st Lt. Royce C. Stevens
TSgt. Herbert F. Heinig

1st Lt. Charles H. King
Maj. Edwin C. Dietz
Pfc. Johnnie T. Orms
Sgt. Richard Winter
TSgt. Lloyd G. Wells
Pfc. Ronald E. Stone
Cpl. Norbert V. Theis
1st Lt. Craig B. Ladd
1st Lt. Robert P. Weaver

### UNITED STATES NAVY

MachMt Harry R. Crites, Jr.

CIVILIANS

Karl V. Hagen, U.S. Dept. of Defense
Capt. Cyril Taylor, Flight Refueling
Capt. William Cusack, Flight Refueling
Rad. Off. D. W. Robertson, Flight
Refueling
Gd. Eng. Theodor Supernat, Lancashire
Acft.
Gd. Eng. Patrick J. Griffin, Lancashire
Acft.
Nav. Off. James Sharp, Lancashire Acft.
Capt. Cyril Golding, Skyways, Ltd.
Rad. Off. Peter J. Edwards, Skyways, Ltd.
Nav. Off. Edward E. Carroll, World Air
Freight
Rad. Off. Kenneth G. Wood, World Air
Freight

Capt. Clement W. Utting, Flight Refueling
Capt. Reginald M. H. Heath, Flight
Refueling
Nav. Off. Alan J. Burton, Flight Refueling
Flt. Eng. Kenneth A. Seaborne, Flight
Refueling
Gd. Eng. Edward O'Neil, Lancashire Acft.
Capt. Robert J. Freight, Lancashire Acft.
Eng. Off. Henry Patterson, Lancashire
Acft.
1st. Off. Henry T. Newman, Skyways, Ltd.
Capt. William R. Lewis, World Air Freight
Eng. Off. John Anderson, World Air
Freight

# Notes

PROLOGUE

1. Forest Pogue, *The Supreme Command* (Washington: Government Printing Office, 1952), 446.

2. Ruth Andreas-Friedrich, *Berlin Underground: 1938–1945,* trans. Barrows Mussey (New York: H. Holt, 1947). Ruth Andreas-Friedrich, *Battleground Berlin: Diaries, 1945–1948,* trans. Anna Boerresen (New York: Paragon, 1990). Some of the individuals, such as her lover, Leo Borchard (referred to as Andrik) and her daughter, Karin (referred to as Heike), can be identified. In those cases, the individual's correct name has been used in this text. In other cases, the code names she used have been employed.

3. Ibid., 272.

4. Ibid., 273.

5. *Current Biography,* July 1952.

6. Andreas-Friedrich, *Berlin Underground,* 298.

7. Ibid., 309–10.

8. Robert Jackson, *The Berlin Airlift* (Wellingborough, England: Patrick Stevens, 1988), 9.

CHAPTER ONE

1. Jean Edward Smith, *Lucius D. Clay: An American Life* (New York: Henry Holt, 1990) 50.

2. James F. Byrnes, *Speaking Frankly* (New York: Harper Brothers, 1947), 47.

3. William L. Shirer, *The Rise and Fall of the Third Reich* (New York: Harper Brothers, 1952), 852–61.

4. Winston S. Churchill, *The Grand Alliance* (Boston: Houghton Mifflin, 1953), 630–31.

5. Jean Edward Smith, *The Defense of Berlin* (Baltimore: Johns Hopkins Press, 1963), 12.

6. Robert Sherwood, *Roosevelt and Hopkins* (New York: Harper Brothers, 1948), 427–42.

7. Smith, *Defense of Berlin,* 14.

8. Ibid., 16.

9. Ibid., 19.

10. Ibid., 20.

11. Pogue, *Supreme Command,* 465.

12. Walter Issacson and Evan Thomas, *The Wise Men* (New York: Simon and Schuster, 1986), 249.

13. David McCullough, *Truman* (New York: Simon and Schuster, 1992), 214.

14. Ibid., 225–44.

15. Harry S Truman, *Year of Decisions– 1945,* Vol. 1 of *Memoirs* (New York: Signet, 1955), 31.

16. Smith, *Defense of Berlin,* 59–62.

17. Ibid., 62–63.

18. Winston S. Churchill, *Triumph and Tragedy* (Boston: Houghton Mifflin, 1953), 573.

19. Ibid., 573.

20. Truman, *Year of Decisions,* 246.

21. Cornelius Ryan, *The Last Battle* (New York: Simon and Schuster, 1966), 484–85.

22. Andreas-Friedrich, *Battleground Berlin,* 16.

23. Ibid., 16.

24. Ibid., 17.

25. Ryan, *Last Battle,* 493.

26. Ibid., 493–95.

27. Andreas-Friedrich, *Battleground Berlin,* 13.

28. Lucius D. Clay, *Decision in Germany,* (New York: Doubleday, 1950), 263–65.

29. Curt Reiss, *The Berlin Story,* (New York: Dial Press, 1952), 26–28.

30. Andreas-Friedrich, *Battleground Berlin,* 19.

CHAPTER TWO

1. *Time,* 25 June 1945.

2. Andreas-Friedrich, *Battleground Berlin,* 31.

3. Ibid., 34.

4. Smith, *Defense of Berlin,* 73.

5. Truman, *Year of Decisions,* 335.

6. Ibid., 335–36.

7. Churchill, *Triumph and Tragedy,* 603.

8. Clay, *Decision in Germany,* 21–22.

9. Ibid., 22.

10. Smith, *Defense of Berlin,* 76.

11. Ibid., 77.

12. Andreas-Friedrich, *Battleground Berlin,* 39.

13. Churchill, *Triumph and Tragedy,* 605–6; Truman, *Year of Decisions,* 337–38.

14. Truman, *Year of Decisions,* 339; Smith, *Defense of Berlin,* 80.

15. Reiss, *Berlin Story,* 83–84.

16. Office of Military Government, U.S. Sector Berlin, *Four Year Report* (Berlin: OMGUS, 1949).

17. Henrick Bering, *Outpost Berlin* (Carol Stream, Ill.: edition q, inc., 1995), 31; OMGUS *Four Year Report.*

18. Bering, *Outpost Berlin,* 31.

19. Frank Howley, *Berlin Command* (New York: G. P. Putnam's Sons, 1950), 3–4.

20. Howley File, *Philadelphia Inquirer;* Howley, *Berlin Command,* 17.

21. Howley, *Berlin Command,* 17.

22. Ibid., 25.

23. Ibid., 28.

24. Ibid., 28–32.

25. Ibid., 32.

26. Ibid., 36–42.

27. Truman, *Year of Decisions,* 340.

28. Herbert Feis, *Between War and Peace* (Princeton: Princeton University Press, 1960), 147; Clay, *Decision in Germany,* 24–26.

29. Clay, *Decision in Germany,* 25; Howley, *Berlin Command,* 42–43.

30. Smith, *Defense of Berlin,* 83.

31. Ibid., 84.

32. Clay, *Decision in Germany,* 26.

CHAPTER THREE

1. Howley, *Berlin Command,* 42.

2. Ibid., 43.

3. Ibid.

4. Ibid., 45.

5. Andreas-Friedrich, *Battleground Berlin,* 51.

6. Howley, *Berlin Command,* 49.

7. Ibid., 50–51.

8. Ibid., 52.

9. John J. Maginnis, *Military Government Journal: Normandy to Berlin,* ed. Robert A. Hart (Amherst: University of Massachusetts Press, 1971), 173.

10. *History of the 852nd Aviation Engineer Battalion* (Berlin: Privately printed, c. 1945), 2–3.

11. John Harmanson and Andrew Glaze, special edition of *The Berlin Tabulator,* 30–31 May 1989, 3.

12. Ibid., 3.

13. Ibid., 4–5.

14. Ibid., 13.

15. Ibid., 13; Lt. Col. A. G. Hazen, *853rd Aviation Engineer Battalion Completion Report, OAF Field R-95—Tempelhof, Berlin, Germany,* 10 September 1945, 3.

16. Hazen, op. cit., 3.

17. Ibid., 4.

18. Ibid.

19. Ibid.

20. Harmansen and Glaze, *Berlin Tabulator*, 3.

21. Jackson, *Berlin Airlift*, 33.

22. Bering, *Outpost Berlin*, 7.

23. Howley, *Berlin Command*, 52–54.

24. Ibid., 54.

25. Ibid., 55.

26. Ibid., 56.

27. Ibid., 57.

28. Ibid., 58.

29. Ibid.

30. John H. Backer, *Winds of History* (New York: Van Norstrand Reinhold, 1983), 24.

31. Ibid., 25.

CHAPTER FOUR

1. Howley, *Berlin Command*, 204.

2. Backer, *Winds of History*, 103.

3. Ibid., 103.

4. Murphy, *Diplomat among Warriors*, 296.

5. Richard Collier, *Bridge across the Sky: The Berlin Blockade and Airlift, 1948–1949* (London: Macmillan, 1978), 4.

6. Andreas-Friedrich, *Battleground Berlin*, 72.

7. Clay, *Decision in Germany*, 207.

8. Jack Bennett, "The German Currency Reform," *Annals of the American Academy of Political Science*, 44.

9. Franklin M. Davis, Jr., *Came as a Conqueror: The United States Army's Occupation of Germany, 1945–1949* (New York: Macmillan, 1967), 151.

10. Bennett, "German Currency Reform," 44; Davis, *Came as a Conqueror*, 150.

11. Davis, *Came as a Conqueror*, 151.

12. Oram Hutton and Andrew Rooney, *Conquerors' Peace* (Garden City: Doubleday, 1947), 38.

13. Davis, *Came as a Conqueror*, 153–55.

14. Reiss, *Berlin Story*, 93.

15. Howley, *Berlin Command*, 66–67.

16. Ibid., 67–68.

17. Ibid., 68–69.

18. Ibid., 70.

19. Smith, *Clay: An American Life*, 267–76.

20. W. Phillips Davison, *The Berlin Blockade: A Study in Cold War Politics* (Princeton: Princeton University Press, 1958) 33–37.

21. Ibid., 37.

22. Davis, *Came as a Conqueror*, 119.

23. Ibid., 120–24.

24. Truman, *Year of Decisions*, 362–63.

25. Hazem, *Completion Report—Tempelhof*, 3.

26. Truman, *Year of Decisions*, 376–77.

27. Ibid., 378.

CHAPTER FIVE

1. Charles L. Mee, Jr., *Meeting at Potsdam* (New York: Dell, 1976), 50–51.

2. Ibid., 53.

3. Ibid., 43–44; 90.

4. Ibid., 90–91.

5. Ibid., 92–96.

6. Truman, *Year of Decisions*, 415–16.

7. Mee, *Meeting at Potsdam*, 173.

8. Truman, *Year of Decisions*, 386.

9. Howley, *Berlin Command*, 25.

10. Bering, *Outpost Berlin*, 30.

11. Ibid., 30.

12. OMGUS, *Four Year Report;* Bering, *Outpost Berlin*, 35.

13. Howley, *Berlin Command*, 82.

14. *Stars and Stripes*, 15 November 1948.

15. Mee, *Meeting at Potsdam*, 144–45.

16. Ibid., 67.

17. Ibid., 188–89.

18. Truman, *Year of Decisions*, 424; Mee, *Meeting at Potsdam*, 189.

19. Mee, *Meeting at Potsdam*, 192.

20. Ibid., 192.

21. Ibid.

22. *Current Biography*, June 1949.

23. Truman, *Year of Decisions*, 439.

24. Andreas-Friedrich, *Battleground Berlin*, 71.

25. Mee, *Meeting at Potsdam*, 216.

26. Ibid., 223–24.

27. Robert Murphy, *Diplomat among Warriors* (New York: Pyramid, 1965), 312.

28. Ibid., 312.

29. Harry S Truman, *Off the Record* (New York: Harper and Row, 1980), 56–57.

30. Truman, *Year of Decisions*, 454–55.

31. Andreas-Friedrich, *Battleground Berlin*, 82.

32. Ibid., 83.

33. Ibid., 86.

CHAPTER SIX

1. Don Cook, *Forging the Alliance: NATO, 1945–1950* (London: Secker and Warberg, 1989), 28.

2. Truman, *Year of Decisions*, 214–17.

3. Cook, *Forging the Alliance*, 25.

4. Ibid., 28.

5. Ibid.

6. Ibid., 29.

7. Ibid., 24–29.

8. Edward N. Peterson, *The American Occupation of Germany: Retreat to Victory* (Detroit: Wayne State University Press, 1978), 84–86.

9. Smith, *Lucius Clay*, 223–25.

10. Backer, *Winds of History*, 28.

11. Ibid., 28.

12. Peterson, *American Occupation*, 55–57.

13. Smith, *Lucius Clay*, 687–89.

14. Hutton and Rooney, *Conquerors' Peace*, 51.

15. Davis, *Came as a Conqueror*, 145.

16. *Newsweek*, 23 September 1946.

17. Davis, *Came as a Conqueror*, 146.

18. Hutton and Rooney, *Conquerors' Peace*, 50.

19. Andreas-Friedrich, *Battleground Berlin*, 98.

20. *Times* (London), 6 September 1945.

21. "The Peace: Russia, Reparations, and the Reich," *Newsweek*, 23 September 1946.

22. Vladislav Zubok and Constantine Pleshakov, *Inside the Kremlin's Cold War: From Stalin to Khrushchev* (Cambridge: Harvard University Press, 1996), 48.

CHAPTER SEVEN

1. Andreas-Friedrich, *Battleground Berlin*, 88.

2. Ibid., 89.

3. Ibid., 93.

4. Ibid., 95.

5. Norman M. Naimark, *The Russians in Germany: A History of the Soviet Zone of Occupation, 1945–1949* (Cambridge: The Bellknap Press of Harvard University Press, 1995), 102.

6. Bering, *Outpost Berlin*, 56.

7. Howley, *Berlin Command*, 92–93.

8. Maginnis, *Military Government Journal*, 323.

9. Howley, *Berlin Command*, 82–83.

10. Ibid., 88–90.

11. Ibid., 92–93.

12. Ibid., 86–87.

13. *The Sunday Bulletin* (Philadelphia), 4 September 1949.

14. Howley, *Berlin Command*, 87.

15. Andreas-Friedrich, *Battleground Berlin*, 95–96.

16. Cook, *Forging the Alliance*, 31–32.

17. Ibid., 32–33.

18. George F. Kennan, *Memoirs: 1945–1950* (Boston: Little, Brown, 1967), 286.

19. Ibid., 287.

20. Cook, *Forging the Alliance,* 35.

21. Truman, *Year of Decisions,* 603–4.

22. Ibid., 605.

23. Ibid., 605–6; Truman, *Off the Record,* 79–80.

24. Truman, *Year of Decisions,* 606.

25. Andreas-Friedrich, *Battleground Berlin,* 107.

26. Ibid., 107.

CHAPTER EIGHT

1. Naimark, *The Russians in Germany,* 227.

2. Ibid., 278.

3. George Clare, *Before the Wall: Berlin Days, 1946–1948* (New York: Dutton, 1990), 118–120.

4. Howley, *Berlin Command,* 102.

5. Maginnis, *Military Government Journal,* 344.

6. Ibid., 344.

7. Ibid., 344–45.

8. Howley, *Berlin Command,* 92.

9. Ibid., 92–93.

10. Maginnis, *Military Government Journal,* 326–28.

11. Kennan, *Memoirs,* 293.

12. Cook, *Forging the Alliance,* 37.

13. Kennan, *Memoirs,* 293.

14. Ibid., 550.

15. Ibid., 556.

16. Cook, *Forging the Alliance,* 63–64.

17. Andreas-Friedrich, *Battleground Berlin,* 114–15.

18. Ibid., 116.

19. Ibid.

20. Davison, *The Berlin Blockade,* 42.

21. Ibid., 43.

22. Ibid.

23. Philip Windsor, *City on Leave: A History of Berlin, 1945–1962* (London: Chatto and Windus, 1963), 69.

24. Davison, *Berlin Blockade,* 44; Windsor, *City on Leave,* 70.

25. Ibid.

26. Howley, *Berlin Command,* 106.

27. *Current Biography,* October 1949.

28. Davison, *Berlin Blockade,* 45.

CHAPTER NINE

1. Howley, *Berlin Command,* 119.

2. Ibid., 121.

3. Ibid., 123.

4. Ibid., 96–97.

5. *New York Times,* 30 July 1946.

6. Davison, *Berlin Blockade,* 10.

7. Ibid., 10.

8. Susan Cooper, "Snoek Piquant," in *Age of Austerity,* Michael Sissions and Philip French, eds. (Hammondsworth, England: Penguin, 1963) 38–41.

9. Cook, *Forging the Alliance,* 51.

10. John Charmley, *Churchill's Grand Alliance: The Anglo-American Special Relationship, 1940–1957* (New York: Harcourt Brace, 1995), 223.

11. Robert James, ed., *Winston S. Churchill: His Complete Speeches,* vol. 7 (New York: 1974), 7285–93.

12. Charmley, *Churchill's Grand Alliance,* 223.

13. *Time,* 8 July 1946.

14. *Time,* 21 October 1946.

15. Howley, *Berlin Command,* 121–122.

16. Andreas-Friedrich, *Battleground Berlin,* 130.

17. Howley, *Berlin Command,* 127–29.

18. *Newsweek,* 28 October 1946.

19. Ibid.

20. Ibid.

21. Bering, *Outpost Berlin,* 58.

22. Joseph B. Phillips, "Luncheon in Berlin," *Newsweek,* 21 October 1946.

23. *Newsweek,* 28 October 1946.

24. Smith, *The Defense of Berlin,* 95.

25. Kennan, *Memoirs,* 108.

26. Naimark, *The Russians in Germany,* 224.

27. Ibid., 223.

28. Ibid., 224.

29. Ibid., 220.

CHAPTER TEN

1. *Newsweek,* 18 November 1946.

2. OMGUS, *Four Year Report,* 65.

3. Ibid., 63.

4. *Newsweek,* 3 November 1947, 41.

5. Bering, *Outpost Berlin,* 69–70.

6. Howley, *Berlin Command,* 110–12.

7. *Newsweek,* 29 July 1946, 33.

8. Ibid., 33.

9. Ibid.

10. *Newsweek,* 12 August 1946, 51.

11. Antoinette May, *Witness to War: A Biography of Marguerite Higgins* (New York: Beaufort Books, 1983), 116.

12. *Newsweek,* 3 November 1947, 41.

13. OMGUS, *Four Year Report,* 64.

14. Howley, *Berlin Command,* 111.

15. Andreas-Friedrich, *Battleground Berlin,* 141–45.

16. Anthony Read and David Fisher, *Berlin Rising: Biography of a City* (New York: W. W. Norton, 1994), 256.

17. Ibid., 257.

18. Ibid., 258.

CHAPTER ELEVEN

1. Herbert Feis, *From Trust to Terror: The Onset of the Cold War, 1945–1950* (New York: W. W. Norton, 1970), 182.

2. Ibid., 190.

3. Dean Acheson, *Present at the Creation: My Years in the State Department* (New York: Signet, 1970), 219.

4. Issacson and Thomas, *The Wise Men,* 395.

5. Cook, *Forging the Alliance,* 73.

6. Harry S Truman, *Years of Trial and Hope:* Vol. 2 of *Memoirs,* (New York: Signet, 1956), 128.

7. Feis, *From Trust to Terror,* 212.

8. *State Department Bulletin,* 23 March 1947.

9. Acheson, *Present at the Creation,* 298.

10. Feis, *From Trust to Terror,* 218.

11. Cook, *Forging the Alliance,* 78.

12. Feis, *From Trust to Terror,* 220.

13. Howley, *Berlin Command,* 144.

14. Ibid., 147.

15. Ibid.

16. Charles E. Bohlen, *Witness to History, 1929–1969* (New York: Norton, 1973), 263.

17. Kennan, *Memoirs,* 326.

CHAPTER TWELVE

1. Issacson and Thomas, *The Wise Men,* 79.

2. Kennan, *Memoirs,* 550.

3. Kennan, *Memoirs,* 326.

4. Ibid., 336.

5. Ibid., 336–40.

6. Hans-Jurgen Schraut, "U.S. Forces in Germany, 1945–1955," in *U.S. Military Forces in Europe: The Early Years, 1945–1970,* Simon W. Duke and Wolfgang Kreiger, eds., (Boulder, Colo.: Westview Press, 1993), 154.

7. Ibid., 157.

8. Ibid., 158.

9. Ziemke, *The American Occupation,* 335–36.

10. Davis, *Came as a Conqueror,* 166.

11. Hutton and Rooney, *Conquerors' Peace,* 42.

12. Davis, *Came as a Conqueror,* 170.

13. Interview, James O'Gorman, September 1996.

14. *Newsweek,* 2 June 1947, 28.

15. Hutton and Rooney, *Conquerors' Peace,* 39.

16. Ibid., 36.

17. Ibid.

18. Ibid., 35.

19. Ibid., 39.

20. Schraut, "U.S. Forces in Germany," 161.

21. Hutton and Rooney, *Conquerors' Peace,* 43–45.

22. Schraut, "U.S. Forces in Germany," 163.

23. *Newsweek,* 30 June 1947, 25.

24. Forrest C. Pogue, *George C. Marshall: Statesman, 1945–1959.* (New York: Penguin, 1987), 211–14.

25. Ibid., 217.

26. Ibid., 219.

27. Ibid., 219.

28. Cook, *Forging the Alliance,* 94–95.

29. Andreas-Friedrich, *Battleground Berlin,* 178.

30. Ibid., 179.

31. *Newsweek,* 11 August 1947, 20.

CHAPTER THIRTEEN

1. Davison, *Berlin Blockade,* 50.

2. Howley, *Berlin Command,* 156.

3. Ibid., 236.

4. Ibid., 151.

5. Ibid., 156.

6. Ibid., 155–56.

7. Melvyn P. Leffler, *A Preponderance of Power: National Security, the Truman Administration, and the Cold War.* (Stanford: Stanford University Press, 1992), 190.

8. Feis, *From Trust to Terror,* 262.

9. Ibid., 263.

10. Ibid., 276–77.

11. Ibid., 281.

12. May, *Witness to War,* 118–20.

13. Ibid., 121.

14. Ibid., 120–22.

15. Leffler, *A Preponderance of Power,* 192.

16. Pogue, *George C. Marshall,* 236.

17. Kennan, *Memoirs,* 378–79.

18. Howley, *Berlin Command,* 157.

19. Ibid., 155.

CHAPTER FOURTEEN

1. *Newsweek,* 2 February 1948.

2. Ibid.

3. John C. Campbell, *The United States in World Affairs: 1948–1949* (New York: Harper, 1949), 105.

4. *Newsweek,* 8 March 1948.

5. Ibid.

6. Cook, *Forging the Alliance,* 120.

7. Curtis LeMay, *Mission with LeMay: My Story* (New York: Doubleday, 1965), 411.

8. Davison, *Berlin Blockade,* 73.

9. Ibid., 19.

10. Ibid.

11. *Newsweek,* 22 March 1948.

12. Ibid.

13. Cook, *Forging the Alliance,* 123.

14. Davison, *Berlin Blockade,* 85–86.

15. *Newsweek,* 29 March 1948.

16. Collier, *Bridge across the Sky,* 2–6.

17. *Newsweek,* 29 March 1948.

CHAPTER FIFTEEN

1. Howley, *Berlin Command,* 200–01.

2. Collier, *Bridge across the Sky,* 20.

3. *Stars and Stripes,* 21 April 1948.

4. Collier, *Bridge across the Sky,* 21.

5. *Newsweek,* 12 April 1948.

6. Howley, *Berlin Command,* 162–63; *Newsweek,* 12 April 1948.

7. *New York Times,* 8 April 1948.

8. *New York Times,* 10 April 1948; *Stars and Stripes,* 10 April 1948.

9. *Stars and Stripes,* 12 April 1948.

10. *New York Herald-Tribune,* 14 May 1948.

11. Ibid.

12. *New York Herald-Tribune,* 3 June 1948.

13. Ibid.

14. Davison, *Berlin Blockade,* 17.

15. *New York Herald-Tribune,* 21 May 1948.

16. Davison, *Berlin Blockade,* 64.

17. Collier, *Bridge across the Sky,* 93–94.

18. *Newsweek,* 28 June 1948.

19. Howley, *Berlin Command,* 178–81.

20. Ibid., 182.

21. *Newsweek,* 28 June 1948.

22. *New York Herald-Tribune,* 17 June 1948; *Newsweek,* 28 June 1948.

23. Howley, *Berlin Command,* 183.

CHAPTER SIXTEEN

1. *Newsweek,* 28 June 1948.

2. *Stars and Stripes,* 30 May 1948.

3. Howley, *Berlin Command,* 184.

4. Collier, *Bridge across the Sky,* 64.

5. Ibid., 7.

6. *Newsweek,* 28 June 1948.

7. Andreas-Friedrich, *Battleground Berlin,* 206.

8. Ibid., 218; *New York Times,* 17 June 1948.

9. Collier, *Bridge across the Sky,* 40.

10. Davison, *Berlin Blockade,* 91.

11. *New York Times,* 20 June 1948.

12. Davison, *Berlin Blockade,* 93.

13. Andreas-Friedrich, *Battleground Berlin,* 223.

14. Bennett, "The German Currency Reform," 50.

15. *New York Times,* 28 June 1948.

16. Bennett, "The German Currency Reform," 52.

17. Andreas-Friedrich, *Battleground Berlin,* 225.

18. Reiss, *Berlin Story,* 159.

19. Davison, *Berlin Blockade,* 96.

20. Andreas-Friedrich, *Battleground Berlin,* 226.

21. Davison, *Berlin Blockade,* 96.

22. Ibid., 97.

23. Ibid.

24. *New York Herald-Tribune,* 24 June 1948.

CHAPTER SEVENTEEN

1. Smith, *Lucius Clay,* 495–96.

2. Ibid., 496.

3. Howley, *Berlin Command,* 196.

4. Ibid.

5. Interview, James O'Gorman, September 1996.

6. Howley, *Berlin Command,* 200.

7. Davison, *Berlin Blockade,* 100.

8. Ibid., 101.

9. *Time,* 5 July 1948.

10. Collier, *Bridge across the Sky,* 54.

11. *New York Herald-Tribune,* 25 June 1948.

12. LeMay, *Mission with LeMay,* 415.

13. Clay, *Decision in Germany,* 366.

14. Ibid.

15. Issacson and Thomas, *The Wise Men,* 456.

16. Reiss, *The Berlin Story,* 158–59.

17. Smith, *Lucius Clay,* 501–02.

18. Ibid., 501.

19. Ibid., 502.

20. Smith, *Lucius Clay,* 500–01; LeMay, *Mission with LeMay,* 415; Murphy, *Diplomat among Warriors,* 355. Murphy gives the date of this conversation as mid-July, after he and Clay returned from a trip to Washington, but the first coal deliveries by American aircraft took place on July 7, prior to the journey to Washington. The principals, Clay and LeMay, write that it took place on June 25, so Murphy's recollection of the date is obviously in error.

21. Smith, *Lucius Clay,* 503.

22. Robert Rodrico, *The Berlin Airlift,* (London: Cassell, 1990), 21.

CHAPTER EIGHTEEN

1. David Wragg, *Airlift: A History of Military Air Transport,* (Shrewsbury, England: Airlife Publishing, 1986), 9–10.

2. Ibid., 36–37.

3. Smith, *Lucius Clay,* 500.

4. LeMay, *Mission with LeMay,* 415.

5. Ibid., 390.

6. Davison, *Berlin Blockade,* 108.

7. Andreas-Friedrich, *Battleground Berlin,* 229.

8. Truman, *Years of Trial and Hope,* 148.

9. Omar Bradley, *A General's Life* (New York: Simon and Schuster, 1983), 476.

10. Davison, *Berlin Blockade,* 110.

11. Bradley, *A General's Life,* 481.

12. William H. Tunner, *Over the Hump* (New York: Duell, Slone and Pearce, 1964), 159.

13. Millis, *Forrestal Diaries,* 454–55.

14. McCullough, *Truman,* 630–31.

15. Roger D. Launius, "The Berlin Airlift: Constructive Air Power," *Air Power History,* Spring 1989, 10.

16. Robert D. Wilcox, unpublished diary made available to author.

17. Collier, *Bridge across the Sky,* 76.

CHAPTER NINETEEN

1. Frank Donovan, *Bridge in the Sky* (New York: David McKay, 1968), 46.

2. Davison, *Berlin Blockade,* 113.

3. Wilcox diary.

4. Wilcox diary.

5. *Time,* 12 July 1948.

6. *New York Times,* 1 July 1948.

7. Rodrico, *Berlin Airlift,* 45.

8. Ibid., 46.

9. Tunner, *Over the Hump,* 78.

10. Ibid., 93.

11. Ibid., 140.

12. Ibid., 159.

13. Issacson and Thomas, *The Wise Men,* 458.

14. Ibid., 458.

15. *Newsweek,* 19 July 1948.

16. Interview, Peter Howley, April 1997.

17. Andreas-Friedrich, *Battleground Berlin,* 232.

18. Ibid., 232.

19. Ibid., 231.

20. This story appears in various sources (Howley, *Berlin Command,* 238–39; *Newsweek*) and is reported to have occurred at various times during the blockade. The earliest mention of it is in Ruth Andreas-Friedrich's diary, *Battleground Berlin,* in the entry of June 29, 1948.

CHAPTER TWENTY

1. Clay, *Decision in Germany,* 372.

2. *Time,* 5 July 1948.

3. Clay, *Decision in Germany,* 373; *Time,* 5 July 1948; *Newsweek,* 5 July 1948.

4. Clay, *Decision in Germany,* 373.

5. Ibid., 367.

6. Rodrico, *Berlin Airlift,* 34–35.

7. Collier, *Bridge across the Sky,* 78–79.

8. *New York Times,* 16 July 1948.

9. *Stars and Stripes,* 8 July 1948.

10. *Stars and Stripes,* 10 July 1948.

11. Wilcox diary.

12. *Stars and Stripes,* 10 July 1948.

13. Davison, *Berlin Blockade,* 124.

14. *Time,* 12 July 1948.

15. *Stars and Stripes,* 10 July 1948.

16. Halvorsen, *Berlin Candy Bomber,* 97.

17. Ibid., 98.

18. Tunner, *Over the Hump,* 158–60.

19. Ibid., 160.

CHAPTER TWENTY-ONE

1. Davis, *Came as a Conqueror,* 204.

2. Ibid., 205–06.

3. "A Special Study of Operation Vittles," *Aviation Operations Magazine,* April 1949, 70.

4. Davis, *Came as a Conqueror,* 209–10.

5. "Special Study," *Aviation Operations,* 69–72.

6. *Stars and Stripes,* 15 July 1948.

7. *Stars and Stripes,* 13 July 1948.

8. Interview, James O'Gorman, October 1996.

9. Jackson, *Berlin Airlift,* 48.

10. *Time,* 19 July 1948.

11. Howley, *Berlin Command,* 205.

12. Ibid., 206.

13. *Stars and Stripes,* 14 July 1948.

14. *Stars and Stripes,* 19 July 1948.

15. *Time,* 19 July 1948.

16. Charles C. V. Murphy, "The Berlin Airlift," *Fortune,* November 1948.

17. *New York Times,* 13 July 1948.

18. Halvorsen, *Berlin Candy Bomber,* 99–105.

19. Davison, *Berlin Blockade,* 128.

20. *Stars and Stripes,* 19 July 1948.

21. *Stars and Stripes,* 24 July 1948.

22. Halvorsen, *Berlin Candy Bomber,* 109.

23. Ibid., 113.

24. Truman, *Years of Trial and Hope,* 149.

25. Ibid., 150–51.

26. Tunner, *Over the Hump,* 163.

CHAPTER TWENTY-TWO

1. *Stars and Stripes,* 25 July 1948.

2. *Stars and Stripes,* 26 July 1948.

3. Ibid.

4. *Stars and Stripes,* 29 July 1948.

5. Davison, *Berlin Blockade,* 171–72; *Stars and Stripes,* 27 July 1948.

6. Tunner, *Over the Hump,* 165.

7. *Stars and Stripes,* 1 August 1948.

8. LeMay, *Mission with LeMay,* 406.

9. Tunner, *Over the Hump,* 166.

10. Ibid., 167.

11. Ibid., 166.

12. Ibid., 167.

13. Ibid., 162.

14. Ibid., 171.

15. Ibid., 170.

16. Ibid., 171.

17. Halvorsen, *Berlin Candy Bomber,* 114.

18. Pogue, *George Marshall: Statesman,* 308.

19. *Newsweek,* 9 August 1948.

20. Rodrico, *Berlin Airlift,* 100.

21. Tunner, *Over the Hump,* 174–76.

22. Ibid., 168.

23. Murphy, "The Berlin Airlift," *Fortune,* November 1948.

CHAPTER TWENTY-THREE

1. *Stars and Stripes,* 14 August 1948.

2. Ibid.

3. Tunner, *Over the Hump,* 152–54.

4. Ibid., 172.

5. Pogue, *George Marshall: Statesman,* 311.

6. Andreas-Friedrich, *Battleground Berlin,* 238.

7. *New York Times,* 14 August 1948.

8. *New York Times,* 20 August 1948.

9. *New York Times,* 21 August 1948.

10. *New York Times,* 20 August 1948.

11. *New York Times,* 22 August 1948.

12. *New York Times,* 16 August 1948.

13. Halvorsen, *Berlin Candy Bomber,* 129.

14. Ibid., 130.

15. Tunner, *Over the Hump,* 173–75.

16. *Stars and Stripes,* 16 August 1948.

17. *Air Force Times,* 28 August 1948.

18. Jackson, *Berlin Airlift,* 55–59.

19. Rodrico, *Berlin Airlift,* 45–47.

20. *Stars and Stripes,* 24 August 1948.

CHAPTER TWENTY-FOUR

1. Tunner, *Over the Hump,* 180.

2. *New York Herald-Tribune,* 26 August 1948.

3. Shlaim, *The United States and the Berlin Blockade,* 323.

4. Ibid., 325.

5. *New York Herald-Tribune,* 26 August 1948.

6. *New York Herald-Tribune,* 27 August 1948.

7. *New York Herald-Tribune,* 25 July 1948.

8. Davison, *Berlin Blockade,* 180.

9. *New York Herald-Tribune,* 27 August 1948.

10. Smith, *Moscow Mission,* 252.

11. *New York Herald-Tribune,* 28 August 1948.

12. *New York Herald-Tribune*, 29 August 1948.

13. Ibid.

14. Ibid.

15. Ibid.

16. *New York Herald-Tribune*, 1 September 1948.

17. Davison, *Berlin Blockade*, 163.

18. Shlaim, *The United States and the Berlin Blockade*, 328.

19. *New York Herald-Tribune*, 2 September 1948.

20. Andreas-Friedrich, *Battleground Berlin*, 241.

21. *New York Herald-Tribune*, 4 September 1948.

22. Tunner, *Over the Hump*, 182–83.

23. Ibid., 183.

24. Ibid., 193.

25. *New York Herald-Tribune*, 6 September 1948.

CHAPTER TWENTY-FIVE

1. *New York Times*, 7 September 1948.

2. *New York Herald-Tribune*, 7 September 1948.

3. Riess, *Berlin Story*, 216.

4. *New York Herald-Tribune*, 7 September 1948.

5. *New York Herald-Tribune*, 9 September 1948.

6. Riess, *Berlin Story*, 217.

7. *New York Herald-Tribune*, 10 September 1948.

8. *Stars and Stripes*, 10 September 1948.

9. Unpublished diary of Kenneth Slaker, furnished to author.

10. Ibid.

11. Collier, *Bridge across the Sky*, 104–05.

12. *Newsweek*, 20 September 1948.

13. *Stars and Stripes*, 11 September 1948.

14. *New York Herald-Tribune*, 10 September 1948.

15. *Newsweek*, 20 September 1948.

16. *Stars and Stripes*, 11 September 1948.

17. Ibid.

18. Millis, *Forrestal Diaries*, 487.

19. Truman, *Off the Record*, 148–49.

20. Millis, *Forrestal Diaries*, 487–88.

21. Slaker diary.

CHAPTER TWENTY-SIX

1. Slaker diary.

2. Ibid.

3. *New York Herald-Tribune*, 15 September 1948.

4. *New York Herald-Tribune*, 16 September 1948.

5. Ibid.

6. *Stars and Stripes*, 18 September 1948.

7. *Philadelphia Inquirer*, 14 September 1948.

8. *New York Herald-Tribune*, 17 September 1948.

9. *Stars and Stripes*, 16 September 1948.

10. *Stars and Stripes*, 18 September 1948.

11. *Stars and Stripes*, 19 September 1948.

12. Ibid.

13. Shlaim, *The United States and the Berlin Blockade*, 343–44.

14. Pogue, *George Marshall: Statesman*, 405–7.

15. *Newsweek*, 4 October 1948.

16. Ibid.

CHAPTER TWENTY-SEVEN

1. *Stars and Stripes*, 8 November 1948.

2. *Time*, 18 November 1948.

3. Andreas-Friedrich, *Battleground Berlin*, 246.

4. Ibid., 247.

5. *New York Herald-Tribune*, 4 October 1948.

6. Ibid.

7. *Time*, 18 October 1948.

8. *New York Herald-Tribune*, 5 October 1948.

9. *Time*, 18 October 1948.

10. Ibid.

11. *New York Herald-Tribune*, 5 October 1948.

12. *New York Herald-Tribune*, 9 October 1948.

13. *Newsweek*, 1 November 1948.

14. "Special Study," *Aviation Operations*, 116–17.

15. *New York Herald-Tribune*, 2 October 1948.

16. Tunner, *Over the Hump*, 189.

17. Shlaim, *The United States and the Berlin Blockade*, 364.

18. Ibid., 363.

19. Tunner, *Over the Hump*, 187.

20. Ibid., 188–89.

CHAPTER TWENTY-EIGHT

1. LeMay, *Mission with LeMay*, 406.

2. Tunner, *Over the Hump*, 190–91.

3. Smith, *Lucius Clay*, 503–04.

4. Tunner, *Over the Hump*, 199.

5. Ibid., 192.

6. Ibid., 192–93.

7. "Special Study," *Aviation Operations*, 60–62.

8. Halvorsen, *Berlin Candy Bomber*, 149.

9. Ibid.

10. Slaker diary.

11. *Stars and Stripes*, 12 August 1948.

12. Interview, Thomas Flowers, September 1996.

13. Tunner, *Over the Hump*, 214.

14. *Stars and Stripes*, 6 November 1948.

15. Rodrico, *The Berlin Airlift*, 95–96.

16. *Stars and Stripes*, 20 November 1948; "A Special Study of Operation Vittles," 17–24.

17. Pogue, *George Marshall: Statesman*, 409.

18. Ibid., 413–14.

CHAPTER TWENTY-NINE

1. Interview, Fain Pool, September 1996.

2. *Air Force Times*, 18 December 1948.

3. Ibid.

4. *Air Force Times*, 2 April 1949.

5. *New York Times*, 21 November 1948.

6. *New York Times*, 29 November 1948.

7. Clay, *Decision in Germany*, 382–83.

8. Reiss, *Berlin Story*, 194–95.

9. Ibid., 197–98.

10. *Time*, 13 December 1948.

11. Reiss, *Berlin Story*, 201.

12. Howley, *Berlin Command*, 226.

13. *Newsweek*, 13 December 1948.

14. Howley, *Berlin Command*, 226–27.

15. *Newsweek*, 13 December 1948.

16. Howley, *Berlin Command*, 228.

17. Interview, Jack Fellman, September 1996.

18. Reiss, *Berlin Story*, 219–21.

19. Ibid., 203.

20. Andreas-Friedrich, *Battleground Berlin*, 253.

CHAPTER THIRTY

1. Rodrico, *Berlin Airlift*, 218.

2. Ibid., 109.

3. Ibid., 124; Collier, *Bridge across the Sky*, 147.

4. *Newsweek*, 1 November 1948.

5. Halvorsen, *Berlin Candy Bomber*, 158.

6. Ibid., 159.

7. Collier, *Bridge across the Sky*, 149.

8. Tunner, *Over the Hump*, 196–97.

9. Howley, *Berlin Command*, 234–36.

10. *Philadelphia Inquirer*, 23 December 1948.

11. Antonio T. Criscuolo, "What Do These People Mean To Us?" *The Legacy: Newsletter of the Berlin Airlift Veterans Association*, Vol. 5, Issue 3.

12. Ibid.

13. Andreas-Friedrich, *Battleground Berlin*, 256.

14. *Newsweek*, 17 January 1949.

15. "Special Study," *Aviation Operations*, 65–66.

## CHAPTER THIRTY-ONE

1. Tunner, *Over the Hump,* 197.

2. Ibid.

3. Halvorsen, *Berlin Candy Bomber,* 167.

4. Rodrico, *Berlin Airlift,* 147–48.

5. Ibid., 147.

6. Collier, *Bridge across the Sky,* 141.

7. Howley, *Berlin Command,* 236.

8. Ibid., 241.

9. Howley, "My Four-Year War with the Reds," *Collier's,* 3 December 1949.

10. Ibid.

11. Jackson, *Berlin Airlift,* 133.

12. Ann Stringer, "Berlin Today: One Family's Story," *New York Times Magazine,* 2 January 1949.

13. *Newsweek,* 14 February 1949.

14. *New York Times,* 24 November 1948.

15. Howley, *Berlin Command,* 239.

16. Issacson and Thomas, *The Wise Men,* 470.

17. Ibid., 470–71.

18. Acheson, *Present at the Creation,* 354–55.

## CHAPTER THIRTY-TWO

1. *Philadelphia Inquirer,* 21 March 1949.

2. Ibid.

3. Acheson, *Present at the Creation,* 356.

4. Ibid., 357.

5. Tunner, *Over the Hump,* 221.

6. Ibid., 221.

7. Ibid.

8. Ibid., 222.

9. *Newsweek,* 15 May 1949.

10. *New York Times,* 13 May 1949.

11. Ibid.

12. Backer, *Winds of History,* 281.

13. *Congressional Record,* 27 May 1949.

14. Acheson, *Present at the Creation,* 295.

15. Jackson, *Berlin Airlift,* 124.

16. Collier, *Bridge across the Sky,* 9.

17. Howley, "My Four-Year War with the Reds," *Collier's,* 3 December 1949.

18. *The Sunday Bulletin* (Philadelphia), 4 September 1949.

19. Ann and John Tusa, *The Berlin Airlift,* (New York: Atheneum, 1988), 370.

20. Letter, Gen. William H. Tunner to Association of Graduates, USMA, 16 January 1979, Tunner Alumni File, West Point Library.

21. Tusa, *Berlin Blockade,* 375.

22. Philip K. Robles, *United States Military Medals and Decorations,* (Rutland, Vt.: Charles K. Tuttle, 1971), 95.

23. Tunner to Association of Graduates, USMA, 16 January 1979.

## CHAPTER THIRTY-THREE

1. D. M. Giangreco and Robert E. Griffin, *Airbridge to Berlin,* (Novato, Ca.: Presidio, 1987), 204.

2. Ibid., 204.

3. Bering, *Outpost Berlin,* 139.

4. Ibid., 133–40.

5. Peter Wyden, *Wall* (New York: Simon and Schuster, 1989), 71.

6. Ibid., 75.

7. Ibid.

8. Ibid., 77.

9. *New York Times,* 26 July 1961.

10. Curtis Cade, *The Ides of August* (New York: M. Evans, 1978), 116–17.

11. Wyden, *Wall,* 81.

12. Bering, *Outpost Berlin,* 151.

13. Ibid., 157.

14. Ibid.

15. Cate, *Ides of August,* 393.

16. Westbrook Pegler, "As Pegler Sees It," King Features Syndicate, 1 July 1961.

17. Cate, *Ides of August,* 403.

18. Wyden, *Wall,* 227.

19. *New York Times,* 27 July 1963.

20. Bering, *Outpost Berlin,* 237.

21. Ibid., 239.

22. Ibid., 242.

# INDEX

# About the Author

Michael D. Haydock holds a degree in history and political science from the University of the State of New York and recently retired from public service. He now works as a consultant and freelance writer and serves on the faculty of Empire State College. He is a frequent contributer to *American History*, *Military History*, and *VFW* Magazine, and his articles have appeared in *Air Force Times*, *Army Times*, *American Heritage of Invention & Technology*, *Buffalo Spree*, the *Bermuda Maritime Museum Quarterly*, *Confrontation*, *Wild West*, and *World War II*. He has written and aided in the production of several documentaries for the History Channel®.

He lives in upstate New York.